AF597462

*Chilton's*

# Repair and Tune-Up Guide

## for the

# TOYOTA

*Illustrated*

PRODUCED BY THE AUTOMOTIVE BOOK DEPARTMENT

**CHILTON BOOK COMPANY**
PHILADELPHIA NEW YORK LONDON


Published in Philadelphia by Chilton Book Company,
and simultaneously in Ontario, Canada,
by Thomas Nelson & Sons, Ltd.

Manufactured in the United States of America

*Second Printing, August 1971*

Library of Congress Catalog Card No. 73-124092

ISBN 0-8019-5339-1

## ACKNOWLEDGMENTS

The Chilton Book Company expresses appreciation to the following firms for their generous assistance:

TOYOTA MOTOR DISTRIBUTORS, INC.
Torrance, Calif.

ED FISHER MOTORS
Parkesburg, Pa.

## NOTE

Although the information in this book is based on factory sources and is as complete as it was possible to make it at time of publication, the possibility exists that later changes were made which could not be included here. It must be recognized that such changes are the manufacturer's prerogative, and that the manufacturer cannot be held responsible for them.

# Contents

TOYOTA CORONA

RT43L
4-DOOR SEDAN

KE15L
FASTBACK

KE16L
STATION WAGON

TOYOTA COROLLA

KE10L
2-DOOR SEDAN

TOYOTA CROWN

RT52L
2-DOOR HARDTOP

MS-55L
4-DOOR SEDAN

MS-53L
4-DOOR STATION WAGON

FJ40LV-A
2-DOOR HARDTOP

FJ40L-A
2-DOOR VINYL TOP

TOYOTA LAND CRUISER

FJ55LG
4-DOOR STATION WAGON

# Chapter 1

# Identification, Troubleshooting and Tune-Up

## Part I Identification

All cars have a model plate attached to the inside of the engine compartment, usually on the inner right front fender well. Late models (1967 to present) also have a decal on the valve cover, showing certain important tune-up data as well as the all-important engine model number. The engine serial number and type is also stamped on the right side of the cylinder block below No. 1 cylinder.

## Part II Troubleshooting

When an engine refuses to start, or performs poorly, the trouble usually can be located by following a step-by-step process of elimination (as shown in the chart below).

The trouble is usually found in any one (or more) of the following systems:

1. Cranking system (starter)
2. Ignition system (distributor)
3. Fuel system (carburetor, fuel pump)
4. Engine compression (valves)

### Cranking System Tests

Turn ignition switch *on* and activate the starter; if engine turns over at a normal rate but refuses to fire, proceed to next test (ignition system).

If engine turns over slowly, or not at all, check the following:

*Battery* Engine will turn over normally at first but slow down rapidly. Turn on headlights; if they dim out as starter is turned, battery is discharged, or terminals are loose or dirty.

*Switches* With a pair of pliers or a heavy wire, short across the two heavy posts of the starter solenoid terminals. If the starter does not work (and the battery is good) then the starter itself is defective.

*Starter motor* If motor spins, but does not engage or turn the engine, look for a bad starter drive (Bendix). Observe the size of the sparks at the shorted terminals; a healthy spark means that the starter drive gear is stuck in the flywheel ring gear, or that the starter is shorted internally. The first malfunction can be corrected by putting the transmission in high gear, releasing the handbrake and rocking the car back-and-forth to disengage the stuck gears (manual transmission only). The second malfunction requires the removal and repair of the starter. Few, or no, sparks indicate an open circuit in the motor itself (brushes), a broken battery post or cable, or a dead battery.

# General Specifications

| Model Designation | | Corolla | Corona | Crown | Corona | Corolla | Stout Pick-up | Mark II | ½ T. Pick-up | Ld. Cruiser | Ld. Cruiser |
|---|---|---|---|---|---|---|---|---|---|---|---|
| Series Designation | | KE | RT | MS | RT | KE | RK | RT | RN | FJ | FJ |
| Engine Designation | | 3K-C | 3R-C | 2M | 3R-B | K-C | 3-R | 8R-C | 8R-C | FJ (early model) | FA |
| No. of cylinders | | 4 | 4 | 6 | 4 | 4 | 4 | 4 | 4 | 6 | 6 |
| Type of valve gear | | ohv | ohv | sohc | ohv | ohv | ohv | sohc | sohc | ohv | ohv |
| Firing order | | 1–3–4–2 | 1–2–4–3 | 1–5–3–6–2–4 | 1–2–4–3 | 1–3–4–2 | 1–2–4–3 | 1–3–4–2 | 1–3–4–2 | 1–5–3–6–2–4 | 1–5–3–6–2–4 |
| Bore and Stroke | in. | 2.95 x 2.60 | 3.46 x 3.07 | 2.95 x 3.35 | 3.46 x 3.07 | 2.95 x 2.40 | 3.46 x 3.07 | 3.39 x 3.15 | 3.39 x 3.15 | 3.54 x 4.00 | 3.54 x 4.00 |
| | mm. | 75 x 66 | 88 x 78 | 75 x 85 | 88 x 78 | 75 x 61 | 88 x 78 | 86 x 80 | 86 x 80 | 90 x 101.6 | 90 x 101.6 |
| Displacement | cc. | 1,166 | 1,897 | 2,253 | 1,897 | 1,077 | 1,897 | 1,858 | 1,858 | 3,878 | 3,878 |
| | cu. in. | 71.1 | 115.8 | 137.5 | 115.8 | 65.7 | 115.8 | 113.4 | 113.4 | 236.7 | 236.7 |
| Horsepower @ RPM (SAE) | | 73 @ 6,000 | 90 @ 4,600 | 115 @ 5,200 | 90 @ 4,600 | 60 @ 6,000 | 95 @ 5,000 | 108 @ 5,500 | 108 @ 5,500 | 145 @ 4,000 | 155 @ 4,000 |
| Torque @ RPM (ft. lbs.) | | 74.2 @ 3,800 | 110 @ 2,600 | 127 @ 3,600 | 110 @ 2,600 | 61.5 @ 3.800 | 110 @ 3,400 | 117 @ 3,600 | 117 @ 3,600 | 217 @ 2,000 | 230 @ 2,000 |
| Compression ratio (to 1) | | 9.0 | 8.0 | 8.8 | 8.0 | 9.0 | 8.0 | 9.0 | 9.0 | 7.8 | 7.8 |
| Compression pressure @ RPM (psi) | | 170 @ 250 | 156 @ 200 | 156 @ 250 | 156 @ 250 | 171 @ 250 | 156 @ 250 | 164 @ 250 | 164 @ 250 | 145 @ 200 | 150 @ 200 |
| Valve clearance (in.) | intake | 0.008 | 0.008 | 0.007 | 0.008 | 0.008 | 0.008 | 0.008 | 0.008 | 0.008 | 0.008 |
| (hot) | exhaust | 0.012 | 0.014 | 0.010 | 0.014 | 0.014 | 0.014 | 0.014 | 0.014 | 0.014 | 0.014 |
| Intake valve opens BTDC | | N.A. | 10° BTDC | 16° | 23° | 16° | 18° | 15° | 15° | 17° | 17° |
| Intake valve closes ABDC | | N.A. | 50° ABDC | 48° | 53° | 50° | 58° | 45° | 45° | 53° | 53° |
| Exhaust valve opens BBDC | | N.A. | 50° ABDC | 46° | 63° | 50° | 58° | 50° | 50° | 55° | 55° |
| Exhaust valve closes ATDC | | N.A. | 10° ATDC | 8° | 13° | 16° | 18° | 10° | 10° | 15° | 15° |

| | | | | | | | | | | | |
|---|---|---|---|---|---|---|---|---|---|---|---|
| Point gap + or — .002" | | N.A. | 0.016-0.020 | 0.016-0.020 | .018 | 0.016-0.020 | 0.016-0.020 | 0.016-0.020 | 0.016-0.020 | 0.016-0.020 | 0.016-0.020 |
| Dwell angle + or — 2° | | 52° | 52° | 41° | 52° | 52° | 52° | 52° | 52° | 41° | 41° |
| Spark plug gap | | 0.031 | 0.031 | 0.031 | 0.028-0.031 | 0.028-0.031 | 0.031 | 0.031 | 0.031 | 0.031 | 0.031 |
| Ignition timing | | 5° ATDC @ 650 rpm | 5° BTDC/650 rpm-auto. TDC/750 rpm-manual | TDC @ 650 rpm | 12° BTDC @ 650 rpm | 5° ATDC @ 650 rpm | 12° BTDC | TDC @ 650 rpm | TDC @ 650 rpm | 7° BTDC @ 600 rpm | 7° BTDC @ 600 rpm |
| Idle speed | manual | 650 | 750 | 650 | 550 | 650 | 550 | 650 | 650 | 600 | 600 |
| | automatic | 650 | 650 | 650 | 550 | 650 | 550 | 650 | — | — | — |
| Steering ratio | | 18.1 to 1 | 20.8 to 1 | 20.5-23.6 to 1 (variable) | 20.8 to 1 | 18.1 to 1 | 18.0 to 1 | 19.5-21.5 to 1 (variable) | 19.48 to 1 | 21.0 to 1 | 21.0 to 1 |
| Tire size/No. ply | | 6.00 x 12 4 ply | 6.00 x 13 4 ply | 6.95 x 14 4 ply | 6.00 x 13 4 ply | 6.00 x 12 4 ply | 7.00 x 15 6 ply (10 ply rear) | 6.00 x 13 4 ply | 6.00 x 14 6 PR LT (8 PR rear) | * | * |
| Tire pressure F/R (psi) | sedan<br>wagon | 22/22<br>22/24<br>(28 loaded) | 22/22 | 24/22 | 22/22 | 18/18 | 25/35 | 22/22 22/26 wagon | — | * | * |
| Differential ratio (automatic and manual) | sedan & coupe<br>wagon & automatic | 4.222<br>4.444 | 3.700 | 4.375 (auto.)<br>4.111 (manual) | 3.7 to 1 | 4.444 | RK 43—5.714<br>RK 41—4.875<br>RK 1003—6.167 | 3.700–Manual<br>3.900–Automatic | 4.111 | 4.11 front<br>4.11 rear | 4.11 front<br>4.11 rear |
| Alternator capacity (Watts) | | 360 | 456 | 480 | 456 | 360 | 456 | 480 | 300 | 480 | 480 |
| Battery capacity (Amp./hr.) | | 40 (50 W/A.C.) | 40 (50 W/A.C.) | 40 (50 W/A.C.) | 40 | 40 (50 W/A.C.) | 40 | 38 (40 & 60 opt.) | 40 (60 opt.) | 50 | 50 |

*Loaded psi: FJ40 (L) (U) (7.10 x 15/4)—18/25
(7.60 x 15/4)—17/25
(7.60 x 15/6)—17/28
(7.00 x 16/6)—24/32

FJ 43 (L) (7.60 x 15/4)—17/30
(7.60 x 15/6)—17/30
(7.00 x 16/6)—24/42

FJ 45 (L) P-B (7.00 x 16/6 front)—32
(7.00 x 16/8 rear)—62

## Starter System Diagnosis

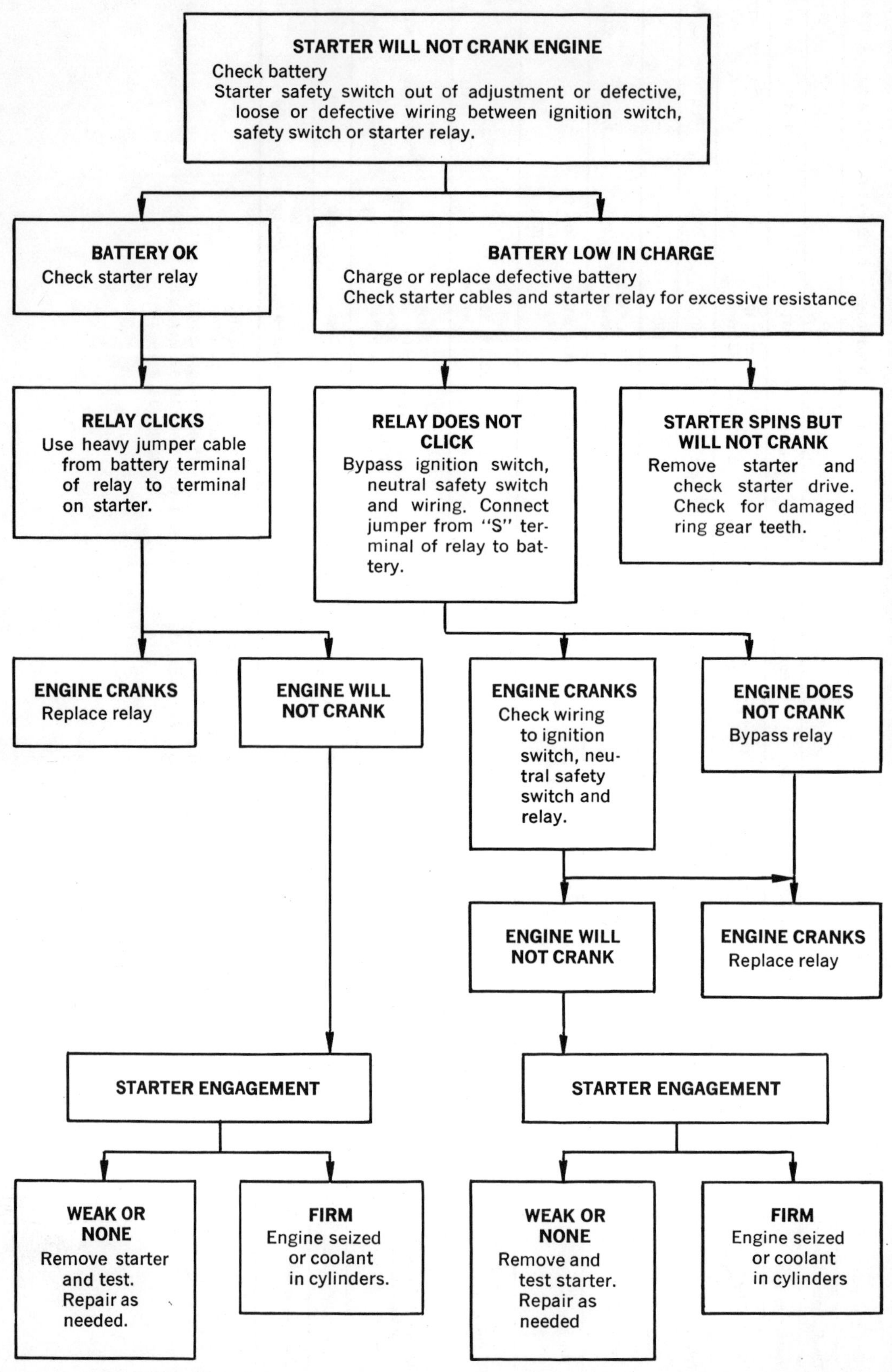

## Starter System Diagnosis

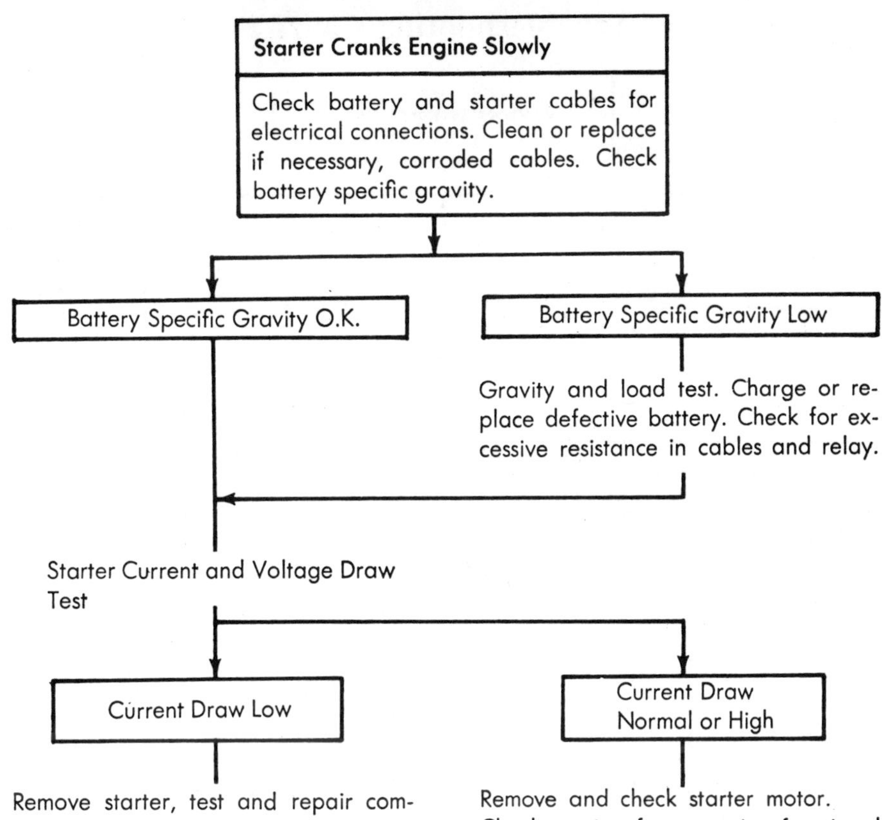


### Ignition System Tests

Disconnect high tension wire from spark plug and hold it about ¼–½″ from engine block. *NOTE: It may be necessary to remove the insulating tip of the cable.* A hot (blue) spark jumping the gap is an indication of a normally functioning ignition system.

If the spark is weak, or completely absent, continue testing as follows: *NOTE: In wet weather thoroughly dry off all high tension wires, distributor and coil connections; remove distributor cap and dry inside.*

*Primary circuit* Remove distributor cap and rotor. Rotate engine until points are fully closed. Switch on ignition and pull wire from coil at distributor cap (center post). Hold this wire about ½″ from engine block, then open and close points with the tip of a screwdriver, taking care to touch the point arm only. A good, "hot" spark from the wire to ground indicates that the primary circuit is good. A weak, or no, spark indicates a defective coil.

*Ignition points* Inspect points for pitting, wear and burning (blue in color). Rotate engine until points are open and slide blade of screwdriver against point arm, this time making sure to ground tip against base plate. A good spark at the coil wire indicates a bad set of points, a weak, or no, spark, however, is indicative of a bad coil.

*Condenser* If, during the previous test, the screwdriver tip sparked against the base plate, the condenser is good. No spark indicates a shorted condenser or an open primary circuit. Remove condenser from base plate, leaving wire connected. With points open, move screwdriver tip up and down against point arm. If sparking occurs between the screwdriver and the base plate, the condenser is shorted and must be replaced. No spark indicates an open circuit, usually a broken "pigtail" (the small wire that connects the point arm to the primary terminal at the distributor housing).

*Secondary circuit* This circuit is tested only *after* the primary circuit has been checked and found to be satisfactory. Turn

## Troubleshooting Chart 1

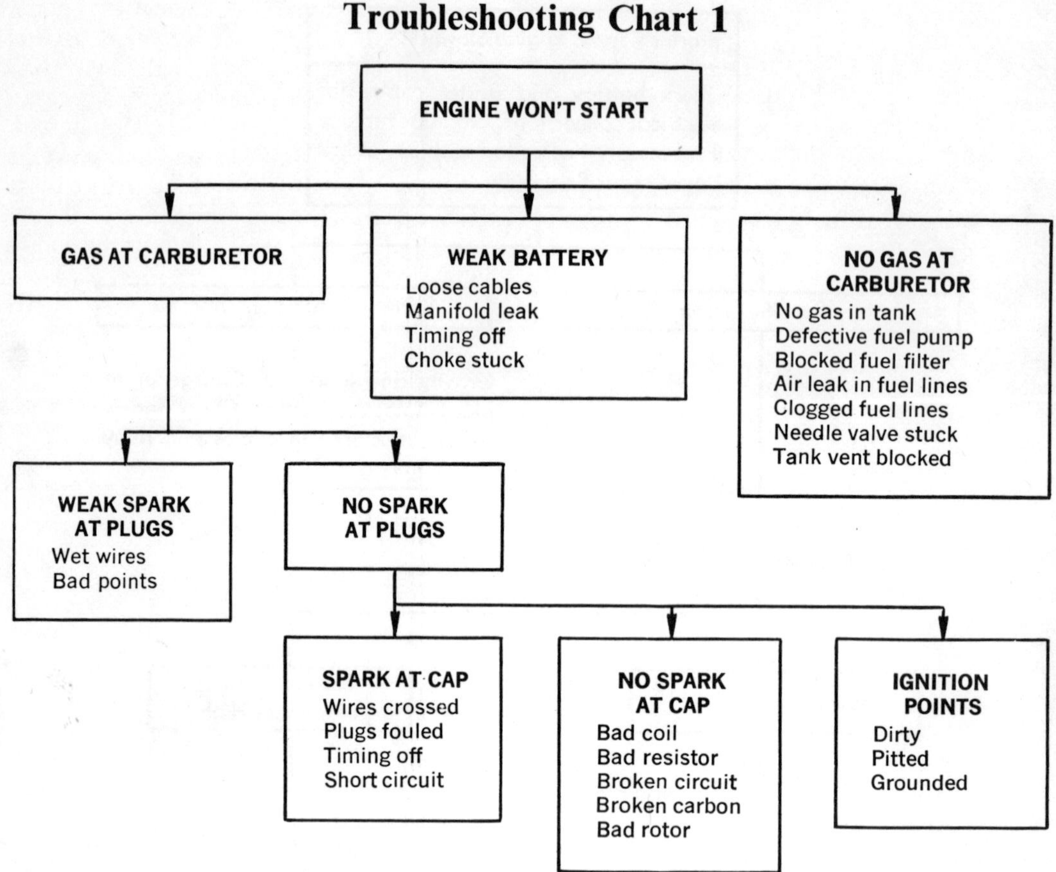


engine until points are closed. Switch on ignition, then hold distributor end of high tension coil wire about ½″ from ground. Open and close points, with screwdriver against point arm only (without grounding out); no spark indicates a bad coil-to-distributor high tension wire or a bad coil. Check coil tower and high tension wire for possible corrosion. A good spark indicates the problem to be in the distributor cap, rotor or spark plugs. *NOTE: Faulty spark plug wires, unless wet, seldom keep an engine from starting under normal conditions.*

Install rotor onto distributor shaft and hold high tension wire about ¼″ above rotor. Switch on ignition and crank starter. If a spark jumps to the rotor, rotor should be replaced. No spark here indicates that the trouble is with the distributor cap. Inspect both rotor and cap for signs of wear, due to misalignment, and/or cracks. Look for carbon deposits around the towers of the cap.

### Fuel System Tests

Make sure there is enough gas in the tank, then remove air cleaner and check manual operation of choke. Open and close throttle several times. Short solid "squirts" of fuel through the discharge nozzle indicate that the fuel system is in good order. No fuel discharge indicates no fuel in the carburetor. *NOTE: In rare cases, the accelerator pump itself may be defective and not discharge, although the carburetor is full of fuel.*

Inspect fuel filter bowl. Look for dirt and water and remove bowl and clean. When installing, make sure the bowl gasket is properly seated. Reversing the old gasket can help restore a good, airtight seal.

Pull out high tension wire at coil (to prevent engine starting) and remove fuel line at carburetor inlet. Crank engine and catch fuel in a can. If there is no fuel discharge, or only a weak dribble of fuel, disconnect fuel line at pump inlet side (from tank) and blow into it. Check all fuel lines (under car) for leaks. If all lines are clear and not leaking, fuel pump itself is defective.

Too much fuel can also keep the engine from starting. If the base of the carburetor is wet, open throttle wide and look into carburetor throat. If excess gas is found at the bottom of the intake manifold, the engine is flooded. In most cases, flooding is due to pumping the accelerator pedal just prior to starting. Open the choke, keep accelerator pedal depressed and crank engine until it starts. Other causes of flooding are too high float level, defective (punctured) float, sticking needle valve, or fuel percolation. After a long, hard drive, excessive underhood temperature may cause a rapid expansion of fuel in the manifold. This causes the engine to stall and prevents restarting. Check spark plugs; a wet plug, smelling strongly of gasoline, is a sure indication of at least one of the above conditions.

(1)

**Normal Engine.**
Around 18 to 20 vacuum with slight fluctuation at idling speed.

(2)

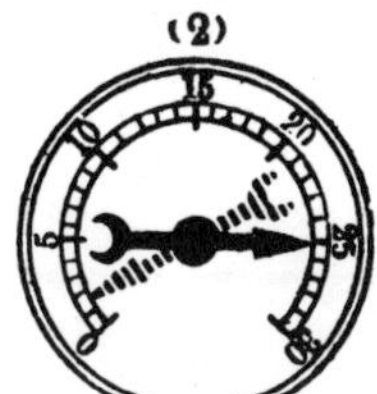

**Piston Ring in Normal Condition.**
Drops to 2 and then springs back to 25, when accelerating engine.

(3)

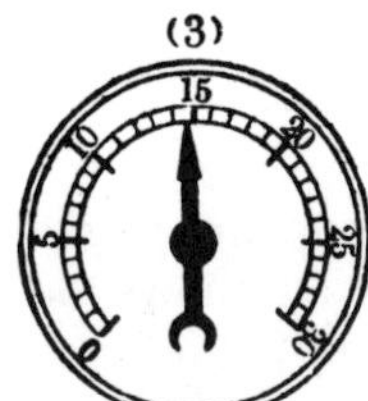

**Oil and Rings in Poor Condition.**
Remains in lower reading in Case 2.

(4)

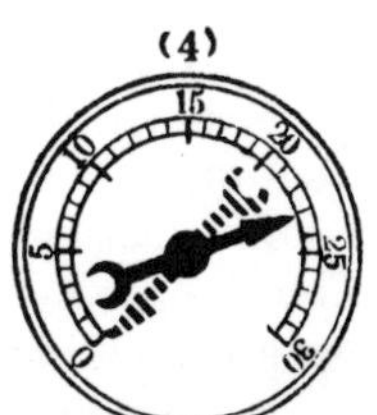

In case 3, gauge hand drops to zero and comes back to about 23 when opening and closing throttle.

(5)

**Sticky Valve.**
Drops occasionally four divisions from normal reading.

(6)

**Burnt Valve.**
Drops regularly several divisions.

(7)

**Leaky Valve.**
Drops about two divisions.

(8)

**Loose Valve Stem Guide.**
Vibrates fast between 14 and 18.

(9)

**Weak Valve Spring.**
From 10 to 22 when accelerating engine, and becomes greater as increasing speed.

(10)

**Late Timing of Valves.**
Remains steady between 8 to 15.

(11)

**Late Ignition Timing.**
Remains steady between 14 to 17.

(12)

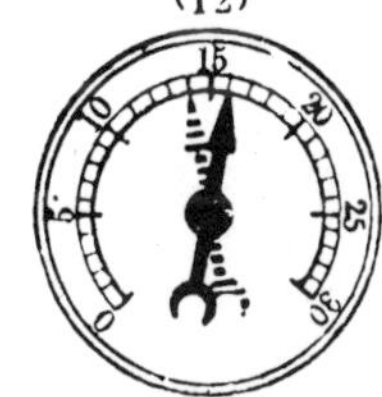

**Spark Plug Gap too Small or Breaker Point Contact Improper.**
Floats between 14 and 16.

(13)

**Leaky Gasket of Intake Manifold or Carburetor.**
Indicates 5 or less.

(14)

**Leaky Cylinder Head Gasket.**
Floats regularly between 5 and 19.

(15)

**Choked Muffler.**
Normal at first, drops to zero and then builds up to 16.

(16)

**Carburetor is Out of Adjustment.**
Floats slowly between 13 and 17.

Vacuum gauge interpretation

**Engine Compression Test**

This test requires the use of a simple vacuum gauge connected to the intake manifold of the engine and a compression test gauge connected to the cylinders (in turn). Both these gauges are relatively easy to use, but the correct interpretation of vacuum gauge readings requires some experience. Vacuum gauges are used to identify a number of engine defects, while the compression gauge is used mainly to pinpoint faulty cylinders. Vacuum gauges are influenced by barometric pressure and will read 1 in. Hg. lower per 1,000 feet altitude. Refer to the accompanying chart for a detailed explanation and interpretation of the most commonly experienced vacuum gauge readings. The compression gauge shows the pressure inside the cylinders in pounds per square inch (psi). Before starting, the battery should be checked for fuel charge and the valve clearances checked. If the car has an automatic choke, block it open. To use this gauge, remove all spark plugs from the warmed up engine and insert the rubber gauge tip into each plug hole (in turn). Turn the engine over at least four or five revolutions, with the throttle wide open, and note and compare readings obtained. If there is less than 15 psi difference between cylinders, the engine can be considered normal. If the difference is greater than 15 psi, squirt about two ounces of engine oil into the cylinder. Turn engine over a few times to allow the oil to spread around the pistons, then repeat the compression test. An increase in compression of more than 5 psi indicates poorly sealing rings. If a cylinder reads low, and adding oil does not result in an appreciable rise in compression pressure, the problem is usually a burnt valve. Two adjacent low compression cylinders are an indication of a blown head gasket.

# Part III
# Tune-Up

A certain number of tools are required in order to perform a good tune-up. These include timing light, feeler gauges, tachometer, dwell meter, volt-ammeter, ohmmeter, compression gauge, vacuum gauge, specific gravity tester (battery) and radiator pres-

## Troubleshooting Chart 2

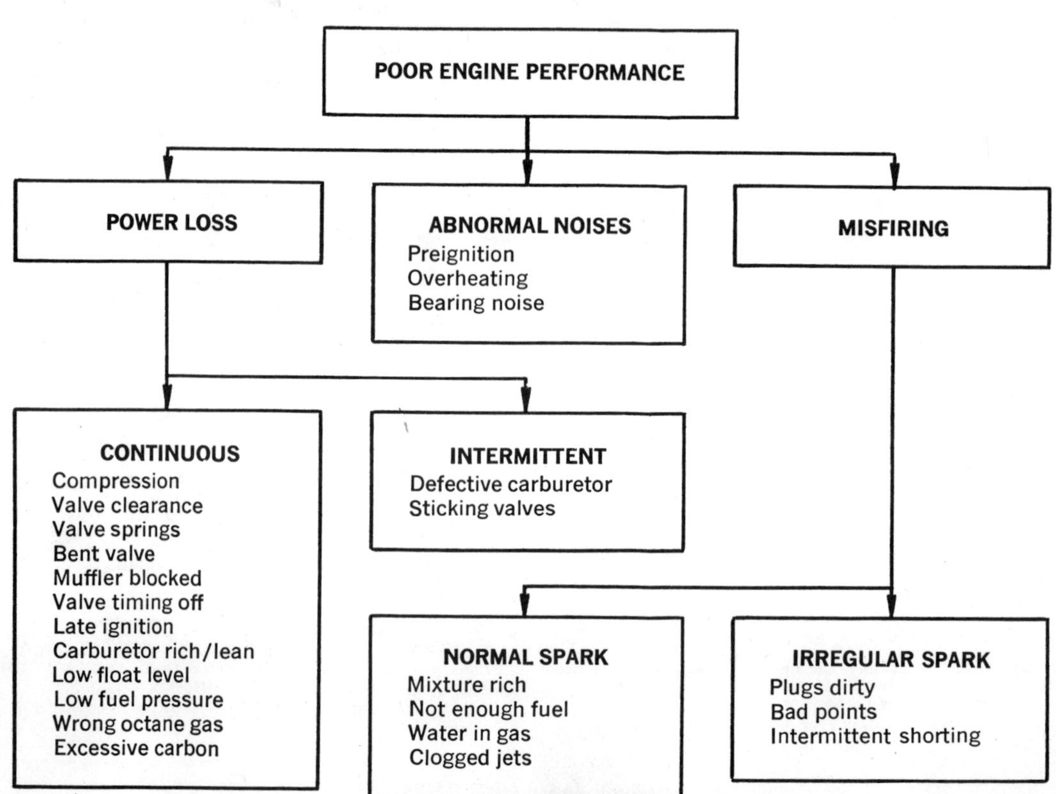

sure gauge. The sequence of tune-up jobs is as follows:

1. Battery
2. Engine oil level
3. Coolant and radiator
4. Fanbelt
5. Fuel filter
6. Air cleaner
7. Distributor and coil (points)
8. Spark plugs
9. Compression test
10. Carburetor
11. Ignition timing
12. Valve clearance
13. Smog control equipment

**Battery**

Check battery specific gravity and connections. Make sure all hold-down bolts are tight, but don't crack the case.

**Oil Level**

Warm up engine and check oil level — if dipstick shows no oil, insert it again, and take another reading. Make sure oil has had sufficient time to drain back into the crankcase. An overfilled crankcase will cause spark plugs to foul and the oil to foam. Check oil for gasoline and/or water contamination. *NOTE: Detergent oil becomes black after five minutes normal operation.*

**Coolant Level and Radiator**

Check condition of coolant; if it looks muddy, flush and replace. Most present day antifreezes are of the permanent type and will last for two years. Test radiator for pressure leaks; also tighten all hoses and hose clamps. If hoses feel stiff and hard (or mushy) it is time to replace them. Screw-

## Troubleshooting Chart 3

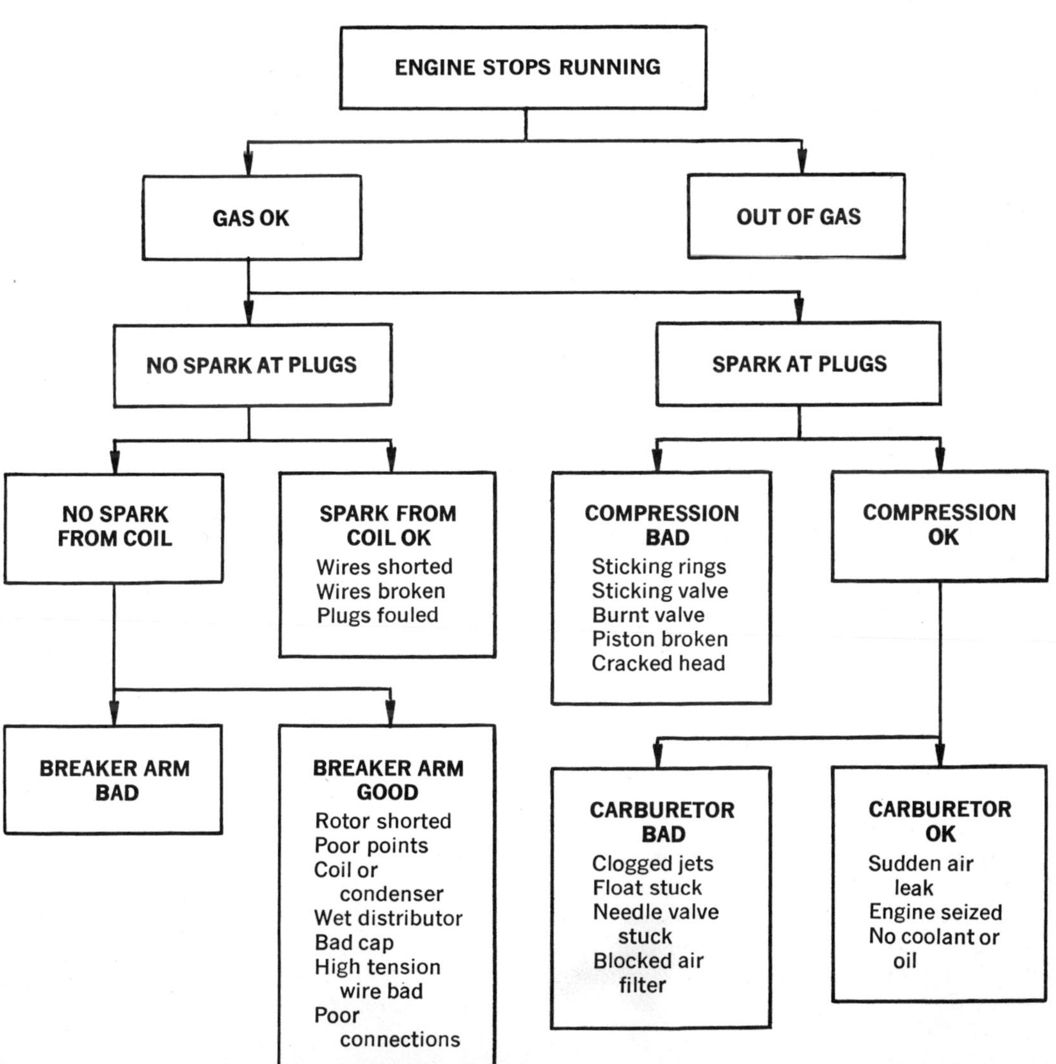

type hose clamps may be used again, but spring clamps should be replaced once they have been removed. Test the radiator cap itself; it should withstand 7 psi. (8R-C engine: 13 psi. FA, FJ engines: 4 psi.) When draining the radiator, remember to drain the engine block at the same time.

**Fanbelt**

If the inside of the belt has a glazed and shiny surface, the belt should be replaced. Check and adjust belt tension so that the longest section of the belt can be depressed ½″ by normal hand pressure (20 lbs.). A loose fanbelt causes overheating and a discharged battery.

**Fuel Filter**

Take off the filter bowl, clean the inside and replace element as necessary. If there is water in the bowl, or heavy accumulations of rust, scale and dirt, replace filter regardless of mileage; otherwise replace about every 12,000 miles or once a year. Be sure to seat the bowl gasket properly.

**Air Cleaner**

Shake off all dust and dirt and blow out (from inside) with compressed air. Replace every 20,000 miles under normal conditions.

**Distributor and Coil**

When removing spark plug wires from the distributor or the plugs, grasp the terminal firmly and pull wire off carefully. Carbon resistance wires are used throughout and, if mishandled, will break internally and become resistive. Check all high tension wires with an ohmmeter and discard any that show more than 25,000 ohms between terminals.

Corolla and Mark II models have two vacuum lines connected to distributor. Test and adjust the distributor in accordance with procedures in Chapter 4. *NOTE: Replace, do not file, points with more than 1,000 miles service. Filing ruins the protective point surface and hastens pitting.* Check the coil for signs of arcing around the tower. Accumulations of dirt on top of the coil may allow moisture to collect. Pull the high tension wire out of the coil and inspect the end; if green and corroded, replace it.

**Spark Plugs**

Remove all plugs and keep in proper sequence. While the plugs are out, take a compression test and write down the pressure of each cylinder. Look at the plugs and compare compression with how the plug looks. Spark plugs may be cleaned by sand-blasting, but too much blasting will remove some of the insulation from the center electrode and ruin an otherwise still serviceable plug. Bend the ground electrode out of the way slightly to allow complete cleaning. Always file the tip and set the spark plug gap with a feeler gauge. A plug showing signs of overheating should be replaced with a plug having a higher heat range (i.e., colder), and vice-versa. Spark plug gap wear is generally estimated to be 0.001″ per 1,000 miles of service, under normal conditions. For short distance city driving, use a hotter plug and adjust the gap to the lower limit. For highway driving, use a colder plug and set the gap wider. Adjust gaps carefully and tighten the plugs to 20 ft. lbs. Install fresh plugs into a hot engine slowly, finger-tight only. Wait for engine heat to expand plugs, then tighten to 20 ft. lbs. For further information on spark plugs, see Chapter 4.

**Ignition Timing**

Use a timing light to set ignition timing, as it is more accurate method than static timing and allows distributor advance to be observed throughout the engine speed range. Be sure to set the octane selector on the distributor to *zero* (center marks) before timing. The timing must be adjusted according to the type of gasoline used. To facilitate reading the timing marks, it is best to clean off the crank pulley and dab a spot of white paint onto the correct timing mark. The best proof of a correctly timed engine is a road test; run the car at about 20 mph and depress the accelerator quickly. If the timing is correct, a slight "pinging" sound will be heard which will fade away as the engine picks up speed. If the pinging is too loud and lingers too long, turn the octane selector towards "R". If there is no pinging at all, turn the selector towards "A". One 360° turn of the selector knob is equal to 5°.

*NOTE: This test does not apply to vehicles with emission control.*

## Adjusting Valve Clearance

### 2M and M Engines

First, align the indent hole on the front side of the camshaft No. 1 bearing cap with the timing line on the camshaft gear flange. At this point, the groove on the crankshaft damper and the "zero" mark on the timing

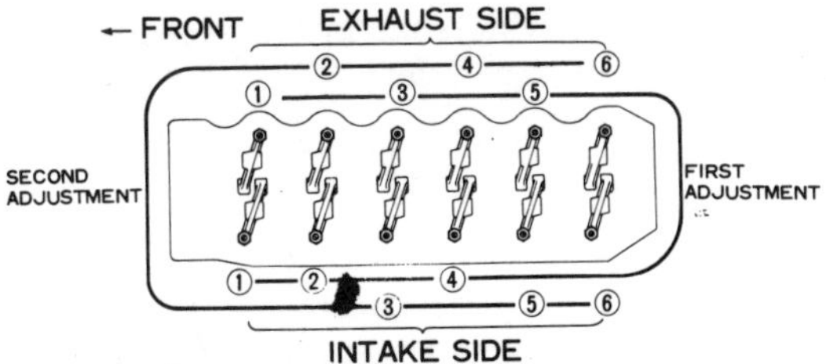

Adjusting 2M valve clearance.

chain cover also should be in alignment. With the marks lined up, No. 1 piston will be at TDC and the intake valves (1), (2) and (4) in the illustration can now be adjusted to 0.004″C and the exhaust valves (1), (3) and (5) can be adjusted to 0.007″C. Rotate the crankshaft one full revolution (in the normal direction of rotation) and again line up the marks on the crankshaft damper and timing chain cover. The intake valves (3), (5) and (6) and the exhaust valves (2), (4) and (6) can now be adjusted. After adjustment is completed, tighten the locknuts to 12–16 ft. lbs.

### F Engine

The engine must be at normal operating temperature (170–185°F.) and the cylinder head bolts and manifold bolts must be tightened to specifications before adjusting valves. Start the engine and set idle speed to 500 rpm, then check the clearance on the running engine by sliding a feeler gauge between the rocker arm and valve stem. The feeler gauge should be able to be pulled out with slight resistance. If not, ad-

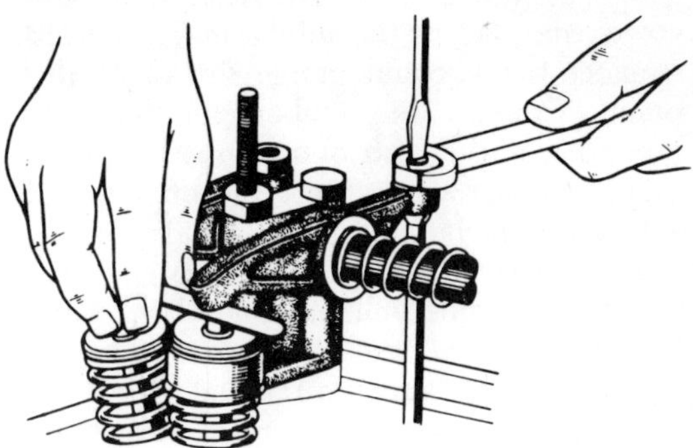
Adjusting F, 2R, 3R, 5R and KC valve clearance.

just by loosening locknut and turning adjusting screw until proper clearance is attained.

### KC, 3RB and 3RC Engines

The procedure is identical to that for the F engine, except that the idle speed must be set to 550 rpm.

### 8RC Engine

Turn piston to TDC (No. 1 cylinder) on compression stroke, then adjust rocker arms (1), (2), (3) and (5); turn crankshaft one complete revolution in the normal direction of rotation, then adjust rocker arms (4), (6), (7) and (8).

*Sticking valves* can be detected by using a timing light. Connect the light to No. 1 cylinder spark plug wire, start the engine and direct the light onto the suspected valve stems. If the valve is not sticking the stem will always show up in the same spot; sticking valves will be irregular in motion. With practice, it is even possible to detect the speed at which the valves float.

## Carburetor Adjustment

Carburetor adjustment and repair is found in Chapter 5. However, idle speed adjustment is simplified by use of a vacuum

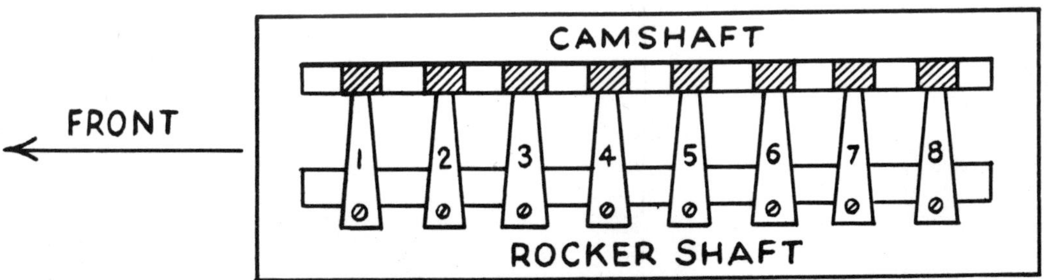

Adjusting 8R valve clearance (Mark II).

gauge, as well as the usual tachometer. Unscrew the plug in the intake manifold and connect the vacuum gauge fitting at this point. Connect the tachometer leads to ground and the distributor-to-coil primary (low voltage) wire. Start the engine and adjust the carburetor throttle valve screw to obtain the lowest possible idle speed at which the engine will run smoothly. Now, turn the idle *mixture* screw to obtain the highest possible vacuum reading. Both adjustment screws must be turned to get the best idle speed/vacuum reading. *NOTE: On cars equipped with pollution controls, set idle speed to specified limits only.*

### Compression Test

Compression testing is done only with a fully warmed up engine. The battery must be fully charged to ensure an engine speed of at least 250 rpm. Keep the throttle valve and choke wide open when testing compression. Should the compression test show one (or more) cylinders to be below the specified readings, squirt some engine oil into the cylinder being tested and repeat the test. A noticeable increase in compression indicates that the piston rings are worn. If there is no appreciable increase in compression it means that valves are burned or not seating properly. Difference in compression between any two cylinders should not exceed 15 psi.

### Smog Controls

All late model cars are equipped with smog (air pollution) control devices. The one unit most likely to cause trouble is the *positive crankcase ventilation* valve (PCV valve). Wash valve in solvent every 6,000 miles and replace once a year or every 12,000 miles. The rest of the system is fully described in Chapter 5.

# Chapter 2
# Engine

All Toyota engines conform to standard designs, both overhead valve (OHV) and single overhead camshaft (SOHC) types being used. All are water cooled and equipped with a single two-barrel downdraft carburetor (except the early FJ series).

*COROLLA, KC* This 1100 cc. engine has an aluminum cylinder head with wedge-shaped combustion chambers, five main bearing crankshaft, aluminum three-ring pistons and a four-bearing camshaft. A full-flow lubricating system is used and there is no vibration damper. A new 1200 cc. en-

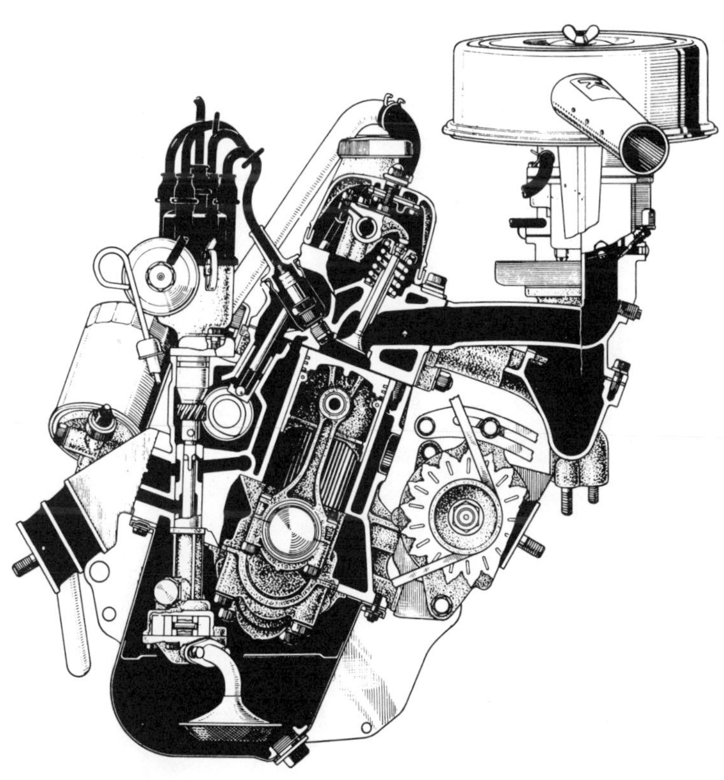

Corolla KC engine.

gine, the 3K-C with emission control, is available for 1970.

*CORONA, 3R* An all cast-iron, 1900 cc. OHV engine having three main bearings, no vibration damper and tub-shaped combustion chambers. Engine has slotted three-ring pistons, five-bearing camshaft and full-flow lubrication system. Difference between the 3R-B and the 3R-C—C is equipped with emission controls.

*CROWN, 2M* A six-cylinder SOHC engine having aluminum head and hemispherical combustion chambers, seven main bearing crankshaft, vibration damper, full-

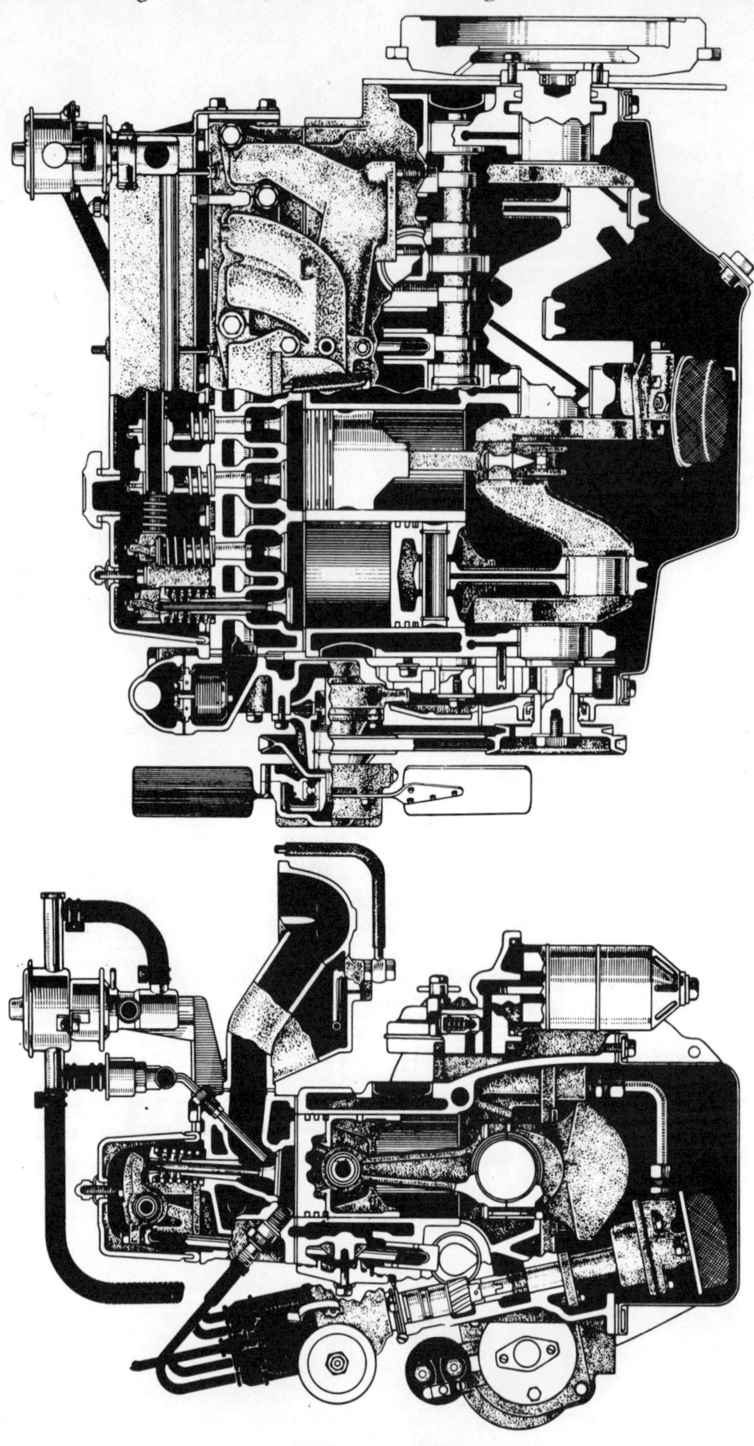

Corona 3RC engine.

flow oil system and three-ring pistons. Crankshaft thrust is taken at the center main bearing by special washers.

*CORONA MARK II, 8R-C* This is a new engine imported late in 1969. It is an all cast-iron engine having 1858 cc. displacement with a single overhead camshaft (SOHC) and a five main bearing crankshaft without vibration damper. Engine has flat-top pistons and wedge-shaped combustion chambers with a 9:1 compression and full-flow lubrication. There are four camshaft bearings, and two double roller chains drive the camshaft.

*LAND CRUISER, FJ* A large (237 cu. in.) OHV engine with cast-iron chambers, four main and four camshaft bearings, two compression and two oil rings on aluminum pistons. This engine is long stroked and slow revving, but has good torque output and is ideally suited for this type special vehicle.

## Removing the Engine

It is advisable to remove both engine and transmission together, unless special transmission supports are available. *NOTE: The following steps are common to all engines. Special operations for specific models are indicated separately.*

Remove hood, radiator grille and radiator support, then remove battery from car (for protection) and disconnect all electrical wiring. To save assembly time, mark each disconnected wire and terminal with a small tag. Now, drain coolant and engine oil. Disconnect radiator and heater hoses and remove radiator. Disconnect and remove, as necessary, all fuel lines, choke and accelerator control cables and wires. Disconnect rear transmission mounts and remove drive shaft, then remove fan. Disconnect exhaust pipe(s). Install lifting hooks or eyebolts. *NOTE: Since the engine must be sharply tilted in order to clear the firewall, it will be necessary to jack up the car and support it on jack stands.*

*FJ Series* Remove engine crankcase stone guards. Remove gearshift linkage, transfer control intermediate rod from control shaft, and engine ground strap. Disconnect front motor mounts and rear engine supports, then remove passenger seat and gasoline tank assembly. Remove transmission cover and parking brake lock plate from firewall; disconnect speedometer cable. Unhook clutch release spring and remove clutch release cylinder. Remove crossmember.

## Disassembling the Engine

Detach the transmission from the engine. If the pressure plate is to be used again, mark its position on the flywheel prior to removal. Remove carburetor, fuel pump, alternator, water pump, coil and distributor, intake and exhaust manifolds, oil filler tube (on FJ series), valve cover and gasket. *NOTE: FJ, take off the rocker shaft oil delivery pipe and screen.* Remove rocker shaft support bolts and lift off the shaft assembly, then remove pushrods.

On SOHC engine, remove crankshaft pulley and key, drop oil pan and remove oil pump intake screen and tube. Next remove

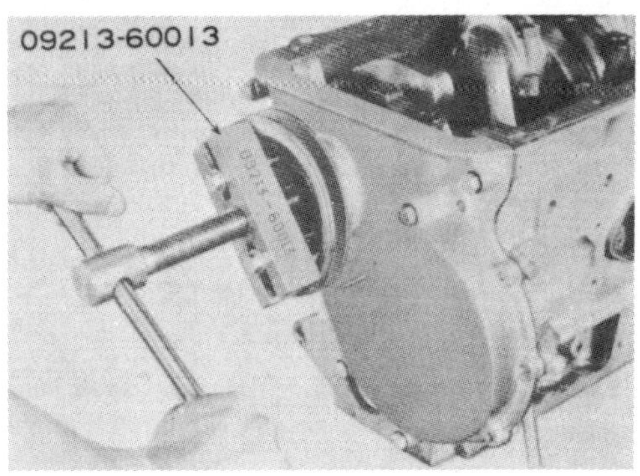

Removing crankshaft pulley with special puller.

the cylinder head bolts as shown. *CAUTION: Do not remove bolts one at a time, first loosen them in sequence. This will prevent warping the head.*

After removing the cylinder head and gasket, place head on a clean surface (wood blocks) to prevent damage. Remove the valve lifters and store in correct sequence, together with previously removed pushrods. Remove the timing chain cover and gasket and the rear oil seal retainer, chain tensioner and damper, then the chain itself. Remove oil pump drive eccentric and connecting rod caps. Use ridge reamer to cut carbon ridge at top edge of cylinder bore, then push pistons and rods out from the bottom. Re-

# Engine Rebuilding Specifications

| Engine Model | Main Bearing Journal Dia. (in.) | Con Rod Bearing Journal Dia. (in.) | Camshaft Journal Dia. (in.) | Cylinder Bore Dia. (in.) | Piston Ring Side Clearance (in.) | Piston Ring End-Gap (in.) | Rocker Shaft Dia. (in.) | Main Bearing oil Clearance (in.) | Rod Bearing oil Clearance (in.) | Crankshaft End-Play (in.) | Maximum Runout of Flywheel (in.) | Piston to Bore Clearance (in.) | Con Rod to Crankpin Side-Play (in.) |
|---|---|---|---|---|---|---|---|---|---|---|---|---|---|
| 2M<br>M | 2.3616–2.3622 | 2.0466–<br>2.0472 | 1.3771–1.3778 | 2.9527–<br>2.9535<br>① | .0012–.0028/1st<br>.0008–.0024/2nd<br>oil ring–"O" | compression rings<br>.006–.014<br>oil rings<br>.008–.020 | .7272–<br>.7281 | .0007–<br>.0017<br>Limit<br>.003 | .0006–<br>.002<br>Limit<br>.003 | .0020–<br>.0100 | .008 | .0012–<br>.0020 | .0043–<br>.0097 |
| F<br>(A&J) | 2.6366–2.6378/1<br>2.6957–2.6969/2<br>2.7547–2.7559/3<br>2.8138–2.8150/4 | 2.1252–<br>2.1260 | 1.8880–1.8888/1st<br>1.8289–1.8297/2nd<br>1.7699–1.7707/3rd<br>1.7108–1.7116/4th | 3.5415–<br>3.5435<br>② | .0016–.0031/1st<br>.0016–.0031/2nd<br>.0016–.0031/3rd<br>.0016–.0033/4th | .0059–.0177/1st<br>.0059–.0157/2nd<br>.0059–.0177/3rd<br>.0059–.0157/4th | .7270–<br>.7280 | .0012–<br>.0018<br>Limit<br>.004 | .0008–<br>.0024<br>Limit<br>.004 | .0012–<br>.0051 | .008 | .0012–<br>.0020 | .004–<br>.009 |
| 3R<br>3R-B<br>3R-C | 2.3634–2.3640 | 2.1648–<br>2.1654 | 1.8291–1.8297/1st<br>1.8192–1.8198/2nd<br>1.8094–1.8100/3rd<br>1.7996–1.8002/4th<br>1.7898–1.7904/5th | 3.4645–<br>3.4651 | .0012–.0027/1st<br>.0012–.0027/2nd<br>.0010–.0027/3rd | .0078–.0158/1st<br>.0059–.0137/2nd<br>.0059–.0137/3rd | N.A. | .0008–<br>.0022 | .0010–<br>.0024 | .002–<br>.009 | .008 | .0012–<br>.0020 | .0067–<br>.0110 |
| K-C | 1.9585–1.9685 | 1.6526–<br>1.6535 | 1.7011–1.7018/1st<br>1.6913–1.6920/2nd<br>1.6814–1.6823/3rd<br>1.6716–1.6722/4th | 2.955–<br>2.957 | .001–.003/1st<br>.0008–.002/2nd<br>.0006–.002/3rd | .006–.014 | N.A. | .0006–<br>.0016<br>Limit<br>.004 | .0006–<br>.0016<br>Limit<br>.004 | .0016–<br>.0087<br>Limit<br>.0118 | .008 | .001–<br>.002 | .004–<br>.008 |
| 8R-C | 2.3613–2.3622 | 2.0857–<br>2.0866 | 1.3768–1.3778 | 3.3857–<br>3.3861<br>③ | .001–.003/1st<br>.001–.003/2nd<br>.001–.003/3rd | .004–.012 | N.A. | .0008–<br>.0020<br>Limit<br>.003 | .0008–<br>.0020<br>Limit<br>.003 | .002–<br>.010<br>Limit<br>.012 | .008 | .001–<br>.002 | .0043–<br>.0097 |

① Bore diameter covers total range of No. 1 and No. 2 sizes.

② Bores marked "O." Other sizes:

| Mark | Size |
|---|---|
| 1 | 3.5515–3.5535 |
| 2 | 3.5615–3.5635 |
| 3 | 3.5715–3.5735 |
| 4 | 3.5815–3.5835 |

③ For 85.965 mm. pistons.

assemble caps to rods and make sure they are marked. Remove flywheel, main bearings and thrust washers.

From the head, remove valve springs and valves. Store in numbered rack unless they are to be replaced. Disassemble the rocker shaft, then the pistons.

Cylinder head bolt removal sequence.

## Inspecting the Engine

*Cylinder head* Remove, with a wire brush, all carbon deposits from the combustion chambers. Clean head thoroughly and check for cracks around the valve seats. Check the flatness of the head surface with a straightedge. If it is deformed more than 0.008″, the head should be resurfaced. Also, check

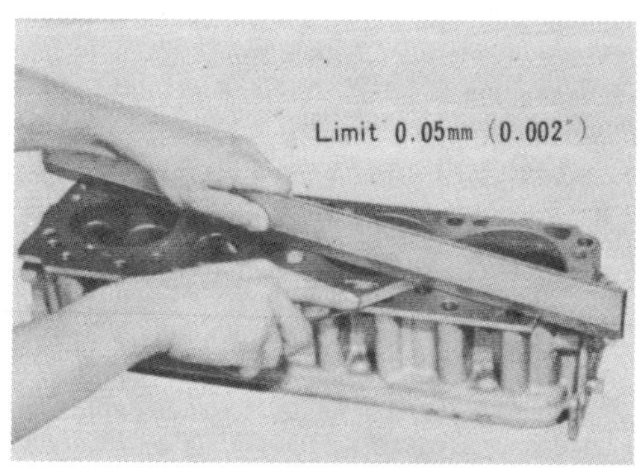

Checking cylinder head with straightedge.

for distortion of the manifold surface in the same manner.

*Valves* Check valve guides for excessive play. Insert the cleaned valve into its guide so that it is almost seated, then rock sideways. If the play at the upper end of the valve stem exceeds .003-.004″, the guides can be considered worn and should be replaced. Worn valve guides can be broken off at the top and driven out with a suitable punch. If possible, preheat the head to avoid any unnecessary stress (180-212° F.). Install snap-ring onto new guide and drive into head from the top (towards the block side). New guides must be reamed to the exact dimensions. *NOTE: Worn valve guides cause loss of power, oil burning and other performance ills.*

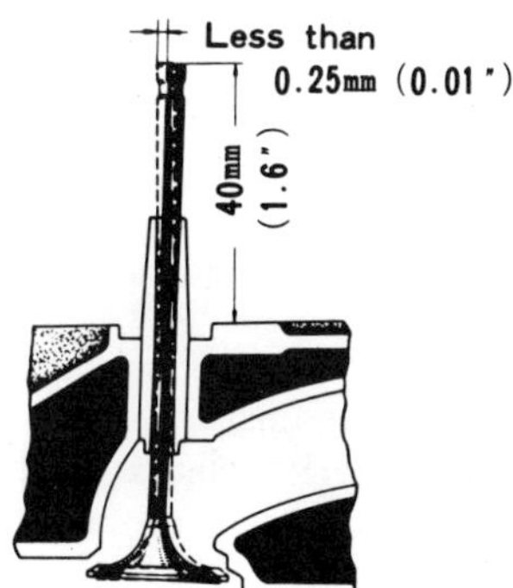

Checking valve guide play.

*Valve seats* Proper seating of the valves is necessary for good performance. Reface seats with coarse and fine grinding stones and be sure to undercut and overcut the seat as per specifications. Valve should seat exactly in the center of the seat with a narrow area of contact. If the seat is too high, use a flat cutter to lower it. Use the steep cutter to raise a low seat.

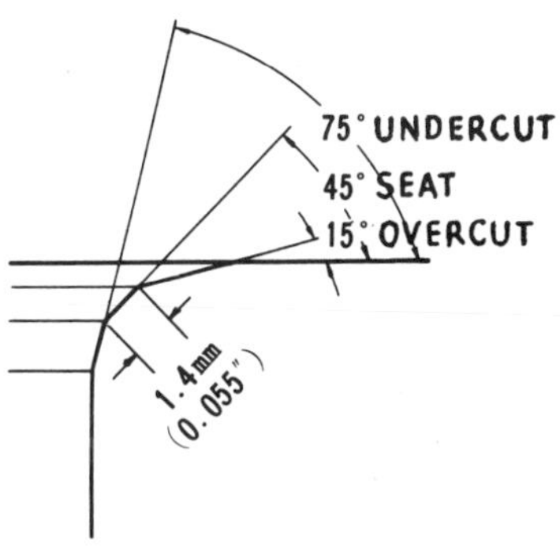

Valve seat angles, showing the three cutting phases.

*Valves* Clean with stiff wire brush to remove all accumulated carbon and dirt. Check stems for bending and heads for wear and edge thickness. Reface valves on refacing machine, then lightly lap valves and seats with valve compound. *NOTE: Thor-*

*oughly remove compound after lapping.*

*Valve springs* Check valve spring free length, check for squareness and, if possible, for load characteristics. Place the spring and a steel square on a flat surface and slide the square up to the spring. Rotate the spring slowly against the square—if there is more than 0.079″ clearance between the spring and the square replace the spring.

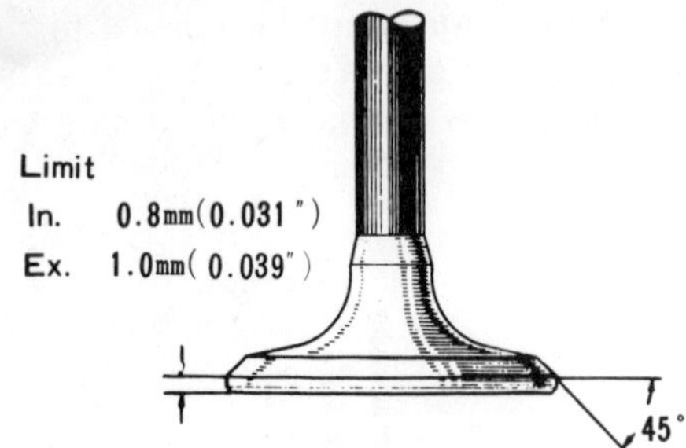


Valve head angle and edge thickness.

*Rocker shaft and arms* Check for wear at the tip of the rocker arms. Rocker arms may be refaced on a special attachment of the valve grinder, provided they are not worn beyond limits. Measure the shaft with a micrometer and replace if worn, then check springs for rust and tension loss.

*Intake and exhaust manifolds* Clean with solvent and remove old gaskets. Check for cracks and corrosion. If distortion is greater than .015″, the manifold must be refaced or replaced.

*Valve lifters and pushrods* Check pushrods for bending; inspect the ends for roughness or excessive wear. Lifters should fit into their block bores with a clearance not greater then 0.004″. Oversize lifters are available—ream the lifter hole to the correct size first. *NOTE: Valves allow an engine to breathe. Anything interfering with this will cause loss of performance.*

*Engine block* Throughly clean block inside and out. Blow out all passages with compressed air. Look for cracks, cuts and gouges on the working faces, then replace all freeze plugs. Check top surface for warpage—more than 0.006″ necessitates resurfacing. Check cylinder bores for roundness, taper or wear. If limits are exceeded, rebore to nearest oversize. Pistons and rings are supplied in oversizes up to 0.060″ and cylinder sleeves are available in two sizes. Small nicks and scratches on the cylinder walls can be honed out. Clean block after honing and use light oil on working surfaces to prevent rust.

*Crankshaft* Clean shaft and blow out oilways with compressed air. Look for deep gouges or nicks which could seriously upset crankshaft balance. Inspect main journals and crankpins for scoring, signs of overheating, etc. Use a micrometer to measure wear, roundness and taper. Check shaft for bending. Inspect and/or replace the bronze bushing at flywheel side of shaft.

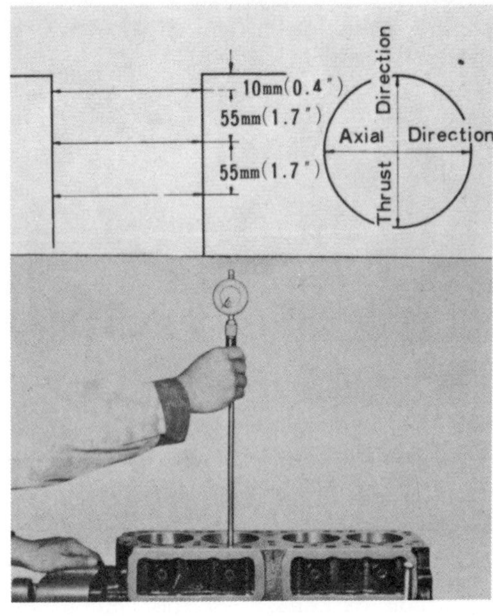


Checking cylinder bore for wear.

*Main bearings* Clean off and dry all main bearing seats in block. (Avoid use of oil for this operation.) Place upper bearing halves in their seats in block, place crankshaft onto bearings, insert strip of PLASTIGAGE (avoid oil hole) and install lower bearing

Checking bearing clearance using PLASTIGAGE.

half with cap. *CAUTION: Do not rotate the shaft.* Tighten to proper torque and remove bearing half, then compare the width of the PLASTIGAGE with the scale. If bearing clearance is excessive, fit the correct undersize bearing (both halves). *Do not file bearing caps to adjust clearance.* Check alignment of oil holes, oil all surfaces prior to installation and check crankshaft end-play.

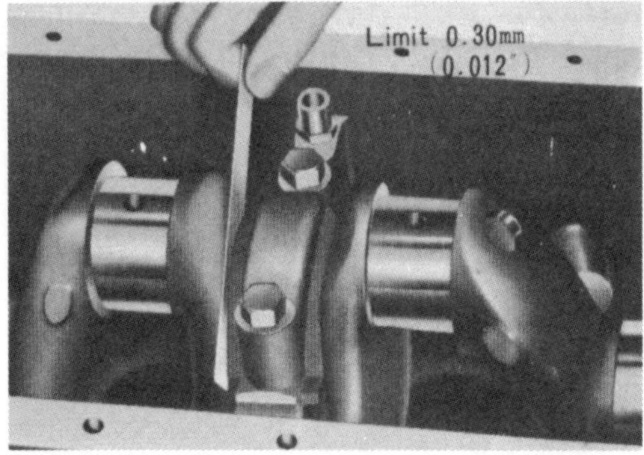


Checking crankshaft end-play.

*Pistons, piston pins and rings* After driving out piston pin, tag it for installation into the same piston. Clean the piston top with a wire brush and use a ring groove cleaning tool (or a broken ring) to remove accumulated carbon from the ring grooves. Clean out oil holes in the oil grooves. Use a micrometer to measure the piston diameter (at right angles to the pin axis). Check for roundness by measuring across the pin axis just below the oil ring.

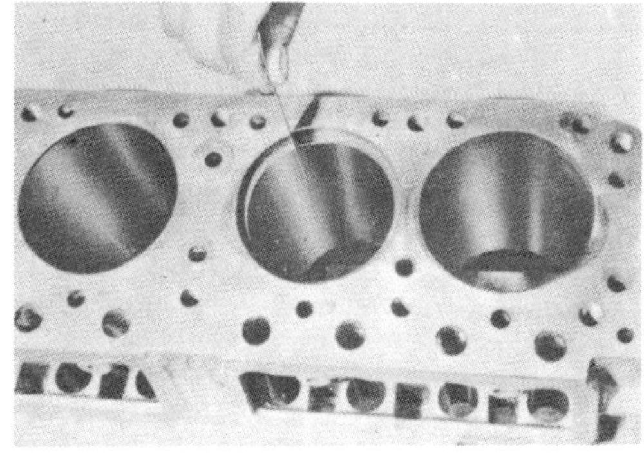

Checking piston ring end gap using a feeler gauge.

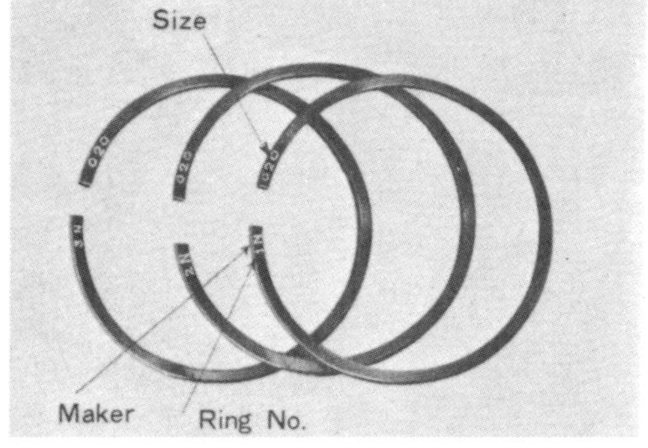


Toyota piston rings.

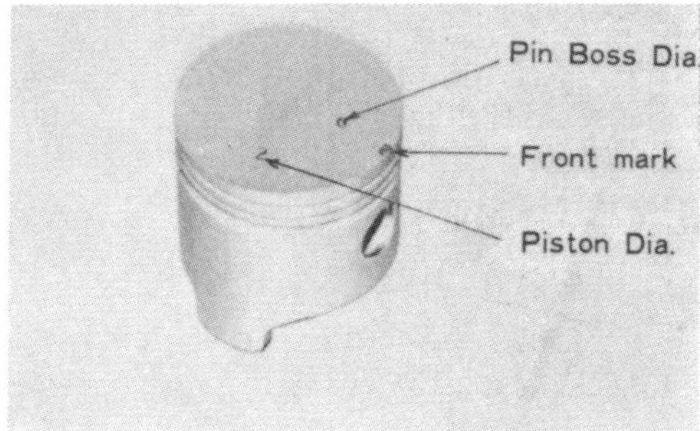


Piston code interpretation.

Pistons have three marks on top face: a notch indicating front, the size stamping of piston and another stamped number showing size of the piston pin bore. Check ring fit in grooves (side clearance). Insert each ring to be measured into the bore and, with inverted piston, push ring down about 1″. Measure end gap. Next, push ring down into bore about 4″ from top and measure end gap again. If there is more than 0.008″ difference, bore taper is excessive and cylin-

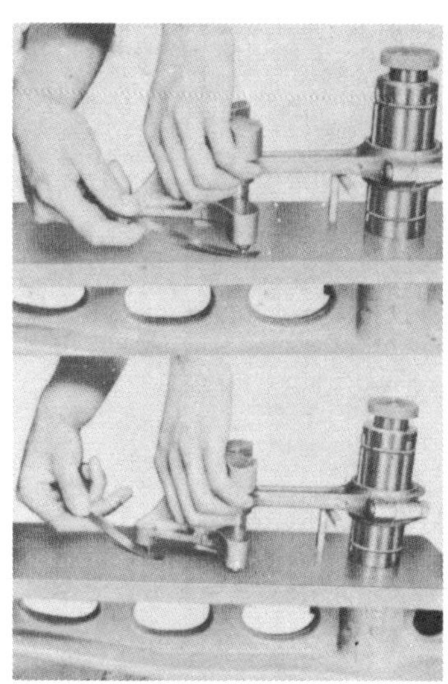

Checking connecting rod for straightness. Bent rods are usually replaced.

der should be rebored. Install piston pin by hand, after preheating piston to 140° F.

*Connecting rods* Clean rods and check for damage. Blow out oil holes. Check rods twisting or bending. Limits are generally 0.002″ per 4″ of rod length. Rods can be straightened and any replacement rods must weight within 2 ozs. of the old rod. Replace small end bushing if new pins are fitted. Check connecting rod bearings (big end) with PLASTIGAGE in the same manner as main bearings were checked, then check side play of rod on crankshaft. If clearance is excessive, the rod must be replaced.

*Camshaft and timing chain (K-engine only)* A double-roller type timing chain with two dampers (tension and vibration) is used.

It is best to set the piston of No. 1 cylinder at TDC and to disconnect the battery be-

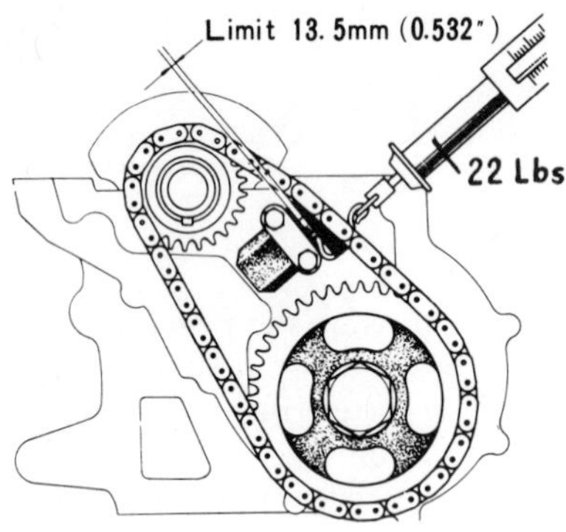


Checking timing chain deflection.

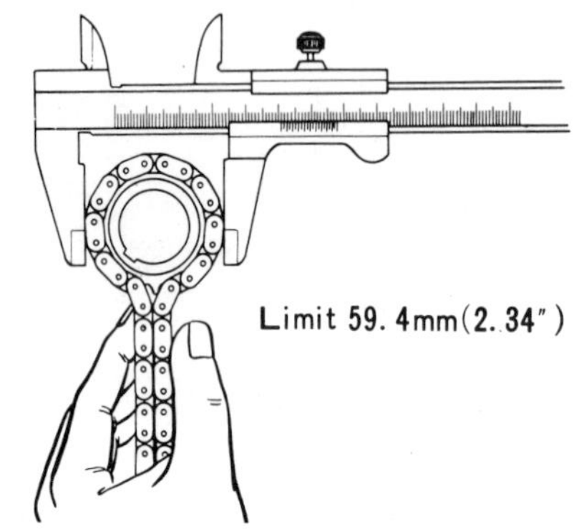


Checking sprocket for wear.

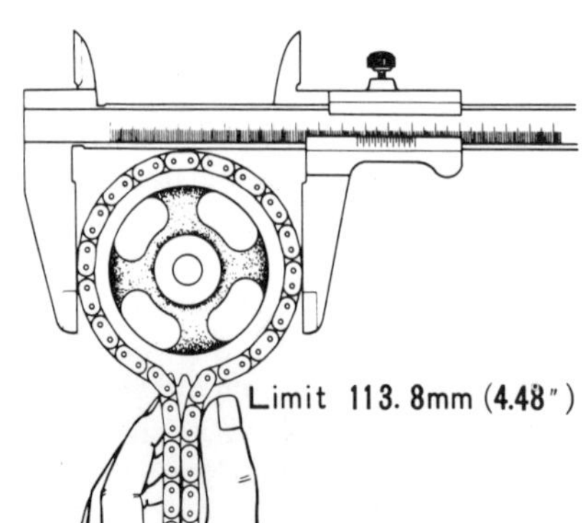


Checking sprocket for wear.

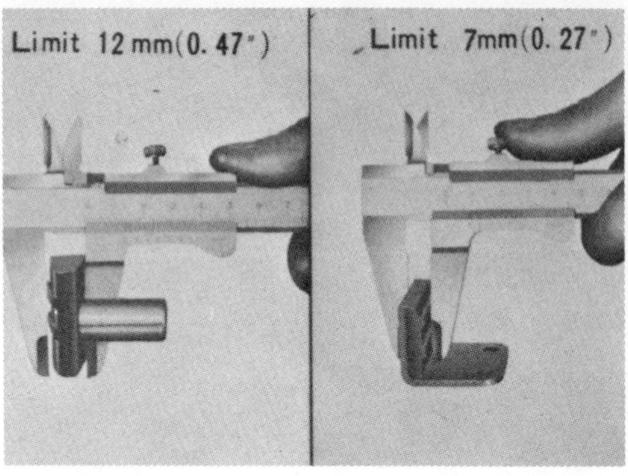


Checking dampers; left is tension unit, right is vibration unit.

Timing mark alignment, Corolla engine.

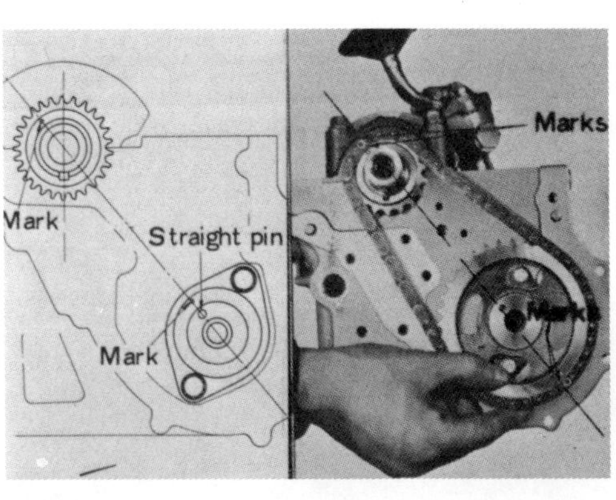


Installing timing chain, Corolla.

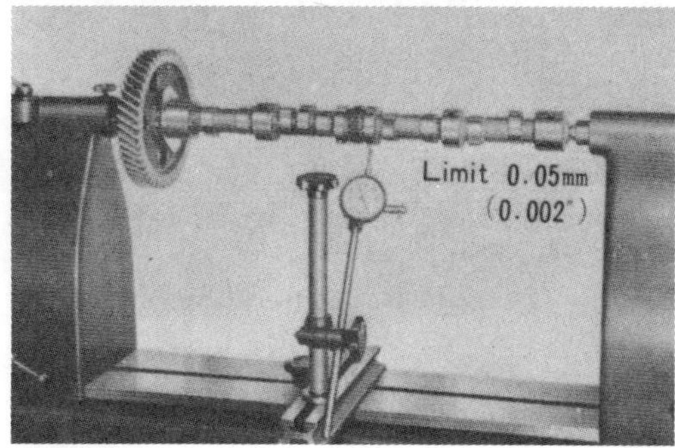


Checking camshaft runout on lathe.

fore removing timing gears and chain. Also, check timing chain deflection (stretch) before disassembling.

Check for wear, broken rollers and chipped gear teeth and replace as necessary. Test chain and sprocket outer diameters as shown and replace worn damper pads. Remove spring from tensioner and lightly oil plunger. Fit plunger into body and block the two oil holes with a finger, then pull plunger about halfway out. A good plunger should be sucked back quickly. Replace tensioner assembly if this is not the case. *NOTE: Timing marks on all sprockets and chain must be lined up correctly, as shown, during assembly.*

*Camshaft* Check runout of camshaft and straighten or replace the shaft if eccentricity exceeds 0.002″. Inspect all lobes for wear and pitting. Check distributor drive gear

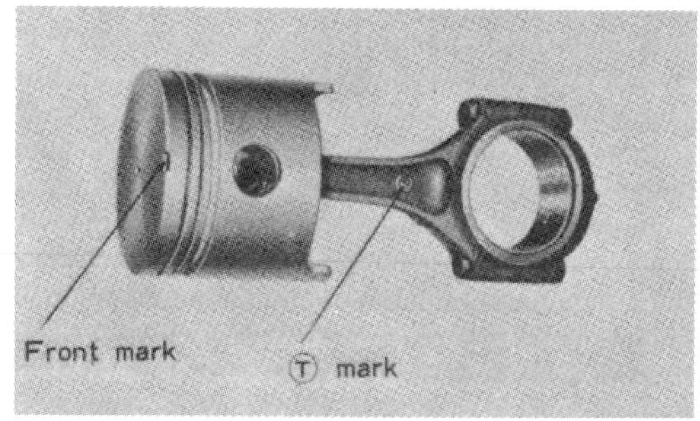


Piston and connecting rod, showing "T" mark location.

and replace camshaft if gear is worn. Check camshaft end-play and adjust by changing thrust plate. Check all journals for wear and size. Bearings are available to 0.020″ undersize. Inspect timing gear and replace if worn or cracked. Timing gear runout limit is 0.008″ and backlash should not exceed 0.008″.

## Assembling the Engine

Thoroughly clean all parts, especially oil passages, oil holes, bearings, bearing seats and cylinder walls. Apply clean engine oil to all moving parts of the engine. Use new gaskets and oil seals and use a liquid sealer to ensure sealing of gaskets. Recheck oil clearances and end-play allowances during assembly.

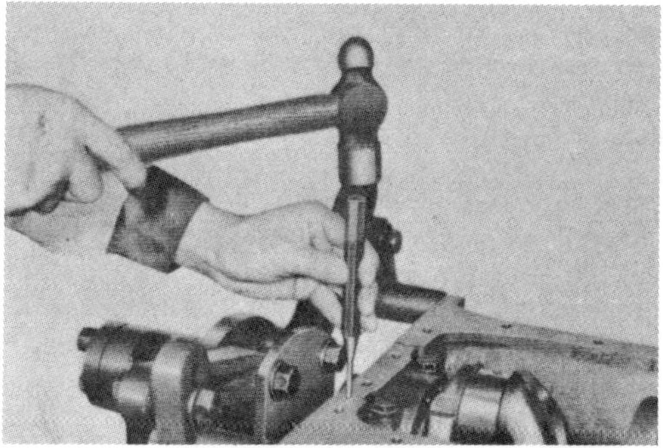

Installing oil seal packings.

Install the springs, rocker arms and supports and the tension and lock springs onto the rocker shaft. The support lock screw hole must face to the front. Install valves into head, along with the inner and outer springs and spring retainers. Compress the valve springs (painted end goes down) and install valve locks and O-rings.

Assemble pistons and rods. (Connecting rod front is marked with a "T", piston ring marks face "up" and piston front side is

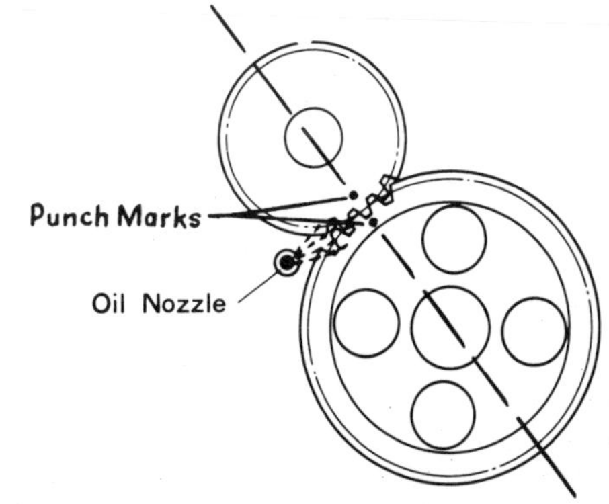


Timing gears and oil nozzle position.

## Engine Torque Specifications

(Ft. Lbs.)

| Engine Model | Cylinder Head Bolts | Intake Manifold Nuts | Exhaust Manifold Nuts | Rocker Shaft Supports | Main Bearing Caps | Rod Bearing Caps | Cam Bearing Caps | Timing Cover Bolts | Flywheel Bolts | Clut Cov Bol |
|---|---|---|---|---|---|---|---|---|---|---|
| 3R 3R-B 3R-C | 80–85 | 14–22 | 14–22 | 15–18 | 75–80 | 43–51 | —— | 7–11.5 | 43–49 | 14- |
| K-C | 36–48 | 14–22 | 14–22 | 13–16 | 39–47 | 29–37 | —— | 4–6 | 39–48 | 7- |
| 2M M | 8mm/11–15 13mm/54–61 | 22–29 | 10–14 | 22–32 | 71–78 | 30–35 | 12–16 | 8mm/11–15 10mm/22–39 | 41–45 | 6- |
| 8R-C | 75–85 | 20–25 | 20–25 | 12–17 | 72–80 | 42–48 | 12–17 | 11–15 | 43–48 | 6- |
| F(A&J) | 83–98 | 14–22 | 14–22 | 10mm/25–30 8mm/14–21 | 1, 2, 3/90–108 rear/76–94 | 35–55 | —— | 12 | 43–51 | 2 |

notched.) Install connecting rod bearings and caps, then hand-tighten the cap nuts. Install rear oil seal into groove at rear of cylinder block, using a suitable tool, then cut off the protruding ends flush with block.

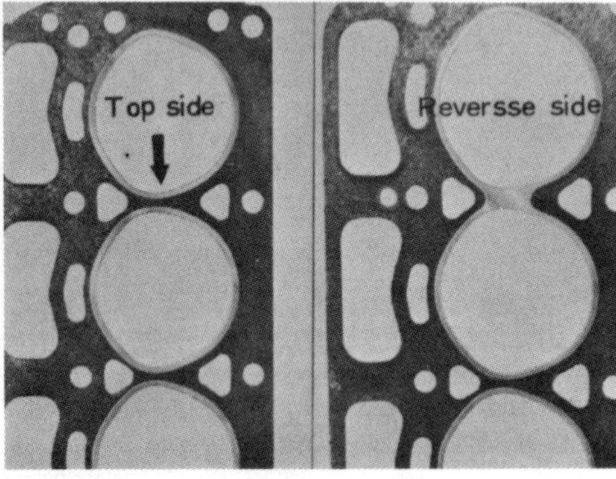


Corolla cylinder head gasket.

Install upper halves of main bearings and install upper halves of crankshaft thrust bearings with oil grooves facing "out". Install crankshaft and place the lower halves of the main and thrust bearings in position. Gradually tighten the main bearing cap nuts to specifications. *NOTE: Arrow on main bearing caps must face to front.* Check crankshaft end-play.

Using gasket cement, install the two rear main bearing packings into the block. Install pistons into bores using a suitable ring compressing tool. Piston ring gaps should face away from thrust side of piston. Tighten connecting rod cap nuts to specifications, and install front end plate and gasket.

Install camshaft assembly and align the timing gears as marked. Tighten thrust plate to 14.5 ft. lbs. and recheck the backlash. Install timing gear oil nozzle into cylinder block and align discharge hole to-

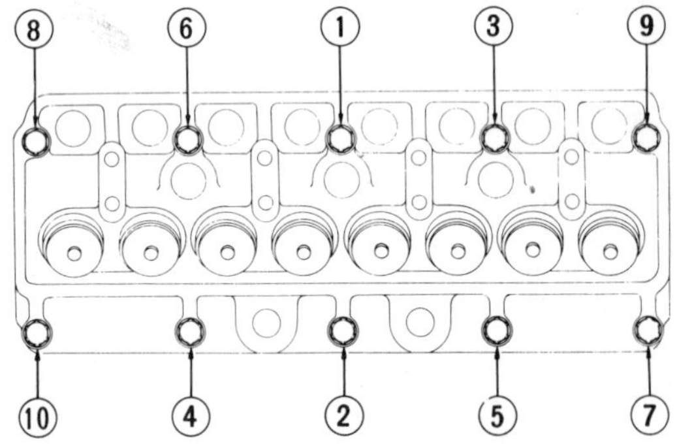


Corolla (KC engine) cylinder head bolt tightening sequence.

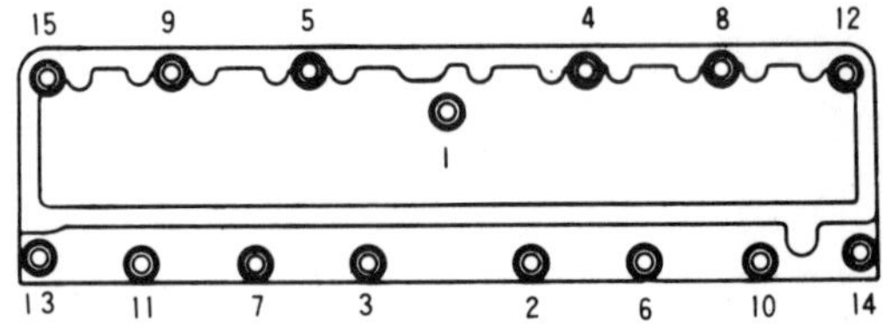


Land Cruiser (F engine) cylinder head bolt tightening sequence.

wards the timing gears. Stake in place with a centerpunch. Install timing gear cover and crankshaft pulley, using a new oil seal. Tighten pulley nut. Install oil pump as-

Corona (3R, 3RB engine) cylinder head bolt tightening sequence.

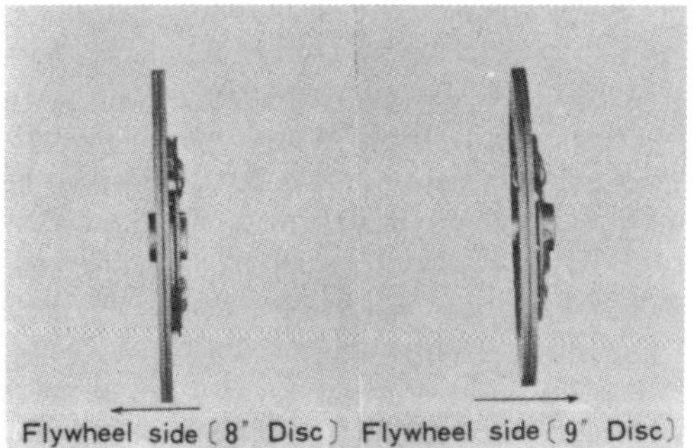


Clutch disc position.

sembly and outlet pipe, then install oil pan and gasket.

Install cylinder head and gasket and tighten, in correct sequence, to specified torque. Install valve lifters, pushrods and rocker shaft assembly, followed by pushrod covers, oil pressure sending unit, temperature sending unit, engine draincock vent tube and dipstick tube. Tighten manifolds and gaskets from center outwards, then install carburetor, covering it with a clean cloth to prevent entry of dirt or small objects.

Install choke stove pipes into manifold. Next install (not necessarily in order mentioned) oil filter, alternator, engine mounts, water pump and thermostat housing, fanbelt, air injection pump and belt, air injection manifolds and valves, heater pipes, distributor, fuel pump, spark plugs, and any other parts or accessories that were removed, such as flywheel, converter and starter motor. *Do not install valve cover prior to engine installation.*

Removing rocker shaft bolts, M and 2M engine.

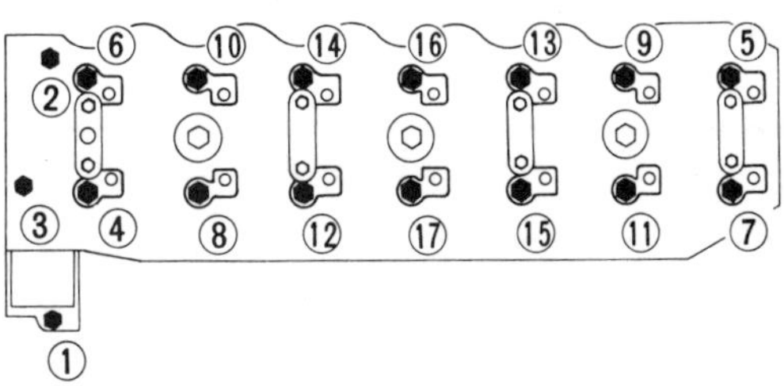


Crown (M, 2M engine) cylinder head bolt removal sequence.

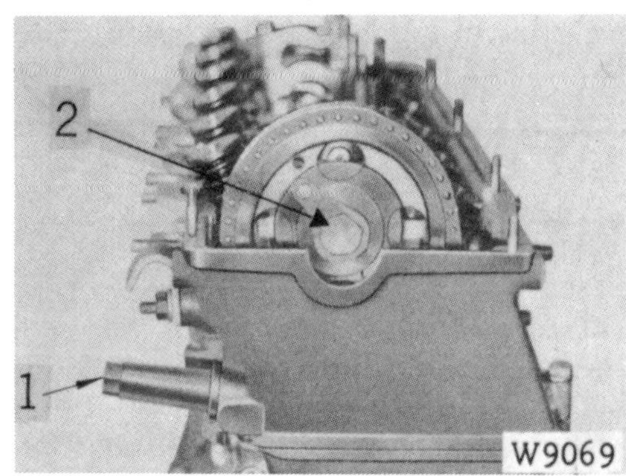


Chain tensioner (1) and timing gear bolt (2).

Removing oil pump drive.

Checking camshaft end-play.

## Installing the Engine

Installation of engine is done by reversing removal order. Before connecting hoist, bolt clutch, or converter, and transmission to the engine. Install oil cooler lines and brackets and bolt clutch release cylinder to clutch fork. Fill transmission with proper quantity and grade of lubricant before installation.

## Special Procedures

### Disassembling the 2M Engine

Disconnect all external parts, as with other engine types, then proceed as follows: remove the valve cover and gasket. *CAUTION: Any time the cover is removed, front of cylinder head should be covered to prevent small objects from falling into the crankcase.* Remove the oil feed pipe union from front of camshaft (two bolts). Loosen and remove the bolts that hold the rocker shaft supports. *NOTE: Do not remove them one at a time; loosen all evenly, then remove.*

Before removing the chain tensioner set the valve timing (with No. 1 cylinder at TDC). Next, remove the camshaft timing gear. *NOTE: This bolt has a LEFT-HANDED thread.* Remove the four camshaft bearing caps and lift out the camshaft. Immediately after removing the camshaft, replace the bearing caps. If the bearings must be taken out of their caps, mark rear of bearings lightly for proper assembly. Remove fuel pump drive, then loosen and remove the cylinder head bolts in sequence. *NOTE: Completely removing the bolts one at a time will cause warping of the head.* When removing the head, lift straight up, as there are two dowel pins for positive head location.

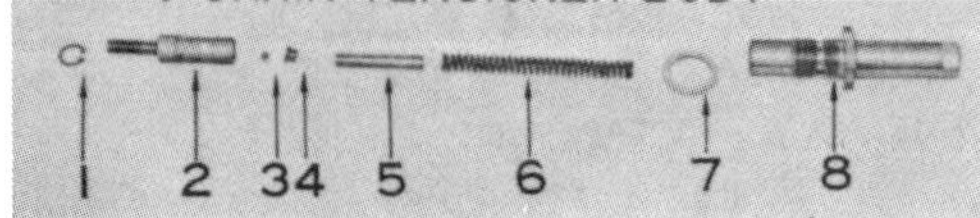


Chain tensioner components.

1. Hole snap ring
2. Chain tension plunger
3. Ball
4. Check ball retainer
5. Chain tensioner bar
6. Compression spring
7. Gasket
8. Chain tensioner body

### Assembling the 2M Engine

These operations are additional to, or different from, those listed for the OHV types. When installing the timing gears, the punch marks on the gear faces must face front (out). Check camshaft end-play between the front support and camshaft gear flange. If the clearance exceeds 0.012″, replace the No. 2 bearing. Normal play is 0.002–0.006″. Inspect the cam lobes for wear. Small irregularities may be honed out with a smooth oilstone.

Use micrometer to measure the cam lobe wear. Limits are 1.535″ intake and 1.496″ exhaust. Check camshaft bearings in their caps with PLASTIGAGE.

Remove chain tensioner snap-ring from front of unit and take out components in order shown. Test the spring—if installed pressure is less than 8.5 lbs., replace spring. If body-to-plunger clearance is more then 0.005″, replace the defective part/s.

## Tensioner Specifications

| | |
|---|---|
| Body inner diameter | 0.590 –0.592″ |
| Plunger diameter | 0.588 –0.589″ |
| Spring free length | 4.331″ |
| Spring installed length | 2.476″ |
| Spring installed pressure | 9.5 lbs. |

Check the rubbing pads of the timing chain vibration dampers for wear and cracks and replace units if necessary. A loose timing chain can cause late (retarded) valve timing and, thus, poor engine performance.

Before installing the timing chain and

testing chain tension, make sure cylinder head is properly tightened and that the chain is tight against the tension pads. Next align the V-notch on the crankshaft pulley with the timing marks on the timing gear cover. Check that the timing mark (notch)

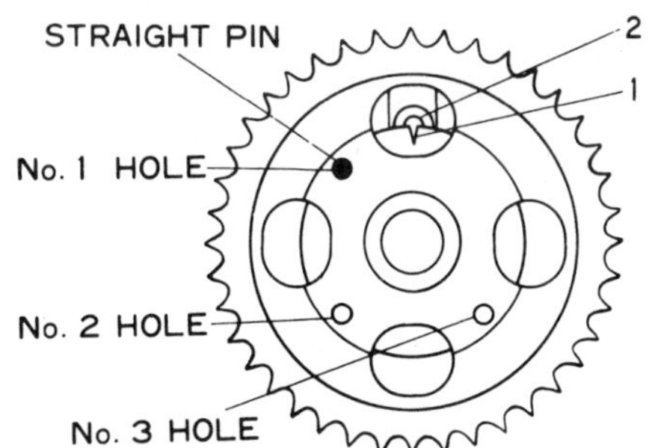


Aligning holes in timing gear.

in the camshaft flange is visible through the indent hole in the camshaft front bearing cap. It is necessary to look straight through the hole (0.160″ diameter).

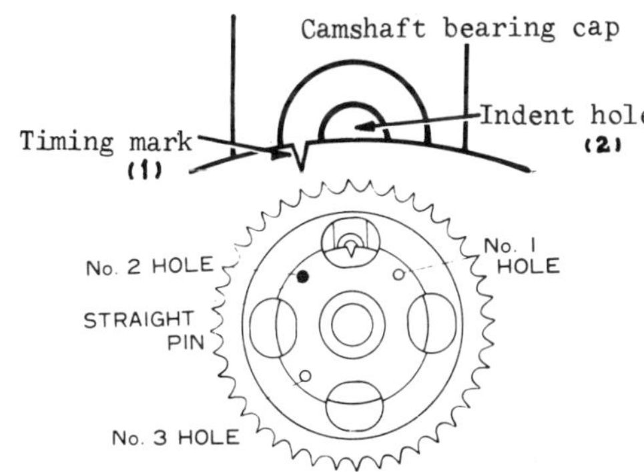


Adjusting timing chain.

If the timing notch is off the mark in a counterclockwise direction, adjust the chain by removing the chain sprocket and rotating it clockwise until the timing mark lines up with the indent hole. There are three indent holes spaced 6° apart. If the timing chain cannot be lined up with the third hole, it is stretched beyond adjustment and must be replaced.

Check the tension gear teeth, shaft and bushing for wear. Measure shaft and bushing—shaft diameter is 0.786″, bushing diameter is 0.787-0.788″, end-play is 0.002–0.026″.

After having installed the pistons, proceed to install timing gear. Install the oil pump shaft assembly into the block and

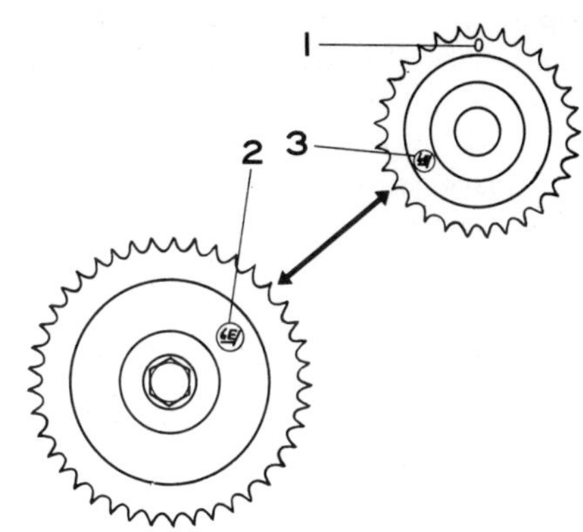


Aligning timing marks; Toyota symbols at (2) and (3), zero mark at (1).

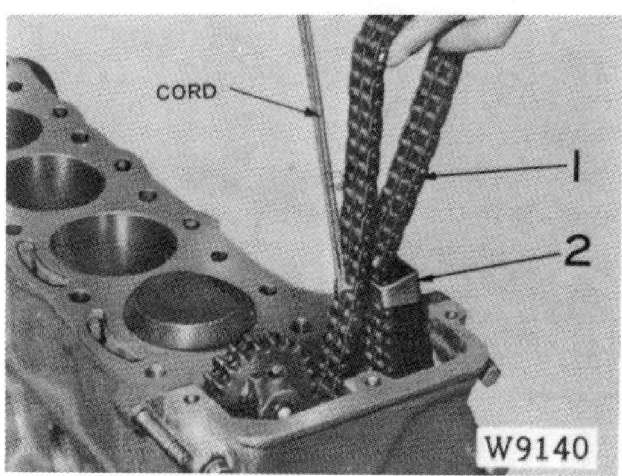


Installing timing chain.

tighten the thrust plate lock bolt. Position No. 1 cylinder at TDC. At this point, the trademark on the crankshaft gear must face, and be in line with, the trademark on the pump drive gear. *NOTE: The timing mark on the crankshaft gear is a plain "0" (not the Japanese Toyota symbol), and in the No. 1 TDC position it will face straight up (12 O'clock).* Next, put the tension gear onto its pin at the upper part of the block. Fit the chain loosely around the gears already installed. *NOTE: The timing chain has no marked links.*

Install the chain vibration damper and damper guide, then secure the guide mounting bolts. Place oil slinger on crankshaft, then install timing chain cover and gaskets. *NOTE: 8mm. bolts equals 7-12 ft. lbs. and 10mm. bolts equals 14-22 ft. lbs.* Now, pull the slack out of the chain and tie chain to the vibration damper with string. Turn the engine over and cover the timing case opening with a clean cloth. *CAUTION:* Do *not rotate engine until chain installation and timing adjustment is completed.* Install the crankshaft vibration damper and tighten the locking bolt to 43–50 ft. lbs. Reset the timing mark on the crankshaft pulley with the "O" mark on the cover.

Install the cylinder head, using a new gasket. It is permissible to use a thin coating of some liquid sealer (Permatex). Do not slide the head onto the block—there are two dowel pins in the block for positive head location. Tighten the head bolts in correct sequence. *NOTE: 8mm. bolts equals 10–15 ft. lbs. and 13mm. bolts equals 54–61 ft. lbs.*

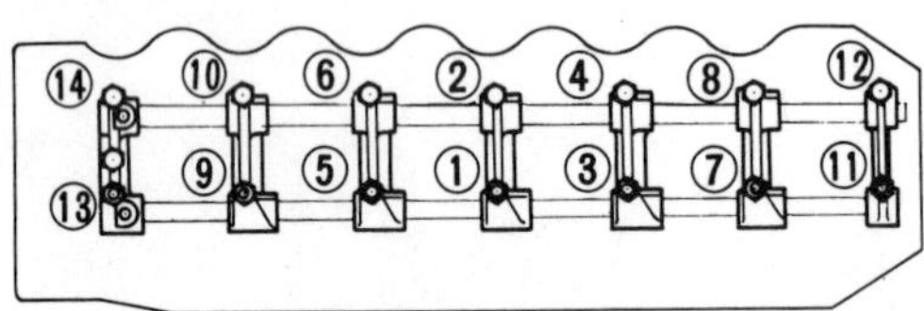


TORQUE: 3~4.5m-kg (22~32 ft-lb)

Rocker arm bolt tightening sequence.

To install the timing chain and gear to camshaft, align the indent hole on the camshaft front bearing cap with the timing notch on the camshaft flange. Recheck the position of the crankshaft timing mark on the pulley. Secure camshaft to prevent movement (which could result in jumped timing), then align the dowel pin on the camshaft flange with the No. 2 hole of the timing gear, release the chain and insert the timing gear into the chain loop so that there is equal tension on both sides of the chain. The gear should seat on the camshaft flange without excessive jiggling which, again, could result in jumped timing. Install and tighten the left-hand thread gear retaining bolt (torque to 47–54 ft. lbs). Bend the lock tab to secure the bolt and remove the covering rag from the timing cover.

Install the chain tensioner, using a new gasket, and torque to 21-29 ft. lbs. Check that the plunger is free to move back at least 0.200″ in its housing. If not, adjust by adding gaskets between the housing and the block.

Install oil filter by hand. If filter base was removed, retighten to 18–25 ft. lbs. Install exhaust manifold and gasket (without Permatex) and tighten nuts to 10–14 ft. lbs. (Loose studs should be tightened to 6–7 ft. lbs.) Install stove pipes for automatic choke and connect them to carburetor. Test the heat pipe where it enters the manifold for air leaks which can damage the choke assembly. Install oil pump and pipes and torque bolts to 22–29 ft. lbs.

Install crankshaft rear oil seal and retainer, then install the oil pan. Torque pan bolts to 3–5 ft. lbs. Check the bronze (pilot) bushing in the flywheel end of the crankshaft, install flywheel and lock plate. Tighten bolts to 41–45 ft. lbs, and secure lock tabs. Install clutch cover assembly and disc (this is a good time to replace a worn disc) and tighten clutch cover bolts to 6–9 ft. lbs. *CAUTION: If no clutch disc aligning tool is available, line up the clutch disc splines using the transmission mainshaft as a pilot. Insert before tightening.*

Install flywheel housing lower cover plate, starter motor and the transmission. Refill engine with oil and proper coolant (use antifreeze all year round) and sealer.

By hand, turn the engine over a few times and check the valve timing. If the timing marks don't line up correctly, repeat the timing operations described in the preceding paragraphs. Install valve rocker assembly and tighten to 22–32 ft. lbs. *NOTE: Replacement studs are tightened to 11–14 ft. lbs. only.* The oil feed bolts of No. 1 rocker support and No. 1 bearing cap are then tightened to 6–9 ft. lbs.

Install the semi-circular plug into the front of the cylinder head, followed by the valve cover gasket and cover. Install fuel pump, using new gasket, then apply liquid sealer to the manifold studs and install gasket and intake manifold. (Tighten nuts to 22–30 ft. lbs.; any loose studs are tightened to 15–18 ft. lbs.)

Install temperature sender into intake manifold—tighten to 25–32 ft. lbs. Install carburetor and connect fuel lines, then install emission controls and connect hoses. Install left engine support and bracket, water pump, bypass hoses, alternator and oil pressure sending unit. Install fan clutch and blades and adjust belt tension.

## Lubricating System

Two types of filters are used: disposable (cartridge) filters on all Corolla and Crown models, and paper replaceable elements on

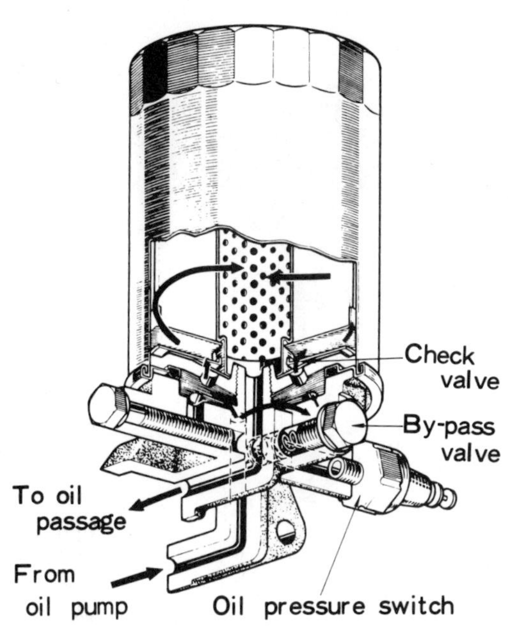

Corolla oil filter.

the Corona and Land Cruiser models. Lubrication of the internal engine parts is full flow (see table footnote) with a trochoid oil pump supplying the pressure. Oil pressure relief valves are situated in the pump body and an additional bypass valve is incorporated with the filter to avoid oil starvation if the element becomes clogged.

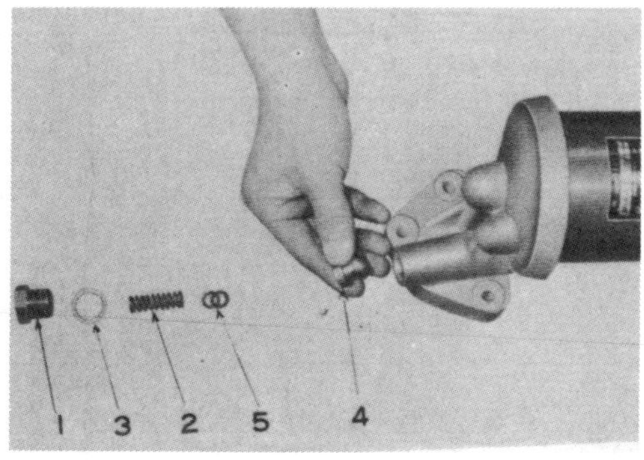

Removing oil bypass valve from filter housing.

*Removing the oil pump* On K series cars, the engine must be removed; on FJ series cars, the engine skid plates, flywheel side and bottom covers and the front drive shaft. All other models require that the motor mounts be disconnected and the engine jacked up far enough to remove the oil pan.

Oil pump removal is simply a matter of taking out all bolts and disconnecting the oil pipes and screens. The drive gear on the 2M type is secured to the shaft with a snap-ring.

*Inspecting the oil pump* Wash the pump thoroughly and allow to air dry. Check for shiny spots which indicate wear and scuffing. Check backlash of gears and measure free length of relief valve spring, then check play between gears and housing, gears and pump cover and between gears themselves. See specification chart for tolerances.

*Installing the oil pump* Always use new gaskets during assembly. Oil all moving parts before installation and prime the oil pump with fresh oil before installing oil pan. Check the pump output before starting the engine by first removing the high tension coil wire, then the oil pressure sending unit. Crank engine with starter. Oil should flow from the opening if the pump is working.

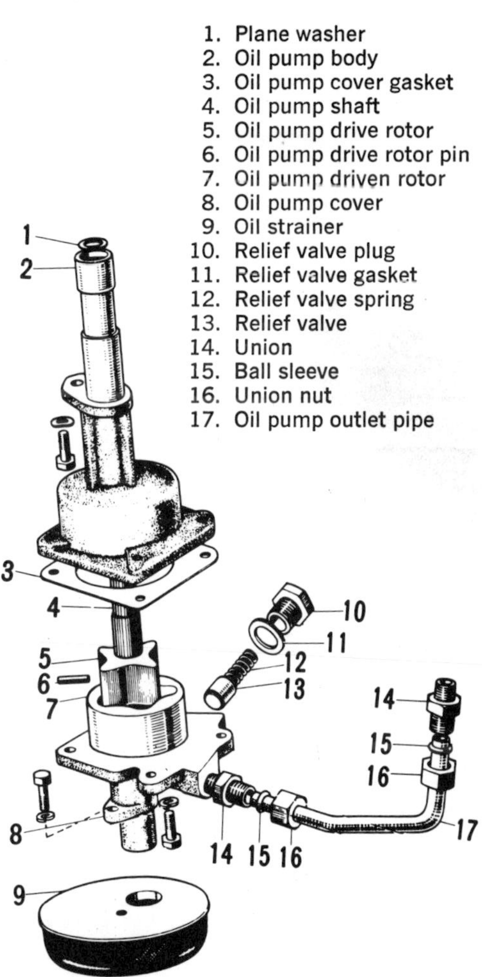

Oil pump components.

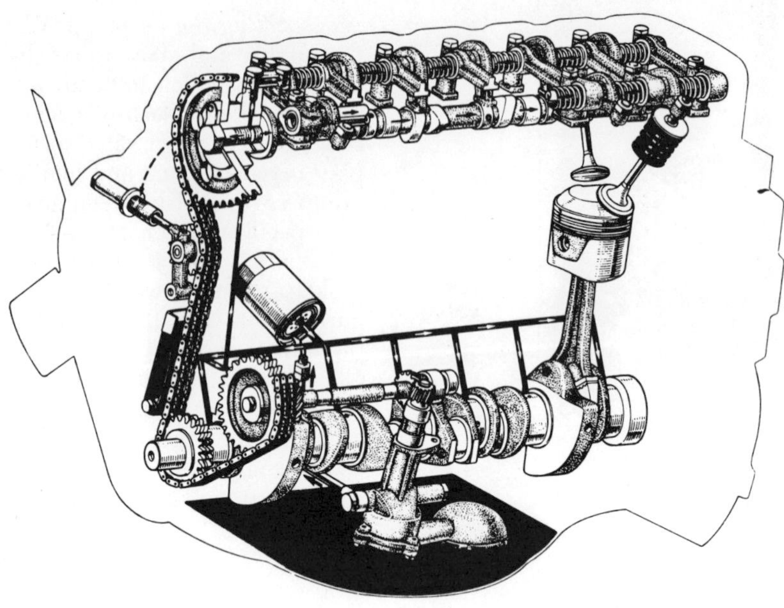

Crown (2M) engine lubricating system, showing direction of oil circulation.

## Oil Pump Specifications

| | Engine Model | | | | |
|---|---|---|---|---|---|
| | *8R-C* | *KC* | *3R* | *2M* | *FA, FJ* |
| Pump type | —Trochoid | | | | Gear |
| Gear to housing (inches) | 0.004–0.006 | 0.004–0.006 | 0.004–0.006 | 0.004–0.006 | 0.001–0.004 |
| Limit: (inches) | 0.008 | 0.008 | 0.008 | 0.008 | 0.008 |
| Gear to gear (inches) | 0.004–0.006 | 0.0016–0.0063 | 0.0026–0.0047 | 0.004–0.006 | 0.018–0.026 |
| Limit: (inches) | 0.008 | 0.008 | 0.008 | 0.008 | 0.037 |
| Gear to cover (inches) | 0.001–0.003 | 0.0012–0.0035 | 0.001–0.003 | 0.001–0.003 | 0.0012–0.003 |
| Limit (inches) | 0.006 | 0.006 | 0.006 | 0.006 | 0.006 |
| Relief valve spring length (free inches) | 1.850 | — | 1.850 | 2.173 | Adjust 44–50 psi |
| Relief valve opens at psi: | 56.9–71.1 | 51–63 | 52.8–61.4 | 57–71 | 44 |
| Filter valve opens at psi: | 11.4–17.1 | — | 11.4–17.1 | 11.4–17.1 | None |

**Note: F series—bypass type with twin gear pump and external, adjustable relief valve.**

# Chapter 3
# Cooling System

## Water Pump

The water pump is of the centrifugal type, having a non-adjustable seal pack. This type pump is best replaced, as a unit, if defective. The pump is mounted on the upper front portion of the engine block. Coolant flows from the pump through the block and cylinder head back to the radiator inlet when the thermostat is open at higher temperatures, or through an internal bypass port in the water pump when the thermostat is closed and the engine cold. *NOTE: The 2M engine has additional circulation around the intake manifold to provide preheated air-fuel mixture to the engine. This gives the greater combustion efficiency needed to meet the U.S. exhaust emission standards.*

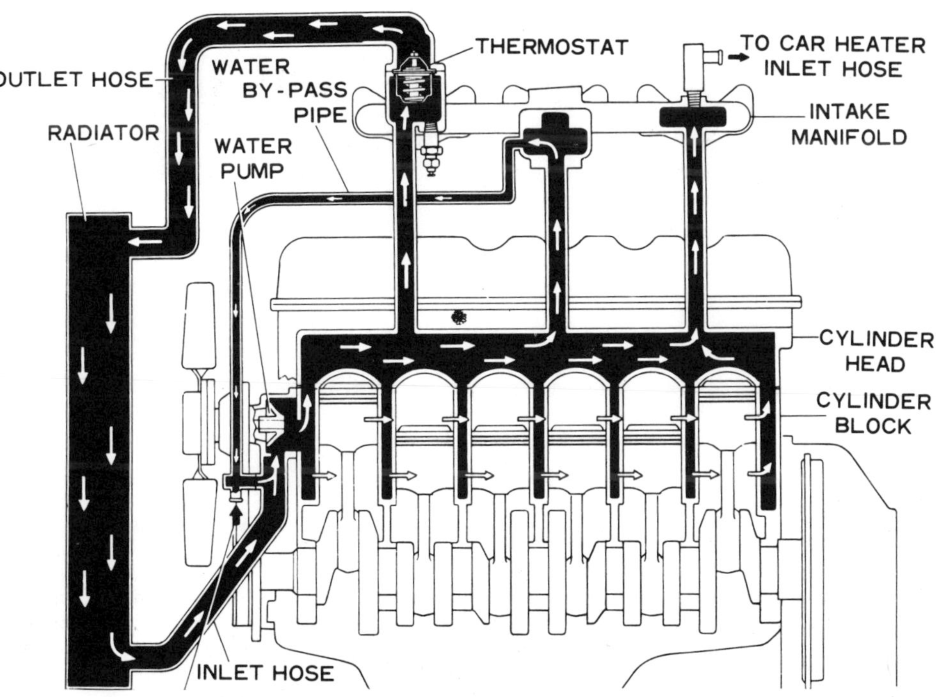


Typical cooling system schematic—2M engine illustrated.

## Diagnosis Guide

A. High Temperature Reading

1. Inaccurate temperature gauge.
2. Fanbelt slipping.
3. Thermostat stuck closed, or opening partially.
4. Leaking cylinder head gasket.
5. Leaking radiator cap.
6. Water pump impeller loose on shaft or broken.
7. Collapsed radiator hose.
8. Clogged radiator.
9. Rust deposits causing low cooling system capacity.
10. Trapped air in cooling system.
11. Excessive internal engine friction.
12. Brakes dragging.
13. Grill clogged with debris.
14. Advanced ignition timing.

B. Low Temperature Reading

1. Temperature gauge defective.
2. Thermostat stuck in open position.

Note: If heater output is normal, disregard low temperature readings in cold weather.

Note: If coolant level stays constant, even though temperature reading is high, suspect a faulty temperature gauge or sending unit.

*Removing the water pump* First drain the cooling system at the radiator drain plug at the bottom of the lower tank—no petcocks are used. Disconnect the radiator and heater hoses, then remove the upper fan shroud, fan blade and V-belt. Remove the air pump belt (where fitted) and the bolts that hold the water pump to the engine. Carefully remove the pump, being careful not to damage the radiator core in the process.

*Disassembling the water pump* Remove pump cover assembly from housing, then remove fluid coupling case from coupling bearing housing. Where no fluid coupling is fitted, simply remove fan pulley hub with a suitable puller. Place fluid coupling pulley in vise, avoiding damage to pulley, and remove fluid coupling. Remove thermostat housing and gasket, then press the impeller from the shaft. Remove snap-ring from impeller and take off the seal pack. *NOTE: In*

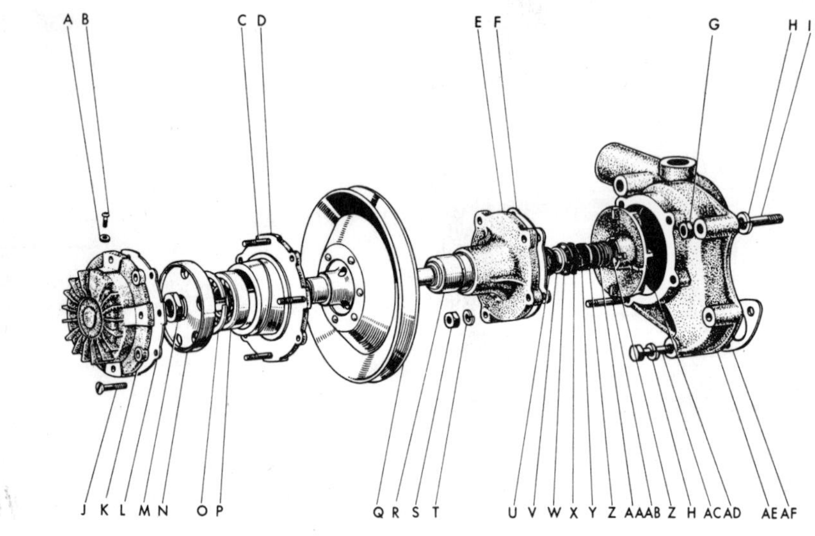


Crown (2M) water pump, showing major components.

A. Plain washer
B. Screw
C. Stud bolt
D. Fluid pulley and bearing case
E. Water pump cover
F. Water pump gasket
G. Nut
H. Lockwasher
I. Stud bolt
J. Screw
K. Fluid coupling case
L. Fluid coupling case gasket
M. Fluid coupling rotor locknut
N. Fluid coupling rotor
O. Fluid coupling bearing stopper
P. Bearing
Q. Fluid coupling pulley
R. Water pump bearing
S. Nut
T. Lockwasher
U. Gasket
V. Water pump floating seat
W. Hole snap-ring
X. Water pump thrust washer
Y. Water pump shaft seal
Z. Water pump spring seat
AA. Compression spring
AB. Stud bolt
AC. Bolt
AD. Water pump impeller
AE. Water pump body
AF. Water pump gasket

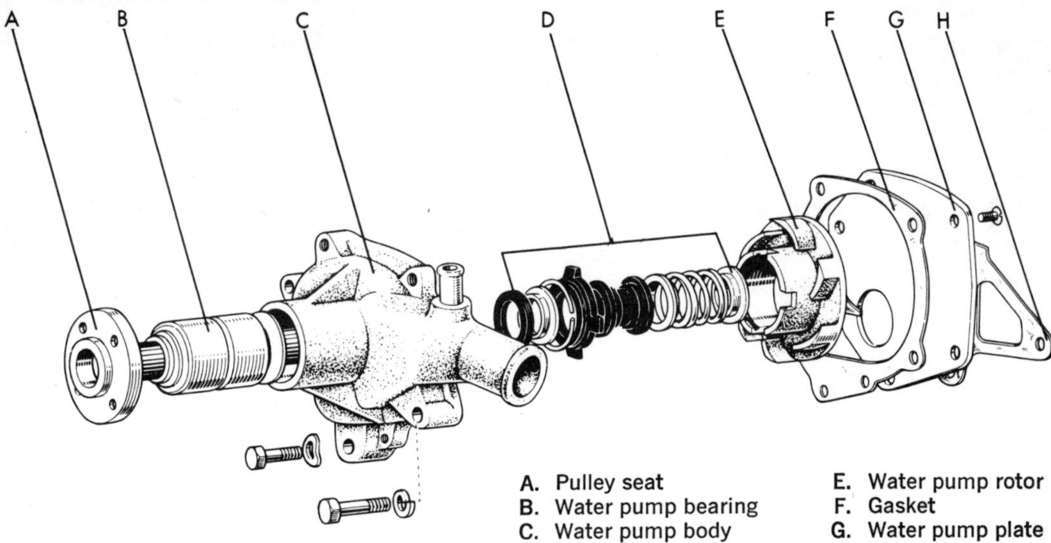


Corolla water pump, showing major components.

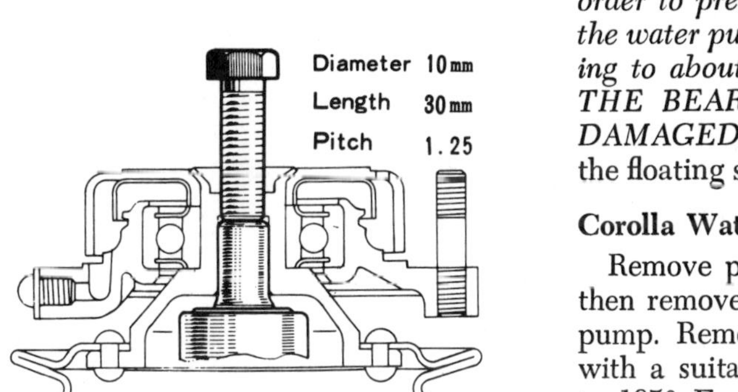


Fluid coupling removal.

*order to press the bearing and shaft out of the water pump housing, first heat the housing to about 185° F. DO NOT REMOVE THE BEARING AND SHAFT UNLESS DAMAGED OR DEFECTIVE.* Remove the floating seal and gasket from housing.

**Corolla Water Pump**

Remove pulley hub with suitable puller, then remove plate and gasket from rear of pump. Remove impeller assembly from rear with a suitable puller, heat pump housing to 185° F. and press out the bearing and shaft from the rear. *NOTE: Thermostat housing is located at front of cylinder head.*

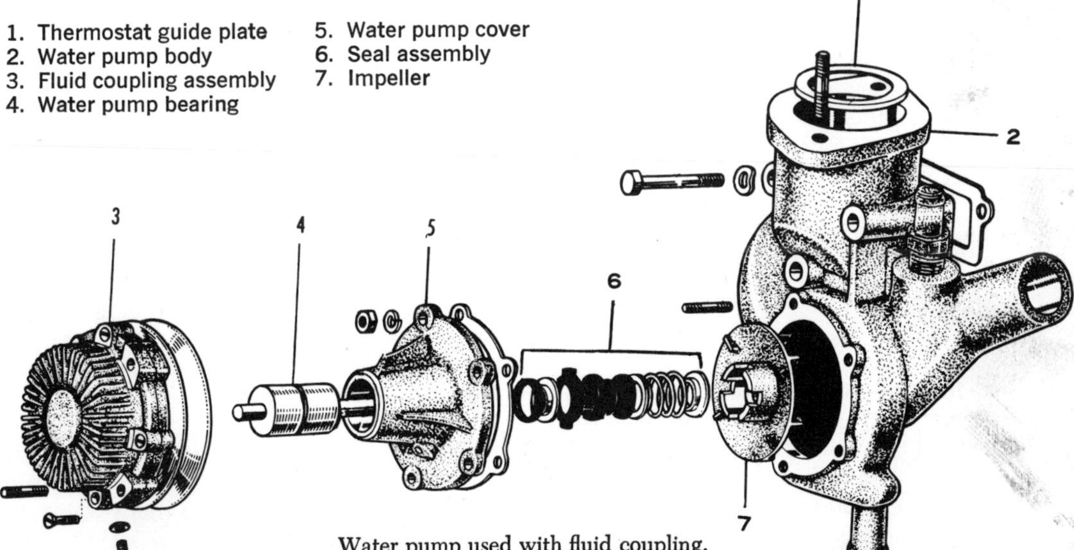


Water pump used with fluid coupling.

### Crown Water Pump

The thermostat housing is located at the intake manifold. Disassembly is the same as for Corona models.

### Land Cruiser Water Pump

The thermostat housing is located at the front of cylinder head. Removal and disassembly is the same as for Corolla model, except that the water pump bearing retaining clip must be removed before pressing out the bearing.

*Inspecting the water pump* Extra care should be exercised when handling the fluid coupling, as it must be replaced if damaged. Wash all parts thoroughly using no solvents. Check water pump housings for cracks, distortion and wear. Check impeller, snap-ring groove, thrust washer and seal surface for wear. Replace all worn components with those from impeller repair kit. Check water pump cover for distortion, cracks and wear at floating seal surface and check bearing for play, noise or wear.

*Assembling the water pump* Install new gasket and floating seal into cover, heat cover to 185° F. and press in bearing assembly until end of bearing is seated flush with face of cover. Mount seal pack on impeller shaft, then apply light coating of silicone to thrust washer and floating seal, press impeller onto shaft until both ends are flush, and check distance between impeller end and inner face of cover (1.12″). Install pulley hub onto shaft (direct drive pump only) or press pulley with fluid coupling bearing case onto bearing shaft until fully seated and install fluid coupling case, with gasket, onto pulley. Install cover assembly onto housing so that drain hole is at the bottom. Check impeller-to-housing clearance. Clearance should be 0.012–0.028″ for all pumps. Install thermostat, gasket and water outlet housing (Corona only).

*Installing the water pump* Bolt pump to engine using new gasket and Permatex, then tighten bolts to 7–12 ft. lbs. Adjust fan belt tension, start engine and test for leaks or noise. Refill radiator with coolant with engine running.

## Radiator

The radiator is of the conventional vertical-flow type with an expansion tank located at the top. An oil cooler is incorporated into the radiator on models with automatic transmission. Test for leaks using a good radiator pressure tester. Do not apply more than 10 psi (MK II–15 psi) pressure at any time. If pressure drops rapidly, look for external leaks; if pressure drop is more gradual, look for internal leaks. Check engine oil for traces of water.

To check for compression or combustion leaks into the cooling system, first run the engine to operating temperature, then install the tester and pressurize system to 10 psi. Any fluctuation of the test gauge indicates a combustion leak. Pull off one spark plug wire at a time—when the fluctuation stops, you have located the faulty cylinder. If more then one cylinder leaks, the fluctuations will become less severe. If tightening the head bolts to proper specification does not stop the leakage, remove the head and replace the head gasket.

*Radiator cap* All radiator caps used on Toyota vehicles are atmospherically vented. A coolant vapor flow of approximately .4–.7 cfm (cubic feet per minute) closes the cap vent and allows pressure to build up to 7 psi. (MK II–13 psi Land Cruiser–4 psi.) (Coolant boiling point increases about 3°F. per 1.0 psi pressure.) Caps should be tested at regular intervals, since defective caps are very often the cause of coolant loss and expensive engine damage.

Never remove the radiator cap when the engine is very hot, as this will depressurize the system and lower the boiling point of the coolant. Serious injuries can result from the rapid escape of steam.

*Removing the radiator* Drain all coolant, disconnect and remove all radiator hoses and disconnect the two oil cooler lines, if fitted. Remove upper shroud section (where fitted) and take off fan blade. Remove bolts that secure the radiator to support and carefully lift out the radiator.

*Repairing the radiator* If more than 20% of the core is damaged, replace the core. Never operate a radiator on plain water, as it will rust quickly.

*Installing the radiator* Reverse removal procedure to install. Tighten hose clamps securely and remember to retighten them after a few hours of engine operation.

## Other Cooling System Components

*Thermostat* A 185° F. thermostat is used on most models. Check and test the thermostat every time the cooling system is serviced, especially when antifreeze is installed. Test as follows: submerge thermostat in antifreeze or water and heat the coolant on a stove. Insert a 0.003″ feeler gauge between the valve and the valve seat and observe the temperature at which the feeler gauge will slip out of the valve. This should be within ±3° F. of the rated temperature and the thermostat must be fully open at 218° F. Always install a new gasket, even if the old thermostat is used.

*Temperature indicator* Coolant temperature readings in the 122–172° F. and the 212–222° F. ranges are considered to be normal. On the car tests are limited to checking thermostat opening temperature. In order to test the indicator throughout its entire range it must be removed from the engine and placed in a container of water.

Heat the water to the temperature check points given in Chapter 4 and check water temperature against scale graduations, after connecting indicator unit to dash gauge and allowing about two minutes for temperature gauge stabilization.

*Fan* The Corolla has a two-section (four-blade) fan. The Crown has a fixed four-blade, the Corona a fixed five-blade, fan. The MK II has a six-blade plastic fan, while Land Cruiser models have both four and five-blade fans. Avoid damaging the blade tips, as this will unbalance the fan, cause noisy running and may damage the water pump bearings.

*Fanbelt* A V-type belt is used to power the water pump, fan and alternator. The air pump uses a separate and shorter belt. Since belts contain rubber they will stretch and, therefore, they must be adjusted from time to time. Adjustment is accomplished by moving the alternator on its bracket to give about ½″ belt deflection between the two pulleys. If a strand tension gauge is used, follow gauge manufacturer's instructions. *NOTE: Do not confuse NEW and USED designation. Once a belt has been run for ten minutes it is considered a used belt and should be adjusted as such.*

*Fluid coupling* On Corona and Crown models, the fan is mounted on a fluid coupling which minimizes power losses due to fan resistance at high engine speeds. The coupling is filled with silicone oil (which can be replaced) and is not serviceable.

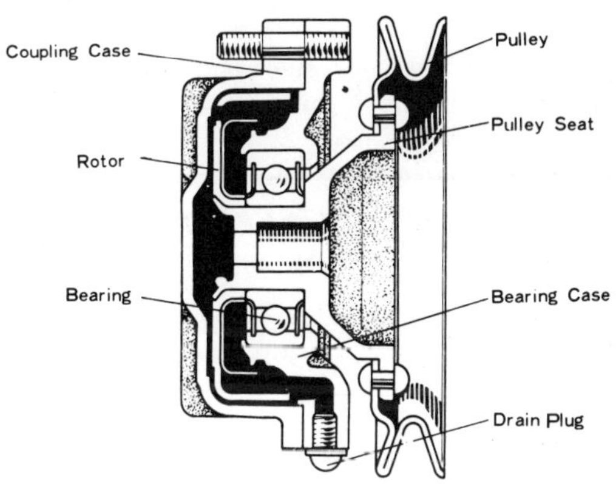


Fluid coupling cross-section.

*Antifreeze* Permanent (ethylene glycol) type antifreeze is installed at the factory and is good for two years. After once draining factory coolant, replace at least once a year. At the onset of cold weather it is advisable to test coolant. Always flush the cooling system with clean water before replacing antifreeze.

## Cooling System Capacity (In Qts.)

| | |
|---|---|
| Corolla | 5 |
| Corona (3R) | 8 |
| Crown | 11 |
| Mark II | 8 |
| Land Cruiser | 10 |

# Chapter 4
# Electrical System

The engine has four electrical subsystems: starting, charging, ignition and battery.

## Starting System

This system includes the starter motor and relay, starter (ignition) switch and the necessary cables and wiring to connect the components. A starter safety switch is incorporated on all automatic transmissions to prevent starting the car in any selector position except "N" (Neutral) and "P" (Park).

### Starter Motor

The starter has an integral positive engagement drive. When the starter is not in

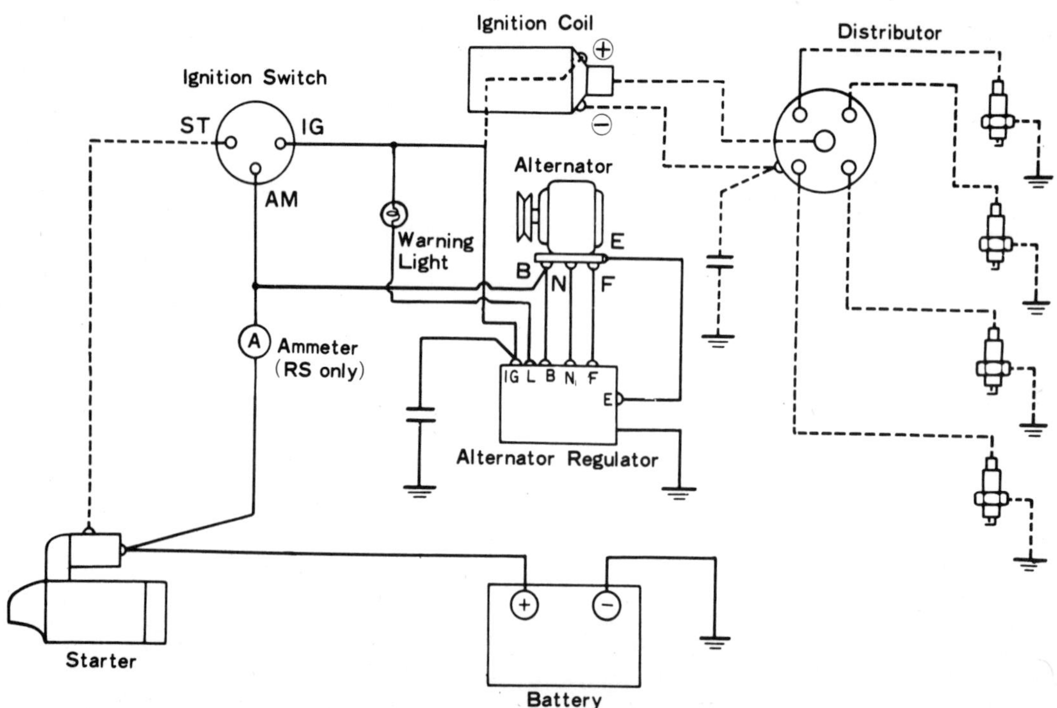


Basic schematic of engine electrical system.

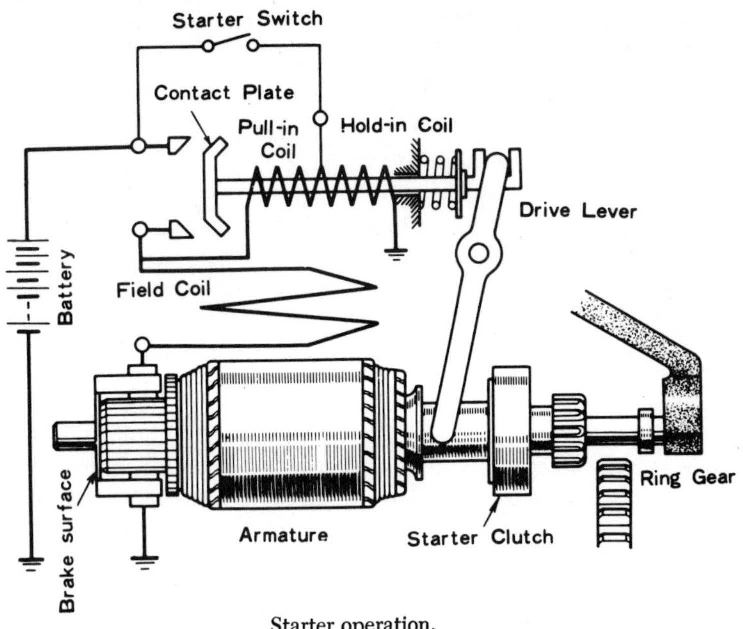


Starter operation.

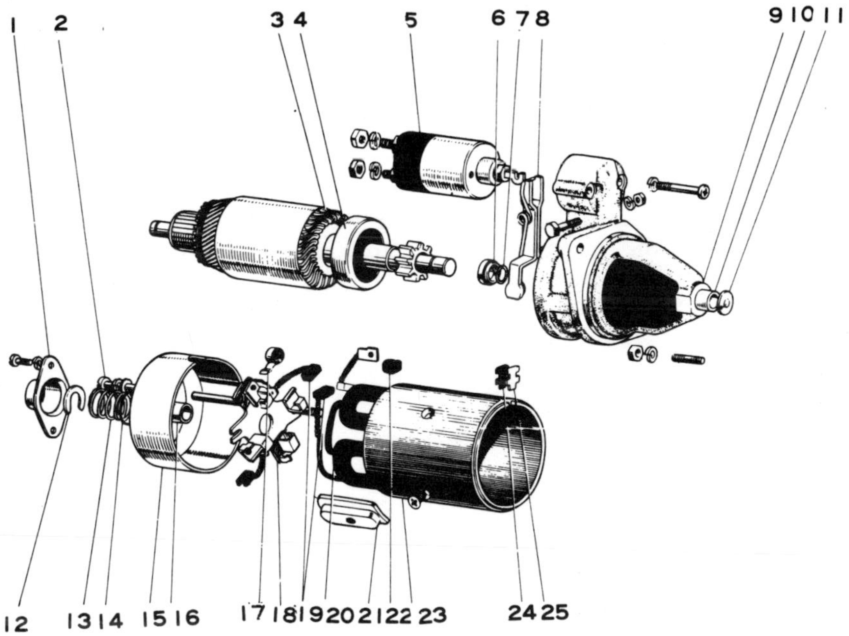


Starter motor components.

1. End frame cover
2. Through bolt
3. Armature
4. Starter clutch
5. Magnetic switch
6. Pinion stop collar
7. Snap-ring
8. Drive lever w/spring
9. Starter drive housing
10. Housing bushing
11. Bushing cover
12. Lockwasher
13. Brake spring
14. Rubber ring
15. Commutator end frame
16. End frame bushing
17. Brush spring
18. Brush holder
19. Brush
20. Field coil
21. Pole core
22. Insulator
23. Yoke
24. Rubber plate
25. Plate

use, one of the field coils is connected directly to ground through a set of contacts. As soon as starter is engaged, a heavy current flows through this grounded field coil, actuating a moving pole shoe attached to the starter drive actuating lever and thus engaging the drive with the flywheel. When the movable shoe is fully seated it opens the field coil grounding contacts and the starter is in normal operation. A holding coil is also used to maintain the movable pole shoe in the fully seated position while the starter is cranking the engine.

**Starter Solenoid**

The starter solenoid is energized when the ignition switch is turned to the START position. Battery voltage is applied to the "S" terminal of the solenoid and the coil is energized, bridging two contacts in the relay and thus completing the circuit between the battery and starter motor. The relay circuit is grounded through the mounting bracket to the starter body; make sure that this connection is both clean and tight.

**Starting Problems and Tests**

These generally can be defined as follows: 1. Starter cranks engine slowly, 2. Starter will not crank engine, 3. Starter cranks at normal speed but engine will not start.

The *Starter System Diagnosis* charts in Chapter 1 should be used to locate the source of the problem if the starter will not crank the engine or if the engine cranks slowly. If the starter motor cranks the engine at normal speed, but the engine will not start, the problem usually can be found in the fuel or ignition systems.

*Starter cable and ground cable tests* To determine if there is excessive resistance in the circuit from the battery positive terminal to the starter motor, connect positive lead of a voltmeter to the positive battery terminal and negative voltmeter lead to the starter motor. Disconnect the ignition coil high tension wire so that engine will not start, then connect a remote control starter switch between the battery terminal and the "S" terminal of the starter relay. Use the remote control switch to crank the engine. Voltmeter reading (V2) should not exceed 0.5 volt. A reading greater than 0.5 volt indicates excessive resistance at the terminal on the starting motor (which is connected to the positive battery terminal). With the positive voltmeter lead connected to the positive battery terminal, connect negative voltmeter lead to the starter terminal of the starter solenoid. Crank the engine. Voltmeter reading (V3) should not exceed 0.4 volt. A reading greater than 0.4 volt indicates excessive resistance in the circuit between the positive battery post and the starter terminal of the starter solenoid. With the positive voltmeter lead connected to the positive battery post and the negative voltmeter lead connected to the battery terminal of the starter solenoid, crank the engine. Voltmeter reading (V1) should not exceed 0.2 volt. A reading greater than 0.2 volt indicates excessive resistance between the

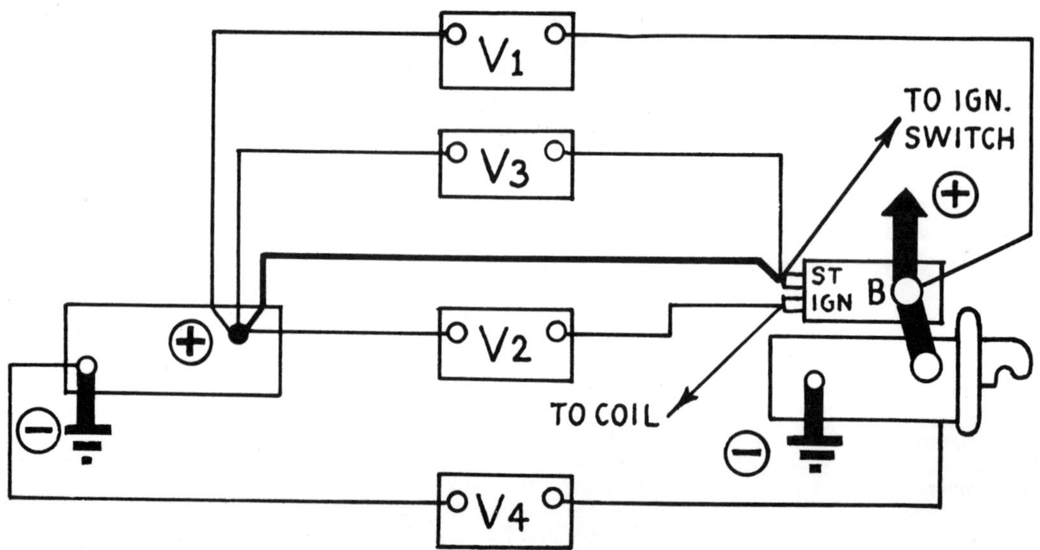


Starter cranking circuit tests.

battery positive post and the battery terminal of the starter solenoid. Connect voltmeter positive lead to the starter motor housing and the negative voltmeter lead to the negative battery post. Voltmeter reading (V4) should not exceed 0.4 volt. If greater than 0.4 volt, move positive lead to ground cable connection at engine. If resistance remains high, clean and retighten connections and repeat test. If voltmeter reading is still high, the ground cable must be replaced.

### Removing Starter Motor

Disconnect the battery-to-starter cable at the battery. Disconnect wires at starter relay, remove retaining nuts and pull out starter. *NOTE: On K-series cars it is necessary to remove the air cleaner, disconnect the choke and accelerator cables at the carburetor, disconnect the front exhaust pipe flange at the exhaust manifold and remove the entire manifold assembly before removing the starter motor; or remove from underneath.*

### Disassembling Starter Motor

All Toyota starters are basically of one design and vary only in size and power rating. Disconnect the field coil wire from the solenoid (magnetic switch) and remove the solenoid. Remove end frame cover, lock plate, washers and the rubber seal ring, then remove the starter yoke. Remove the two through bolts, the commutator end frame and brush holders with washers.

Remove the drive lever set pin, rubber and plate, then remove the armature, drive lever and starter clutch (Bendix drive) in one piece. Remove the snap-ring by pushing the pinion stop collar towards the armature, after which everything will slide off towards the front.

### Inspecting and Testing Starter Motor

Inspect all parts for signs of wear, overheating or any other visible defects. Check clearance between armature shaft and bushings; it should be no more than .008″. Replacement bushings are available in standard size, as well as in two undersizes.

*STD:* 0.493–0.494″
*U/S:* 0.482–0.483″
and 0.474–0.475″

Check commutator for rough, burned or scored surface. If the commutator is out of round by more than 0.012″ it must be turned down on a lathe. The diameter lower limit is 1.450″. Undercut the mica insulation to a depth of 0.020–0.030″ if the existing depth is less than 0.008″. Check brushes and springs.

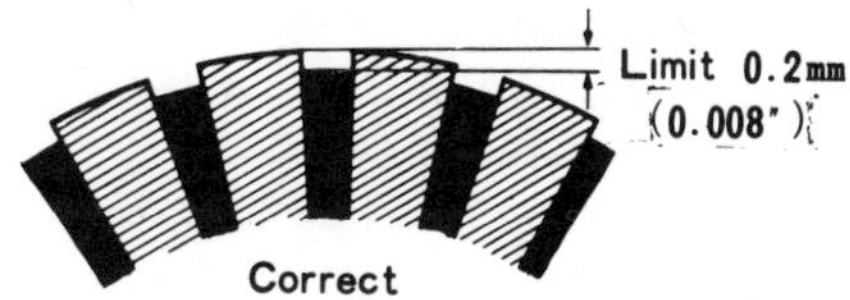

Mica undercutting specifications.

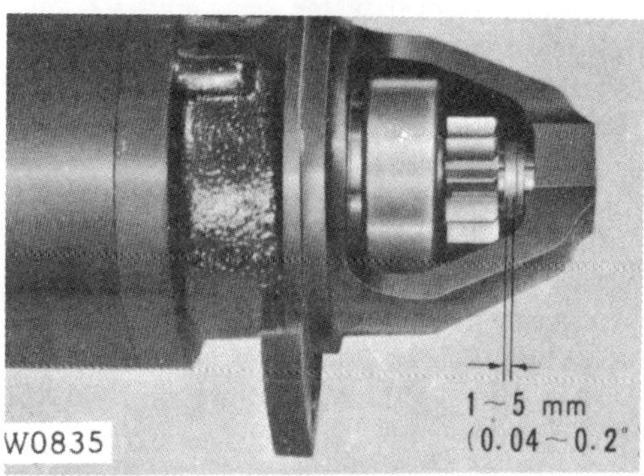


Starter pinion gear clearance.

Use a growler to test the armature for electrical shorts, grounding and balance. Follow the equipment manufacturer's procedure, or use the following general procedure.

#### Ground Test

Place the armature in the growler jams. Turn the power switch to test position and touch one test lead to the armature core and the other lead to each commutator bar in turn. Observe the light; if it goes on when any commutator bar is grounded the armature must be replaced.

#### Short Test

*CAUTION: Never operate a growler in the growler test position without having placed an armature in the jaws.* Place the armature in the jaws. Turn the switch to the growler position. Laying a steel (hacksaw) blade parallel with, and touching, the armature, slowly rotate the armature one or more revolutions in the growler jaws. If the steel blade vibrates in any position, the area is shorted and the armature must be replaced.

### Balance Test

Leaving the armature in the jaws with the switch in the growler position (as above), place the contact fingers of the meter test cable across two adjacent commutator bars. Adjust voltage control until needle registers highest on the scale. Test each pair of commutator bars until all bars have been tested. A reading of zero (0) indicates an open circuit in the pair of bars being tested. In this event, the armature must be repaired or replaced.

### Field Coil Test

Using a circuit tester (ohmmeter), place one test lead on the field coil lead and the other test lead on the other field coil lead. If the needle does not move, an open circuit is indicated and the field coil must be replaced.

### Solenoid Test

Adjust the free length of the plunger to 1.340″ as illustrated. Late Corona models (RT46 and RT52) have a special relay in the starter circuit to overcome certain cold weather starting conditions. Full 12-volt battery current is fed to the coil (bypassing the resistance) to produce the hottest possible spark when cranking the engine.

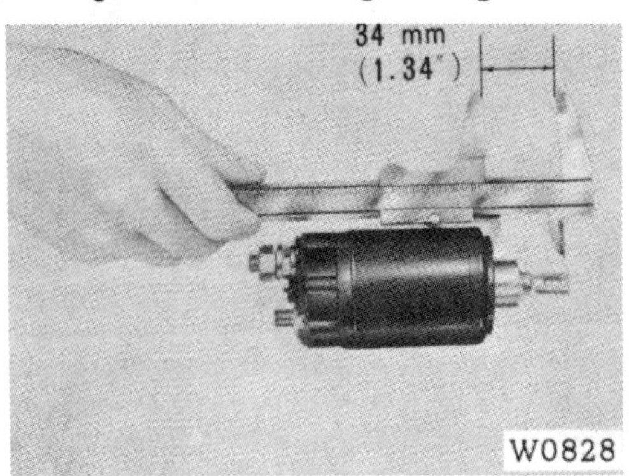


Checking solenoid plunger stroke.

### Brush and Holder Test

Using a circuit tester, check for a shorted holder. If the needle moves when the test leads are connected between the positive and the negative sides, the holder is defective and must be replaced. Check the brush length and replace brushes if shorter than specified. Check brush spring tension and replace springs if not within limits.

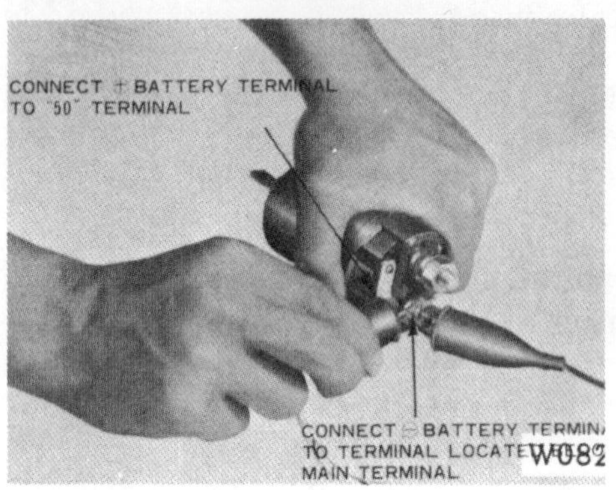


Testing solenoid pull-in coil.

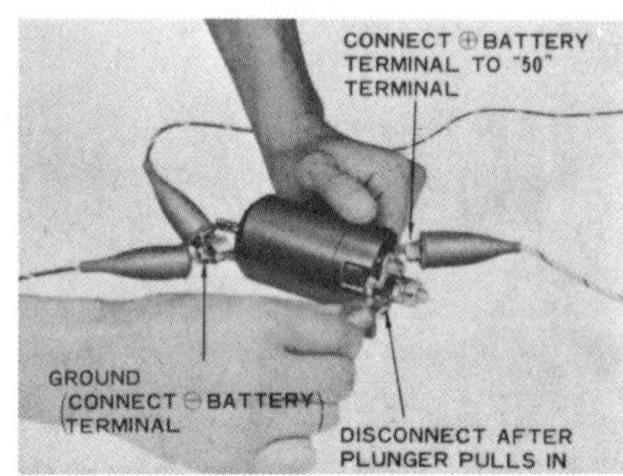


Testing solenoid hold-in coil.

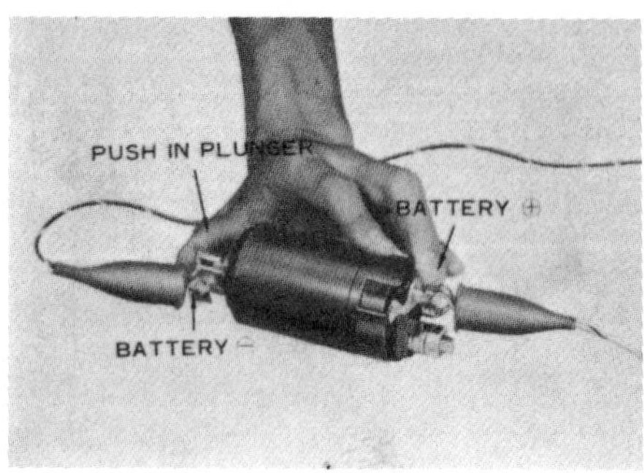


Testing solenoid return.

### Starter Drive Test

Check for worn and chipped gear teeth and loose, uneven or binding starter clutch.

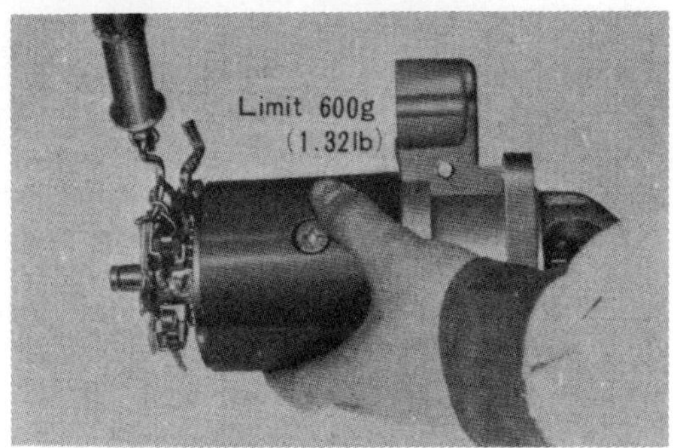


Checking starter motor brush spring tension.

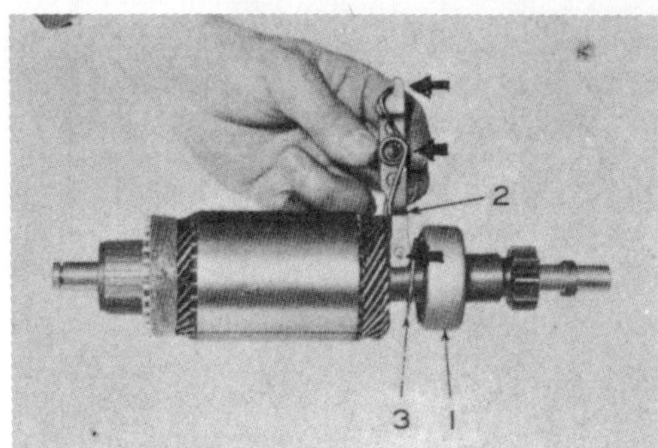


Installing starter drive lever

### Assembling the Starter Motor

Assemble all parts in reverse order of disassembly. Apply a light coating of Dow Corning 33 silicone lubricant (or its equivalent) to the armature splines. Assemble the starter clutch and drive gear onto the shaft,

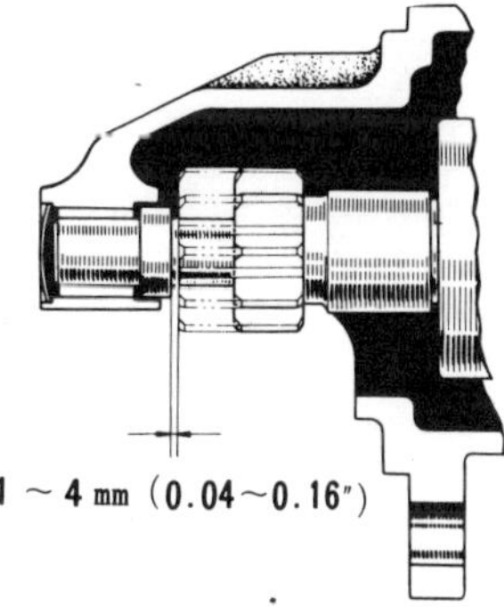


Clutch pinion clearance.

then install the pinion stop nut and the snap-ring. Lock the stop nut into place by staking it in two places with a centerpunch. Check the end-play of the armature at the end protruding from the rear housing.

## Battery

A 12-volt negative ground system is used in all models. Since battery defects account for more than half of all electrical breakdowns, it is of utmost importance to maintain your car's battery in as good condition as is possible at all times. If a booster battery is used for starting, it must be connected correctly to prevent damage to the alternator. (Connect positive to positive, negative to negative.) A *quick* charger should never be used to *start* a car when the car's battery is discharged.

### Charging

Slow charging is still the best method of charging a battery. Properly applied, the

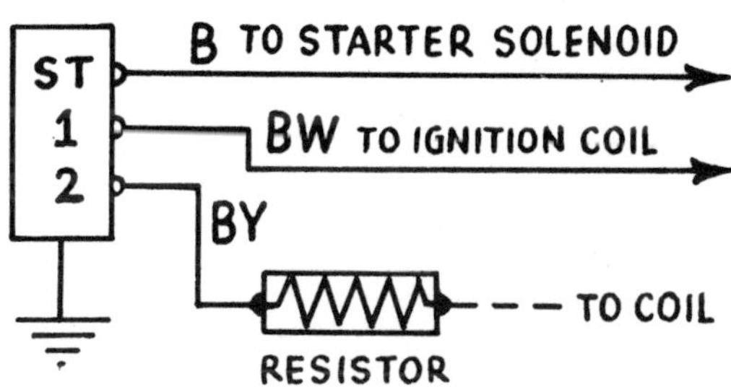


Hard starting relay used in RT46 and RT52 models.

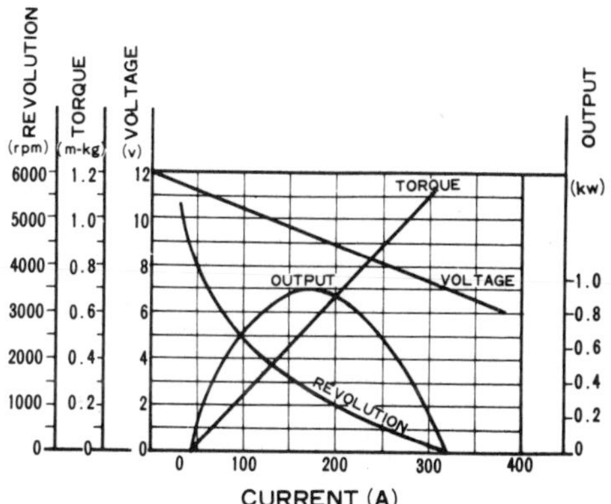


Starter motor characteristics.

slow charge method is safe under all possible battery conditions, provided the electrolyte level in all cells is correct. An acceptable charging rate is 5 Amperes for a minimum period of 24 hours, if the battery is capable of accepting a full charge. A battery has reached a fully charged condition when all cells are bubbling freely and three specific gravity readings, taken at hourly intervals, indicate no increase in specific gravity.

Always disconnect the battery ground cable when fast charging. The charging rate should be controlled so that the temperature of the electrolyte does not exceed 125° F., which would cause excessive gassing and loss of electrolyte. A fast charger cannot, and should not, be expected to charge a battery to capacity within an hour (or less). A fast charger only charges a battery enough to allow its return to service, after which it must be brought to capacity by the vehicle's own charging system. *NOTE: The addition of water, particularly in cold (freezing) temperatures, should not be made unless the car is to be immediately driven so that mixing of water with the acid is complete enough to prevent freeze-up.*

| *Specific Gravity* | *Freeze Points* |
|---|---|
| 1.100 | +18°F. |
| 1.150 | + 6°F. |
| 1.200 | —17°F. |

**Maintenance**

The top of the battery must be kept free of all acid accumulation between the terminals so as to prevent voltage leaks. Simple baking soda, sprinkled on top of the battery and washed off with water, will usually remove dirt and neutralize all acid. *CAUTION: Baking soda will ruin the battery if allowed to seep into electrolyte.* Battery hold-down bolts should be tight enough to keep the battery from shaking, but not so tight as to cause the case to crack. Clean terminals and tight connections are a *must.* Apply a light coat of Vaseline before securing the cable clamps. *CAUTION: Highly explosive gas is present inside the battery at all times. Avoid open flames or sparks when charging or when using jumper cables.* Should your battery freeze up, remove and store it in a warm room for a time to allow a gradual thawing. Never quick-charge a frozen battery, as it is highly explosive in this state. If acid is spilled on the skin, wash it off with a solution of baking soda and water.

**Battery Tests**

Prior to testing, visually inspect the battery for damage (broken container, loose posts, etc.).

HYDROMETER TEST

Standard hydrometer floats are calibrated for a temperature of 80°F. Temperature correction amounts to approximately .004/10°F. For each 10°F. above the 80°F. standard temperature *add* .004, and for each 10°F. below 80°F. *deduct* .004 from the indicated reading. Measure the specific gravity of each cell and, if necessary, make the above corrections. If the specific gravity readings of all cells are above 1.235, but the variation between cells is more than .050, an unserviceable battery is indicated. If the specific gravity of all cells is less than 1.235, recharge the battery.

BATTERY LOAD TEST

Connect a voltmeter between the (fully charged) battery terminals, then start the engine. Voltage during starting should be 8.5 volts or greater. A reading of less than 8.5 volts is an indication of dirty or loose terminals or switch connections.

STARTER VOLTAGE TEST

Connect voltmeter between main starter terminal and ground, then operate starter. Voltage should drop to 8.0 volts. If voltage drops below 8.0 volts, test all starter-to-switch connections and the battery terminals.

BATTERY CABLE TEST

Connect voltmeter between starter terminal and positive battery terminal. Operate starter switch. If voltmeter reading is greater than 0.5 volts, and all connections are tight and clean, replace the starter cable (negative side).

VOLTAGE DROP TEST AT STARTER SWITCH

Connect voltmeter across starter switch terminals and operate starter. If the voltage is greater than 0.5 volt, replace the switch.

HEAVY DISCHARGE TEST

A standard discharge tester with built-in resistance is necessary for this test. If the test indicates a constant (steady) voltage reading of 1.6 volts over a period of five seconds, the battery cell being tested is good. If the specific gravity, however, is less than 1.200, the battery first must be charged.

### Heavy Load Test

The use of a commercial battery tester is recommended. Follow manufacturer's instructions, or the following general procedure. Connect both sets of test leads to the correct battery posts, red to positive and black to negative. Turn load control knob clockwise until ammeter reading is equal to three times the Amp./hr. rating of the battery.

For example: 120 Amps. for a 40 Amp./hr. battery,
150 Amps. for a 50 Amp./hr. battery.

Maintain load for 15 seconds and note the voltmeter reading. Turn control knob to off position. If the voltmeter reading was 9.6 volts or more, the battery has sufficient capacity.

If a tester is not available, the starter itself may be used for testing. Connect a voltmeter across the battery terminals and crank the engine. The reading should be not less than 9.0 volts. All readings are calibrated for 70°F.; if the ambient temperature is below 40°F., reduce specified minimum to 8.5 volts.

## Alternator

The alternator (alternating current generator) is totally different in all major aspects from the DC generator (direct current) in spite of certain physical similarities. The alternator has a rotating field coil and a stationary armature. Brushes are used to carry current into the unit rather than out. Two continuous slip rings are used instead of a segmented commutator and three pairs of silicon diodes (rectifiers) convert the alternating current into direct current. The familiar test methods used for DC generators are no longer valid, and the following precautions must be observed if damage to the alternator system is to be avoided.

1. The wire at the alternator "B" terminal is always hot and is connected directly to the battery.

2. Current to the alternator "F" terminal is controlled by the ignition switch.

3. Do not run engine for any length of time with the "B" terminal disconnected, as the alternator will overheat and the voltage relay coil will burn out. If, for some reason, the engine must be run with the "B" termi-

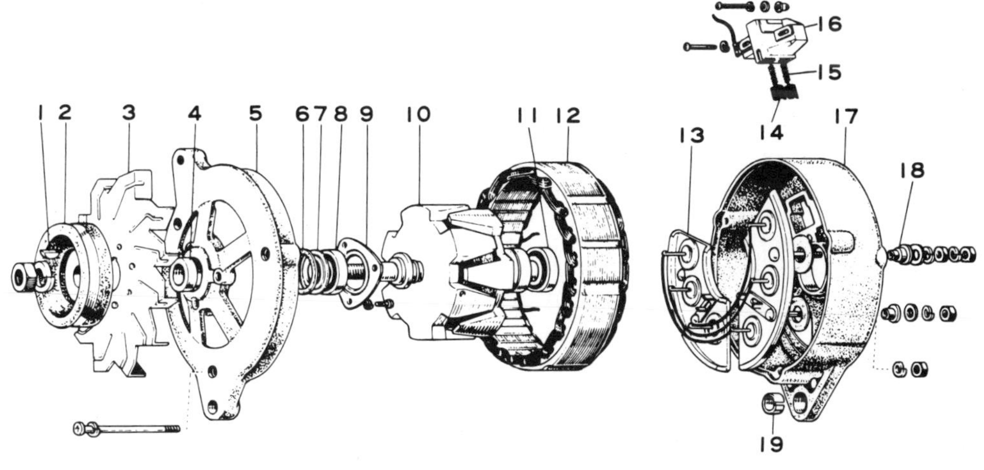


Alternator components.

1. Key
2. Alternator pulley
3. Alternator fan
4. Space collar
5. Drive end frame
6. Felt ring
7. Felt ring cover
8. Bearing
9. Bearing retainer plate
10. Rotor
11. Bearing
12. Stator
13. Rectifier holder
14. Brush
15. Brush spring
16. Brush holder
17. Rectifier end frame
18. "B" terminal insulator
19. Bushing

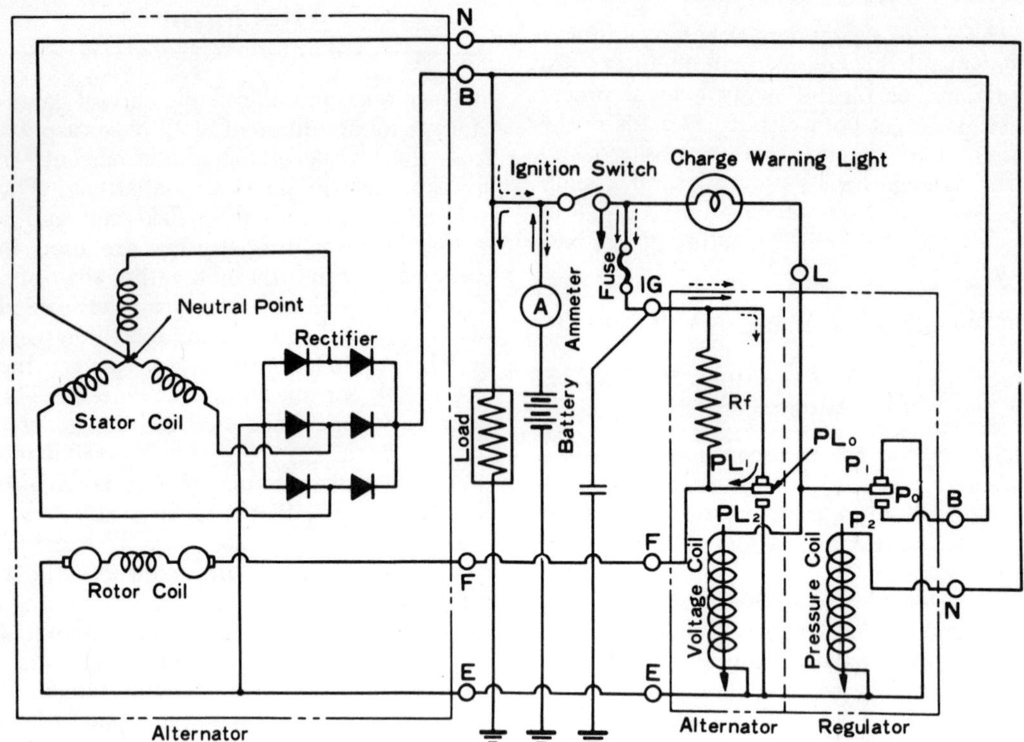


nal disconnected, also disconnect the "F" terminal.

4. Do not connect any condenser or noise suppressor to the "F" terminal.

5. When quick charging, always disconnect the battery ground cable. Also disconnect the cable whenever any arc (electric) welding is to be done on the car.

6. Beware of reversing polarity when *jump starting* the car, especially when using a battery of uncertain polarity. Disconnect ground cable to prevent damage to the system through reversed polarity.

7. Remember that it is possible for a car to run with a battery incorrectly installed. Of course, the diodes will be damaged, the ignition points rapidly burned out and the signal flasher may catch fire. All Toyota models officially imported to the USA have a negative-ground system.

**Alternator System**

Toyota passenger cars and trucks use a system incorporating either a warning light or an ammeter (or both), together with a two-coil voltage regulator, while Land Cruiser models employ a single coil regulator and an ammeter.

**Testing the Alternator (in car)**

First, disconnect the battery ground cable, test condition of battery, fanbelt and wiring. Connect the test meter, using the hookup illustrated or following the meter manufacturer's recommendations. Reconnect the battery ground cable and start the engine. Increase engine speed to 2,000 rpm and observe voltmeter and ammeter readings—at 2,000 rpm, output should be 13.5–14.5 volts @ 10 Amperes or less.

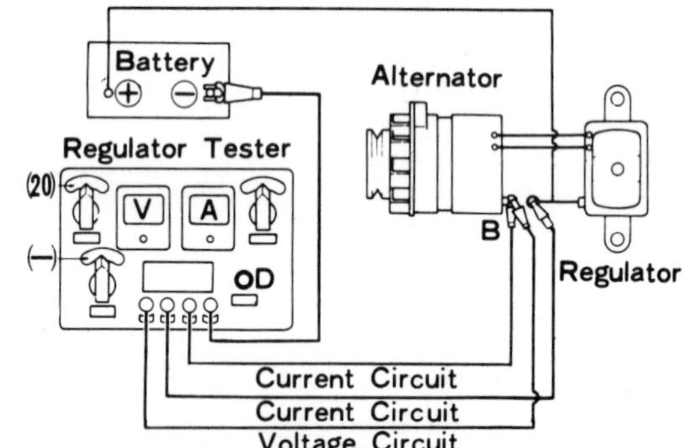


Test circuit for alternator.

### Test Indications

1. Considerably more than 10 Amperes; battery is discharged or has shorted plates.

2. Voltmeter needle vibrates; regulator points dirty, rough or pitted; loose or corroded connections at "F" terminals.

3. Voltmeter reads higher than normal.

a. Voltage regulator high-speed point gap too wide.
b. Voltage regulator low-speed point gap too wide.
c. Poor high-speed point contact.
d. Regulator or relay coil is open.

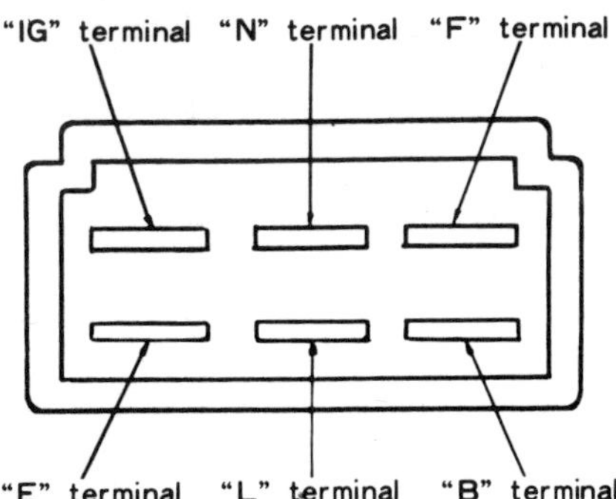


Regulator harness plug terminal identification.

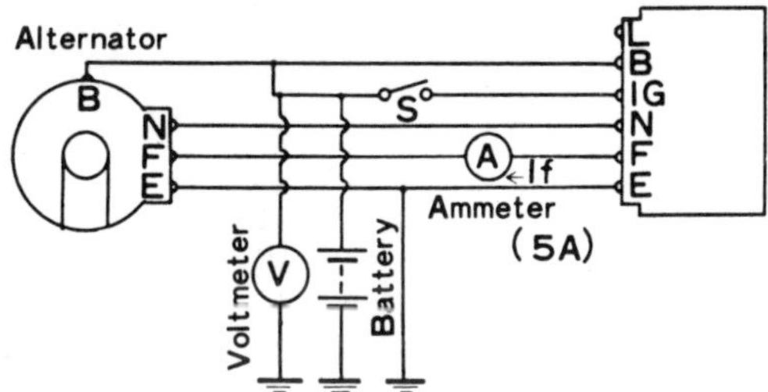


Voltage regulator test circuit.

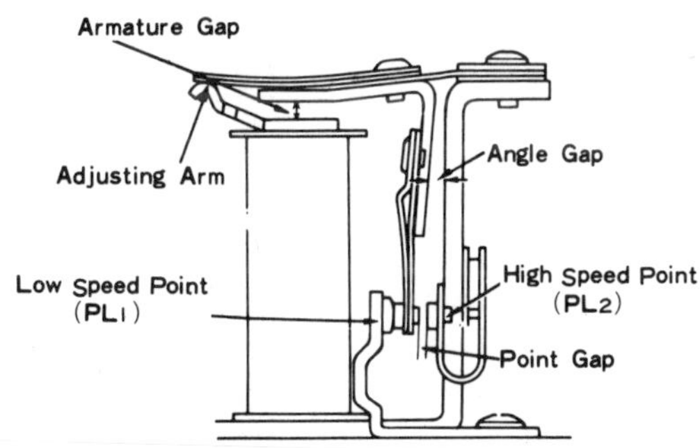


Voltage regulator components.

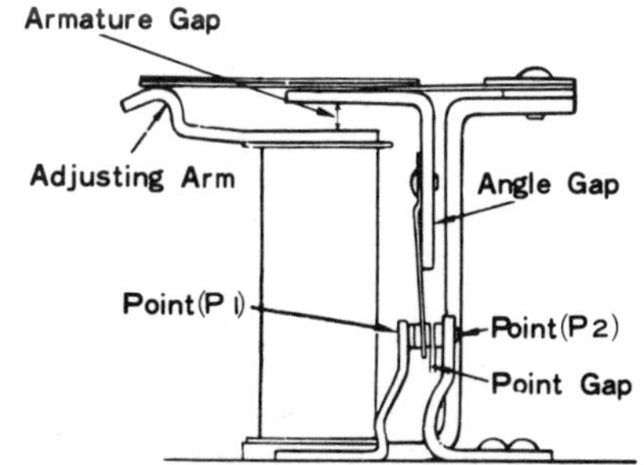


Voltage relay components.

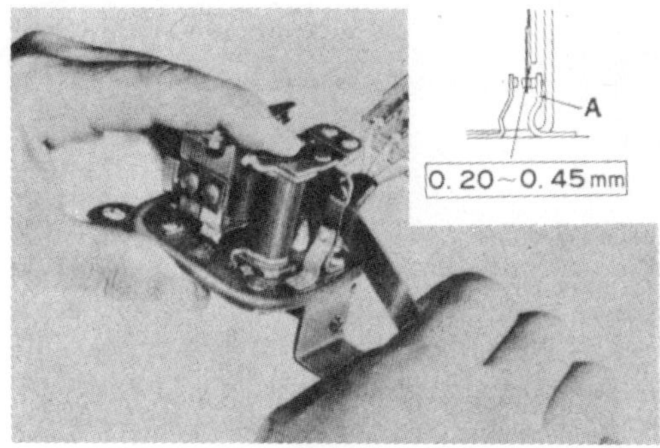


Checking voltage relay spring deflection.

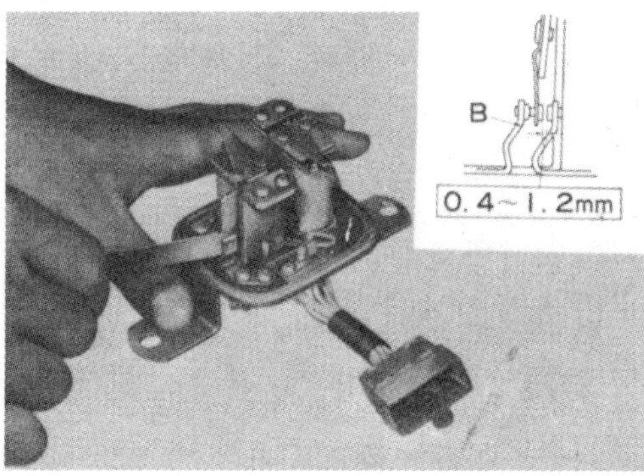


Checking point gap.

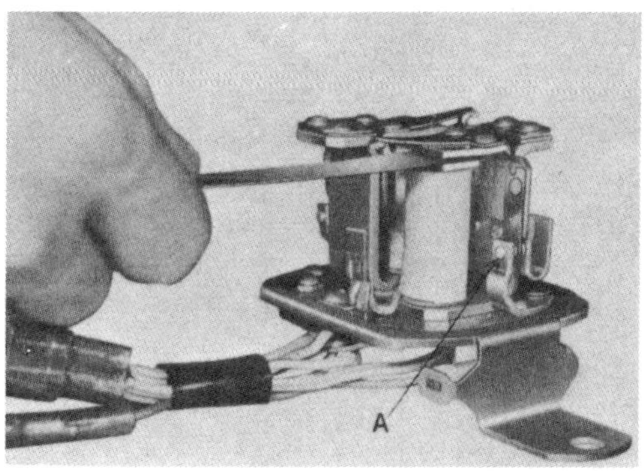


Checking armature gap.

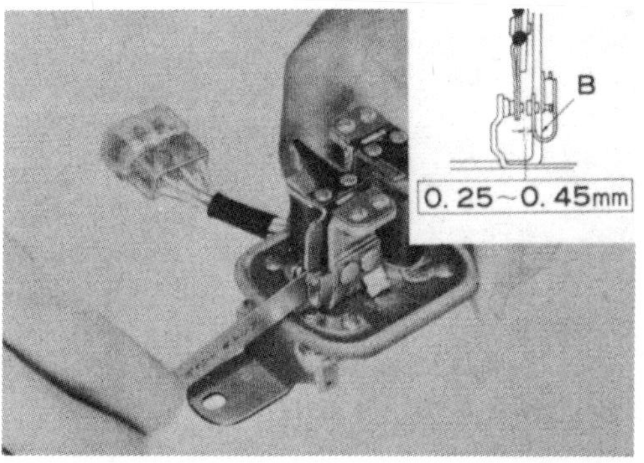


Checking point gap.

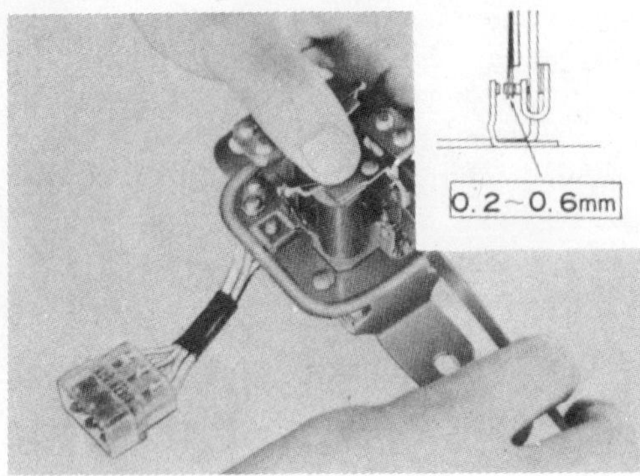


Checking spring deflection.

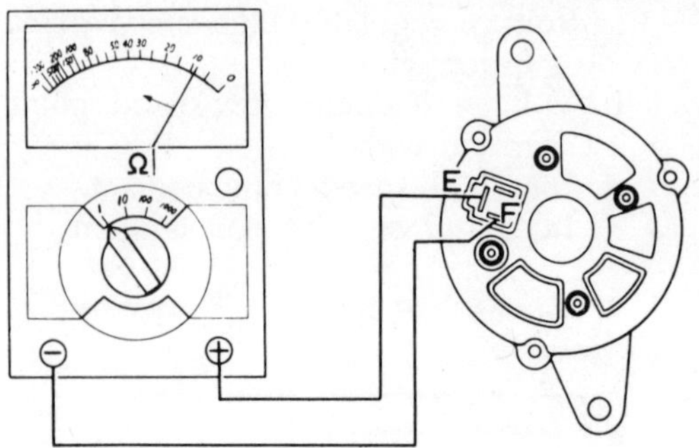

Checking resistance between F and E terminals.

e. Poor connections at "N" or "B" regulator terminals.

f. Regulator low-speed point arm spring pressure too strong.

4. Check resistance between alternator "E" and "F" terminals with circuit tester (ohmmeter). Correct resistance is 6–9 Ohms. Greater resistance indicates dirty or poorly seated brushes and slip rings, or an open rotor coil.

5. Check resistance between regulator "IG" and "F" terminals. Any resistance here indicates bad regulator points.

*Load test* Connect the test meter as illustrated. Start engine and run at 1,100 rpm.

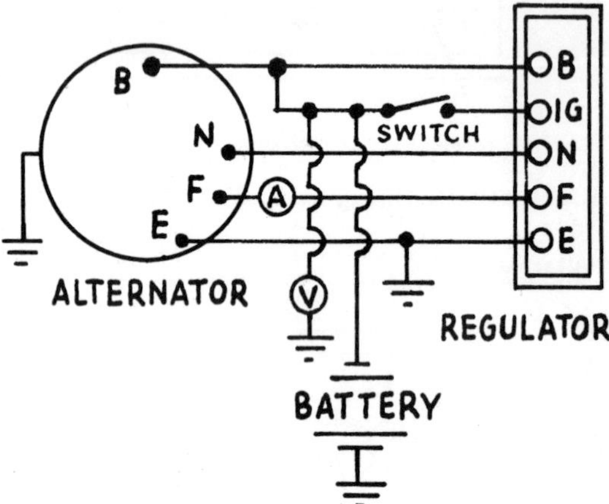


Voltage regulator (two-element with ammeter) test circuit.

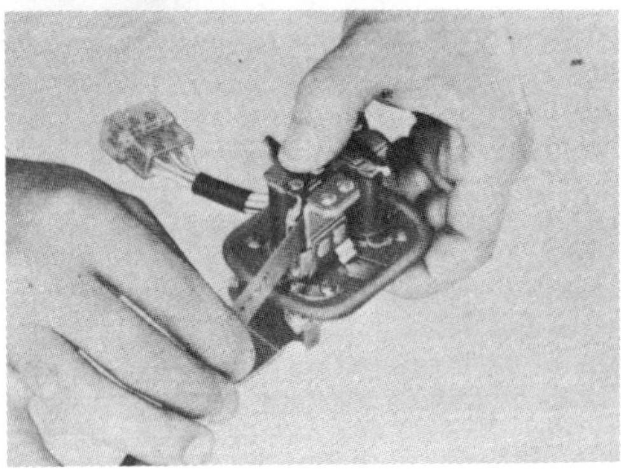

Checking angle gap—0.008″.

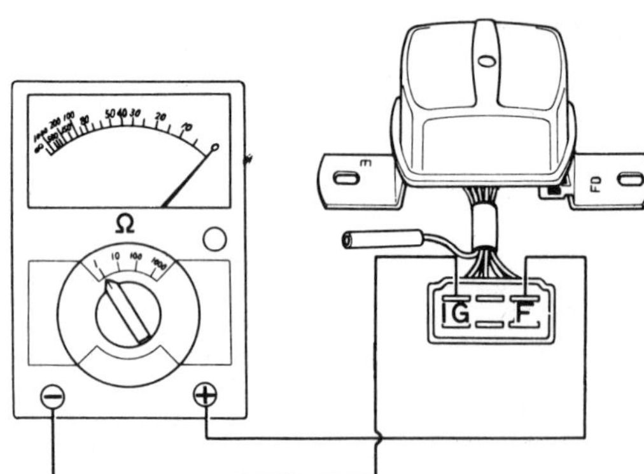


Checking resistance between IG and F terminals.

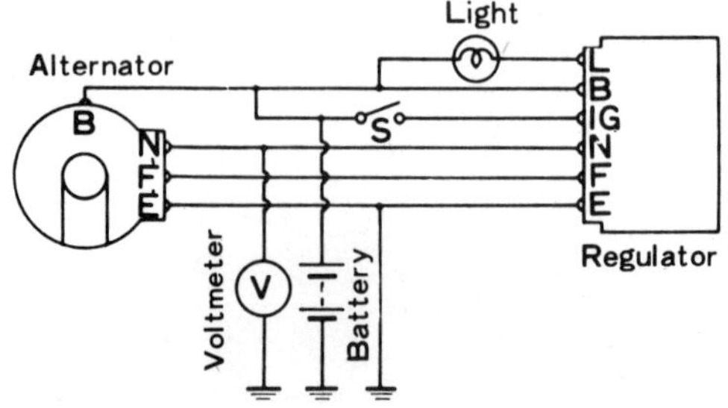


Voltage relay (warning lamp) test circuit.

Switch on headlights (high beam). The ammeter should indicate more than 28 Amperes and the voltmeter 13.5–14.5 volts. If less than 28 Amperes is indicated and the fanbelt is correctly tensioned, the diodes or stator coil might be shorted or open. *NOTE: If the battery is fully charged and the ammeter reading is less than 28 Amperes, disconnect the high tension wire from the coil and turn the starter for about 15–20*

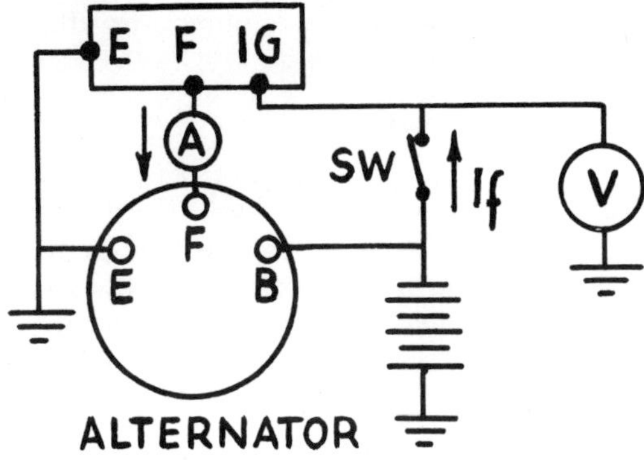

Voltage regulator (single element F-type) test circuit.

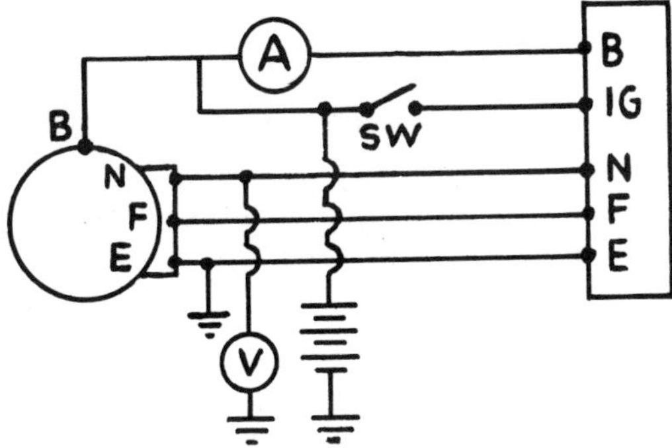

Voltage regulator (two-element with ammeter) test circuit.

*seconds to discharge the battery, then repeat the test.*

**Alternator Service**

*Removing the alternator* Disconnect battery ground cable and alternator wiring. (On J series, also remove oil pipe, oil hose and vacuum hose.) Remove alternator adjusting bar and fanbelt, then remove hold-down bolts and alternator.

*Disassembling the alternator* Remove pulley nut, fan and hub, pulley and key. Remove the three through bolts, insert a screwdriver into the notches of the drive end frame and pry frame away from stator. Tap drive end frame lightly to separate rotor from housing. (On J series, rotor must be separated from rectifier end housing by using a suitable puller.) Drive bearing

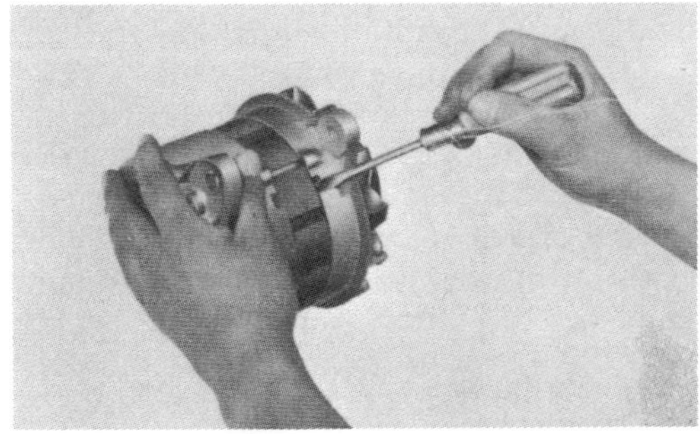
Removing alternator drive end frame.

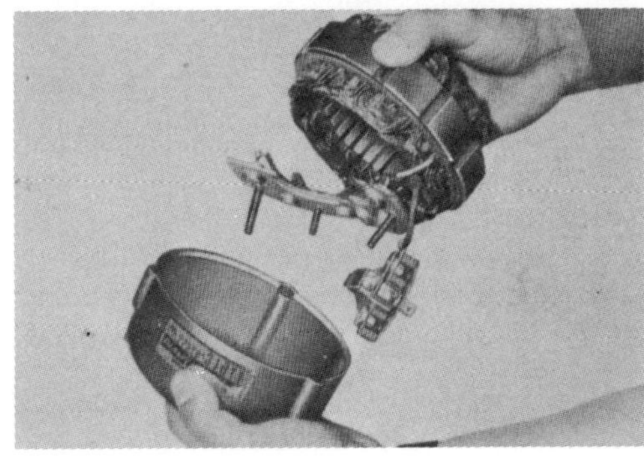
Removing alternator stator and rectifier holder.

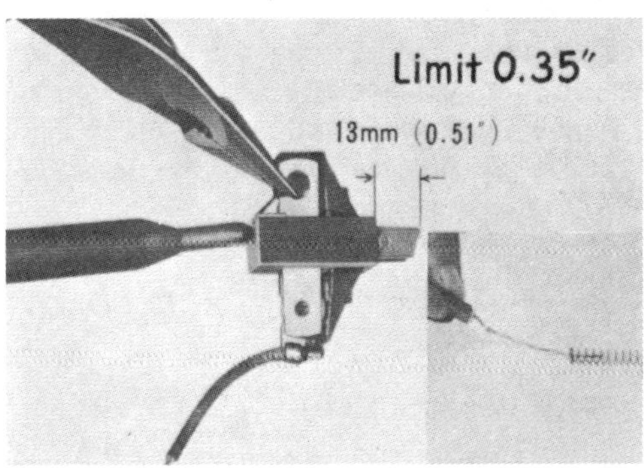

Replacing alternator brush.

from front end frame using a mallet. (Before disassembling stator from rectifier housing, punch or paint marks to assist in correct assembly.) Pull stator coil, positive and negative rectifier plates, brush holder and connections from housing. Unsolder brush connections at holder to remove them. (On F series, the brushes are screwed to the holder.) Press rectifiers (diodes) from holder. (F series diodes are mounted in holders secured to the yoke, which is located between end frame and stator coil.) *CAUTION: When soldering diodes, do not overheat. Temperatures in excess of 300°F. will damage the delicate silicon rectifiers; a 150 Watt iron should be more than sufficient.* Remove rear bearing from rotor shaft, using a suitable puller. (On J series, the bearing will remain in the rectifier housing and must be removed with a puller.)

*Assembling the alternator* Follow the

previous procedures in reverse order, observing the following precautions: make sure that the positive rectifier holder is fully insulated from the housing and/or the negative rectifier holder. A grounded positive holder will short out instantly when alternator is connected into the system. Before installing the rotor into the rectifier housing, push the brushes into the holder and insert a piece of wire (paper clip) into the access hole to keep the brushes retracted. Remove this wire before installing alternator into car.

**Inspecting and Bench Testing Alternator**

BEARINGS

All bearings (except the rear bearing of the 50 Ampere J series) are sealed and need no lubrication. Check for roughness or pitting and replace as necessary.

BRUSHES

Check for cracks, uneven wear and seating, arcing and free movement in holder. Replace if worn to, or below, wear limit (0.2″ from holder). Test insulation of brush holder using a circuit tester.

STATOR COIL

Test coil to core insulation and replace insulation if defective. To test for open stator coil, check the three lead wires for continuity. If meter needle does not move, the stator coil is open and must be replaced.

ROTOR COIL

Connect circuit tester between rotor shaft and one slip ring. If needle moves, rotor is grounded and must be replaced. Next, connect tester between the two slip rings. If needle moves, rotor coils are good. Normal rotor coil resistance is about 3.5 ohms 3RC; 4.1–4.3 for Corolla; 4.8 ohms for the J series alternator.

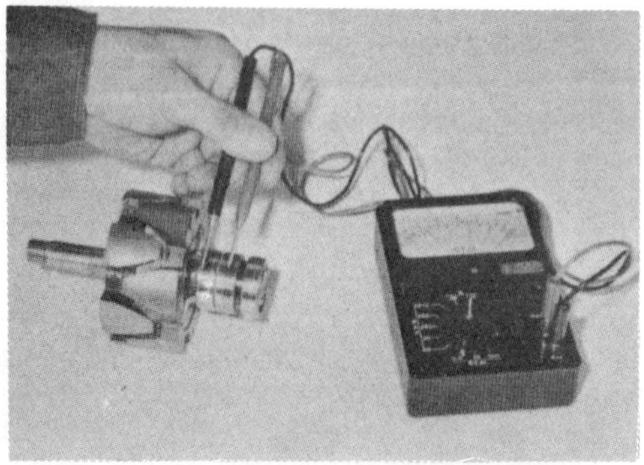

Testing rotor for open and/or short circuit.

RECTIFIER TEST

Connect circuit tester between rectifier lead wire and rectifier holder. Note action of meter needle. Next, reverse the connection and again note meter action; it should be the opposite of the first reading. If meter needle moves in both tests, the rectifier is shorted; if needle moves in neither test, rectifier is open. Replace rectifier in either case. Single rectifiers are available for the J series only, all other rectifiers are available in positive or negative sets of three, mounted in holders.

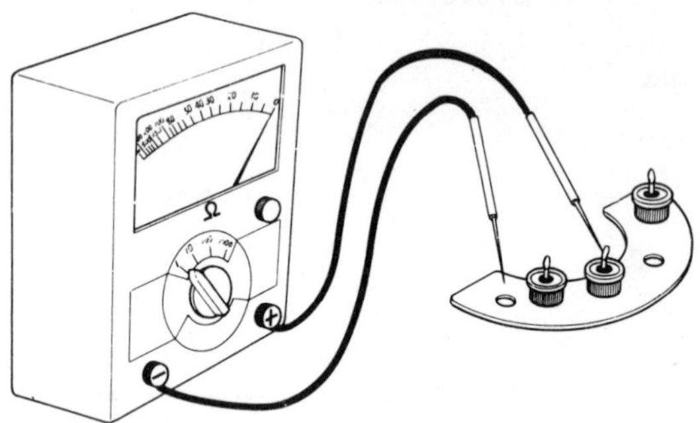

Testing rectifier.

IDENTIFICATION OF RECTIFIERS

*Red* markings denote *positive* diodes (permits current flow from lead wire to holders). *Black* markings denote *negative* diodes (the current flows from the holder to the wire).

## Ignition System

The ignition spark must take place at the right moment, with sufficient intensity to ignite the compressed air-fuel mixture. The ignition coil transforms the low primary voltage into a secondary voltage high enough to supply sufficient spark for all conditions of load and speed (approximately 15,000 volts). The distributor performs two jobs: it distributes secondary (high) voltage to the spark plugs, in proper sequence (firing order), and it opens the ignition points at the proper time to fire the spark plugs. A built-in centrifugal advance unit advances engine timing as engine speed increases; the vacuum advance unit is operated by throttle position and load requirements. The tach-dwellmeter, volt-ammeter, ohmmeter and timing light are a few of the test instruments needed to perform accurate ignition system diagnosis. Most ignition problems are caused by failure of the primary and/or the secondary circuits, incorrect ignition timing or incorrect distributor advance. Circuit problems can be caused by shorts in the wiring, loose or dirty connections in either the primary or secondary circuit, faulty insulation, cracked rotor or distributor cap, bad points and/or worn out spark plugs.

**Distributor**

*Removing the distributor* Disconnect all high tension wires from spark plugs, taking care to mark the No. 1 wire for easy assembly. Disconnect the primary wire and the vacuum advance line at the distributor. *NOTE: On K series, also disconnect the vacuum retard line.* Remove distributor cap and paint mark the distributor body and engine block for correct assembly positioning. Remove distributor clamp and lift the distributor out. *CAUTION: Do not rotate the crankshaft while the distributor is removed.*

1. Distributor cam
2. Governor spring
3. Governor weight
4. Governor shaft and plate
5. Steel washer
6. Bakelite washer
7. Terminal insulator
8. Terminal bolt
9. Condenser
10. Distributor housing
11. Adjuster cover
12. Housing cap spring
13. Oil cup
14. Distributor cap
15. Carbon center piece
16. Rotor
17. Dust proof cover
18. Breaker
19. Contact point
20. Breaker plate
21. Stationary plate
22. Spring set
23. Vacuum advance unit
24. O-ring
25. Washer
26. Spiral gear
27. Pin

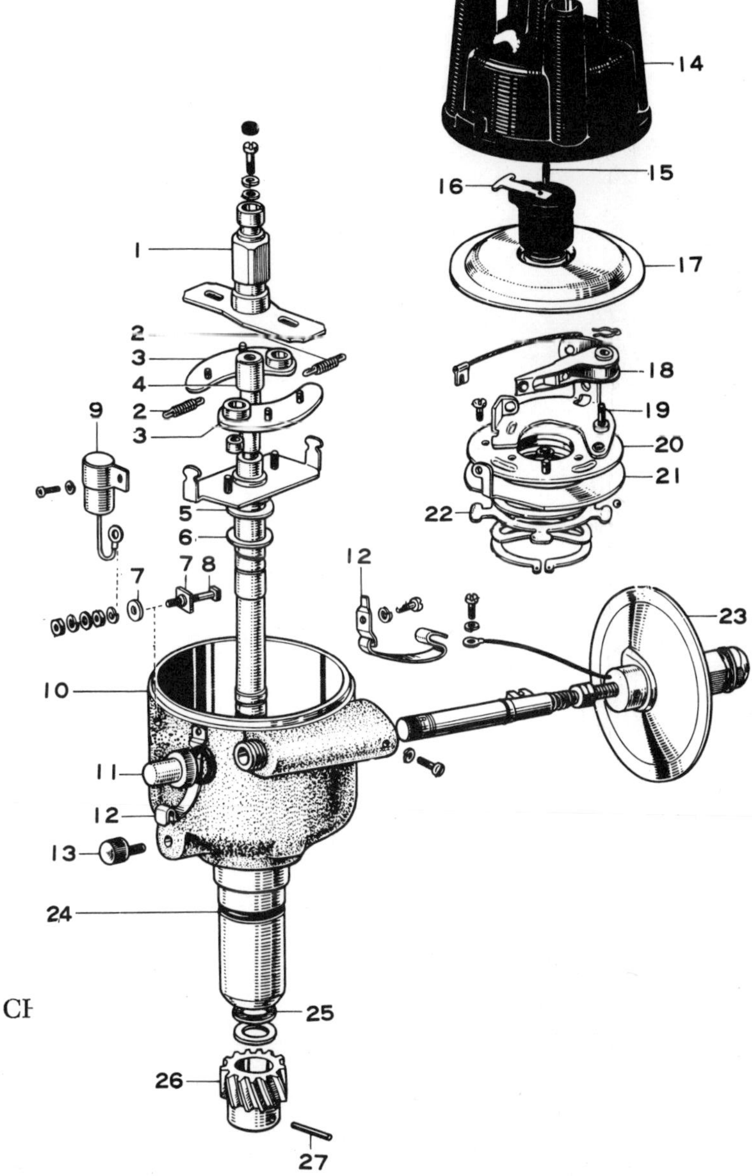

Typical distributor, showing major components.

*Disassembling the distributor* Remove the rotor and the dust cover, then disconnect the vacuum advance lead wire and remove the snap washer that secures the diaphragm link to the base plate. Remove the adjuster cap and the vacuum advance retaining screw, then slide the advance unit out of the distributor. Disconnect the condenser wire, remove the terminal bolt, base plate retaining screws and the condenser. Lift contact points out of the distributor, then remove spring clips and lift the base plate out. Remove cam retaining screw and pull cam off the shaft. With paint, mark one of the governor springs and its anchor. Also mark one weight and its pivot pin. Remove the governor springs carefully and take out the weights. Drive out the pin that holds distributor drive gear to shaft and remove the gear. Now, pull the distributor shaft from the housing.

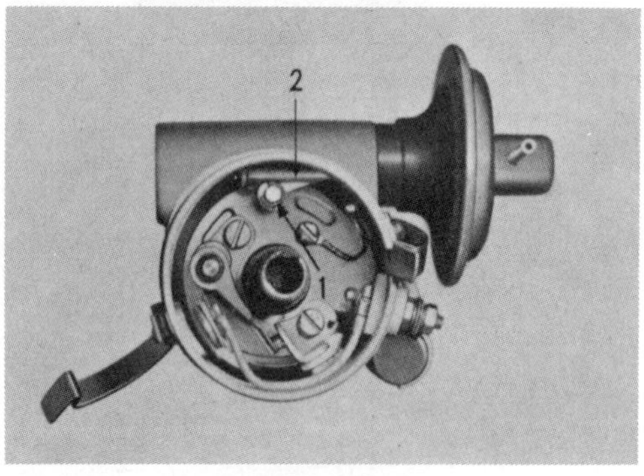


Disassembling vacuum retarder.

*Inspecting the distributor components* Wash all parts thoroughly (with the exception of the diaphragm and the condenser) in clean solvent and dry with compressed air. Check distributor cap for cracks, carbon deposits and burnt or corroded metal terminals. Check center carbon button; it must move freely and should protrude at least .25″. Inspect rotor for damage and corrosion. Inspect contact points for pitting and/or uneven seating. Inspect distributor shaft for runout, which should not exceed 0.002″. Make sure the governor weights can move freely on their pivots and check the cam lobes for signs of wear. Check turning resistance of base plate; it should not exceed 1.1 lbs. Install the washers onto the shaft and install shaft into housing. Insert the pin into the shaft and check the end-play with a gauge; minimum is 0.006″ and maximum 0.020″. If end-play is excessive, remove pin and add shim washers (plastic washer fits between the metal washers).

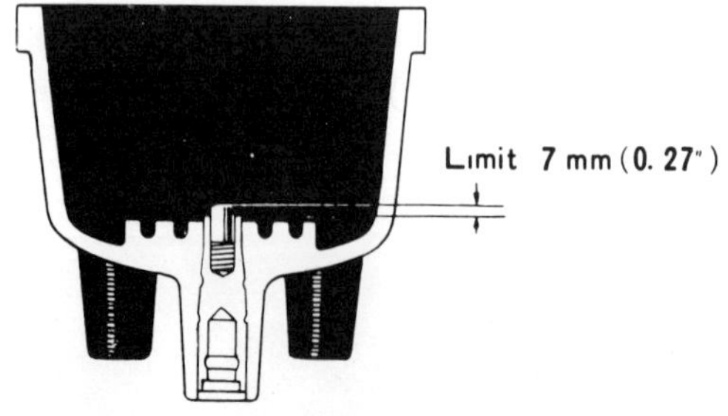


Distributor cap carbon button must protrude at least 0.27″.

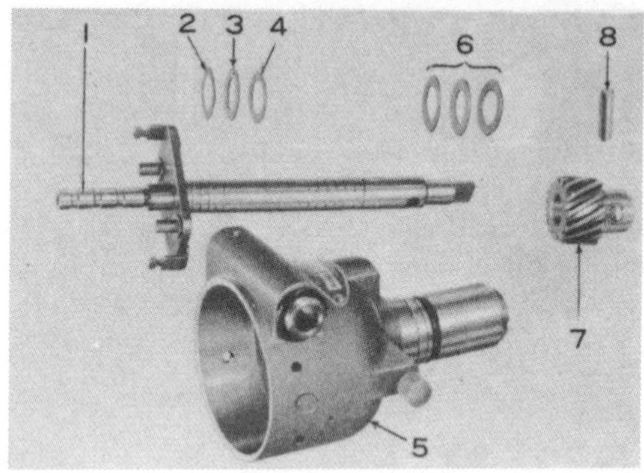


Distributor shaft assembly sequence.

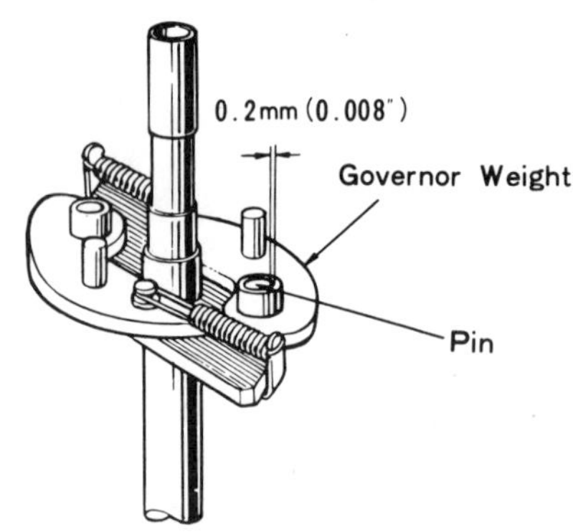


Centrifugal advance governor pin clearance.

*Assembling the distributor* Reverse the order of disassembly, coating distributor shaft with a silicone lubricant and filling the groove in the upper portion of the cam with the same lubricant. Also apply a light coating to the cam surface. After installing the rotor, check the advance mechanism operation by twisting the rotor clockwise and releasing it. It should return to its original position without binding. Check the vacuum advance unit by pushing the rod in as far as possible and then closing the line opening with a finger. If there is a vacuum leak, the rod will return.

*Testing the distributor* After assembly, set the point gap with a feeler gauge by rotating the distributor shaft until the breaker arm plastic rubbing block is at the

Adjusting distributor contact point gap.

top of the cam. Measure the spring pressure of the breaker arm with a tension scale. Always replace the condenser when replacing contact points, especially if points were deeply pitted.

*Installing the distributor* If the crankshaft has not been moved during the time the distributor was out, simply align the paint marks for correct installation. If the crankshaft was rotated, however, it will be necessary to set the ignition timing.

### Ignition Timing

Rotate engine so that No. 1 cylinder is at TDC on compression stroke. Now align the timing mark on the crankshaft pulley with the timing pointer on the front engine cover.

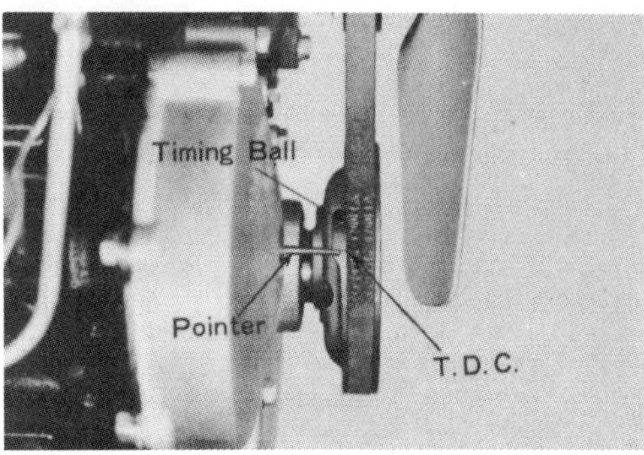


Timing mark location.

Distributor installation position.

(This varies with each engine, so be sure to check specification tables.) Align the oil pump shaft slot with the alignment point punch marked on the distributor base at the block. (The slot position will approximate ten minutes after eight o'clock position.) Set the octane selector dial at zero

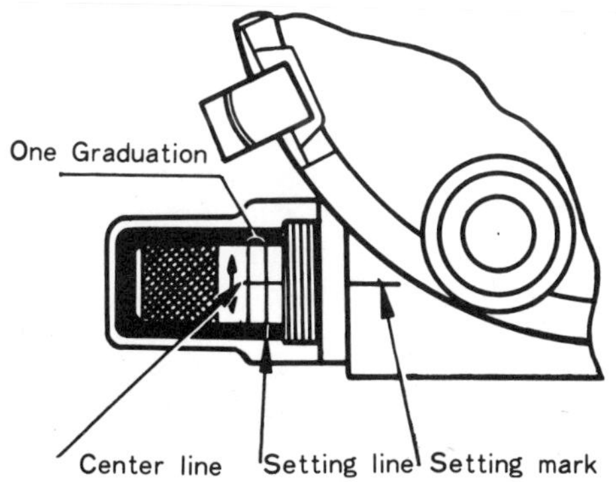


Octane selector in normal position.

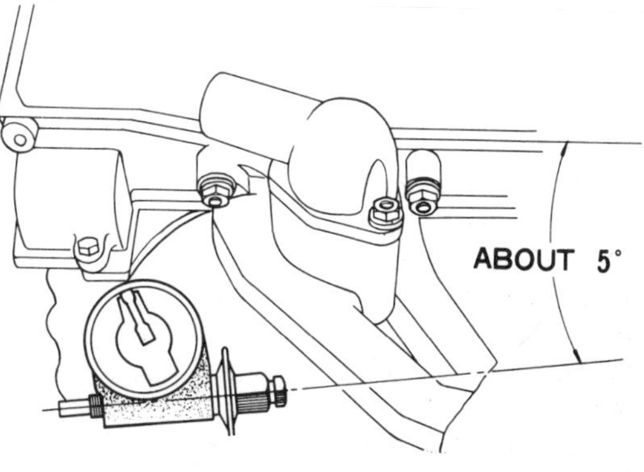


Distributor installation position.

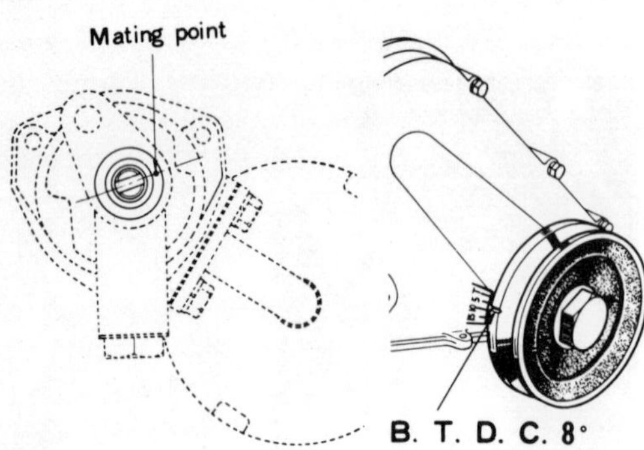

Timing marks and oil pump drive position at 8° BTDC.

position, the distributor at the eleven o'clock position and install the distributor into the block, making sure the drive slot is engaged properly. If distributor is correctly installed, the rotor will now be in the one o'clock position. Rotate the distributor slightly until the points begin to open. Install retaining clamp and tighten screw. Check ignition timing, with engine running, using a strobe light.

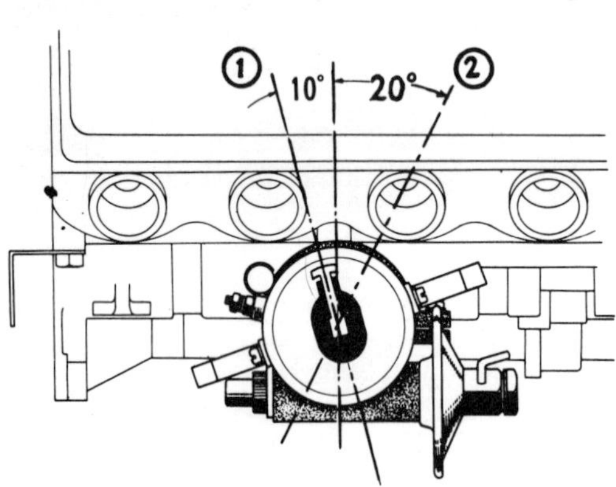

Distributor rotor position; (1) 10° Before (2) 20° After.

*Vacuum advance and vacuum retard units* These are fitted to the Corolla K-C engines only. Remove the cap, rotor and dust cover. Remove the vacuum advance retaining screw and unscrew the advance assembly, then remove unit from distributor housing. (Do not loosen the two nuts.) Remove the snap-ring, then disconnect the retarder rod from the retaining pin and remove the retarder assembly from the distributor housing.

Assemble in reverse order of disassembly. When installing, screw in the advancer all

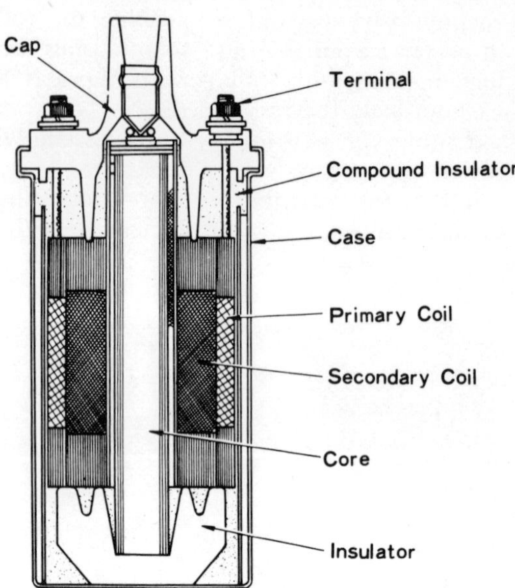

Ignition coil.

the way, then unscrew until the lock hole is lined up.

### Ignition Coil

The ignition coil is a hermetically-sealed, oil-filled unit not requiring special service other than maintaining terminal cleanliness and tight connections. The coil has two windings on a soft iron core: the primary, which consists of a few turns of heavy wire, and the secondary, which consists of many turns of a very fine wire. With the points closed, the primary (low voltage) current flows from the battery through the ignition switch into the primary windings of the coil, then to ground through the closed points. When the points open, the magnetic field built up in the primary windings moves into the secondary windings, producing very high voltage. This high voltage is generated each time the points are opened. It flows through the high tension wire to the center tower of the distributor cap, through the carbon brush into the rotor and, from there, to each spark plug in turn.

*Testing the ignition coil* Before testing a coil, allow sufficient time for it to reach normal operating temperature.

Check the primary resistance with an ohmmeter; it should be 2.55–3.15 ohms. Should resistance exceed 5 ohms, replace the coil. Test the resistance of the secondary windings; this should be 8,400–9,200 ohms. A higher resistance indicates a broken (open) circuit. Check the primary terminal-to-case insulating resistance, which must exceed 100 megohms (1 megohm equals 1,000,000 ohms). After installing coil, run the engine at idle speed and pull off the No. 1 plug wire. The spark should bridge (jump) at least .25″ when held near the engine block.

### Spark Plugs

Be sure to select and install only factory recommended type plugs for best performance. For different types of driving there are different plug heat ranges. Use "hot" plugs for winter or short trip driving, "cold" plugs for high speed or summer driving.

#### Inspection and Adjusting of Spark Plugs

Check the porcelain insulation for cracks and chips and check electrodes for wear. Check for carbon deposits: excessive carbon deposits are an indication of oil burning —replace with "hotter" plugs. If plugs are excessively white or electrode wear is too rapid, replace with "colder" plugs. Always replace gasket when installing old plugs and torque plugs to 25–30 ft. lbs.

*Gap bridging* —(A)— May be traced to flying deposits in the combustion chamber. In some cases, fluffy deposits may accumulate on the plugs during intown driving and when the engine is suddenly put under high load; this material can melt and bridge the gap.

*Scavenger deposits* —(B)— Fuel scavenger deposits shown may be white or yellow in color. They may appear to be harmful, but this is normal with certain brands of fuel. Note that accumulation on the ground electrode and shell areas may be unusually heavy, but the material is easily chipped off. Such plugs can be considered normal and can be cleaned using standard procedures.

*Chipped insulator* —(C)— Usually results from bending the center electrode during gapping. Under certain conditions, severe detonation can also split insulator firing ends.

*Preignition damage* —(D)— Caused by excessive temperatures, produces melting of the center electrode and, somewhat later, the ground electrode. Insulators will appear relatively clean of deposits. Check for cor-

Spark plug damage.

rect plug heat range and overadvanced ignition timing.

*Cold fouling (or carbon fouling)* —(E)— Dry, black appearance of one or two plugs in a set. Check for sticking valves or bad spark plug wires. Fouling of the entire set may be caused by a clogged air cleaner, a sticking exhaust manifold heat valve, or a faulty choke.

*Overheating* —(F)— Dead white or gray insulator which appears "blistered." Electrode gap wear rate will be considerably in excess of .001″/1,000 miles. This may suggest that a cooler heat range should be used; however, overadvanced ignition timing, detonation and cooling system malfunctions can also overheat spark plugs.

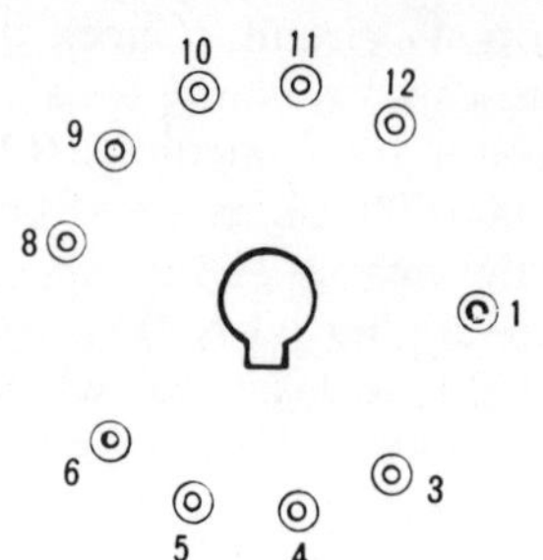


Combination meter terminal identification—Corolla.

1. Water temperature sending gauge
3. Voltage regulator
4. Fuse block (5A)
5. Oil pressure sending gauge
6. Lighting switch
8. Body ground
9. Turn signal switch
10. Turn signal switch
11. Dimmer switch
12. Fuel sending gauge

## Miscellaneous Electrical

### Instrument Panel

Except on Land Cruiser series, the combination meter consists of the speedometer and trip meter, fuel and temperature gauges, oil pressure warning light, alternator (or charge) warning light, left and right turn indicator lights, high beam indicator and the parking brake light.

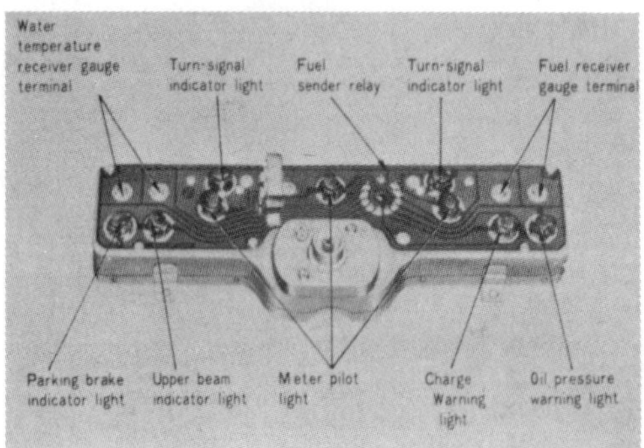


Combination meter rear view.

*Removing the instrument panel* Disconnect the battery ground cable, then unscrew the speedometer cable housing and pull out the inner cable. Next, disconnect all harness connections; remove the ignition switch on early models. (Late models have the switch in the steering column jacket.) Remove two bolts from the steering column jacket. The panel is secured to the dash with four screws. Avoid scratching the column housing during panel removal.

### Speedometer

The speedometer is of the rotating magnet type. At 637 speedometer shaft revolutions, the indicated speed is 40 mph. The odometer will read 0.6 miles (1 km.) per 637 revolutions of the shaft. The tripmeter operates from the same shaft as the speedometer,

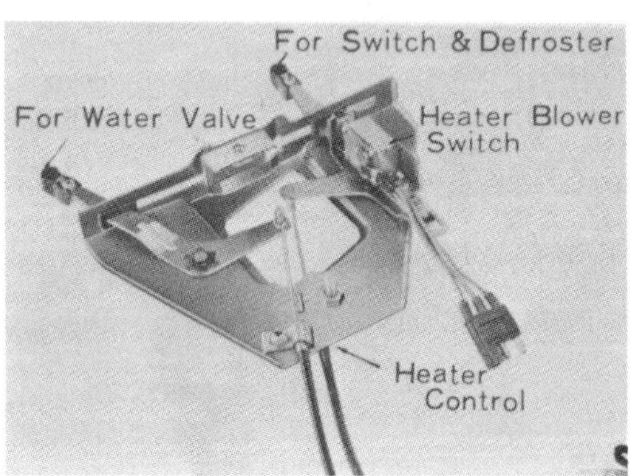


Corolla heater controls.

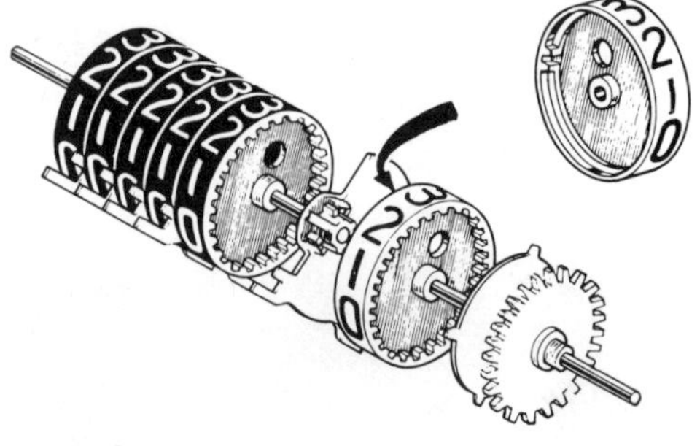

Corona odometer.

and is connected to it through a one-way clutch which allows the tripmeter to be reset to zero.

**Fuel Gauge (dash unit)**

The complete fuel gauge circuit consists of the dash gauge, the tank (sending) unit and a voltage regulator. This regulator also affects the operation of the temperature gauge and it should be tested if either of the two gauges seems erratic.

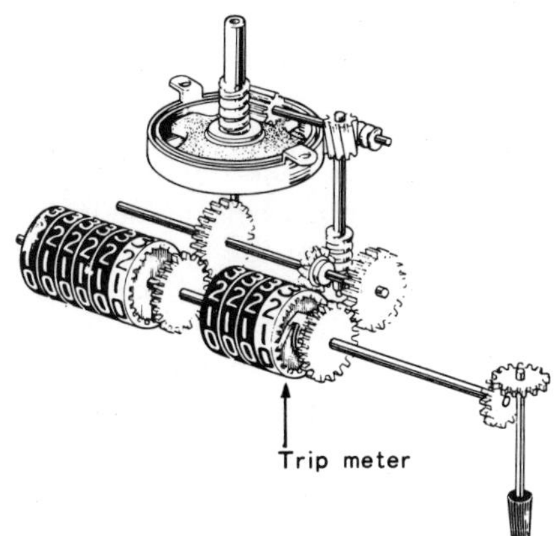


Corona trip odometer.

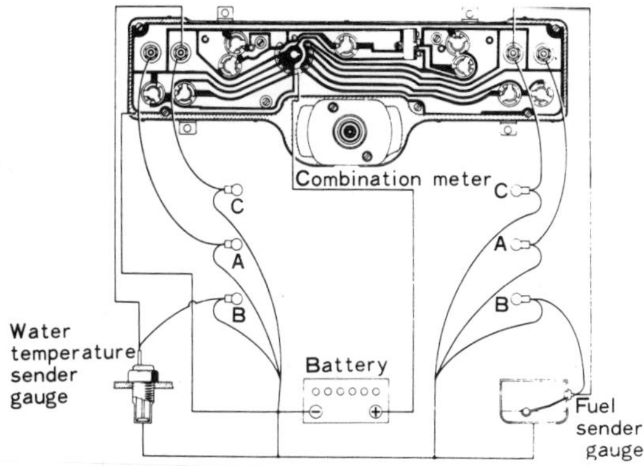


Test points for gauge testing.

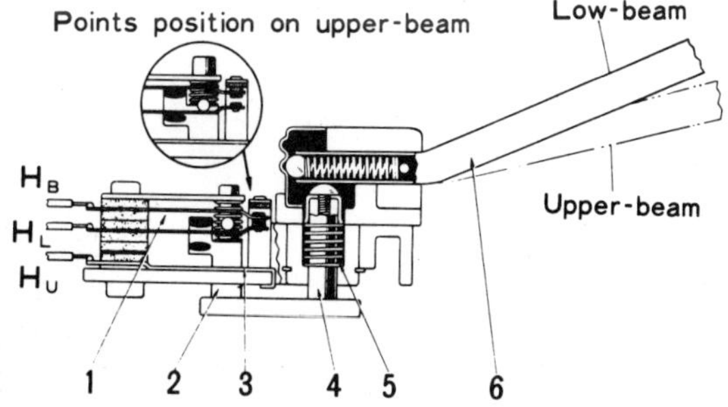


Headlight switch.

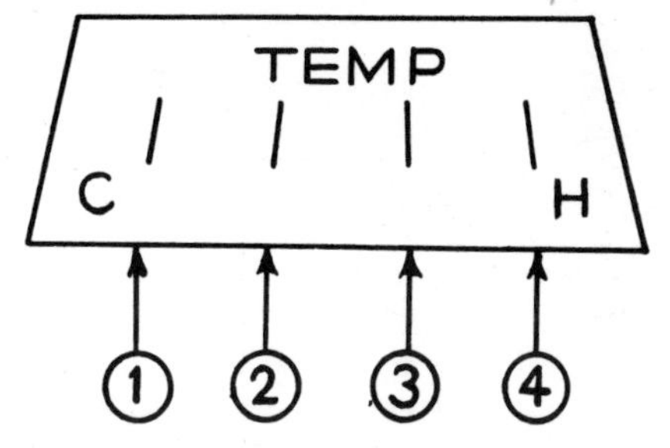


| | *Temperature* | | *Ohms* | | | |
|---|---|---|---|---|---|---|
| | *°C* | *°F* | *K* | *MS* | *MK II* | |
| C | 25 | 77 | | 450/700 | | |
| ↑ | 50 | 122 | | | 136 | ① |
| ↕ | 80 | 172 | 44 | 38/51 | 48 | ② |
| ↓ | 100 | 212 | 22 | 21/24 | 27 | ③ |
| H | 110 | 232 | | | | ④ |

TEMPERATURE GAUGE CALIBRATION

FUEL GAUGE
(Ohms)

| | *K* | *8n* |
|---|---|---|
| E | 110 | 120 |
| ½ | | 45 |
| F | 3 | 17 |

### Testing

*Fuel and temperature gauges* Ground combination meter body, connect a 3-watt test light between the positive terminal of the dash unit (either fuel or temperature) and ground. Test light will go *on* if the sending unit is functioning properly. Next, connect the test light between the sending unit and ground. If the dash gauge needle moves, the dash unit is good.

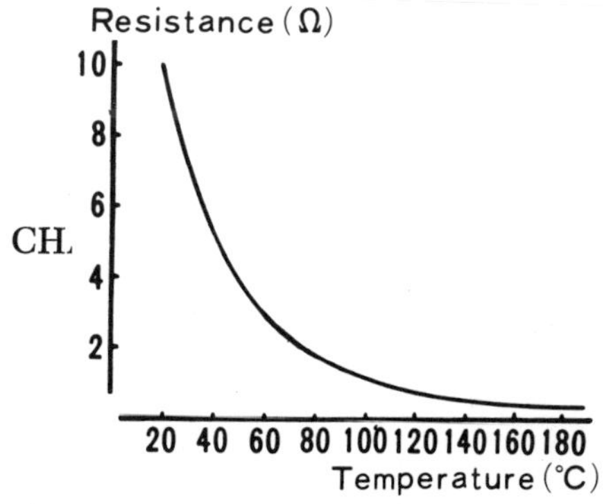


Thermistor temperature/resistance relationship.

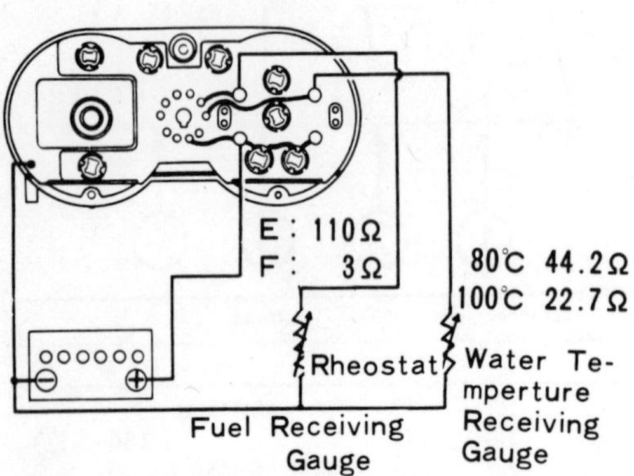


Corolla combination meter test.

On Corolla units, test the combination meter with a test meter having a variable resistance. Check resistance between meter body and each connection of the harness plug. Resistance should be zero, but connectors No. 1, 3, 4, 5 and 12 are grounded through the fuel and temperature gauges and may read 100 ohms. Set the rheostat to 3 ohms. In this position, gauge should register *full.* At 110 ohms, gauge should register *empty.* Test the temperature gauge by setting the resistance to 44.2 ohms, at which point the gauge should register about 172° F. At 22.7 ohms, the gauge should read about 212° F. Gauge dials are designed so that *cold, middle, upper* and *hot* lines correspond to the following temperatures: 122, 172, 212 and 232° F.

*Oil pressure warning circuit* Switch the ignition *on;* the warning light should come on as well. Check if the light bulb or fuse is burned out, then check for broken wiring between ignition switch and light. Next check that the wiring between light and sending unit is not broken. The switch itself can be defective or poorly grounded. If the light does not go out when engine is started, check the oil level in the crankcase. If oil level is good, remove gauge from block and test oil pressure using an oil pressure gauge. If the pressure is more than 2.8–5.7 psi, the sending unit is defective and must be replaced.

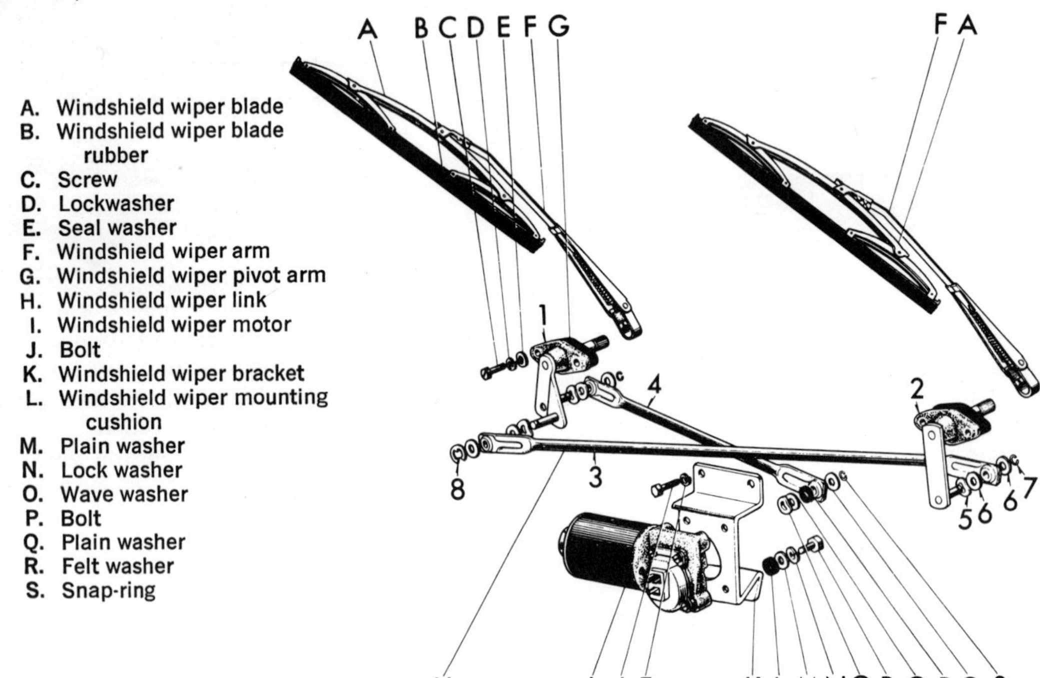


Windshield wiper motor and related components.

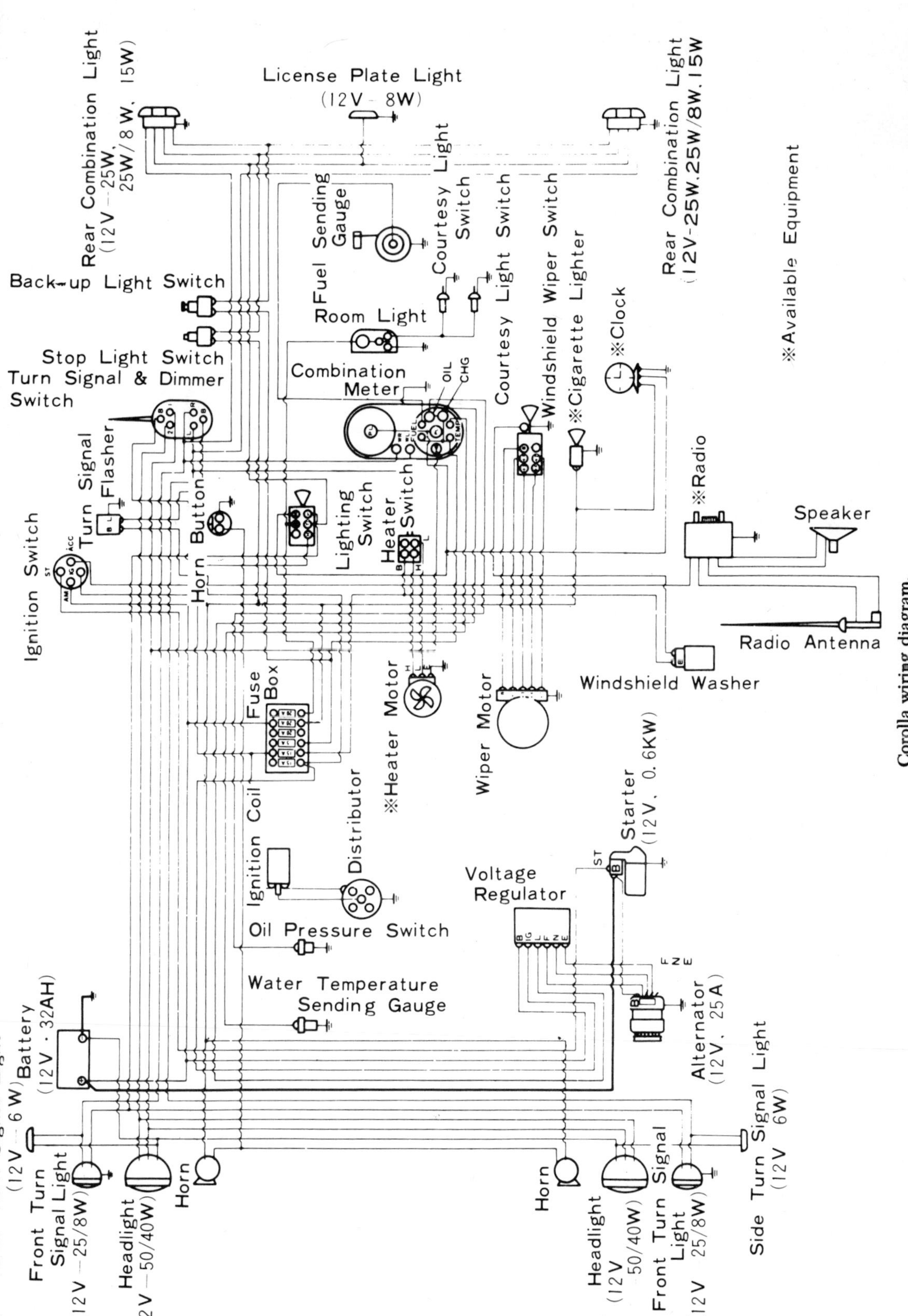


Corolla wiring diagram.

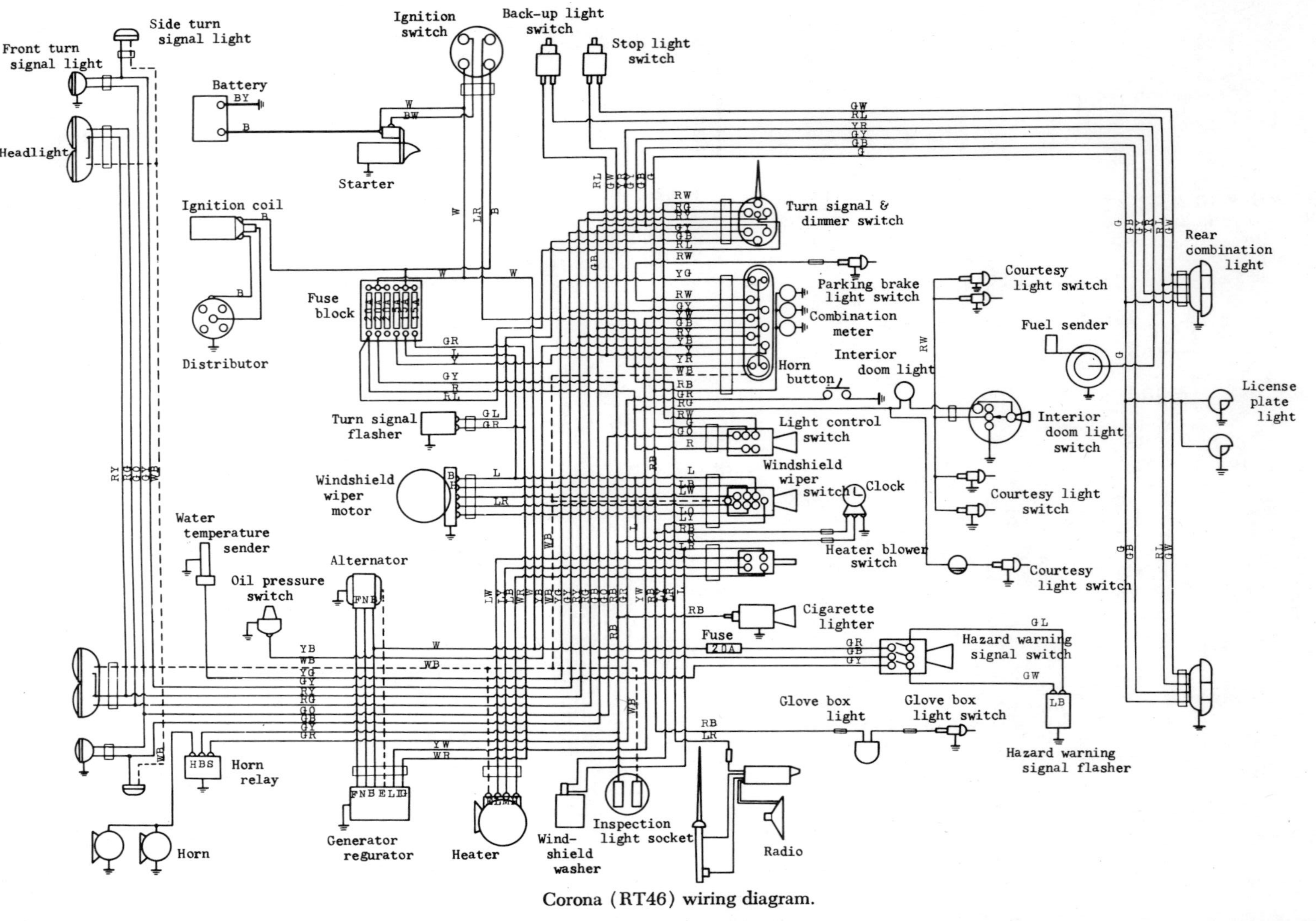

Corona (RT46) wiring diagram.

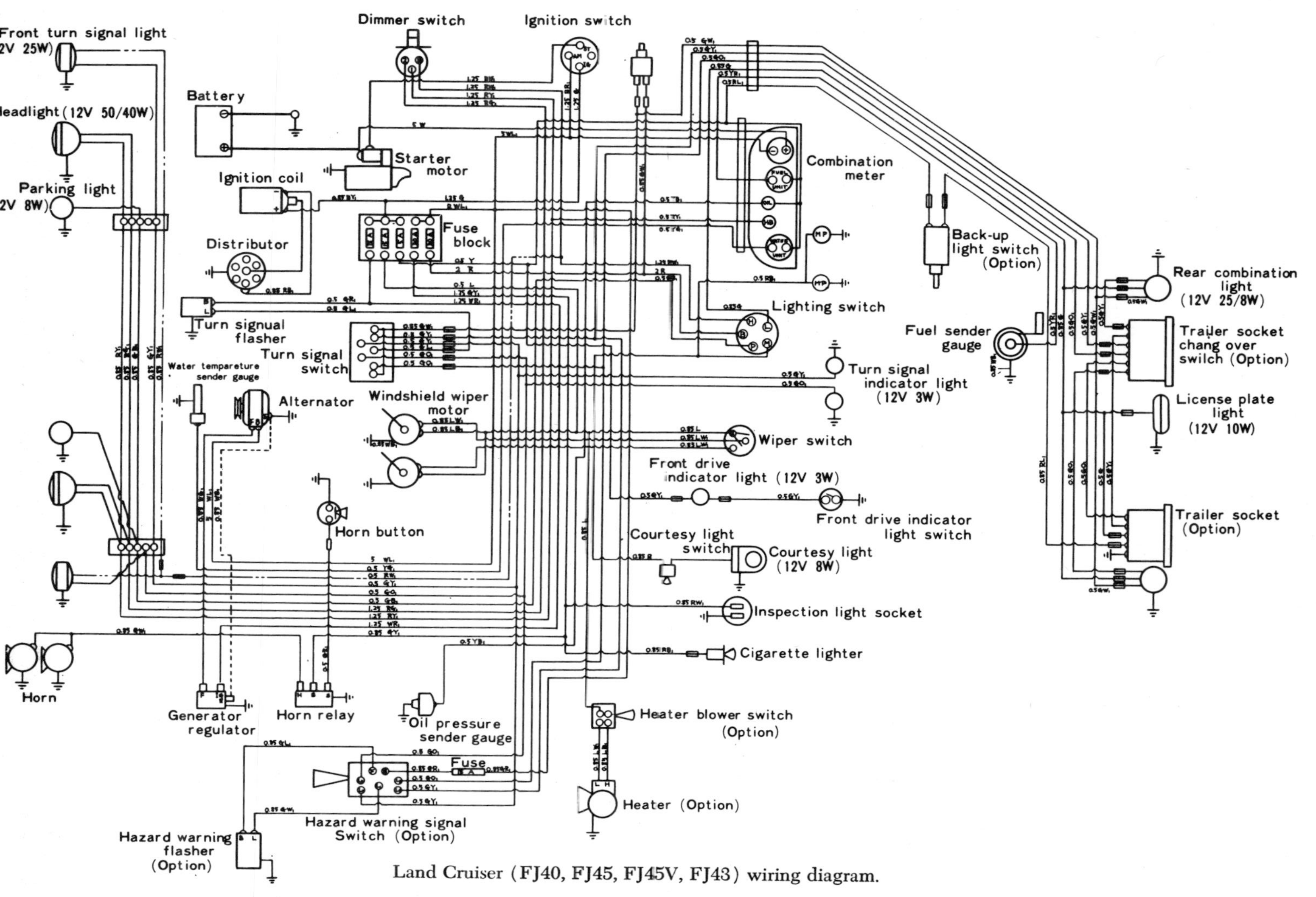


Land Cruiser (FJ40, FJ45, FJ45V, FJ43) wiring diagram.

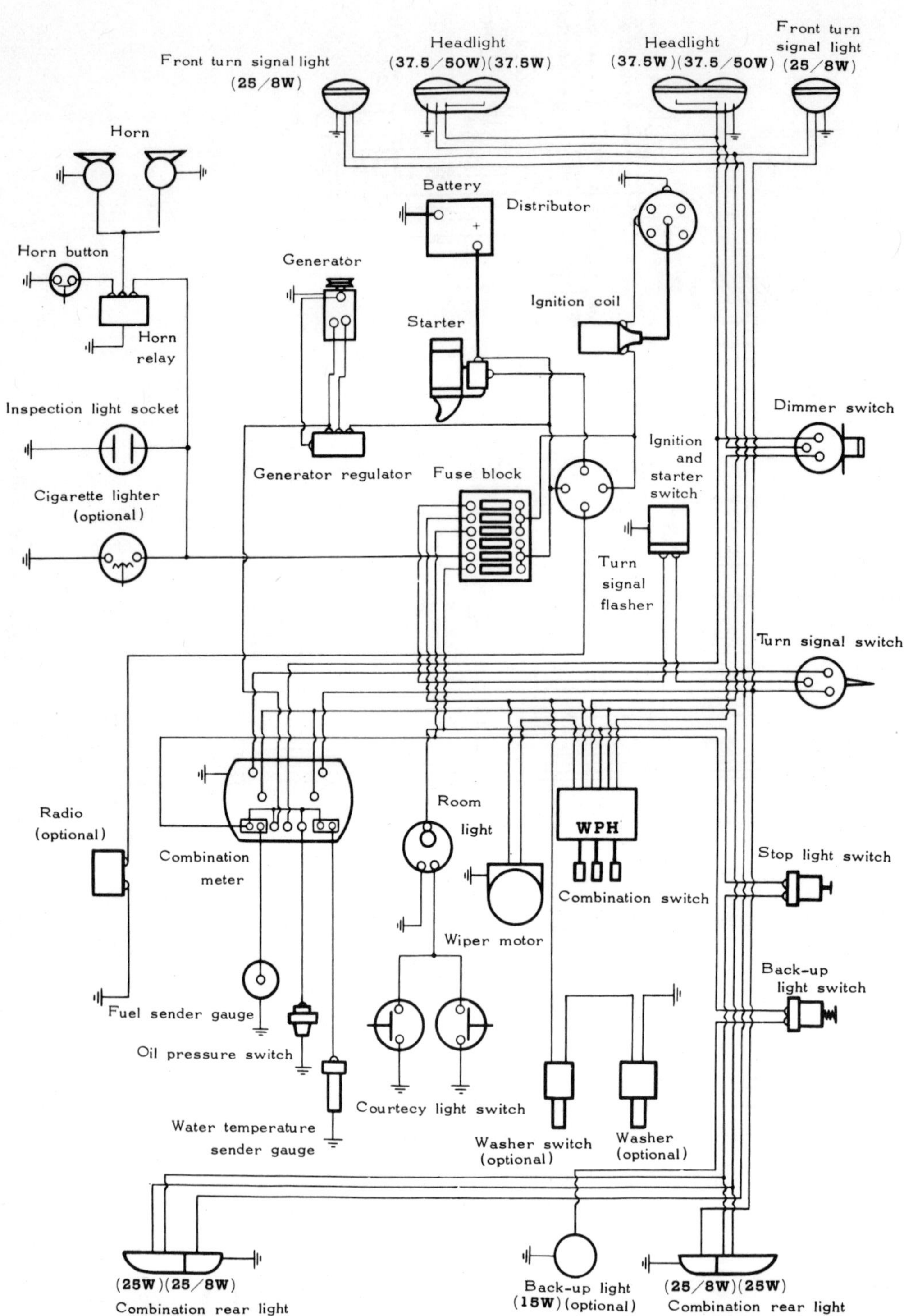


Stout and Lite Stout wiring diagram.

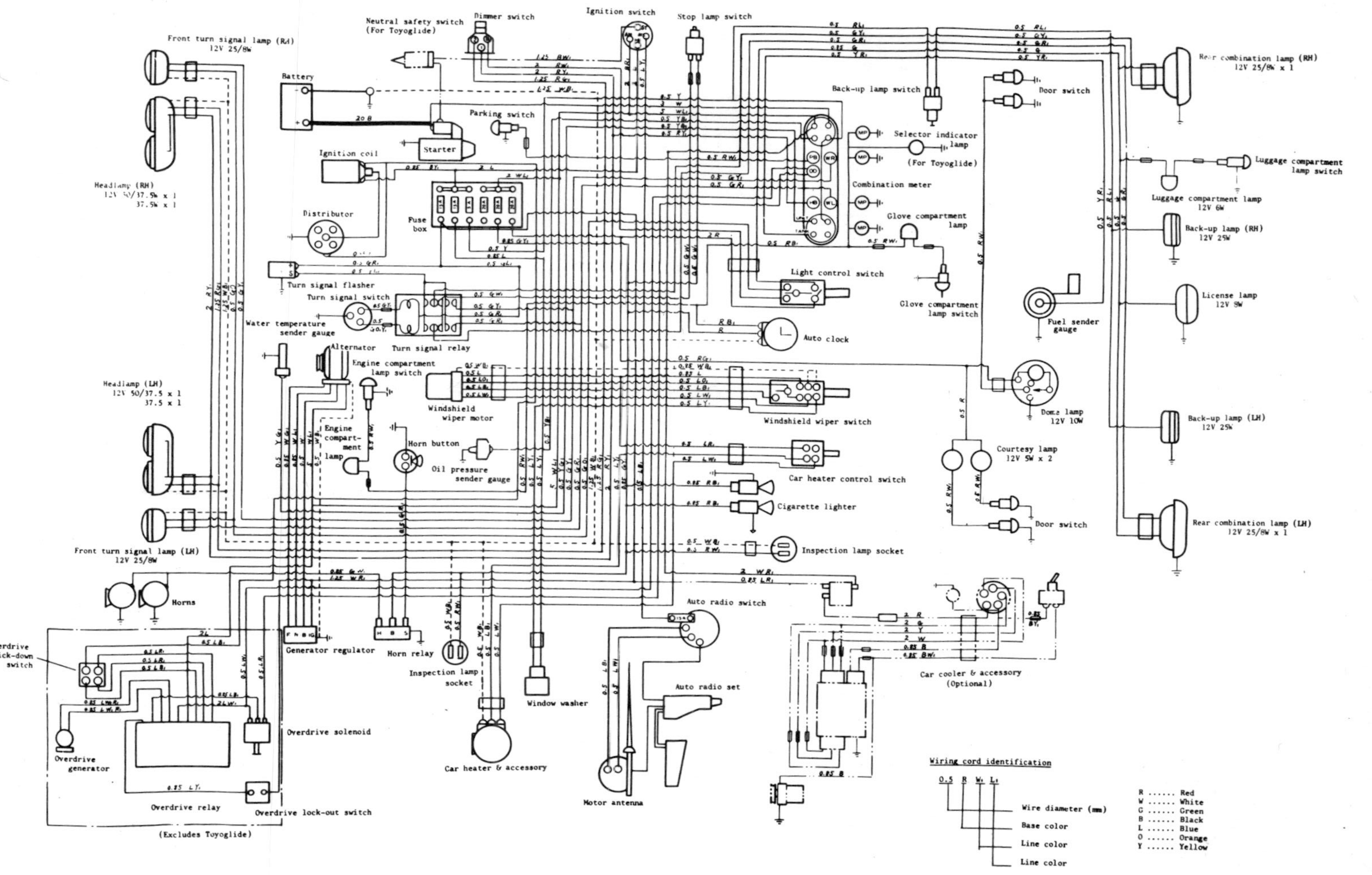


Crown (RS41) wiring diagram.

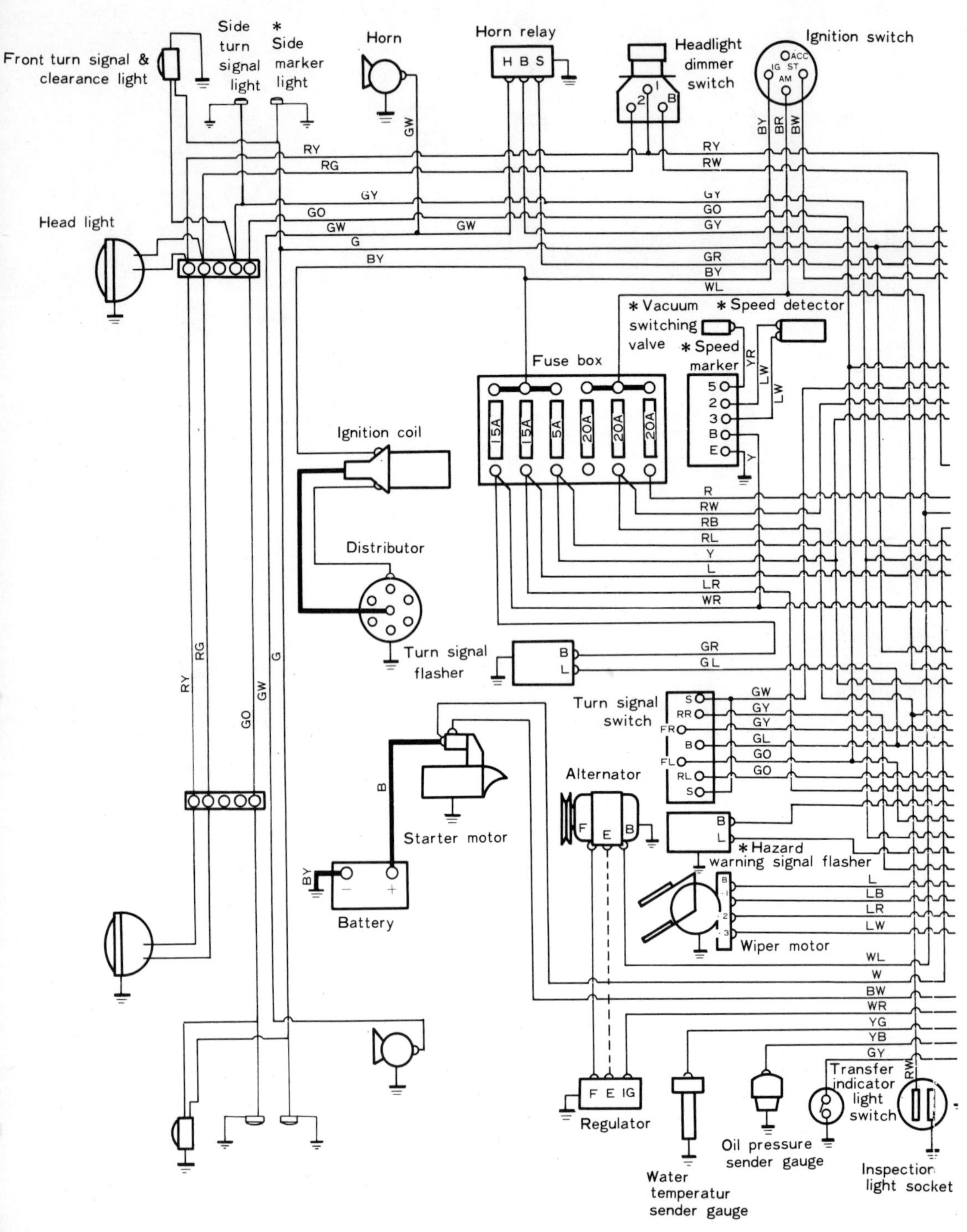
Front turn signal & clearance light
Side turn signal light
* Side marker light
Horn
Horn relay
H B S
Headlight dimmer switch
Ignition switch
ACC IG ST AM
Head light
* Vacuum switching valve
* Speed detector
* Speed marker
Fuse box
15A 15A 5A 20A 20A 20A
Ignition coil
Distributor
Turn signal flasher
Turn signal switch
Alternator
Starter motor
Battery
* Hazard warning signal flasher
Wiper motor
Regulator
F E IG
Water temperatur sender gauge
Oil pressure sender gauge
Transfer indicator light switch
Inspection light socket

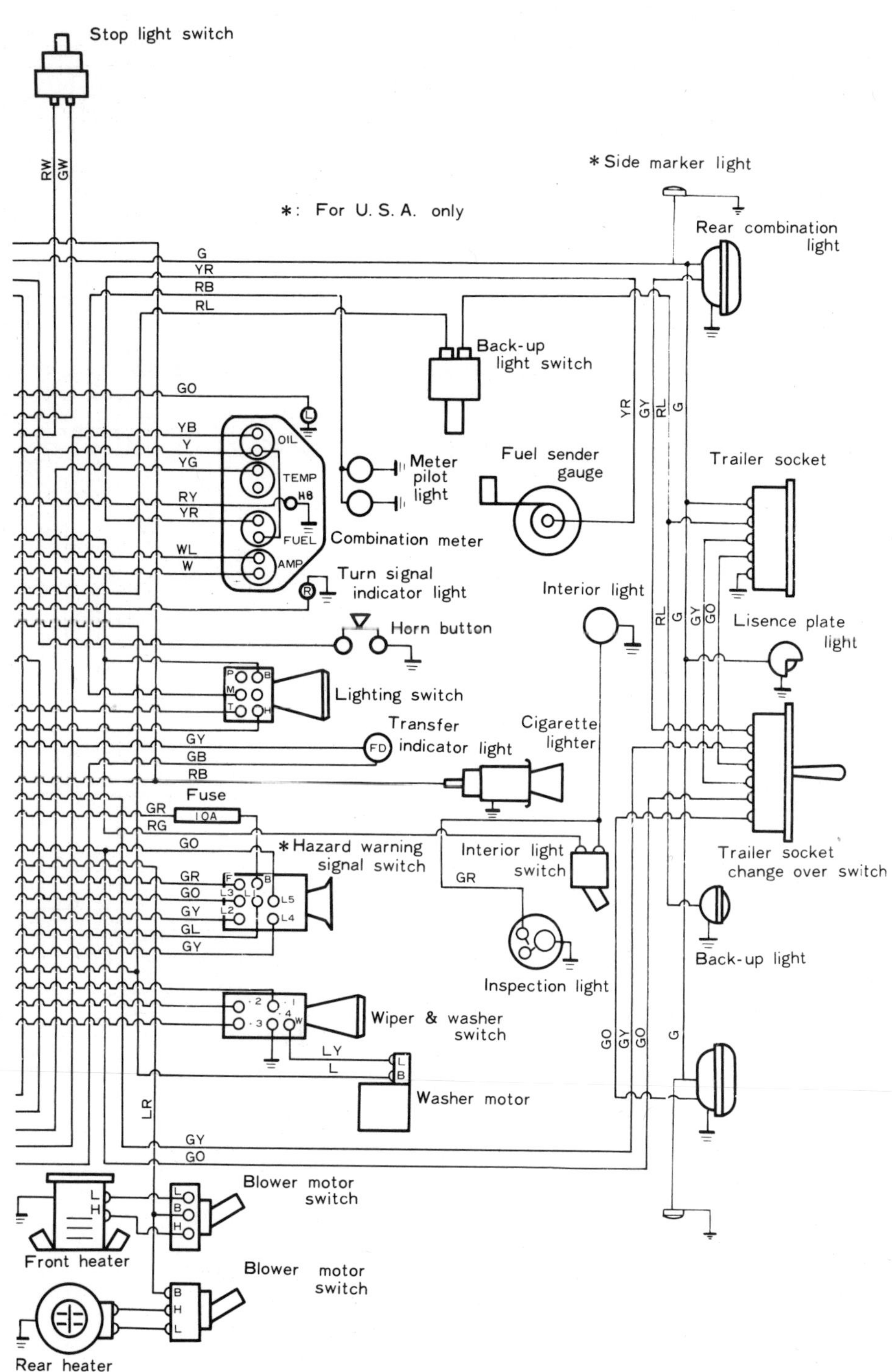


Wiring diagram—155 H.P. Land Cruiser

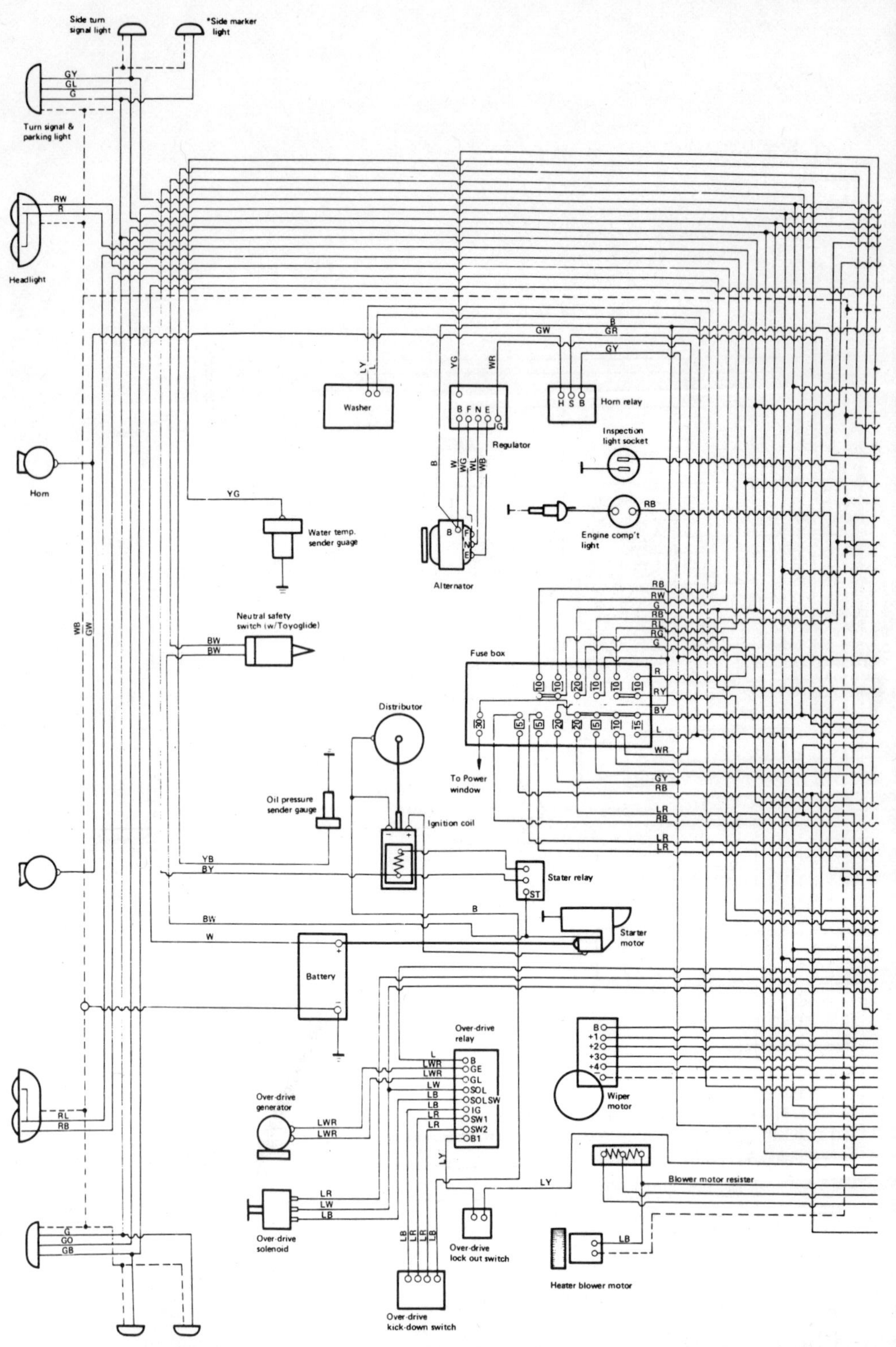


Wiring diagram—1970 Crown

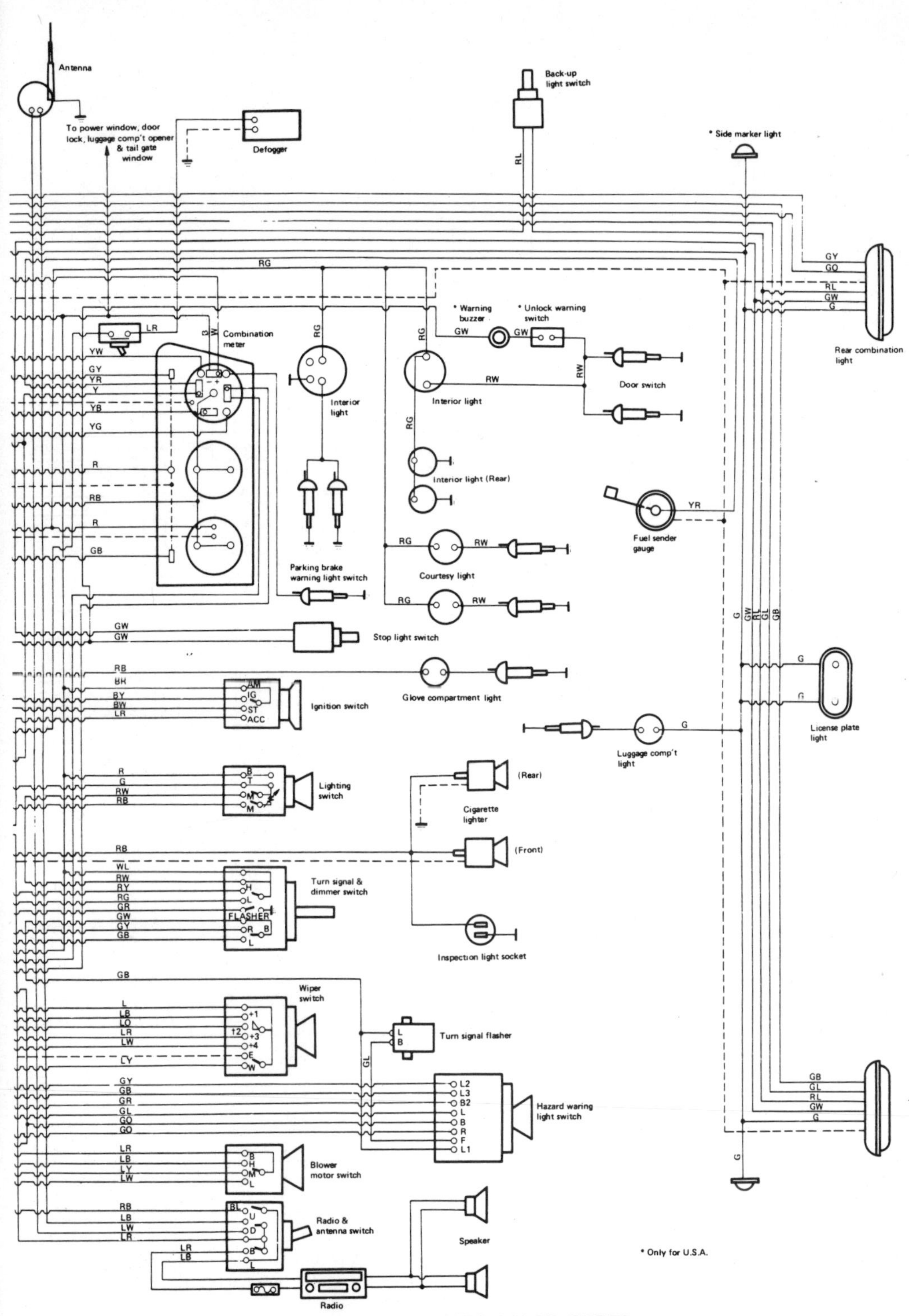


## WIRING HARNESS COLOR CODES

The first alphabet indicates the basic color for the wire, and the second alphabet indicates the spiral line color.

R = red L = light purple Y = yellow O = orange
W = white G = green B = black

Example: RG is for red and green line.

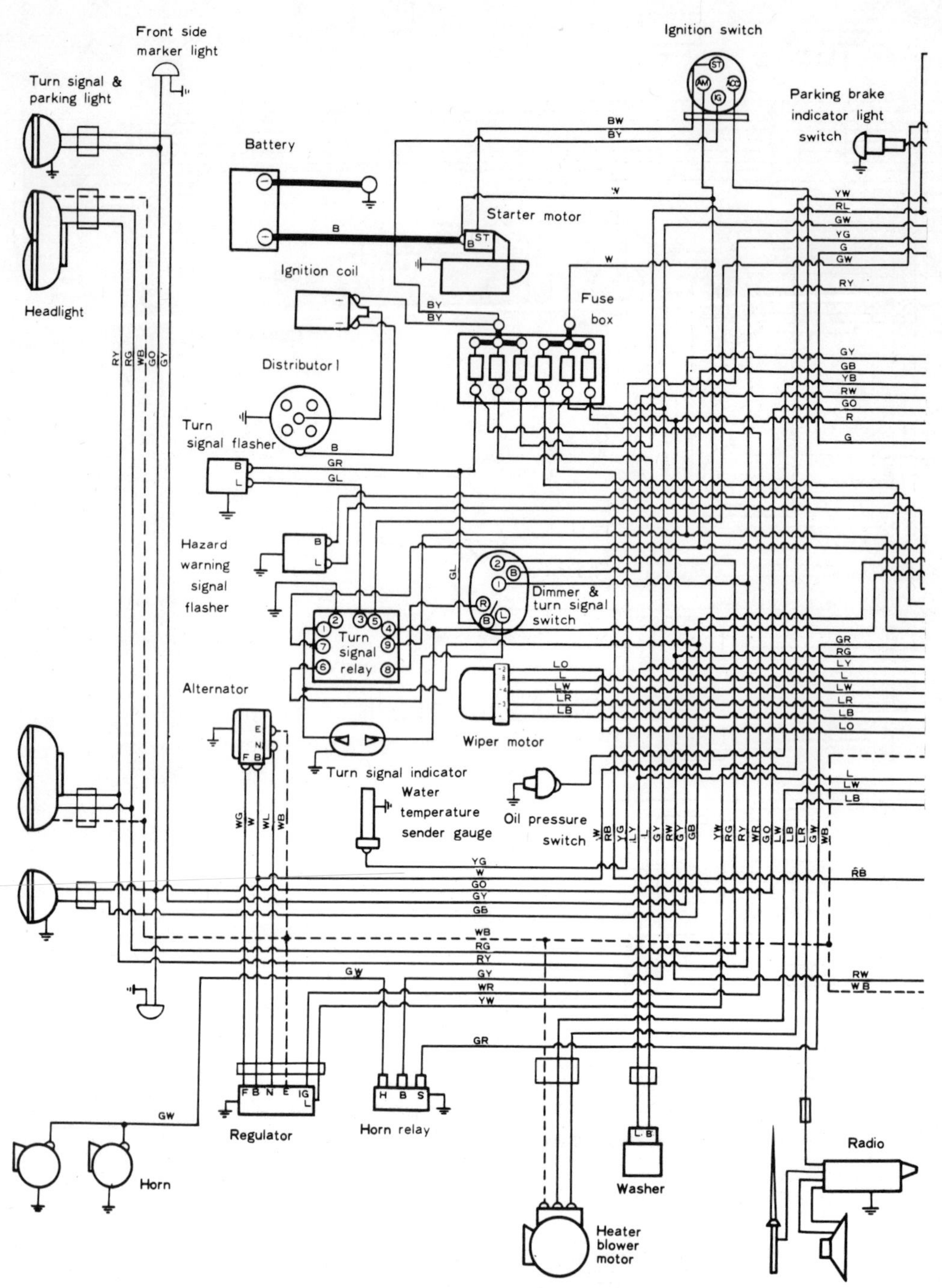


Wiring diagram—1970 Hi Lux pick-up

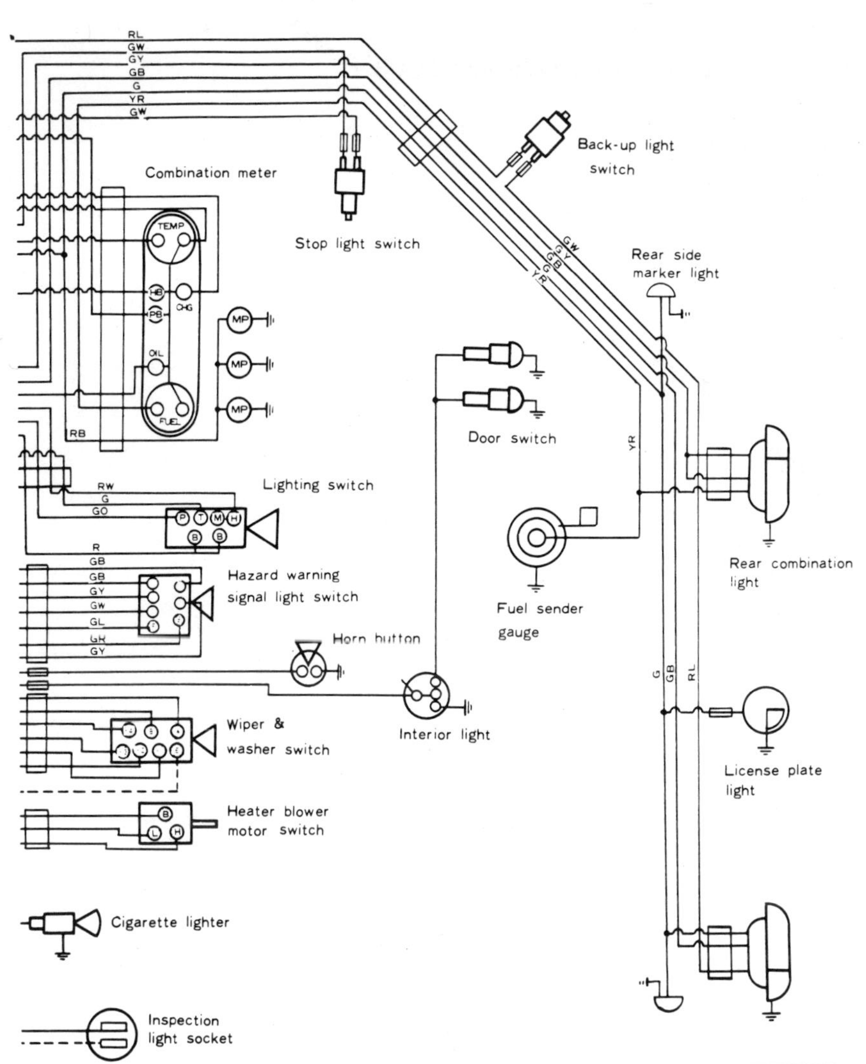


**WIRING HARNESS COLOR CODES**

The first alphabet indicates the basic color for the wire, and the second alphabet indicates the spiral line color.

R=red, W=white, L=light purple, G=green, Y=yellow, B=black, O=orange

Example: RG is for red and green line.

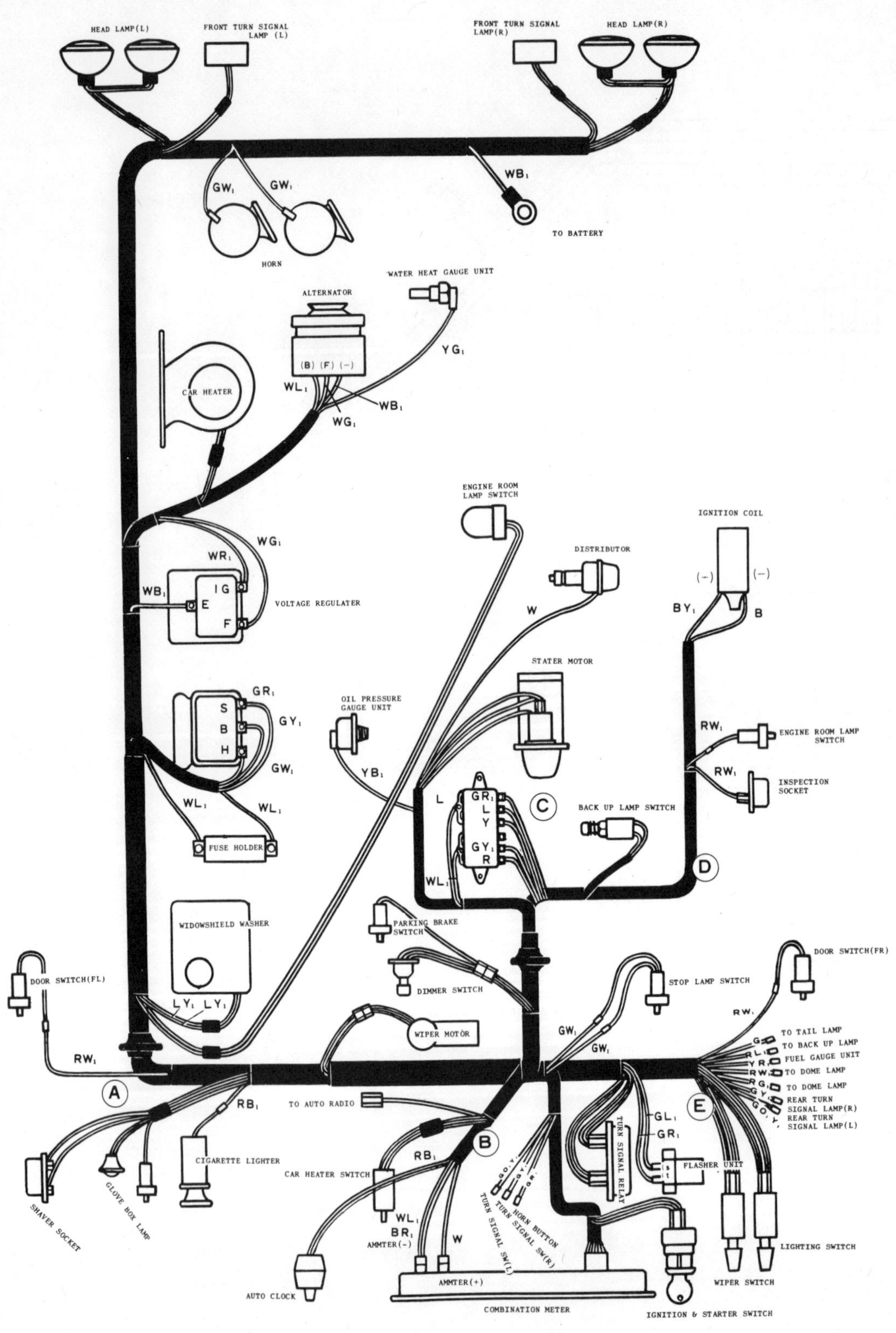


Crown (RS40) wiring harness (front).

# Chapter 5
# Fuel System

The fuel system consists of the fuel tank, filter, pump, carburetor and lines, as well as the air filter. Fuel tanks are fitted under the trunk; on some models they actually constitute the trunk floor, while on others (station wagons) they are fitted into the side behind the fender.

The fuel pump pulls the fuel from the tank through one (or more) fuel filters and delivers it to the carburetor, where it is metered and mixed with air before being drawn into the cylinders.

The air cleaner removes dirt and dust from the air drawn into the engine. A dirty (clogged) filter will have a definite influence on engine performance.

The carburetors used on Toyota models are conventional two-barrel, downdraft types similar to domestic carburetors. The main circuits are: *primary*, for normal operational requirements; *secondary*, to supply high speed fuel needs; *float*, to supply fuel to the primary and secondary circuits; *accelerator*, to supply fuel for quick and safe acceleration; *choke*, for reliable starting in cold weather; and *power valve*, for fuel economy. Although slight differences in appearance may be noted, these carburetors are basically alike. Of course, different jets and settings are demanded by the different engines to which they are fitted.

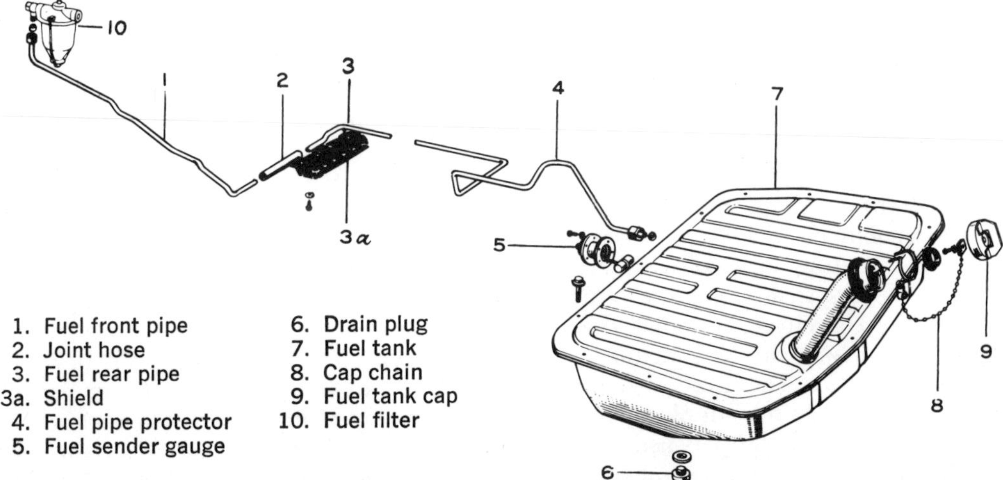


Typical fuel tank and lines—RT43L illustrated.

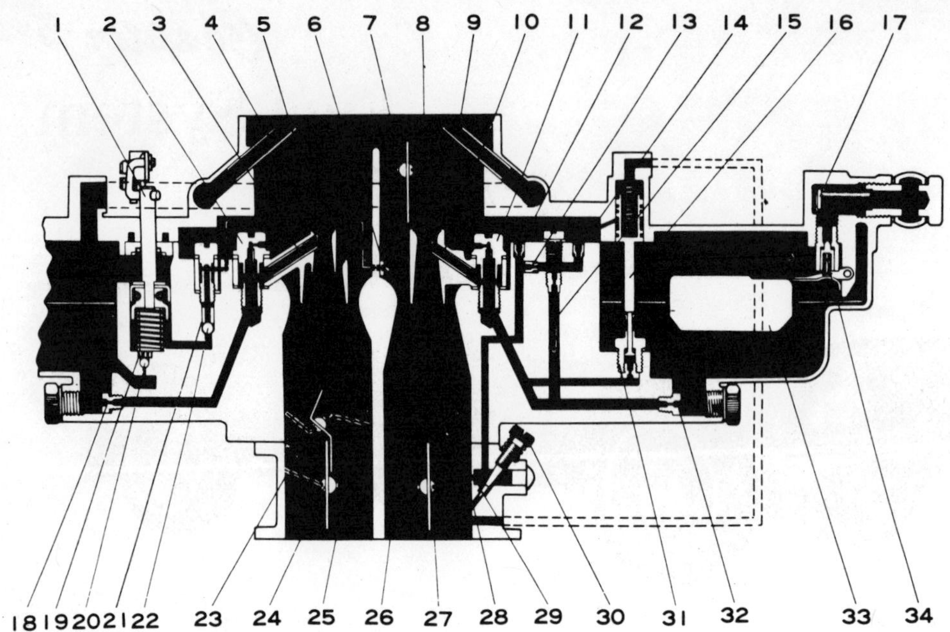


Corona 3RC carburetor.

1. Pump plunger
2. Secondary main air bleed
3. Secondary main nozzle
4. Air vent
5. Secondary small venturi
6. Pump jet
7. Choke valve
8. Primary small venturi
9. Air vent
10. Primary main nozzle
11. Primary main air bleed
12. Slow air bleed No. 2
13. Economizer jet
14. Slow air bleed No. 1
15. Slow jet
16. Power piston
17. Strainer
18. Secondary main jet
19. Check ball retainer
20. Steel ball (inlet)
21. Pump discharge weight
22. Steel ball (outlet)
23. High speed valve
24. Secondary throttle valve
25. Secondary bore
26. Primary bore
27. Primary throttle valve
28. Idle port
29. Slow port
30. Idle adjusting screw
31. Power valve
32. Primary main jet
33. Float
34. Needle valve

## Carburetor Operation

Fuel from the float chamber passes through the primary main metering jet, mixes with air coming from the primary main air jet and is discharged into the venturi through the discharge nozzle. When the throttle is opened quickly (upon acceleration) the accelerator pump supplies an extra amount of fuel to the discharge nozzle. For starting in cold weather, an automatic choke system closes the primary side of the carburetor, restricting the air intake and enriching the fuel mixture.

*Slow speed circuit* The slow speed circuit is designed to maintain a supply of fuel in spite of a closed or slightly opened throttle valve. Fuel from the float chamber flows through the main jet and mixes with air from the air bleed nozzle. It then flows into the idle and slow speed ports and is sucked into the engine. This volume is controlled by the idle adjusting screw. Although the closed throttle plate does not allow any vacuum at the venturi, the small space between the throttle plate and carburetor bore (exactly in front of the idle port) creates a high vacuum. It is this pressure differential between float chamber (atmospheric) and the vacuum at the ports which causes fuel to be discharged. When the throttle valve is opened slightly, its edge moves past the idle port and allows the vacuum to be applied to the slow speed port; thus allowing both ports to operate.

*Primary circuit* This circuit is designed to supply fuel for intermediate, or partial-load, engine requirements. As soon as the throttle valve is opened past a certain point (angle), the vacuum is transferred from the slow speed port to the main fuel discharge nozzle. Fuel from the main jet mixes with

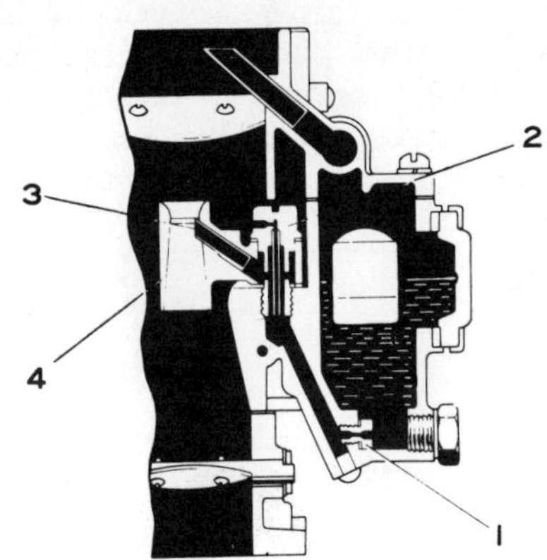

Primary high speed circuit.

air from the air bleed nozzle and is then passed into the discharge nozzle in the small venturi. An emulsion jet or tube is part of the main air bleed system—it assists in mixing air and fuel and also allows escape of fuel that has been vaporized by high engine temperature.

*Secondary circuit* This circuit is designed to supply the additional fuel-air mixture required for high-speed operation. Fuel flow is identical to that in the primary circuit except that it takes place in the secondary side of the carburetor. The important difference here is the additional high speed

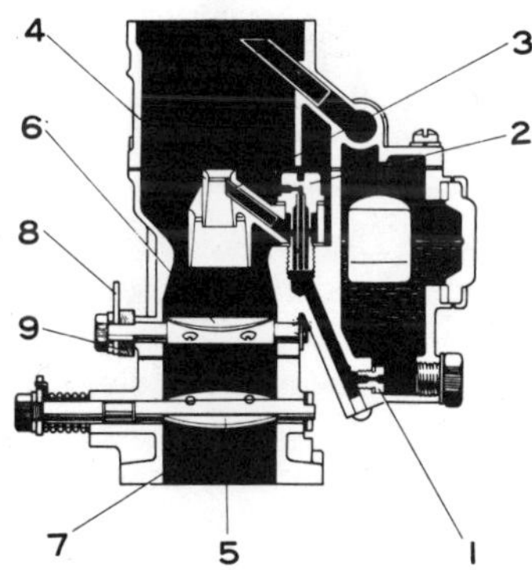

Secondary high speed circuit.

valve plate installed in the secondary side above the throttle plate. In order for this valve to open, it is necessary for the engine speed to be high; the primary throttle valve must be open at least 51° before the linkage starts to open the secondary valve plate. In addition, it is necessary for the airflow through the carburetor to be fast enough to overcome the counterweight on the high speed plate.

*Float circuit* The float chamber serves as a fuel reservoir, having a constant level which is maintained by the action of the float. Fuel enters the float chamber until the rising float closes the needle valve against its seat. Fuel pump pressure is also an important factor, as too high pressure invariably forces the needle away from the seat and causes high fuel levels. The float chamber is vented through the air filter and the float chamber cover incorporates a sight glass to enable checking fuel level without disassembling the unit.

*Accelerator circuit* The sudden opening of the throttle valve when the engine is running causes manifold vacuum to disappear suddenly, just when the need for power is greatest. To overcome this condition, which would cause a "flat spot", lagging and even stalling, the accelerator circuit has been added to the carburetor. It consists of a plunger (or piston) connected to the ac-

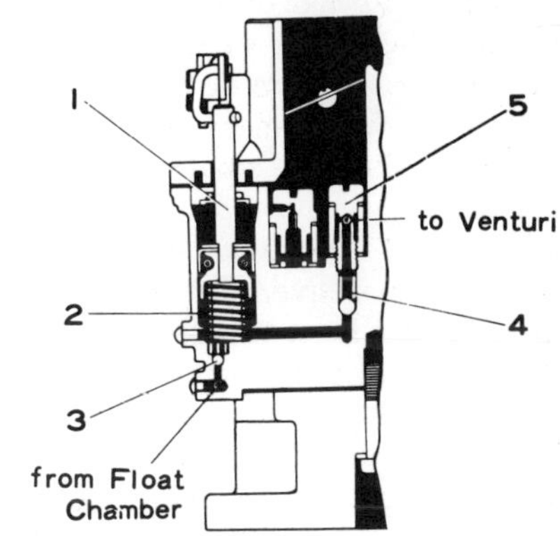

Accelerator circuit.

celerator linkage. When the accelerator pedal is depressed, the linkage forces the plunger down into the fuel-filled pump cylinder, causing the check ball and weight to be lifted. This results in the discharge of fuel into the outer venturi. Closing the throttle causes the plunger to be pulled upwards, drawing fresh fuel into the pump cylinder through another check ball in the bottom of the cylinder. This primes the accelerator pump for the next demand. Although the length of the pump stroke can be adjusted by changing the position of the connecting lever, optimum efficiency is achieved with the throttle valve less than halfway opened.

*Power valve circuit* When full power output is desired at full throttle, it is necessary to enrich the fuel-air mixture. The power valve is designed to supply this extra fuel on demand. The high manifold vacuum present under light-load conditions keeps the power valve closed by acting on the power piston. Vacuum drops as soon as the primary throttle is opened and the power

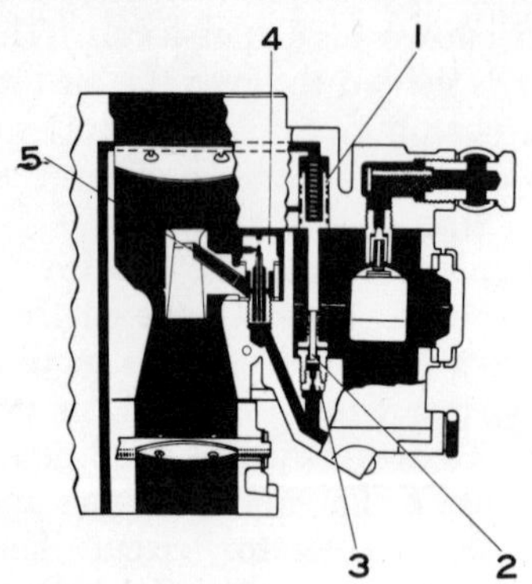

Power circuit.

piston is then pushed down by spring tension to open the power valve. This permits fuel to flow through the power jet and join the fuel from the primary main jet; both then discharge into the small venturi of the primary side.

*Choke circuit* When an engine is cold, the fuel mixture delivered to it by the carburetor in vapor form tends to cling to the manifold and cylinder walls. Thus, the amount of fuel is drastically reduced to the point where the engine is almost impossible to start. The automatic choke fitted to the Toyota carburetor provides the correct mixture necessary to ensure quick and reliable cold starting, as well as proper warm-up performance. *NOTE: The K series engine is equipped with a standard type manual choke, operated by a dash-mounted lever connected to a cable. The cable operates a spring-loaded butterfly valve located over the primary throat of the carburetor.* Tension of the thermostatic coil (bimetal spring) holds the choke valve closed. When

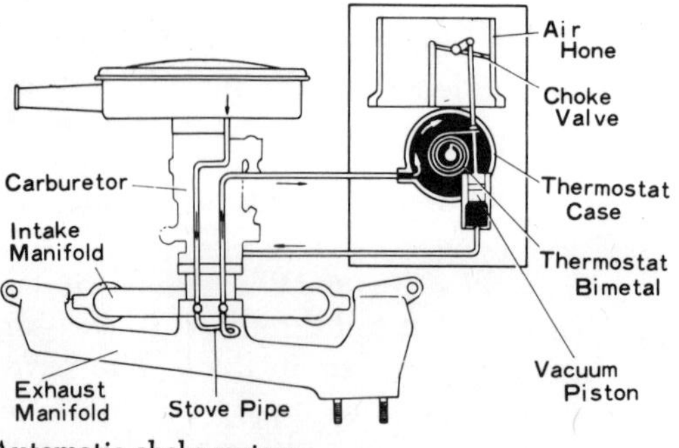

Automatic choke system.

the engine is started, air velocity against the offset valve plate causes the plate to open slightly against thermostatic spring tension. Intake manifold vacuum, acting on the choke piston, also tends to open the

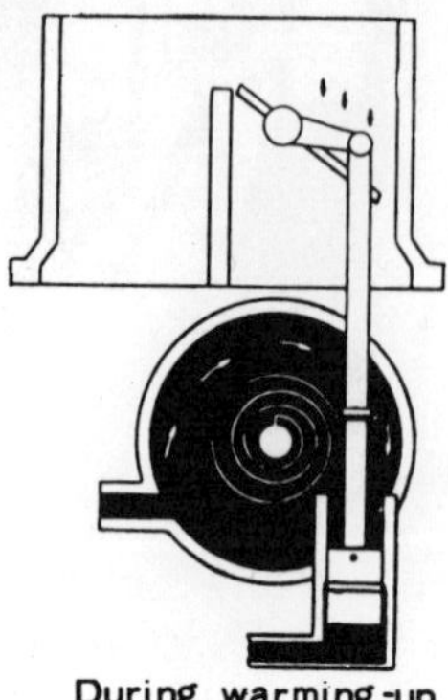

Automatic choke operation.

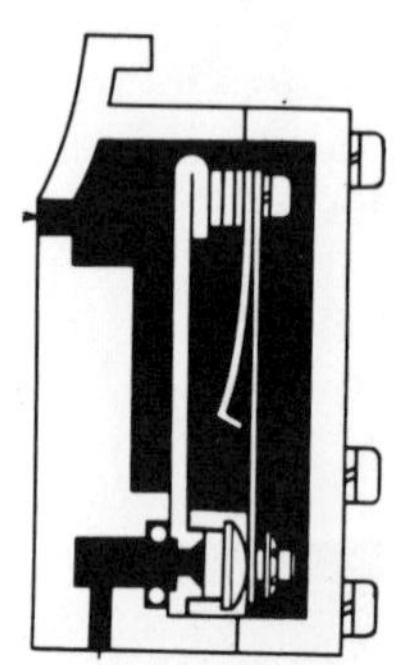
Thermostatic valve.

choke valve. The choke valve remains in the position where the pull of the vacuum on the choke piston, aided by the airflow acting on the choke valve plate, is balanced by the tension of the thermostatic spring. With the engine running, slots in the choke piston cylinder are uncovered, allowing intake manifold vacuum to draw air from the air cleaner through a stove pipe located in the exhaust manifold. This air is passed through the choke housing, where its heat acts on the thermostatic spring causing it to lose some of its tension. The closed choke valve plate creates a very high vacuum in the primary side, causing fuel to be discharged from the main jet (as well as from the slow and idle circuits) to give a very rich mixture, ideal for cold starts. If the engine is accelerated during the warm-up period, the ensuing drop in manifold vacuum allows the thermostatic coil to close the choke momentarily, again providing the

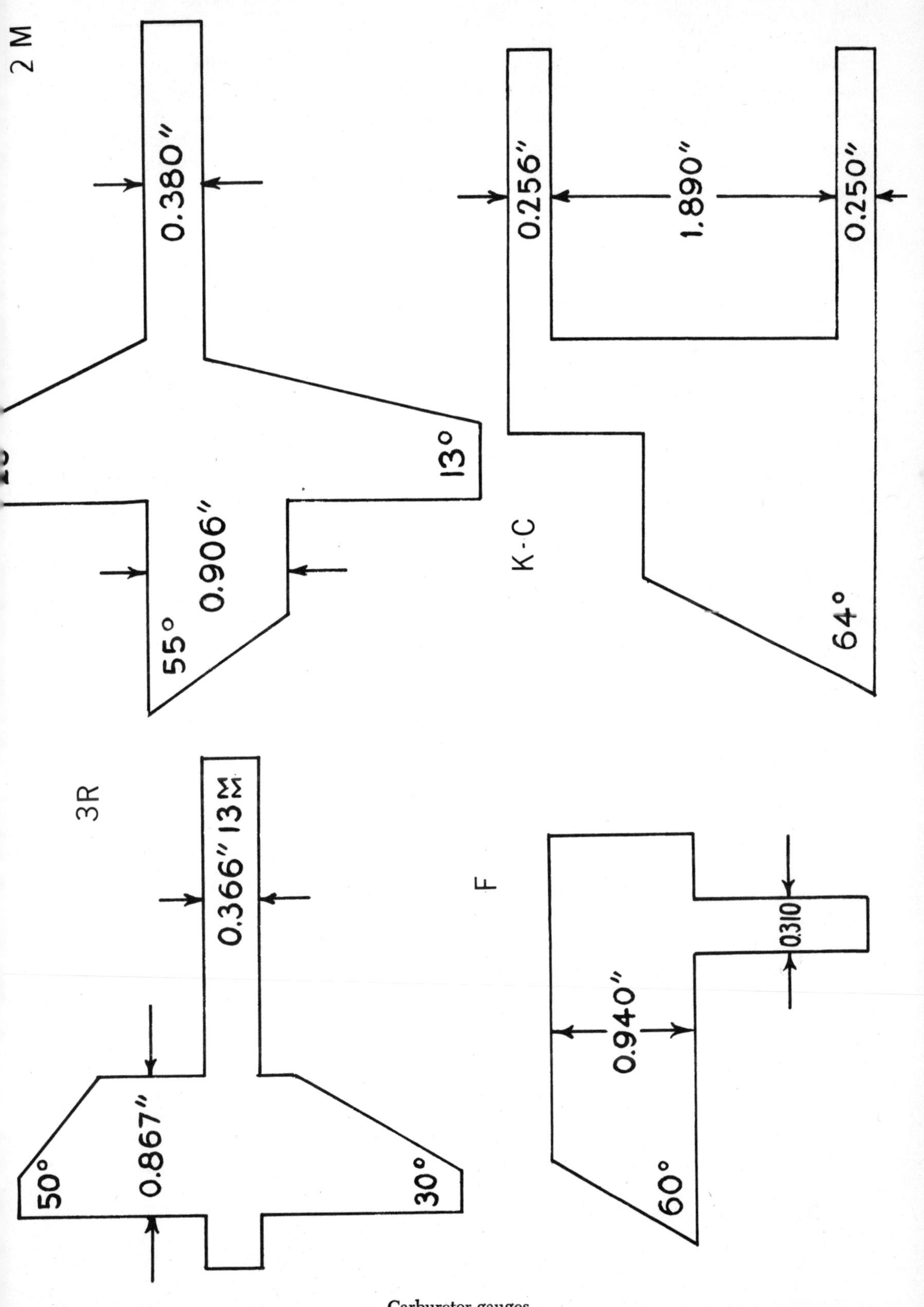


Carburetor gauges.

required rich mixture. A choke baffle plate prevents pieces of dirt and dust carried in with the heated air from being deposited on the vacuum cylinder walls.

When accelerating a cold engine, unless the choke is allowed to open somewhat the engine will stall. A device known as an unloader is incorporated to prevent this. When the accelerator pedal is depressed, the choke shaft is rotated by a cam follower located at the sliding rod, which opens the choke valve 20° against the tension of the thermostatic spring.

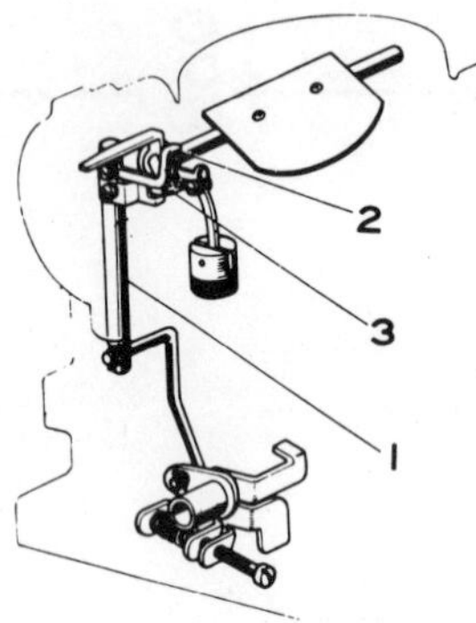

Unloader.

To avoid overheating due to an overly rich mixture, the choke is so designed that the thermostatic spring starts to open the choke valve plate at 140° F. When the choke is *on,* a fast idle cam keeps the throttle valve opened slightly to prevent stalling. It is necessary to depress the accelerator pedal once *before* starting the engine in order to engage this cam. After sufficient warm-up, it is necessary to depress the accelerator once again to disengage the fast idle cam follower and allow the engine to idle normally.

On some 3R series engines, an additional valve is attached to the carburetor to prevent vapor lock. Air from the air cleaner is drawn into the intake manifold through this valve, which consists of a bimetal spring operating a bleed valve. If, during slow driving in hot weather, carburetor temperature rises to the point of fuel vaporization, the thermostatic valve (bimetal spring) opens to allow fresh, outside air into the manifold. This cools the fuel and prevents stalling, poor idling and hard starting. The valve is set to begin opening at 108° F. and to be fully opened at 168° F. During tune-ups, or when checking for an air leak at the manifold, be sure to check this valve.

## Service

### Removing the Carburetor

Remove air filter housing, disconnect all air hoses from filter base and disconnect battery ground cable. Disconnect fuel line, choke pipe and distributor vacuum line. Remove accelerator linkage (with automatic transmission, also remove throttle rod to transmission). Remove the four nuts that secure the carburetor to manifold and lift off carburetor and gasket. Cover the open manifold with a clean rag to prevent small objects from dropping into the engine.

### Disassembling the Carburetor

Before disassembling a carburetor, remember that a certain number of special gauges will be necessary for correct assembly. Remove the accelerator pump connecting link, pump lever and the six screws that secure the top of the carburetor. Lift the carburetor top straight up so as not to damage the float. Pull out the pump plunger and the spring underneath. Remove pump jet screws and jets, turn carburetor upside down and shake out the pump check ball and check weight. Remove the primary and secondary main air bleed jets and the small venturis from both sides. Next remove the slow speed jet plug and the jet which is found under it. Remove the power valve and separate the power jet from the valve. Remove the thermostatic valve and the gasket (do not strip the valve threads), then remove the three flange retaining screws and separate the body from the flange. (Note that one of the screws is drilled and serves as a vacuum feed.) Remove both main jet plugs and the two main jets with their gaskets. Next remove the discharge check ball retainer from beneath the pump cylinder and extract the ball, using a small magnet or a pair of tweezers.

With a ⅛″ drill, drill out the caulked parts of the two screws that secure the high speed valve plate to the shaft, after first removing the outside parts and the retaining ring from the shaft. Unscrew the float chamber sight glass plate and remove it, together with gasket. Remove the idle and throttle adjusting screws. Next, remove the throttle shaft link retaining ring and nut, then remove the primary throttle arm, the fast idle lever and follower and the throttle lever collar. Re-

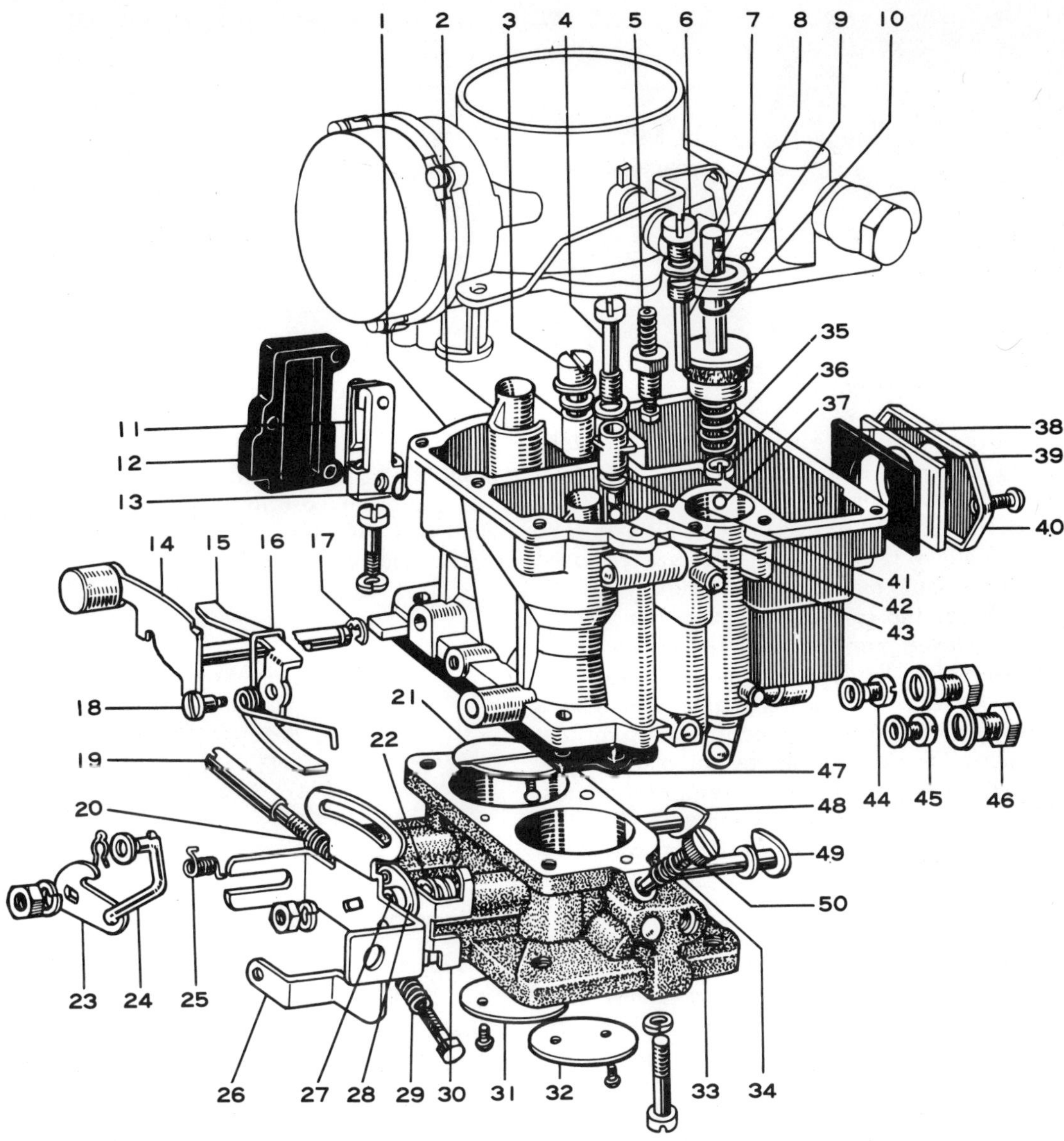


Carburetor used on RS series vehicles.

1. Body
2. Secondary small venturi
3. Primary main air bleed
4. Pump jet screw
5. Power valve
6. Slow passage plug
7. Pump plunger
8. Slow jet
9. Plunger guide
10. O-ring
11. Thermostatic valve
12. Thermostatic valve cover
13. O-ring
14. High speed valve shaft
15. High speed valve stopper lever
16. High speed valve stopper lever spring
17. E-ring
18. Stopper lever securing screw
19. Throttle adjusting screw
20. Throttle adjusting spring
21. High speed valve
22. Retainer ring
23. Secondary throttle lever
24. Throttle shaft link
25. Secondary throttle return spring
26. Primary throttle shaft arm
27. Throttle lever collar
28. Fast idle lever
29. Fast idle adjusting spring
30. Fast idle adjusting lever
31. Secondary throttle valve
32. Primary throttle valve
33. Flange
34. Idle adjusting screw spring
35. Pump damping spring
36. Discharge check valve retainer
37. Steel ball
38. Level gauge gasket
39. Level gauge glass
40. Level gauge clamp
41. Pump jet
42. Pump discharge weight
43. Steel ball
44. Secondary main jet
45. Primary main jet
46. Main passage plug
47. Body flange gasket
48. Secondary throttle shaft
49. Primary throttle shaft
50. Idle adjusting screw

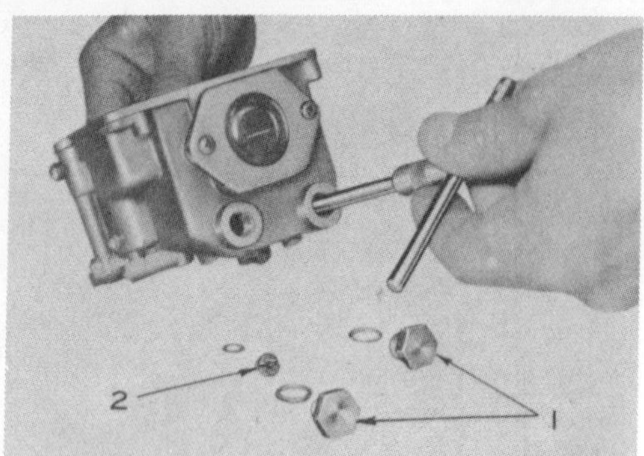


Removing main jet.

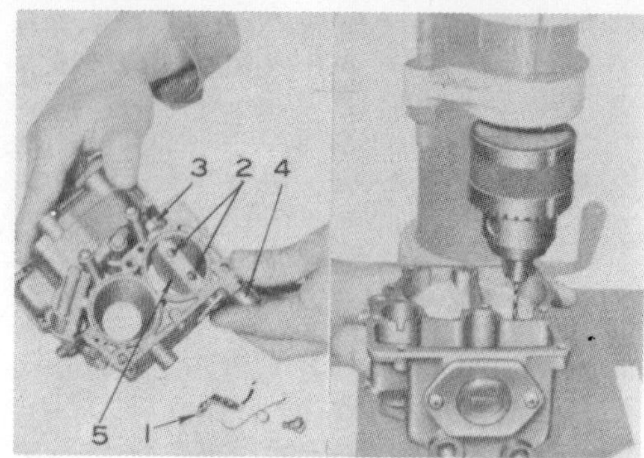


Removing high speed valve.

move the fast idle adjusting bolt and take off the lever and spring. Before removing the primary throttle shaft, the caulked parts of the securing screws must be filed off. The secondary throttle and shaft are removed in the same manner as the primary.

From the carburetor cover, remove the float lever pin, float and the needle valve assembly. Remove the power piston retainer and the power valve and piston spring. Remove wire mesh filter from inlet union. To disassemble the automatic choke, first remove the three screws and the housing, gasket and plate. Remove the fast idle cam follower and the sliding rod (unloader). Pull the vacuum piston out carefully, after first removing the choke valve and shaft in the same manner as the primary throttle valve plate. It will not be necessary to remove the choke casing unless it is cracked.

### Inspecting Carburetor Parts

Clean all parts in fresh carburetor cleaner and blow out all passages with air. Use only a small, soft brush for cleaning in the corners and never use wire for cleaning jets. Replace all gaskets, regardless of appearance. Inspect all die castings for signs of wear, cracks or distortion. Check the upper carburetor cover (air horn) for cracks or distortion, especially where the air filter attaches. Check choke shaft for bends or twists. Check choke mechanism for proper alignment of the bimetal spring; proper position is 17° at 68° F., measured between the tab of the spring and the notch in the housing. *Do not bend the spring* to adjust; make a new notch as required. Check power piston and spring for wear and twist and check the float and float tab for proper alignment. Check needle valve and seat for signs of wear; if there is a visible ring on the conical part of the needle it would be best to install a new needle and seat. Make sure the fuel inlet screen is clean and not deformed.

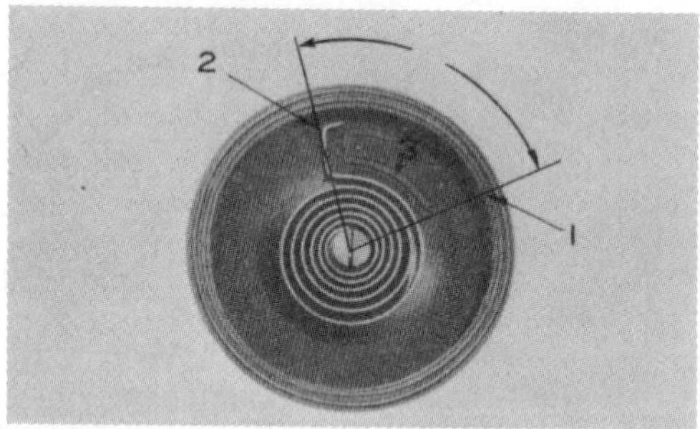


Thermostat bimetallic spring.

Check the main body of the carburetor for cracks and deformation. Check throttle shafts and plates for signs of rubbing against the bore and for play in the shaft bores. Inspect the idle adjusting screw tip and threads.

### Assembling the Carburetor

Before final assembly, wash each part with clean gasoline and blow off with compressed air. All sliding, rotating and moving

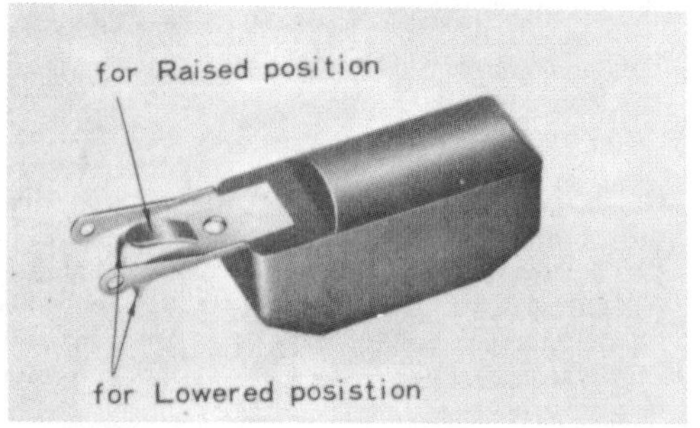


Float tabs.

parts should be coated with light oil or silicone lubricant. Check the operation of each part as it is installed. If the choke housing was removed from the body, reinstall using the flat-headed screw above the piston bore. Next, assemble the connector to the piston by means of the pin, then insert unit into the choke housing. Now, fit the fast idle cam and spring to the oiled choke shaft and install onto the air horn. Secure the choke valve plate to the shaft using the two screws, then check the alignment and free movement and stake the screw ends securely. Assemble the piston connector to choke shaft, screw in place and slip the sliding rod into the thermostat case. Mount the fast idle cam follower, then assemble the dust plate, gasket and spring housing, making sure the choke shaft arm hooks onto the bent part of the coil spring. Turn the choke housing counterclockwise to close the choke and align the notch on the plastic housing with the center mark on the carburetor body.

Install the fuel filter screen and inlet union (do not tighten), then install power piston, spring and retainer onto the air horn. Install needle valve and seat, using new gaskets, and mount the float in such a way as to keep the needle from dropping out. The float level must be adjusted very carefully; if the correct level gauge is unavailable (2M, 3R, 8RC), use a ⅜″ drill under the float, holding the air horn upside down. In the normal position, the float should drop enough to allow a ⅞″ gauge to be inserted between the outer end of the float and the underside of the air horn. To assemble the flange part of the carburetor, begin by fitting the spring to the secondary throttle shaft, then assemble the shaft, throttle lever and link to the flange. Install the valve plate onto the shaft and align the plate.

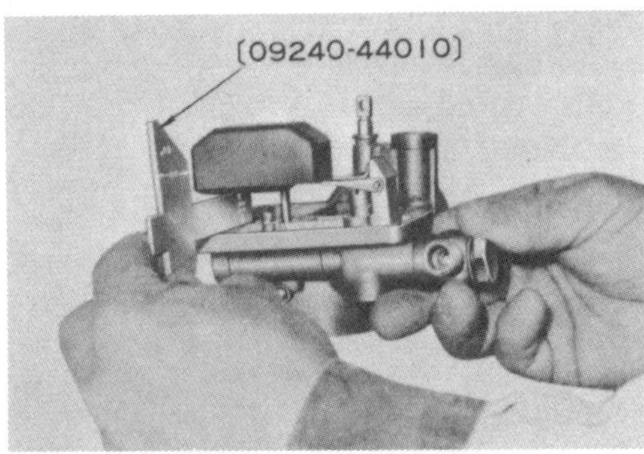


Checking float level.

*NOTE: Do not caulk or stake the screws.* The secondary valve plate is thicker than the primary and the securing screws are therefore somewhat longer. After assembling the primary throttle, check the side play of the shaft; it should be less than 0.008″. Selected shims are available to bring the side play within limits. *NOTE: Excessive play will cause throttle binding.* After making sure that both throttle valves are lined up correctly, proceed to caulk or stake the screws to the shaft.

Assemble the fast idle lever, collar, spring and screw and mount the whole group, together with the primary throttle shaft arm, onto the primary throttle shaft. Make absolutely certain that both throttle valves open fully in synchronization. Next, adjust the throttle shaft linkage so that the secondary throttle begins to open when the primary valve is opened exactly 60°. Screw the throttle adjusting screw into the throttle arm, then screw the idle adjusting screw (with spring) into the flange gently until it hits bottom. Then, back off the screw about three turns.

To assemble the main body section, first install the float chamber cover with the sight glass and gasket. Install the high speed valve, with its shaft and retainer ring, and adjust so that there will be a clearance of 0.004–0.012″ between plate and bore when the valve is fully closed. Adjustment is facilitated if the screws are not tightened before checking. Check valve for free movement in the bore before staking the screws.

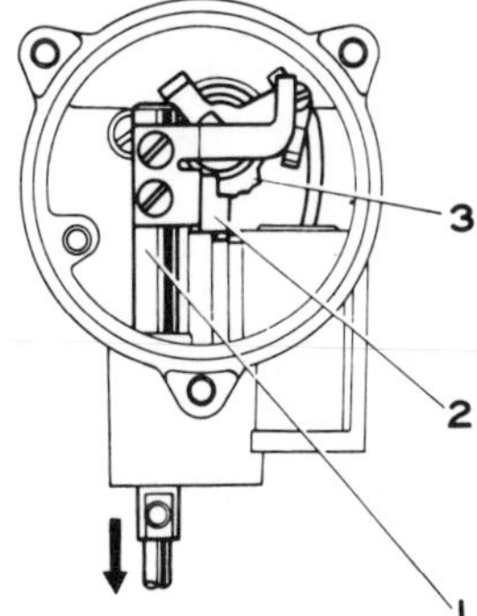


Fast idle.

Assemble high speed valve stop lever and spring. If the carburetor is equipped with a thermostatic valve, install the valve at this time.

Now, install the main jets, gaskets and plugs. The secondary jets are larger than the primary jets, while the plugs are the

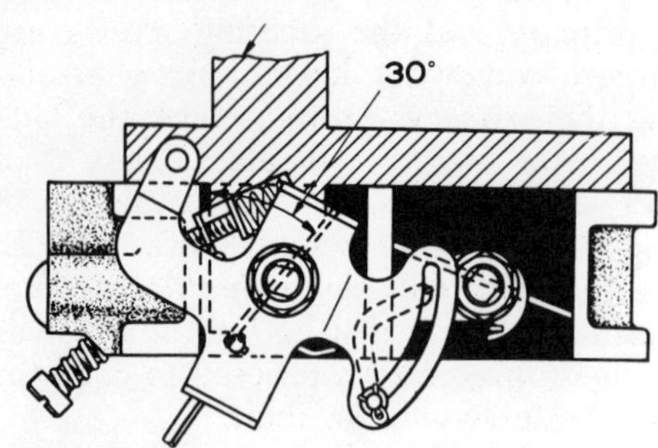

Adjusting secondary throttle valve (3RC).

same. Using a pair of tweezers, install the steel ball and the discharge valve retainer into the pump well. Mount the body on the flange, using a new gasket. *NOTE: The longer bolt goes in from the underside.* Fit the power jet into the power valve, then fit both into the body. Install the slow speed jet and plug, with gasket, then install both

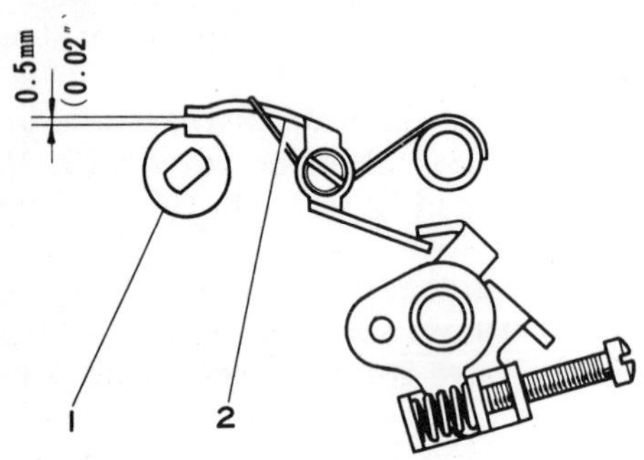

Adjusting high speed valve stopper lever (3RC).

small venturis and secure with the two main air bleed jets. Drop the steel ball and the check ball weight into place and secure both with the pump jet and its gasket. Install pump spring, plunger and guide and mount the air horn onto the main body, also using a new gasket.

Assemble the pump lever, pump connecting link and the fast idle connecting link. *NOTE: There are two holes in the pump connecting link. Use the upper hole for normal, and the lower for cold weather, driving.* At this point, there should be no parts left over other than the old gaskets and jets.

## Adjusting the Carburetor

*Float level* Adjust by bending the tabs; check by looking through sight glass.

*Secondary throttle valve opening* Hold the primary valve at a 30° angle before the fully open position and observe whether the throttle shaft link touches the end of the groove in the throttle shaft arm. If necessary, bend the arm until contact is made without opening the secondary valve, then check for smooth operation.

*High speed stop lever* Check the clearance between the stop and the lever at the point where the secondary valve begins opening; it should be 0.020″. To adjust, bend the stop lever slightly.

*Fast idle speed* With the choke fully closed, adjust the fast idle screw to give 0.040″ clearance between the primary throttle valve and the carburetor bore.

*Unloader* Fit a 50° gauge into the throttle opening and bend the fast idle cam follower

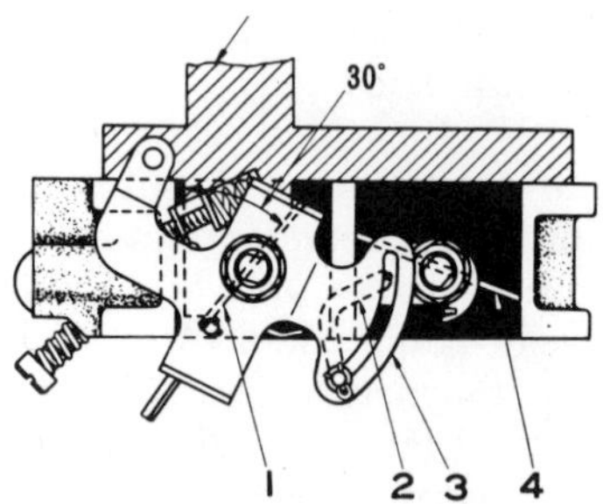

Initial opening angle (3RC).

so that the choke begins to open at the 50° throttle plate opening position.

*Choke* This should be adjusted with the carburetor installed on a running engine. The choke should be fully closed with a cold engine; fully open after the engine comes to proper operating temperature. Adjust by loosening the three choke housing screws and turning the housing clockwise to lean the mixture (make choke open sooner) and counterclockwise to richen the mixture (make choke open later). One mark on the housing equals about 7° F.

## Installing the Carburetor

Reverse the order of the carburetor removal instructions. After engine is warmed up, check for fuel leaks and recheck float level settings. If the car is equipped with an automatic transmission, adjust the throttle valve pressure rod as described in the chapter on automatic transmissions.

## Carburetor Variations

### Carburetor, FJ Series

This carburetor is a conventional, single-barrel downdraft unit having a manual choke. It has six main circuits: 1) float and vent; 2) low speed; 3) high speed; 4) accelerator; 5) choke and fast idle; and 6) power.

The main difference in operation is in the added solenoid valve in the low speed circuit, which prevents engine "run-on" after ignition shut-off (especially with a hot engine). This run-on is due to fuel in the carburetor expanding from engine heat and overflowing into the intake manifold. The solenoid valve closes the economizer jet as soon as the ignition is turned off and opens it as soon as the ignition is turned on again. *NOTE: This is not part of any air pollution control system.*

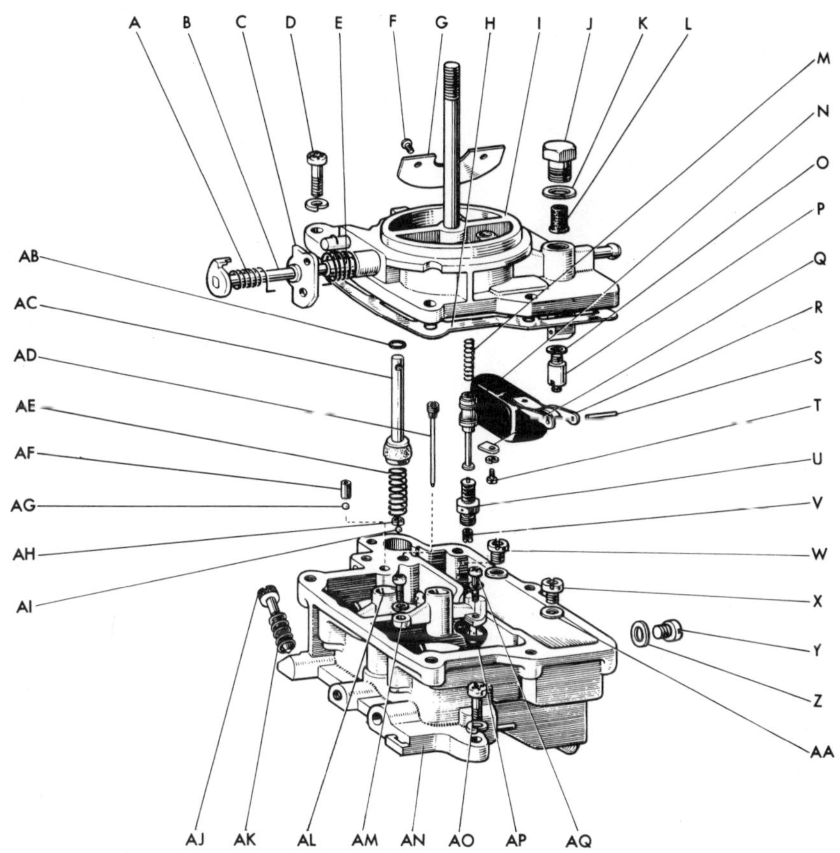


Upper carburetor components—Corolla.

A. Choke valve relief spring
B. Choke shaft
C. Choke lever
D. Screw
E. Choke return spring
F. Screw
G. Choke valve
H. Air horn gasket
I. Air horn
J. Main passage plug
K. Inlet strainer gasket
L. Strainer
M. Power piston spring
N. Power piston
O. Needle valve seat gasket
P. Needle valve
Q. Power piston stopper
R. Float
S. Float lever pin
T. Screw
U. Power valve
V. Power jet
W. Primary main jet
X. Secondary main jet
Y. Drain plug
Z. Gasket
AA. Main jet gasket
AB. O-ring
AC. Pump plunger
AD. Slow jet
AE. Pump damping spring
AF. Pump discharge weight
AG. Check ball
AH. Check ball retainer
AI. Check ball
AJ. Throttle adjusting screw
AK. Spring
AL. Primary small venturi
AM. Secondary small venturi
AN. Main body
AO. Screw
AP. Venturi No. 1 gasket
AQ. Screw

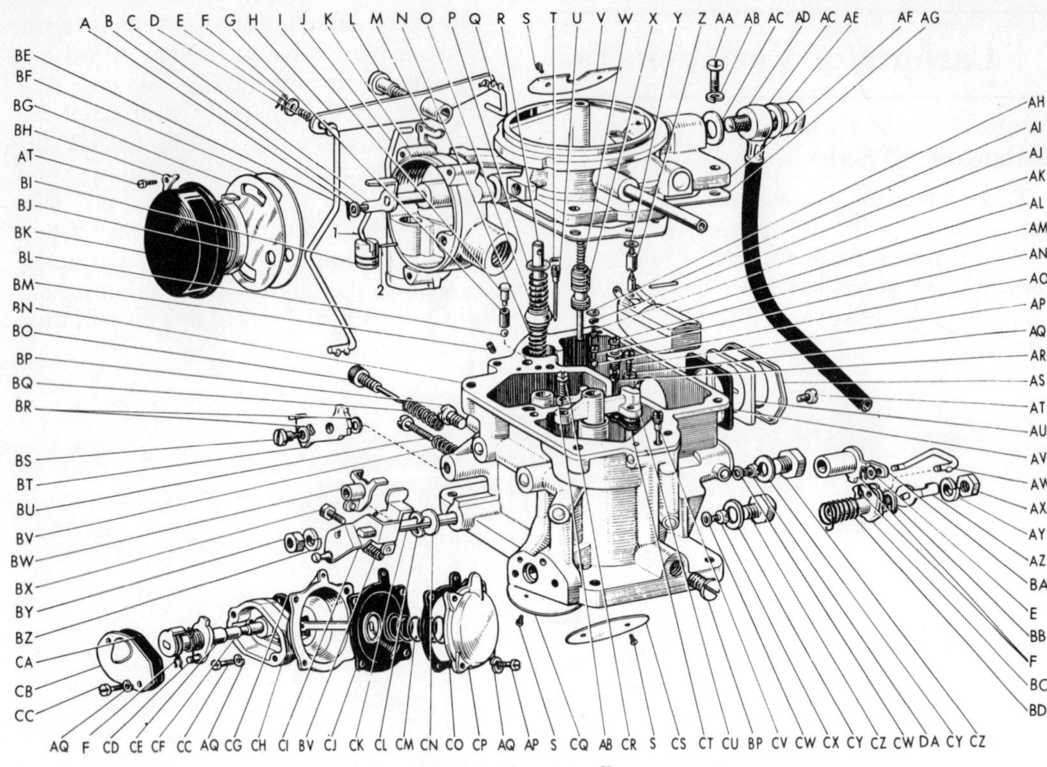


Typical carburetor, showing all components.

A. Cotter pin
B. Plain washer
C. Choke shaft
D. Pump arm pushing spring
E. Pushing spring retainer
F. Snap-ring
G. Pump discharge weight
H. Pump lever
I. Discharge weight stopper
J. Choke lever link
K. Thermostat case
L. Pump lever attaching screw
M. Fast idle cam lever (for choke link)
N. Pump damper spring
O. Pump spring
P. Pump spring retainer
Q. Pump connecting link
R. Pump plunger
S. Valve attaching screw
T. Pin
U. Primary slow jet
V. Choke valve
W. Power piston spring
X. Power piston
Y. Needle valve seat gasket
Z. Needle valve
AA. Screw
AB. Lockwasher
AC. Union fitting gasket
AD. Fuel hose
AE. Strainer
AF. Air horn
AG. Air horn gasket
AH. Power piston stopper
AI. Float lever pin
AJ. Lockwasher
AK. Stopper retaining screw
AL. Float
AM. Power valve
AN. Plug
AO. Steel ball
AP. Screw
AQ. Lockwasher
AR. Power jet
AS. Level gauge glass retainer
AT. Screw
AU. Level gauge glass
AV. Level gauge glass gasket
AW. Connecting link
AX. Throttle lever retaining nut
AY. Lockwasher
AZ. Secondary link arm
BA. Primary link lever
BB. Retainer ring
BC. Secondary link lever
BD. Secondary throttle return spring
BE. Pump connecting link
BF. Coil housing plate
BG. Coil housing gasket
BH. Coil housing retainer
BI. Vacuum piston
BJ. Thermostat bi-metal
BK. Coil housing
BL. Steel ball
BM. Slow passage plug
BN. Body
BO. Idle adjusting screw
BP. Plug
BQ. Idle adjusting screw spring
BR. Spacer
BS. Fast idle cam retaining screw
BT. Fast idle cam
BU. Throttle adjusting screw
BV. Fast idle adjusting spring
BW. Fast idle lever
BX. Fast idle adjusting screw
BY. Nut
BZ. Lockwasher
CA. Gasket
CB. Diaphragm housing cover
CC. Screw
CD. Diaphragm relief lever
CE. Collar
CF. Secondary throttle shaft
CG. Diaphragm housing gasket
CH. Diaphragm housing
CI. Primary throttle lever
CJ. Diaphragm rod
CK. Primary throttle shaft
CL. Retainer ring
CM. Diaphragm spring
CN. Primary throttle shaft shim
CO. Diaphragm gasket
CP. Diaphragm housing cap
CQ. Primary throttle valve
CR. Retaining screw
CS. Secondary throttle valve
CT. Venturi gasket
CU. Secondary small venturi
CV. Secondary slow jet
CW. Main jet gasket
CX. Secondary main jet
CY. Main passage plug gasket
CZ. Main passage plug
DA. Primary main jet
1. Piston connector
2. Piston pin

### Carburetor, FA Series

FA series vehicles are equipped with a two-barrel carburetor similar to the type used on the Corona and Crown models, only the jet and venturi sizes being different.

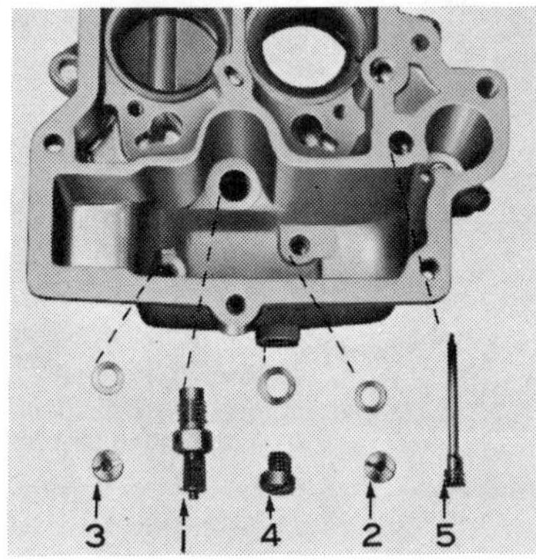


Installing jets.

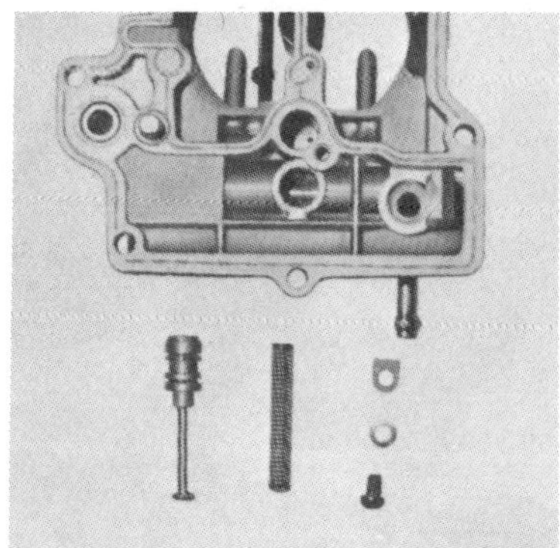

Installing power valve.

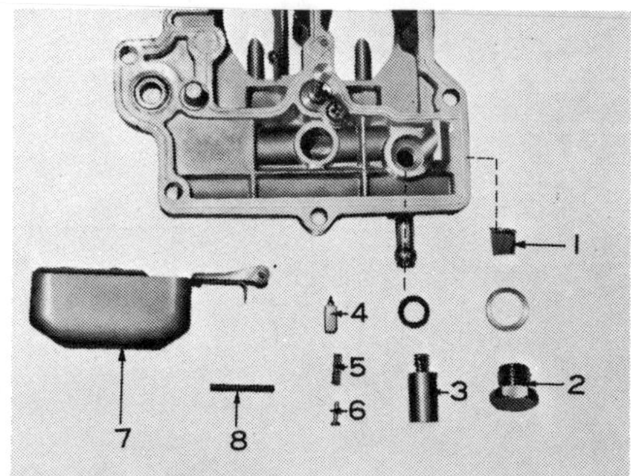


Installing float.

### Carburetor, KC Series

A conventional two-barrel carburetor with manual choke is used. An "Auxiliary Slow System" has been incorporated to prevent excessive discharge of unburnt gases during deceleration. High manifold vacuum acts on a diaphragm (through the vacuum sensing line), opening the spring-loaded valve and allowing both fuel and air to enter the intake manifold. The proper air-fuel ratio needed for proper combustion, within the limits of emission control standards, is thus maintained.

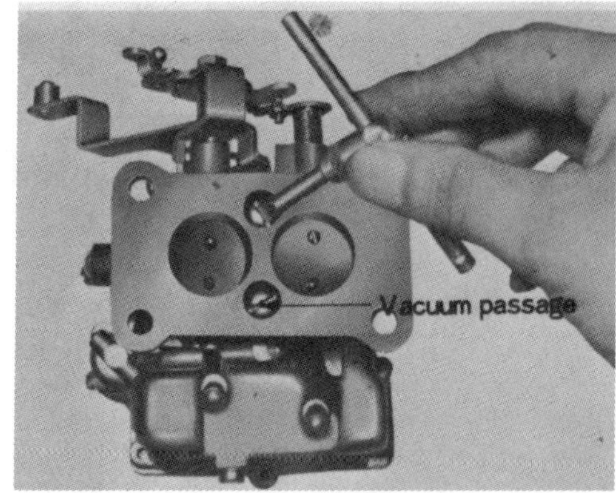


Assembling flange and main body.

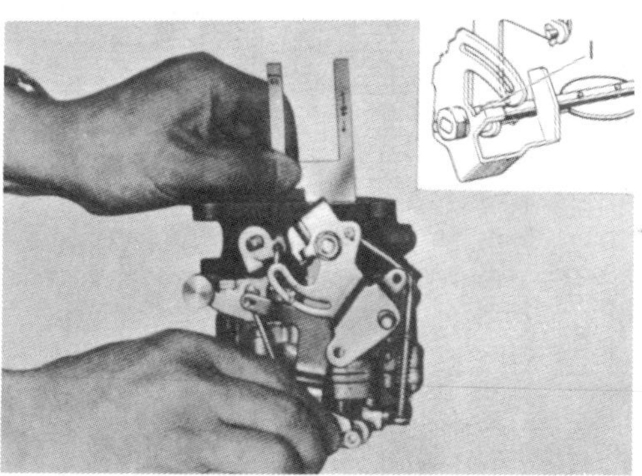

Adjusting fast idle.

*Inspecting the A.S.S. system* Remove the rubber cap and check for air (suction) leaks due to a defective diaphragm. Close off the air hose from the air cleaner and, if there is a change in engine speed, replace the diaphragm. Disconnect the air hose from the air cleaner and rev up the engine. If no air is drawn in during deceleration, the diaphragm is defective.

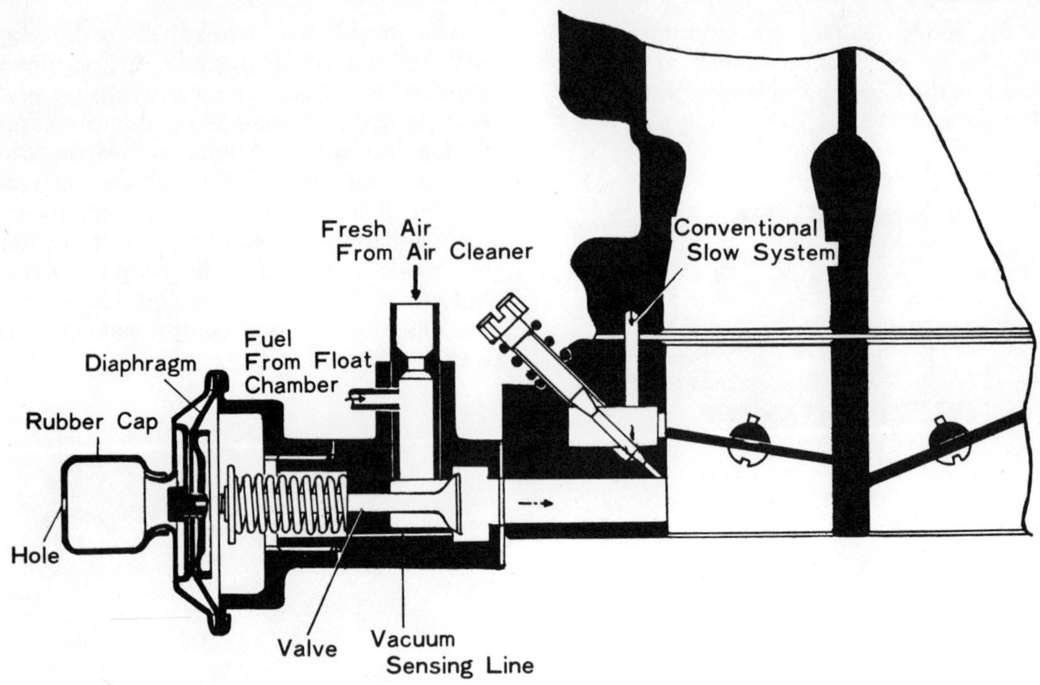


Auxiliary Slow System on Corolla KC engine.

Check the fuel line from float chamber to A.S.S. valve for obstructions. Sometimes the engine will "hunt" or surge at low and medium speeds. This is due to insufficient pressure on the diaphragm spring and the problem can be cured by a simple modification. Remove the valve from the carburetor and unscrew the valve bodies. Depress the brass plate on top of the diaphragm and insert a small C-washer of about 0.025″ thickness under the valve stem head so as to increase the spring pressure. This will serve to keep the valve fully seated regardless of slight variations in manifold vacuum at low and medium engine speeds. *NOTE: If the outside of the diaphragm is wet, replace valve assembly.*

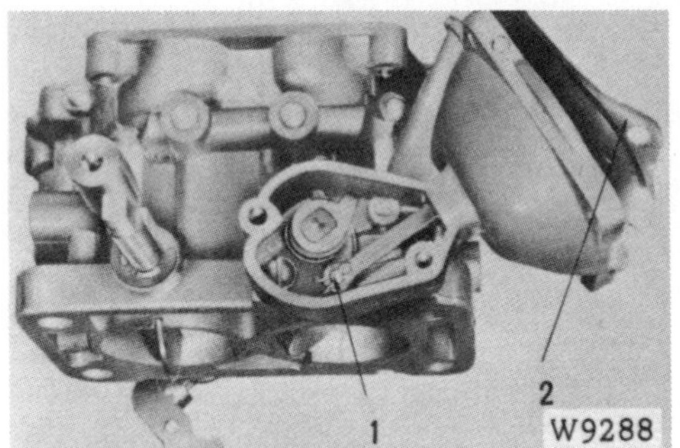


Crown (2M) diaphragm.

### Carburetor, Mark II Series (8R-C)

This carburetor is like the one used on the 3R-C with only a few minor changes and different jet sizes. A *reloader* has been added to prevent the throttle valve from opening during automatic choke operation. The following settings are different from the 3R-C:

*Fast Idle* Primary throttle valve opens 11° when choke is fully closed.

*Unloader* Choke valve should open at 19° when throttle is fully opened.

Adjusting start of secondary throttle valve opening (2M).

*Reloader* Unit should drop freely (of its own weight) when the choke valve is opened by hand.

*NOTE: The reloader lever should disengage smoothly from the stop when the choke valve plate is opened manually (50° from fully closed position).*

**Carburetor, 2M Series**

A conventional two-barrel carburetor is used. The secondary throttle plate is controlled by a vacuum diaphragm and the jets are larger than those on the 3R-C series carburetor. Settings are as follows:

*Float level* Float clearance should be 0.370″ at raised position.

*Fast idle* With choke valve closed, the upper part of the idle cam (3) should touch the fast idle lever (4). If not, bend the link (1). Now, adjust fast idle screw (2) so that the primary throttle valve is opened 11°, giving a clearance with the carburetor body of 0.050″.

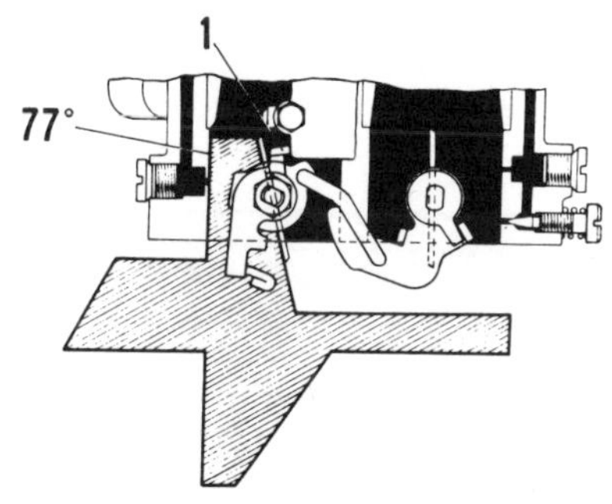


Adjusting fully open throttle valve position (2M).

## Fuel Pump

A diaphragm-type pump is used on all models. It consists of a lower body containing a rocker arm and spring, diaphragm and pull rod. The upper body contains two valves and inlet and outlet fittings, as well as the top cover.

**Removing the Fuel Pump**

It is best to first disconnect the battery to prevent accidental cranking of the engine. Disconnect the two pipes at the pump and remove the two mounting bolts.

**Disassembling the Fuel Pump**

Remove the upper body retaining screws and lift off the upper body. *NOTE: The diaphragm may stick to one or both sides.* From the underside, remove the valve retaining screws and the retainer, valves and gaskets. Press down on the diaphragm and unhook the pull rod from the diaphragm stem, then remove the diaphragm. Drive out the rocker arm pin (towards the knurled end) using a drift and remove rocker arm and spring.

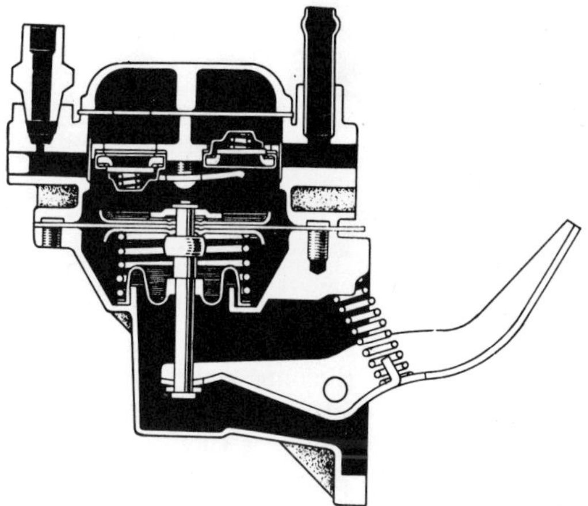

Fuel pump cross-section.

**Inspecting the Fuel Pump**

Wash all parts in clean gasoline and dry off with compressed air. Check the cover for cracks or distortion. Also check both bodies for cracks and worn pin holes or crossed screw threads. Check the diaphragm for tears or stretching, and the pull rod for a distorted eyelet. Check the valves for proper seating.

**Testing the Fuel Pump**

*Pressure test* Remove the fuel outlet line at the pump and connect a pressure gauge to the pump side. Start engine and run for a few seconds—if pressure is not within specifications, replace the diaphragm spring.

*Volume test* Disconnect fuel line at carburetor and connect a gravity feed fuel supply to the carburetor fuel inlet. Connect the fuel pump output line in such a way that the pump output can be collected in a measured container. Start engine and run at specified speed for one minute. If discharge quantity is less than specified, check fuel filter visually for obstructions and perform vacuum test before replacing pump.

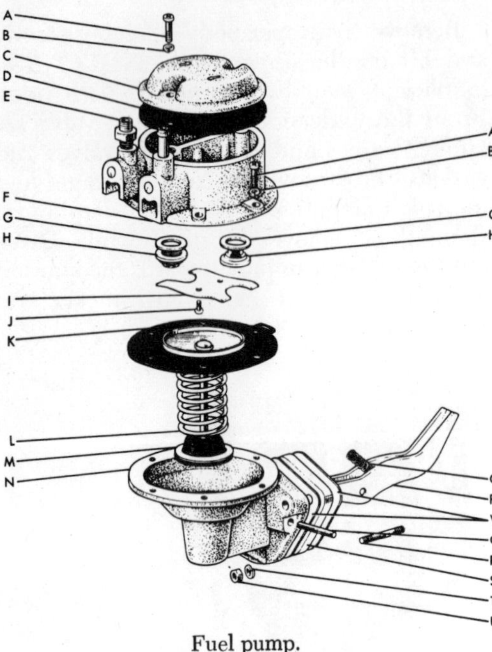

Fuel pump.

A. Cover securing screw
B. Lockwasher
C. Fuel pump cover
D. Fuel pump cover gasket
E. Fuel pump union connector
F. Fuel pump upper body
G. Valve packing
H. Valve
I. Valve retainer
J. Valve retainer securing screw
K. Diaphragm
L. Diaphragm spring
M. Oil seal packing retainer
N. Fuel pump lower body
O. Rocker arm spring
P. Rocker arm
Q. Rocker arm pin
R. Stud bolt
S. Fuel pump insulator
T. Lockwasher
U. Nut
V. Fuel pump gasket

*Vacuum test* Reconnect all fuel lines at pump and carburetor. Disconnect fuel inlet line at filter and connect vacuum gauge to filter inlet side. If vacuum is much higher than specified, the filter is clogged and should be replaced. Low vacuum usually indicates a weak diaphragm spring. If engine is fitted with a felt element, cleaning is best done by blowing out with compressed air from the inside. If the felt is oil soaked or very dirty, it may be washed in clean gasoline and then dried. It is not recommended that felt-type filters be cleaned more than three times.

## Fuel Pump Specifications

| *Model* | *Volume/Min. @ RPM (pts.)* | *Pressure (psi)* | *Vacuum (in. Hg.)* |
|---|---|---|---|
| FJ | 4.4 @ 1,000 | 3.4–4.8 | 19.7 |
| K-C | 1.8 @ 2,900 | 2.84–4.27 | 15.7 |
| 3R, 8R | 3.4 @ 2,500 | 2.8–4.2 | 15.7 |
| 2M | 3.8 @ 1,500 | 3.60–5.00 | 15.7 |

### Assembling the Fuel Pump

Reverse order of disassembly. A quick way to check the valves for proper installation is to make sure the inlet valve bulges towards the diaphragm and the outlet valve away from it. (*In* and *out* are marked on the body.)

### Installing the Fuel Pump

Always use a fresh gasket when installing the pump. Be careful not to cross-thread the pipe fittings; use no wrench until at least two turns are threaded fully. Tighten the mounting bolts again after running the engine, then check fuel pump delivery pressure with gauge.

## Air Filter

Most models are equipped with an air filter having a replaceable paper element. Change element every 12,000 miles, or sooner if the engine is operated under severe dirt and dust conditions. A simple test to determine the degree of filter clogging can be made by holding a 50-Watt light bulb inside the filter element. If the light can be seen through the element, element is still usable. Blowing out the element with compressed air is permissible—washing the element in gasoline is not.

## Fuel Tank

Located in the rear on most models, except trucks and Land Cruiser. On both the Corona and the Corolla series, the tanks are part of the trunk floor. All fuel tanks have drain plugs and electrical gauges are fitted in the front part of the tank. *NOTE: When installing a fuel tank, always use a water-resistant, non-drying sealer between the edges of the tank and the trunk compartment to prevent water entry. When replacing a tank gauge unit, use a gasoline-proof sealer under the gasket (not Permatex).*

**Fuel Tank (Land Cruiser)**

*Removing the tank* Remove driver's seat and disconnect fuel gauge wire. Drain tank, then disconnect fuel outlet line. Disconnect breather (vent) pipe and fuel filler pipe hoses and clamps. Remove the bolts that hold the tank mounting straps. Remove tank and the strap packings. Now, unscrew the fuel tank sending unit and remove it, carefully, from the tank.

On the FJ55V series, tank removal is accomplished by first removing the service hole cover on the rear floor, then disconnecting the wire to the fuel gauge. Then remove the spare tire and drain the tank. Loosen all clamps and connections and remove the spare tire carrier and crossmember beneath the tank. It is then possible to remove the straps and the tank. *NOTE: Small fuel leaks can be plugged with soap for a temporary repair.*

**Inspecting the Tank**

It is safer to have the tank flushed and repaired by a professional repair shop, as gasoline fumes are easily ignited if the tank is abused. Fill the tank with water if repair work, other than soldering, is to be done.

## Fuel Filter

Consists of the filter housing or body, a glass bowl and gasket and the replaceable filter element. A filter in normal operation is never more than one-half full of fuel; more than that indicates that the element is clogged and should be cleaned or replaced. Cleaning is done by washing the element in clean fuel and blowing it out with compressed air. Replace the element every 10,000 miles, or sooner if dirty, waterlogged or clogged. When installing the bowl, make sure the bowl gasket is properly seated in the body or the pump will not be able to draw fuel from the tank. An old gasket can be reused (if no other is available) by reversing it so that it presents a fairly flat surface to the bowl side.

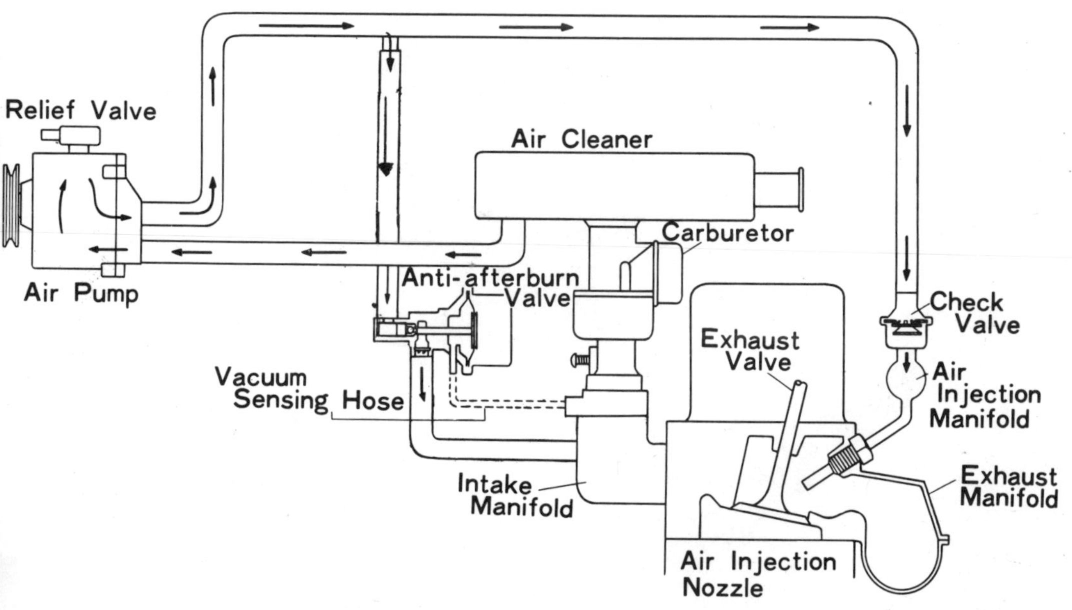


Manifold Air Injection System for emission control.

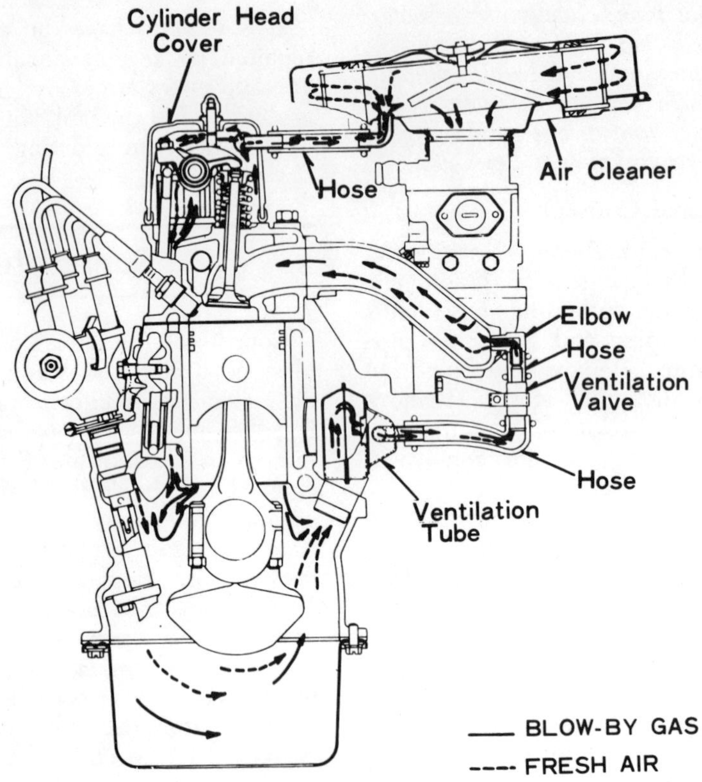


Corona (3RC) PCV system.

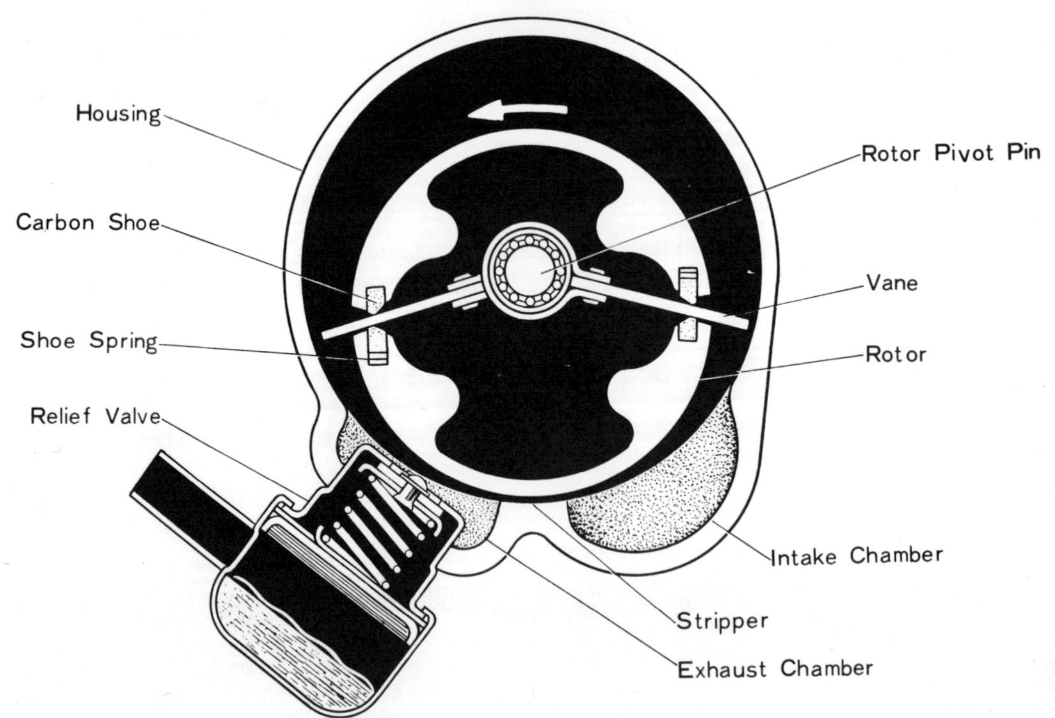


Air pump cross-section.

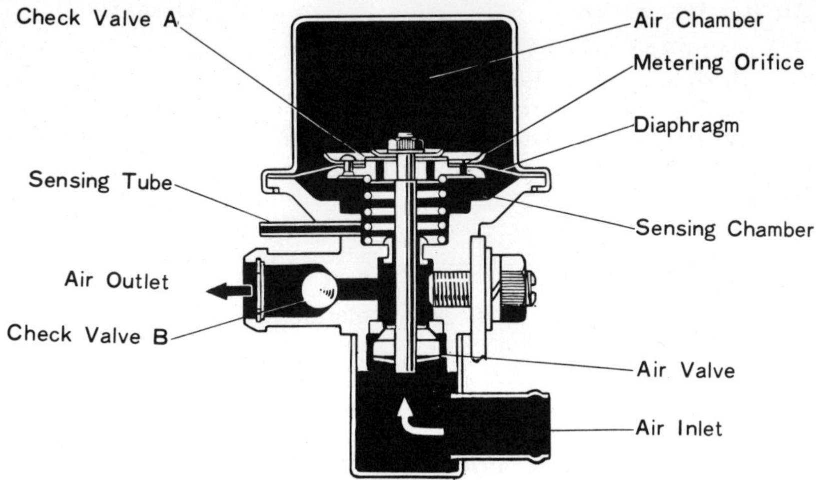


Anti-afterburn valve.

1. Housing cover
2. Rear bearing
3. Rotor ring
4. Shoe spring
5. Carbon shoe
6. Vane
7. Rotor housing
8. Housing cover attaching bolt
9. Rotor ring screw
10. Rear seal
11. Pulley plate
12. Pulley
13. Key
14. Lockwasher
15. Locknut
16. Knock pin

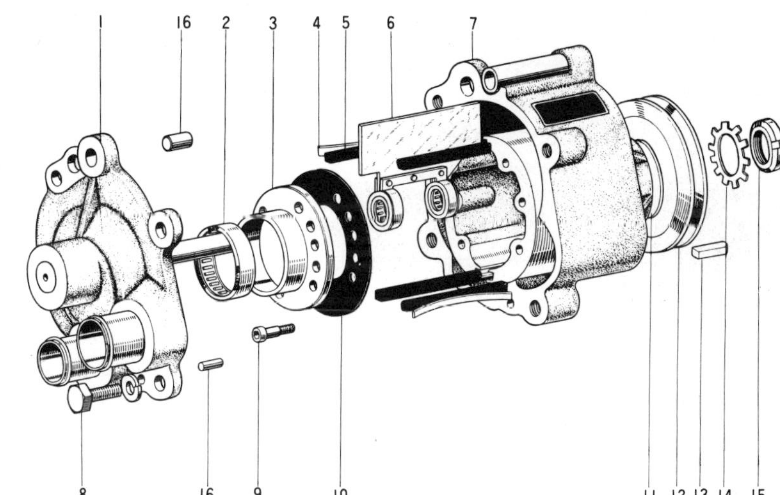


Air pump disassembled.

## Emission Control Systems

Toyota vehicles incorporate one of two different types of exhaust emission control systems—the Air Injection System or the Engine Modification System. The Case Storage System is also used with both of the engine emission control systems. The Air Injection System is used on the Corolla, the Corona and the Crown, while the Engine Modification System is used on the ½-ton Pick-up and the Land Cruiser.

All engines are equipped with *positive crankcase ventilation* systems (PCV). In order to comply with federal standards, all engines since 1968 are equipped with additional controls consisting of an *air injection system* and emission-calibrated *carburetors* and *distributors. NOTE: Carburetors and distributors fitted to "equipped" engines are not interchangeable with those of "non-equipped" engines (3R-C, 2M, KC and F series).* In addition, the cylinder head, exhaust manifold and cooling system is designed to handle the extra heat produced.

### PCV System

The PCV system has two functions, to prevent blow-by gases from escaping into the atmosphere and to ventilate the crankcase with fresh, clean air, scavenging the blow-by gases and thus preventing build up of sludge and other undesirable byproducts.

### Manifold Air Injection System

Designed to control and reduce the emission of hydrocarbons and carbon monoxide by oxidizing (burning) the unburned portion of the combustion gases in the exhaust manifold. Compressed and filtered air, supplied by a belt-driven, rotary-vane pump, is fed continuously into the exhaust ports, where it reacts with the unburned exhaust gases to limit combustion byproducts. The system consists of an air pump, a check valve, anti-afterburn valve, air injection pipes and nozzles, a special carburetor and a calibrated distributor. *NOTE: On Corona models with manual transmission, an additional valve is installed to control airflow during starting.*

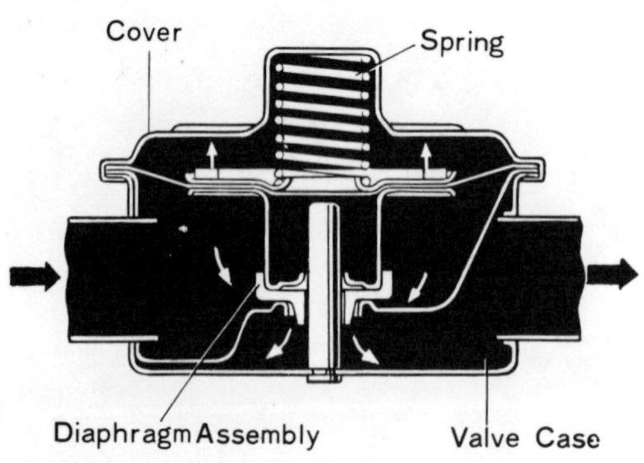

Air control valve.

#### Operation

The anti-afterburn valve (AABV) comes into action during deceleration when the fuel mixture is extremely rich. The high manifold vacuum existing during engine deceleration is used to open a diaphragm to allow fresh air from the air pump to enter the intake manifold, where it dilutes the rich mixture to a more normal ratio. The check valve prevents exhaust gases from entering the air pump in case exhaust pressure exceeds the pump pressure (belt failure). The air control valve (on 3R-C, manual transmission only), located between the air pump and the AABV, prevents the latter from opening at high manifold vacuum (due to closed choke) until the air pump discharge pressure is at least 1.6 psi.

#### PCV System Operation

Ventilating air enters the engine through the valve cover (on 3R-C and F engines), the ventilating tube from the air cleaner (2M engine), or the cylinder head from the air cleaner (K engine). The valve is operated by the pressure differential between the crankcase and the intake manifold.

### Troubleshooting the Emission Control System

*Check valve* Remove from engine and blow through from both sides. Air should pass only in one direction.

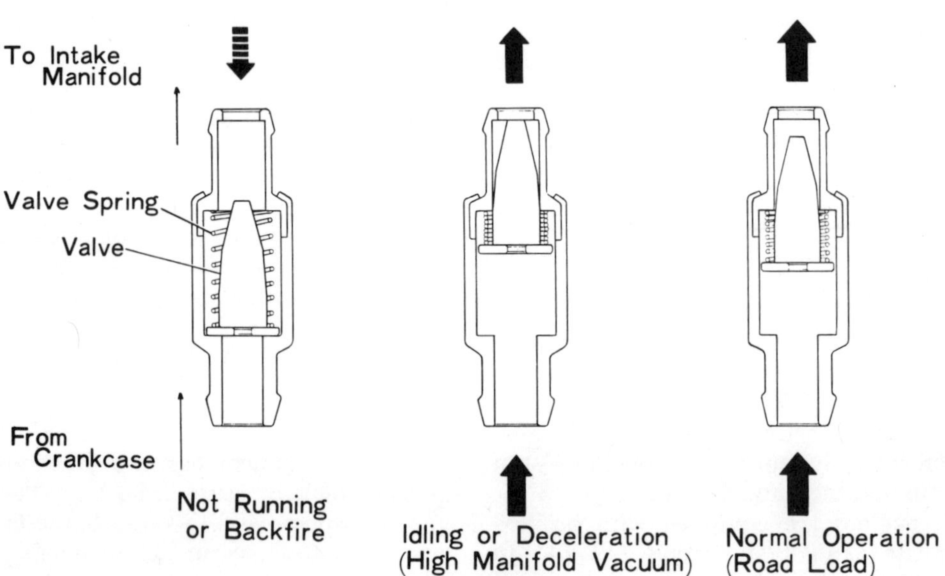

PCV valve operation.

*AABV* Disconnect the inlet hose from the valve and race the engine. Upon releasing the accelerator, air should be sucked into the valve for about five seconds. If air is sucked into the valve for a longer period of time, the valve is defective. The valve also must be replaced if no air is sucked in.

*Pressure relief valve (on air pump)* No airflow should be noticed from idle speed to 3,000 rpm; after 3,000 rpm, some airflow should be present.

*Air injection manifold* Remove by loosening the nuts that hold the manifold to the cylinder head. On F engines, also remove the nuts that hold the injection nozzles to the manifold. On 2M engines, the entire manifold must be removed before removing the injection components.

*NOTE: Nozzles may be removed from the inside of the cylinder head by tapping them out with a hammer.*

*Air control valve (manual transmission Corona models)* Disconnect the AABV hose and check for airflow at idle speeds. If airflow is present, the valve is defective and must be replaced. A stuck valve will cause severe backfiring.

*PCV valve* In cases of hard starting or rough, slow idling, the PCV valve is often at fault. Clean out all hoses and make sure air flows freely through the valve.

### Engine modification System

The Engine Modification System consists of a modified carburetor with a throttle positioner, a modified distributor with vacuum retard and advance diaphragm, a speed detector, a speed marker and a vacuum switching valve. Using this system, the engine is able to run smoothly with a lean fuel mixture, thus greatly reducing the emission of unburned hydrocarbons and carbon monoxide.

### Case Storage System

The Case Storage System is designed to reduce hydrocarbon emission from the fuel system and consists mainly of a vacuum switching valve, a fuel vapor storage case, an air filter, a thermal expansion tank and a modified fuel tank.

## The Exhaust System

Exhaust systems conform to the usual design found on domestic cars. The front exhaust pipe leads the exhaust gases from the exhaust manifold to the pre-muffler, or resonator, then through the center pipe(s) to the main muffler and out through a tail pipe into the open air. *NOTE: Some mufflers are welded to their respective pipes, although this is not always shown in shop manuals.*

Exhaust manifolds are generally of standard design and materials. Gaskets are used to attach the manifold to cylinder head. On

## Emission Control System Periodic Service Intervals

| | *Inspection and Service* | *At the first 1,000 miles* | *Every 3,000 miles* | *Every 6,000 miles* | *Every 12,000 miles* |
|---|---|---|---|---|---|
| 1. | Air pump drive belt | O | O | O | O |
| 2. | Air pump | O | | | O |
| 3. | Anti-afterburn valve | O | | | O |
| 4. | Air bypass valve silencer | | | O | X |
| 5. | Check valve | O | | | O |
| 6. | Air manifold | O | | | O |
| 7. | Air control valve (for 3K–C and 3R–C engine) | O | | | O |
| 8. | Positive crankcase ventilation valve | | | | X |
| 9. | Air filter cleaning (for case storage system) | | | | O |
| 10. | Purge control valve | O | O | O | O |
| 11. | Hoses and tubes | O | | | O |

O — Check and adjust X — Replace

cars equipped with automatic choke, there are provisions for the supply of heated air to operate the choke control. On F series engines, a heat riser valve is incorporated which should be checked every 4,000 miles. To prevent valve from sticking, lubricate it with special spray lubricant or graphite mixed with kerosene. Make sure the weight is seated firmly on the shaft. The valve is open when the weight is seated in its extreme counterclockwise position (seen from the rear). The bimetal coil spring should be pre-loaded at least one-half turn before connecting it to the shaft.

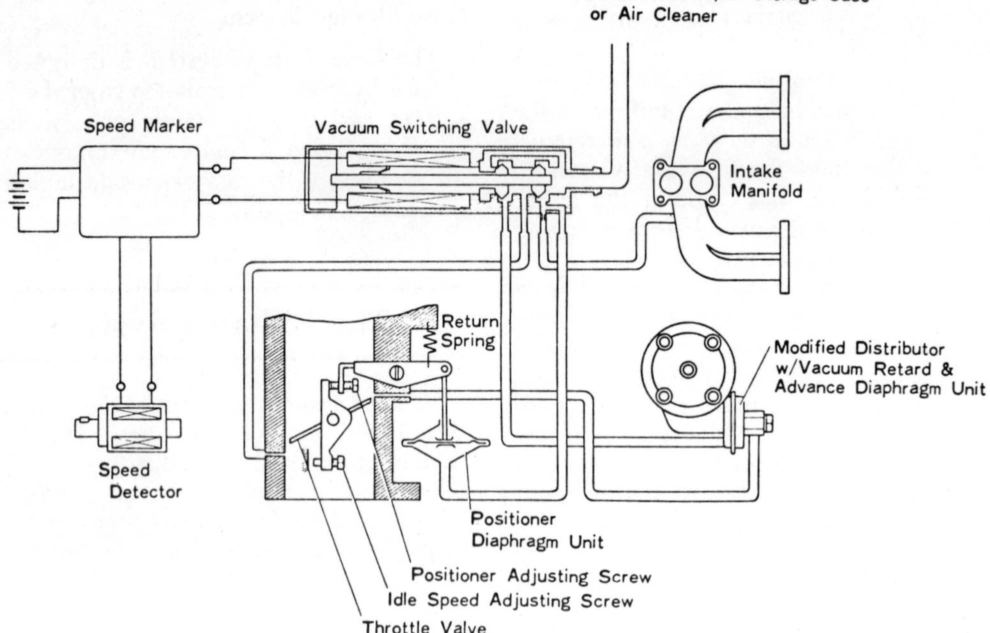


Engine Modification System Schematic.

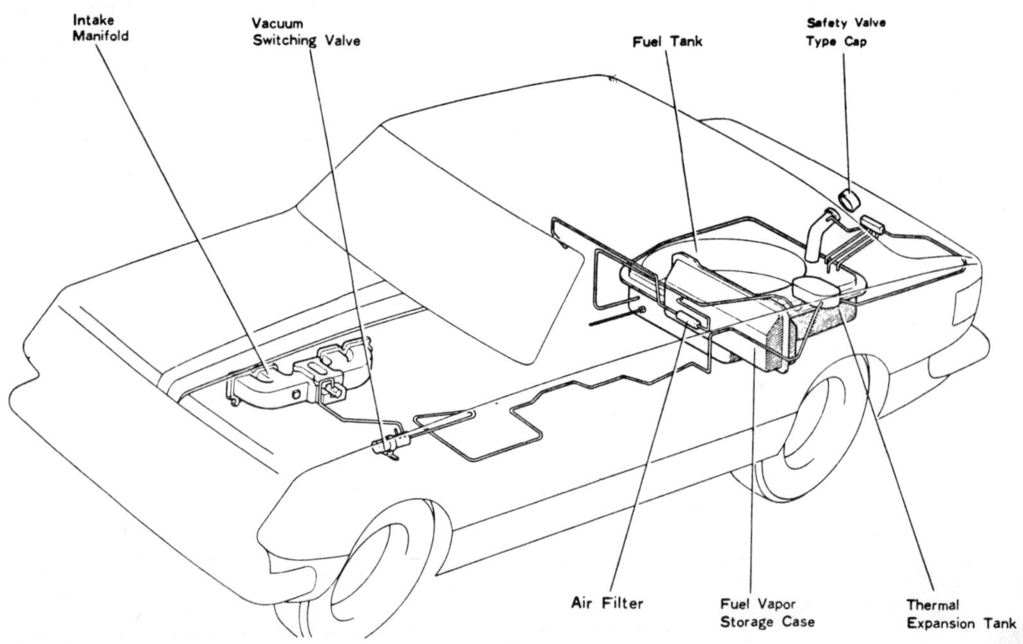


Case Storage System Schematic.

# Chapter 6
# Clutch and Manual Transmission
## Clutch

## Clutch

The clutch is a single-plate, dry-disc type. Two types of pressure plates are in use: some early models, and all F series, use a clutch consisting of a pressure plate with six (nine on the F series) coil-type pressure springs, release levers and pins. Later models all use a diaphragm-spring pressure plate. Clutch release bearings are sealed ball bearing units which need no lubrication and which never should be washed in any

A. Clutch disc assembly
B. Clutch pressure plate subassembly
C. Round rivet
D. Clutch cover subassembly
E. Tension spring
F. Clutch pressure lever
G. Plate washer
H. Nut
I. Radial ball bearing
J. Clutch release bearing hub
K. Release bearing hub clip
L. Bolt
M. Spring washer
N. Clutch release fork assembly
O. W/knurling pin
P. Solid bushing
Q. Release fork support subassembly
R. Cotter pin
S. Clutch pressure plate bolt
T. Compression spring
U. Spring washer
V. Bolt
W. Clutch release fork dust shield
X. Plate washer
Y. Spring washer
Z. Bolt

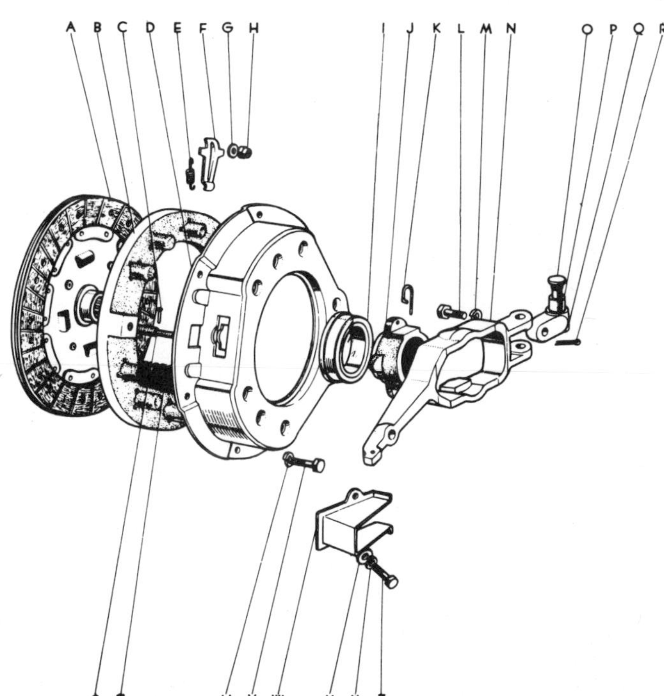


Coil spring clutch.

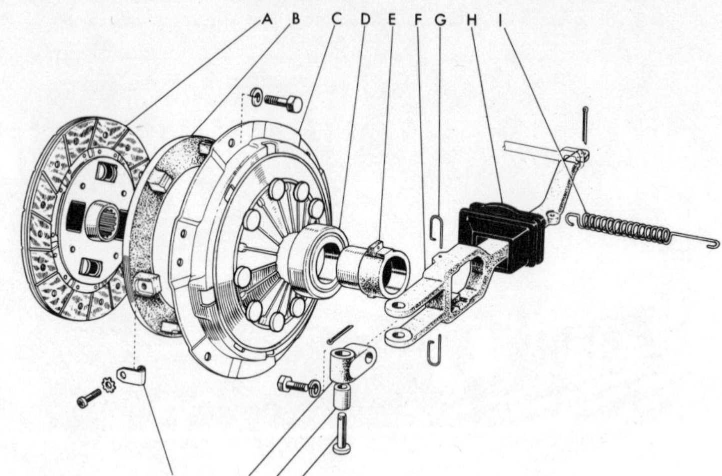


Diaphragm spring clutch.

kind of solvent. All clutches except the one used on the Corolla are hydraulically operated.

## Removing the Clutch

Remove transmission, then remove the clutch cover bolts by first loosening them evenly all around to prevent warping the clutch cover. Lift off the cover and the disc.

## Disassembling the Clutch

Punch mark the cover and flywheel to maintain balance positioning. There is no need to disassemble diaphragm clutches unless the diaphragm spring is damaged or its pressure is below specifications. Replace such defective clutches if necessary, as a unit. To disassemble coil-spring units, place a wooden block on top of cover and press down until enough spring pressure is relieved to allow removal of the nuts that secure the clutch cover bolts. Release pressure slowly and remove cover assembly. Take out pressure springs, pull cotter pins from the release lever pins and remove pins.

Removing clutch cover.

## Inspecting the Clutch

Do not wash the disc. Check disc for lining wear and broken rivets or springs. If there is less than 0.012″ of lining showing above the rivet heads, replace the disc. Runout limit is 0.020″. Check splines and free-travel on gear shaft, then check torsion rubbers for distortion or wear. Wash off all clutch cover parts and check lever tips for wear, distortion or cracks. Test all springs for load and squareness. If the pressure plate bearing surface is blue or shows tiny crack marks, reface or replace the pressure plate assembly. Limit for refacing is 0.030″.

Check the clutch release bearing; if it feels rough or is noisy, replace it. Replace clutch parts after 50,000 miles, as metal components are usually fatigued by that time and may fail in service. Also, inspect the clutch fork fingers for wear, the fork pivot ball and spring for looseness and the pilot bearing in the crankshaft for wear.

## Assembling the Clutch

Apply a light coat of silicone lubricant to all moving parts of the clutch prior to installation. Install the lever pins into the release lever pin holes, then fit the release levers and pressure plate pins. Lock the assembly with cotter pins. Install the release lever yokes onto the levers, then place the pressure plate face down and install the springs onto their seats. Place the clutch

## Clutch Specifications

| *Model* | *K* | *RT* | *MS* | *FJ* |
|---|---|---|---|---|
| Disc diameter | 7.087″ | 7.780″ | 8.820″ | 10.830″ |
| Master cylinder diameter | — | .625″ | .750″ | .750″ |
| Slave cylinder diameter | — | .591″ | .750″ | .750″ |
| Full pedal travel | 5.50–6.00″ | 5.75–6.10″ | 5.50–6.00″ | 6.50–6.70″ |
| Play at fork | — | .150″ | .125″ | .210″ |
| Clutch pressure spring length | — | — | — | 9–1.690″ |
| Clutch pressure | 530 lbs. | 636 lbs. | 860–875 lbs.<br>764–792 lbs. | 93–100 lbs.<br>each |
| Pressure limit | 400 lbs. | 462 lbs. | 700 (616) lbs. | 88 lbs. |
| Release lever height | — | — | 1.360″ | 2.930″<br>(±.002″) |
| Cover to plate (ft. lbs.) | 3–5 | 6–7 | 3–5 | — |
| Cover to flywheel (ft. lbs.) | 7–11 | 6–9.5 | 6–9.5 | 11–16 |

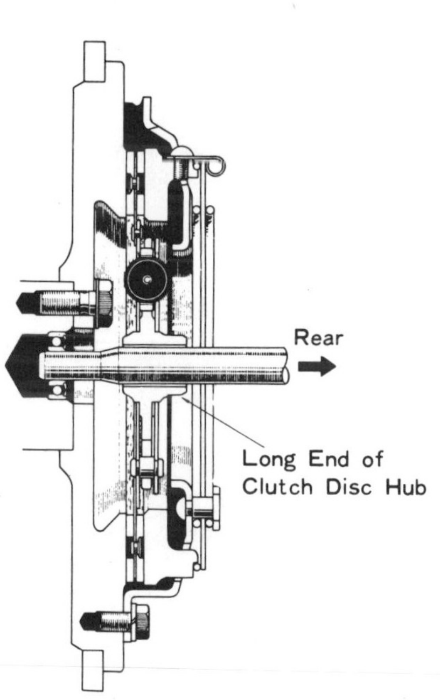


Installing clutch disc.

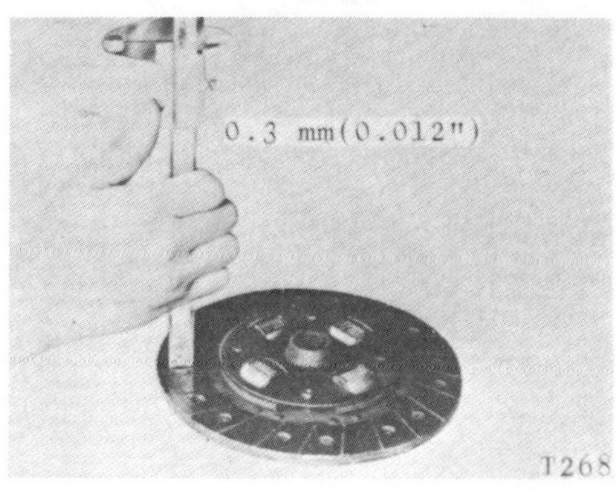


Checking clutch lining wear.

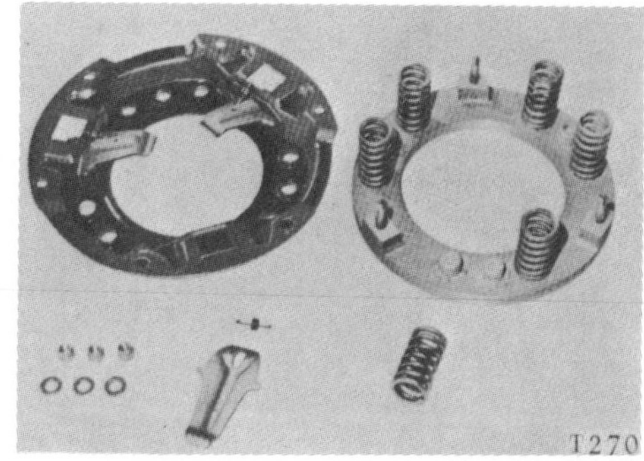


Check all clutch components before assembly.

cover carefully over the pressure plate, aligning the punch marks. Place a wooden block on the cover and press down until the locking nuts can be assembled and tightened, equally all around to prevent warping the cover. Secure the yoke bolts to the cover and torque to 22–32 ft. lbs. Mount the disc and clutch assembly onto the flywheel. Center the disc using a clutch pilot tool, or the transmission input shaft itself if no tool is available. This must be done carefully or the transmission will not line up with the clutch disc splines. Now, adjust the release lever height. The difference between fingers must not exceed 0.002″. Install the release fork into transmission case and connect the spring clips to the bearing, making sure the bearing moves freely on

Adjusting clutch lever height using special gauge.

the shaft. *NOTE: Install the disc with flat surface towards the flywheel.*

### Hydraulic Clutch

The clutch master cylinder is serviced and bled in the same manner as the brake master cylinder.

To remove and replace the slave cylinder, first unhook the release fork spring, then screw in the pushrod until it can be disengaged from the fork; disconnect the flexible hose and remove the mounting bolts and spring bracket. Remove the boot and pushrods, then remove the release piston with its mounted cup. Pull off the cup if necessary.

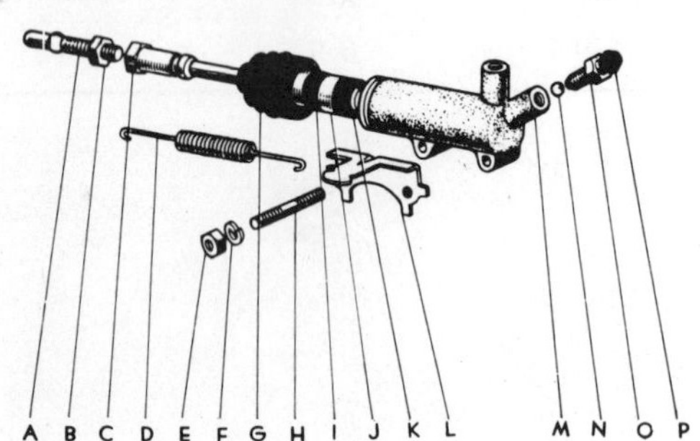


Clutch slave cylinder.

A. Release cylinder pushrod No. 2
B. Nut
C. Release cylinder pushrod No. 1
D. Tension spring
E. Nut
F. Spring washer
G. Release cylinder boot
H. Stud bolt
I. Cylinder cup
J. Release cylinder piston
K. Cylinder cup
L. Release fork retracting spring hanger
M. Clutch release cylinder assembly
N. Ball

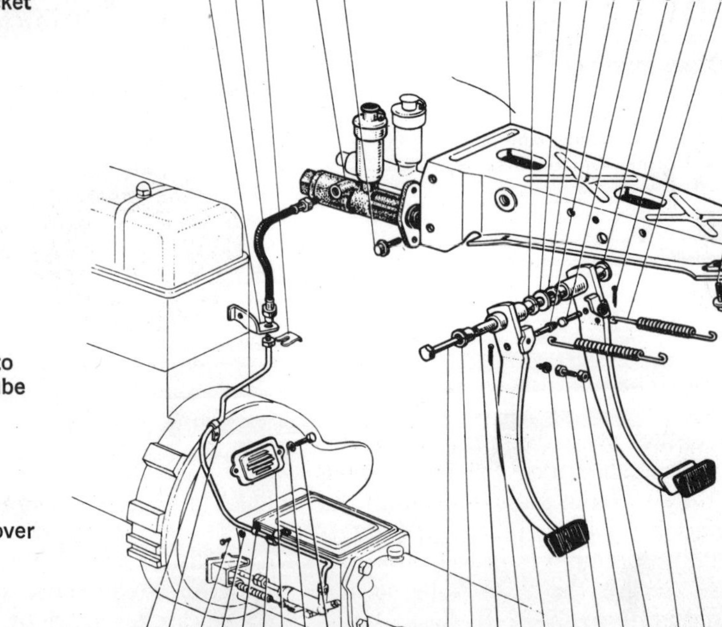


Clutch and brake pedal assemblies.

A. Flexible hose bracket
B. Flexible hose
C. Clip
D. Master cylinder
E. Bolt
F. Pedal bracket
G. Bushing
H. Plain washer
I. Pin
J. Pin
K. Cotter pin
L. Tension spring
M. Bolt
N. Lockwasher
O. Nut
P. Release cylinder to flexible hose tube
Q. Clamp
R. Bolt
S. Lockwasher
T. Clamp
U. Clamp
V. Clutch housing cover
W. Bolt
X. Collar
Y. Clutch pedal
Z. Cushion
AA. Bolt
AB. Nut
AC. Tension spring
AD. Brake pedal
AE. Pedal pad

## Clutch Specifications

| *Model* | *K* | *RT* | *MS* | *FJ* |
|---|---|---|---|---|
| Disc diameter | 7.087″ | 7.780″ | 8.820″ | 10.830″ |
| Master cylinder diameter | — | .625″ | .750″ | .750″ |
| Slave cylinder diameter | — | .591″ | .750″ | .750″ |
| Full pedal travel | 5.50–6.00″ | 5.75–6.10″ | 5.50–6.00″ | 6.50–6.70″ |
| Play at fork | — | .150″ | .125″ | .210″ |
| Clutch pressure spring length | — | — | — | 9–1.690″ |
| Clutch pressure | 530 lbs. | 636 lbs. | 860–875 lbs.<br>764–792 lbs. | 93–100 lbs.<br>each |
| Pressure limit | 400 lbs. | 462 lbs. | 700 (616) lbs. | 88 lbs. |
| Release lever height | — | — | 1.360″ | 2.930″<br>(±.002″) |
| Cover to plate (ft. lbs.) | 3–5 | 6–7 | 3–5 | — |
| Cover to flywheel (ft. lbs.) | 7–11 | 6–9.5 | 6–9.5 | 11–16 |

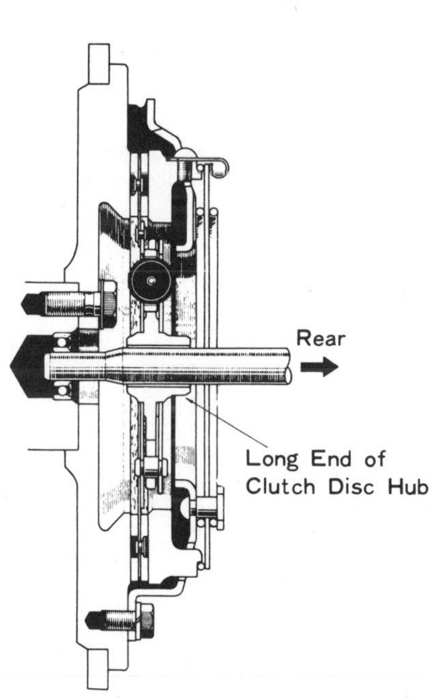


Installing clutch disc.

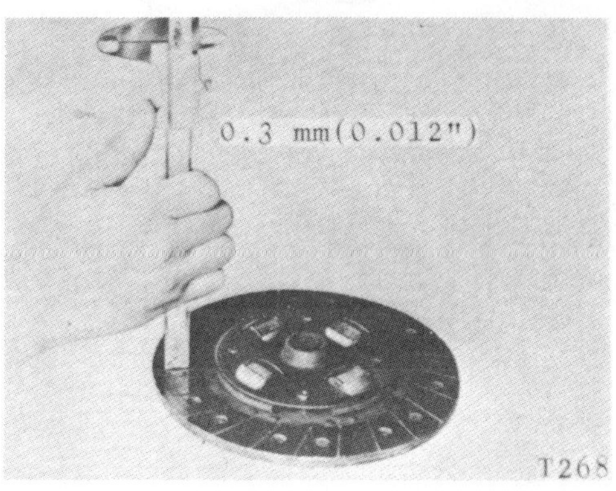


Checking clutch lining wear.

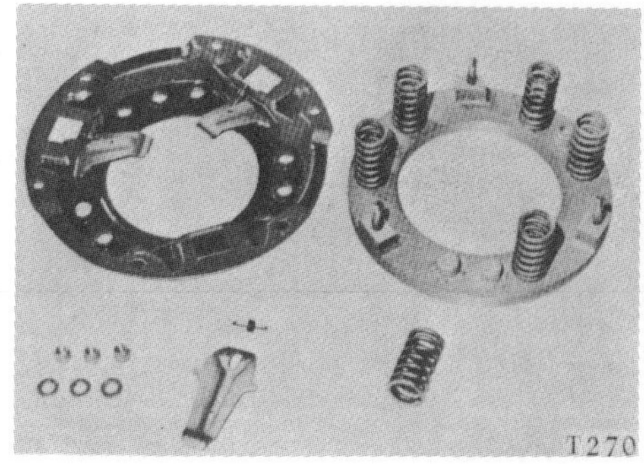


Check all clutch components before assembly.

cover carefully over the pressure plate, aligning the punch marks. Place a wooden block on the cover and press down until the locking nuts can be assembled and tightened, equally all around to prevent warping the cover. Secure the yoke bolts to the cover and torque to 22–32 ft. lbs. Mount the disc and clutch assembly onto the flywheel. Center the disc using a clutch pilot tool, or the transmission input shaft itself if no tool is available. This must be done carefully or the transmission will not line up with the clutch disc splines. Now, adjust the release lever height. The difference between fingers must not exceed 0.002″. Install the release fork into transmission case and connect the spring clips to the bearing, making sure the bearing moves freely on

Adjusting clutch lever height using special gauge.

the shaft. *NOTE: Install the disc with flat surface towards the flywheel.*

**Hydraulic Clutch**

The clutch master cylinder is serviced and bled in the same manner as the brake master cylinder.

To remove and replace the slave cylinder, first unhook the release fork spring, then screw in the pushrod until it can be disengaged from the fork; disconnect the flexible hose and remove the mounting bolts and spring bracket. Remove the boot and pushrods, then remove the release piston with its mounted cup. Pull off the cup if necessary.

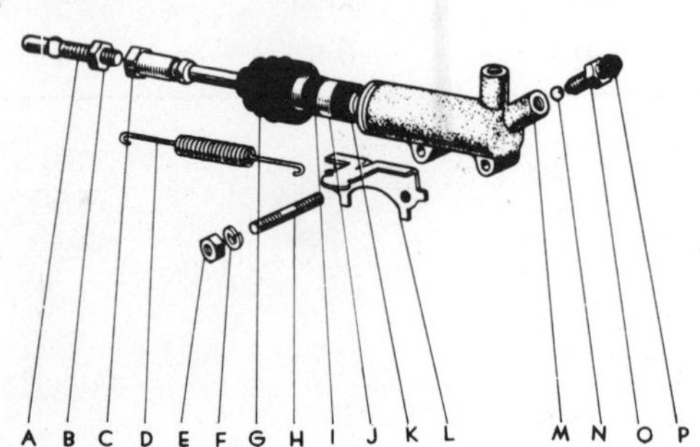


Clutch slave cylinder.

A. Release cylinder pushrod No. 2
B. Nut
C. Release cylinder pushrod No. 1
D. Tension spring
E. Nut
F. Spring washer
G. Release cylinder boot
H. Stud bolt
I. Cylinder cup
J. Release cylinder piston
K. Cylinder cup
L. Release fork retracting spring hanger
M. Clutch release cylinder assembly
N. Ball

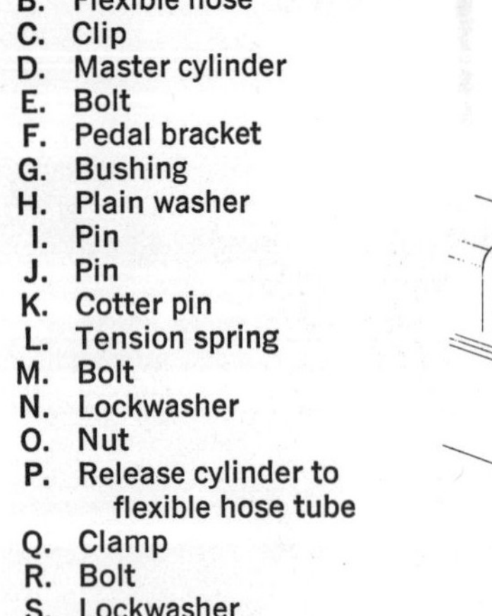

A. Flexible hose bracket
B. Flexible hose
C. Clip
D. Master cylinder
E. Bolt
F. Pedal bracket
G. Bushing
H. Plain washer
I. Pin
J. Pin
K. Cotter pin
L. Tension spring
M. Bolt
N. Lockwasher
O. Nut
P. Release cylinder to flexible hose tube
Q. Clamp
R. Bolt
S. Lockwasher
T. Clamp
U. Clamp
V. Clutch housing cover
W. Bolt
X. Collar
Y. Clutch pedal
Z. Cushion
AA. Bolt
AB. Nut
AC. Tension spring
AD. Brake pedal
AE. Pedal pad

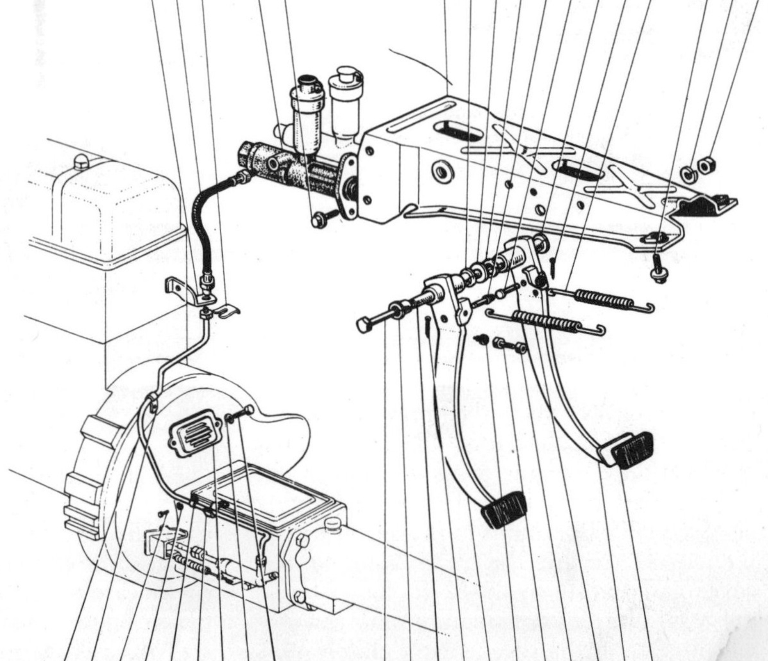


Clutch and brake pedal assemblies.

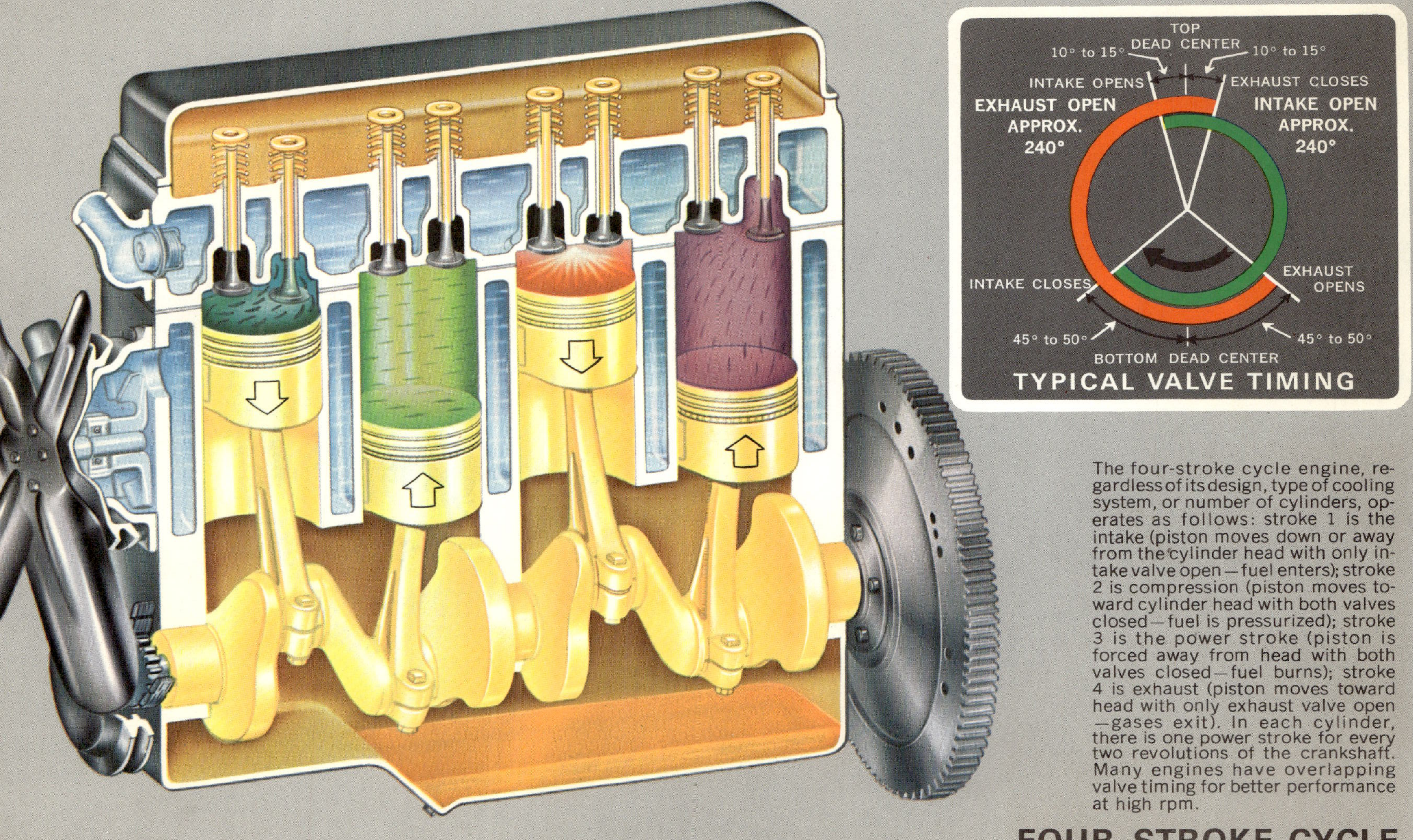


The four-stroke cycle engine, regardless of its design, type of cooling system, or number of cylinders, operates as follows: stroke 1 is the intake (piston moves down or away from the cylinder head with only intake valve open—fuel enters); stroke 2 is compression (piston moves toward cylinder head with both valves closed—fuel is pressurized); stroke 3 is the power stroke (piston is forced away from head with both valves closed—fuel burns); stroke 4 is exhaust (piston moves toward head with only exhaust valve open—gases exit). In each cylinder, there is one power stroke for every two revolutions of the crankshaft. Many engines have overlapping valve timing for better performance at high rpm.

## FOUR-STROKE CYCLE

Wash all parts thoroughly in clean brake fluid or alcohol. *Do not use any other solvents.* Inspect all parts for signs of wear, scuffing or scoring. Inside of cylinder may be honed out, if necessary, but the honing limit is 0.004″. Always use a new cup.

Assemble all parts after coating with fresh brake fluid. Mount cup on piston and insert assembly into cylinder, then place boot on rods and fit to cylinder. Install slave cylinder onto transmission housing and engage clutch release fork. Adjust play between fork and rod per specification, then bleed the clutch hydraulic system.

### Troubleshooting the Clutch

In most problem cases, clutches either slip or do not disengage at all. Check fluid level in master cylinder and operation of release (slave) cylinder. If both are normal, trouble is internal and will require clutch disassembly. Oil leaking onto clutch disc causes chattering and grabbing (or sticking), but so does a bad rear motor mount under certain conditions. Check the motor mounts before removing the clutch. Squeaking noises are usually caused by the pressure springs in the cover assembly. Slipping during shifting is usually the result of worn clutch linings. Make sure the flywheel is not burned in cases of slipping.

## Transmission

### Removing Corolla Transmission

Remove floormat and shift lever boot, then press shift lever cap down and turn it counterclockwise to release. Cover the

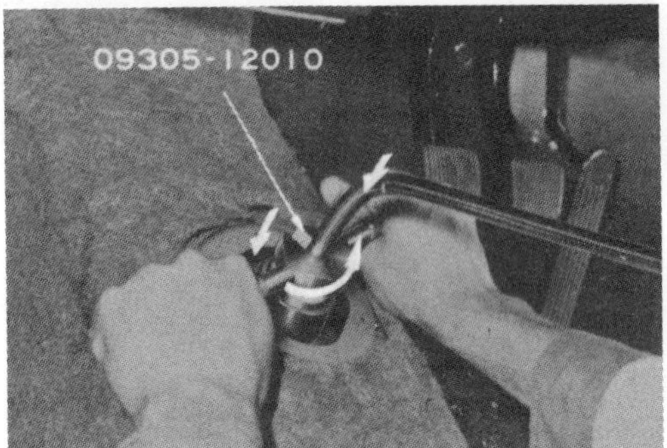


Removing shift lever collar.

opening with a clean rag to prevent entry of dirt, then disconnect back up switch and positive battery cable. Remove radiator inlet hose and turn fan blade to horizontal position. Jack up car and place stands under

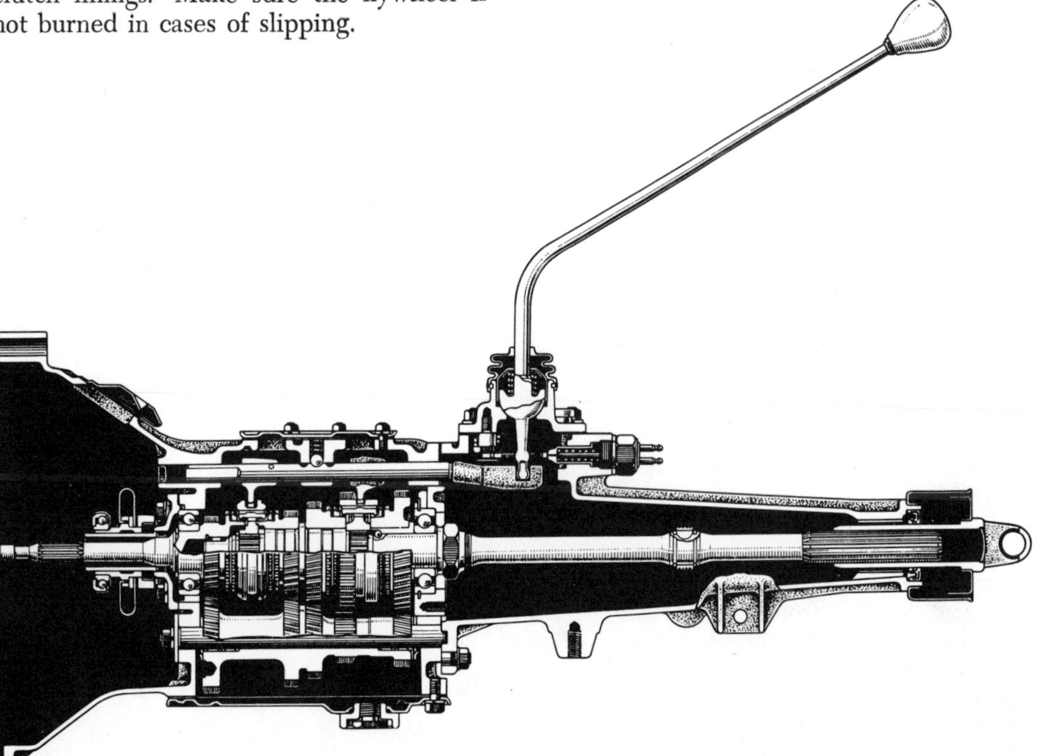

Corolla transmission cross-section.

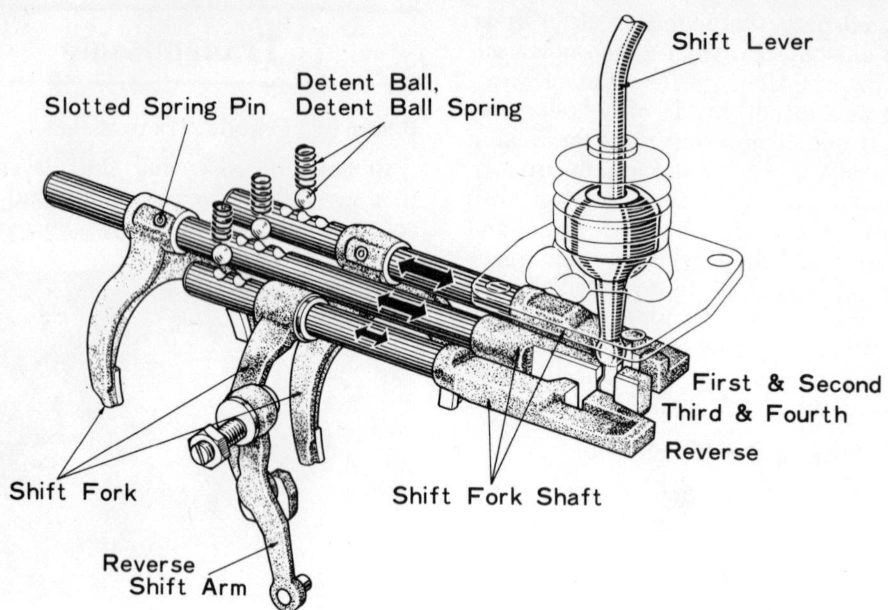


Corolla shift mechanism.

frame, then disconnect exhaust flange. Disconnect and remove drive shaft; plug hole to prevent oil loss. Disconnect speedometer cable and exhaust pipe hanger from extension housing. Place jack under front of transmission and remove two bolts (only) from rear mount. Remove rear transmission support (crossmember) and remove the jack.

Remove starter motor and the two bolts that hold the stiffener plate to the transmission case. Disconnect and remove clutch cable, then remove the two lower and the four upper bolts that hold the transmission to the engine block. *NOTE: Upper bolts are best removed using a 17mm. socket and a 20" extension on ratchet.* Remove transmission to the rear, pulling straight back until free of the clutch and flywheel housing.

**Removing Corona Transmission**

Corona transmission removal is similar to Corolla.

*Special procedures* Remove gear lever knob and boot, then remove shift lever bracket from extension housing; lever and the small bushing from bracket. Disconnect clutch cylinder from housing, but do not disconnect hydraulic hose. Remove handbrake equalizer bracket and cables.

On Corona models having remote control linkage, first jack up car and support it on axle stands. Disconnect battery ground wire, exhaust flange and pipe clamp. Remove parking brake equalizer bracket; disconnect speedometer cable and remove flywheel housing cover. Remove clutch release cylinder and pushrod (do not disconnect the hydraulic line or depress the clutch pedal), then disconnect the shift rods from the shift levers and remove the cross shaft and its support knob. Disconnect the drive shaft and plug the hole to prevent oil leaks. Jack up rear of engine (use a piece of wood to protect oil pan) and remove the rear support member. Remove all bolts and slide transmission to rear until clear of clutch, then lower to floor.

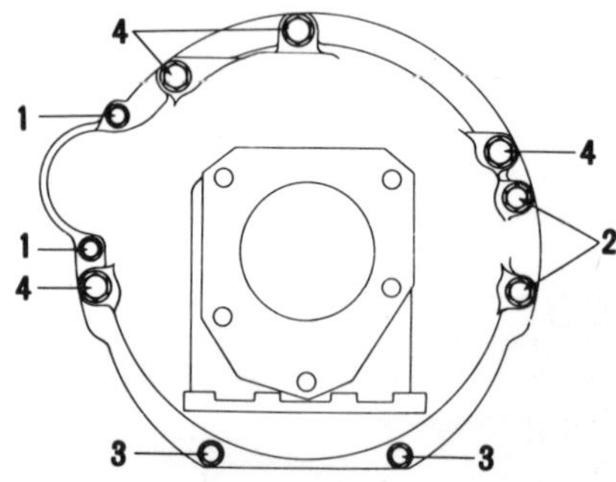


Transmission hold-down bolts.

**Removing Crown Transmission**

Removal is the same as for Corona models, including the procedures concerning remote control linkage, with the following exceptions: the starter motor, torque rod support and torque rod must be removed.

### Removing Land Cruiser Transmission

Remove skid plate and disconnect front and rear drive shafts. Drain the oil, remove the transmission cover, and disconnect all shift levers and links. Disconnect parking brake cable from lever, remove speedometer cable and disconnect wires from front wheel drive indicator switch. Remove all vacuum hoses, remove flywheel housing cover and loosen all bolts that hold transmission to clutch housing. Slide transmission to rear until it clears the clutch housing. *NOTE: The combined weight of transmission and transfer case make it advisable to use a transmission jack for this operation.*

### Disassembling the Corolla Transmission

Remove back up switch and wiring, speedometer pinion and sleeve and clutch fork and bearing with sleeve. Remove transmission oil pan and thoroughly wash inside of gearbox and dry off with air. *NOTE: A number of measurements must be taken before the transmission is disassembled.* Remove shift lever retaining cover from extension housing, then remove extension housing. Remove countershaft cover and front bearing retainer, along with oil seal. First loosen, then remove, all five nuts that hold the transmission case cover. Remove cover slowly or the shift rail detent balls will fly out. Remove lock bolt and reverse idler shaft, along with gear and spacer.

Now, using a dial indicator, measure the gear backlash and end-play. Write these measurements down for later reference during assembly. Drive out countergear shaft, using a brass punch, towards rear of case; remove the two thrust washers and the four needle roller bearings.

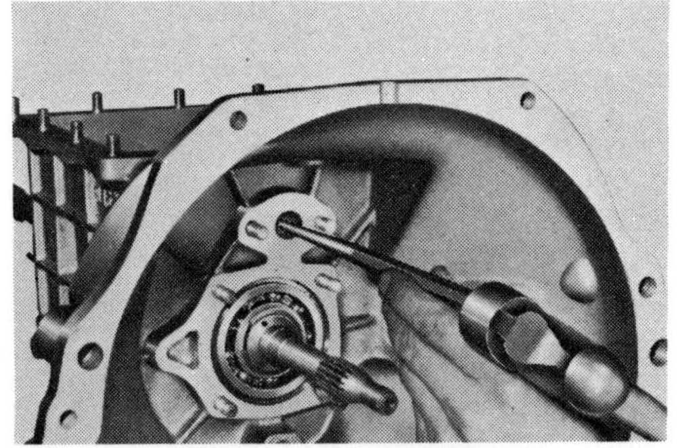

Removing countershaft.

With a small punch ($\frac{3}{16}$" dia.) drive the roll pins from the shift forks.

Remove, in order, reverse shift rail, first-second shift rail and third-fourth shift rail. Remove the three detent balls and the shift forks.

Remove output shaft, together with bearing retainer, then remove needle bearing and synchronizer ring from input shaft (main drive gear) and remove shaft from front of case.

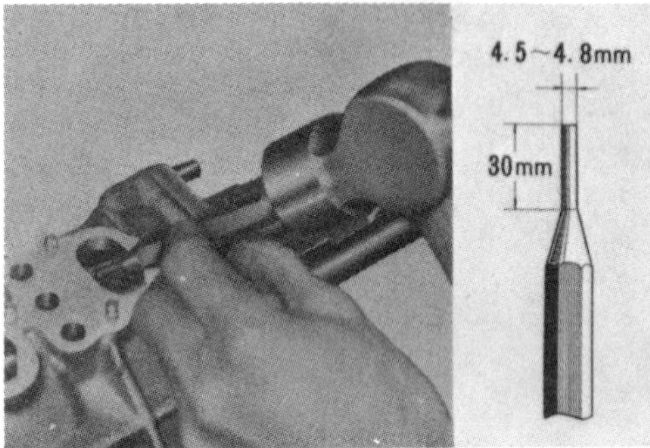


Removing slotted pin.

Before disassembling: measure end-play of first, second, and third gears on mainshaft, then remove snap-ring at front of shaft and pull off third-fourth synchronizer hub, spacer and synchronizer ring. *CAUTION: Synchronizer rings must not be mixed; tag each ring as it is removed.*

Remove snap-ring and speedometer drive gear, along with Woodruff key. Straighten

Removing output shaft.

lock tab and remove locknut from mainshaft (rear). Mark and save all shims.

Remove rear bearing retainer, first gear and bushing with ball, first-second synchronizer mechanism, synchronizer rings and

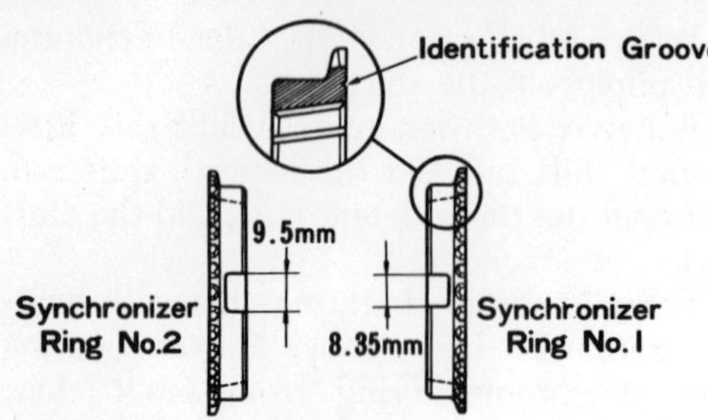


Synchronizer ring differences.

second gear, then disassemble all synchronizer mechanisms.

### Inspecting the Corolla Transmission

Wash all parts and blow off with compressed air, then check for chipped, broken or bent parts.

If there was excessive end-play when it was checked during disassembly, select the proper thrust washers to obtain correct end-play of gears, then check transmission case for wear.

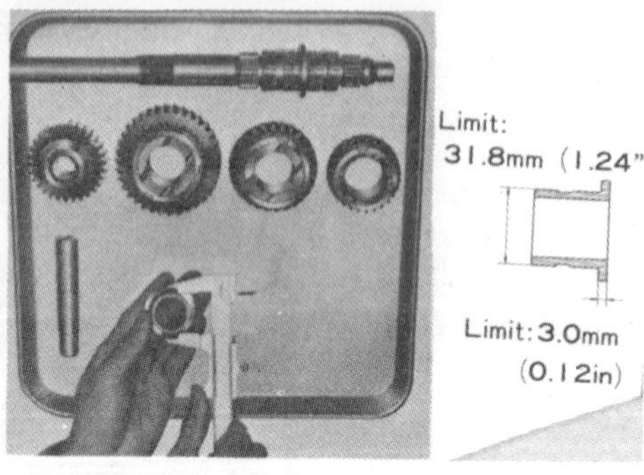


Checking first gear bushing.

## Specifications

| Gear | Normal | Limit |
|---|---|---|
| BACKLASH BETWEEN GEARS AND COUNTERGEAR | | |
| Input (main drive) | 0.004″ | 0.008″ |
| 3rd gear | 0.004″ | 0.008″ |
| 2nd gear | 0.004″ | 0.008″ |
| 1st gear | 0.004″ | 0.008″ |
| Reverse gear | 0.006″ | 0.012″ |
| Reverse idler | 0.007″ | 0.012″ |
| END-PLAY OF GEARS (THRUST CLEARANCE) | | |
| Countergear | .002–.020″ | 0.020″ |
| 1st gear | .004–.012″ | 0.020″ |
| 2nd gear | .006–.012″ | 0.020″ |
| 3rd gear | .004–.010″ | 0.020″ |

OUTPUT SHAFT (MAINSHAFT) DIMENSIONS
Flange wear limit—0.140″
Bearing seat limit—1.240″ diameter
Bend limit—0.001″

COUNTERGEAR
Thrust washer limit—0.067″
*Note: Input shaft bearing snap-rings are available in two sizes to allow proper seating of shaft.*

FIRST GEAR BUSHING LIMITS
Inside diameter—1.240″
Shoulder width limit—0.120″
Gears (all) inside diameter limit—1.260″

SYNCHRONIZER HUB GROOVE WIDTH
Shift fork seat limit—0.300″

SHIFT FORK TIP WIDTH
Wear limit—0.260″

SHIFT FORK TO HUB CLEARANCE
Wear limit—0.030″

SYNCHRONIZER RING TEST
Clearance between ring and gear—must be greater than 0.016″
*Note: Light hand pressure seating only.*

REVERSE IDLER GEAR
Bushing wear limit—0.710″
Shaft wear limit—0.700″

CLUTCH RELEASE BEARING RETAINER
Outer diameter limit—1.090″ (replace if scored)

REAR EXTENSION HOUSING BUSHING
New bushing reaming limits—1.260–1.261″
Clearance between drive shaft flange and bushing—0.0004–0.0024″
Bushing wear limit—1.270″
*Note: Old bushing must be removed by heating housing in boiling water. Slot of new bushing faces upwards.*

### Assembling the Corolla Transmission

Always use new oil seals and gaskets. Apply thin coats of Permatex to all gaskets and mating surfaces and lightly oil all gears,

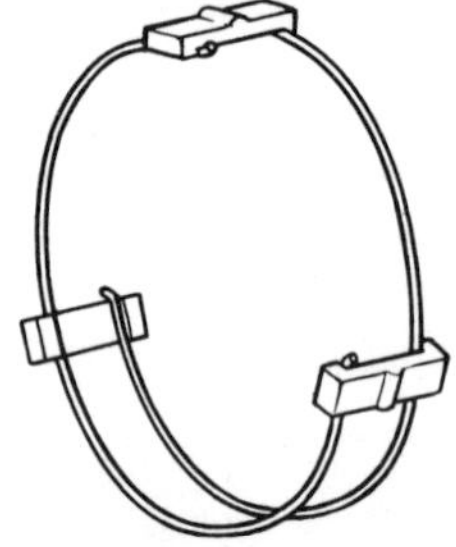

Shift keys and springs.

bearings and bushings before installation. Grease or oil all oil seal contact surfaces.

1. Place synchronizer hub into sleeve, fit the three shift keys (open end facing inwards) into the slots in the sleeve and install shift key retaining springs with open ends 120° apart. *NOTE: The third-fourth synchronizer hub is fitted with the wide*

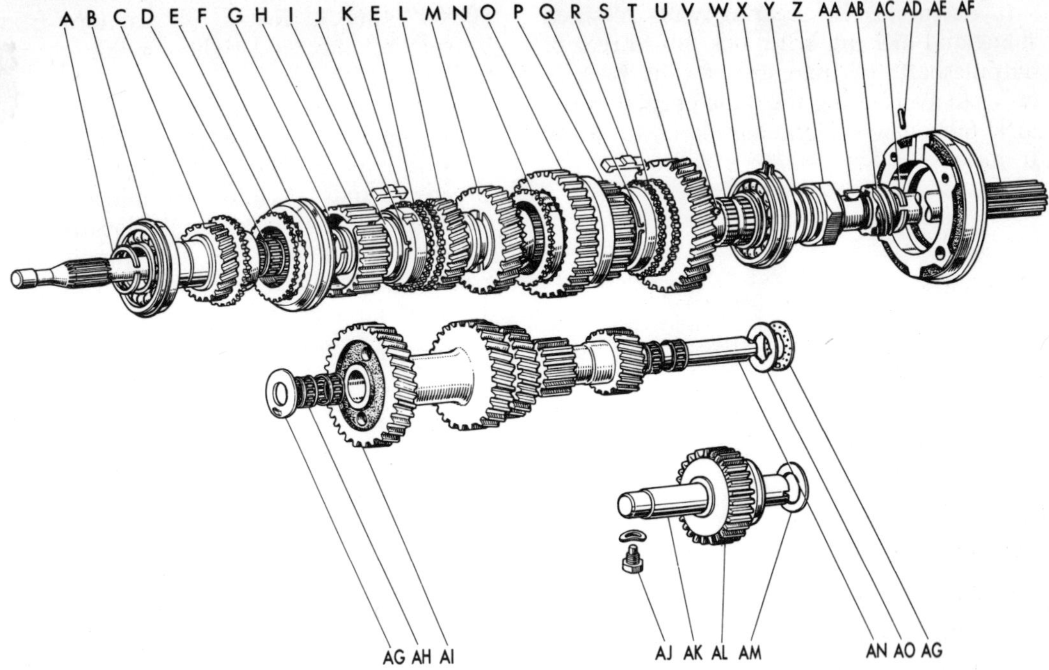

Transmission components.

A. Shaft snap-ring
B. Bearing (transmission front)
C. Input shaft
D. Needle roller bearing
E. Synchronizer ring No. 3
F. Transmission hub sleeve
G. Shaft snap-ring
H. Transmission clutch hub No. 2
I. Clutch hub spacer
J. Synchromesh shifting key spring No. 2
K. Synchromesh shifting key No. 2
L. Side gear
M. Second gear
N. Synchronizer ring No. 2
O. Reverse gear
P. Transmission clutch hub No. 1
Q. Synchromesh shifting key spring No. 1
R. Synchromesh shifting key No. 1
S. Synchronizer ring No. 1
T. First gear
U. Ball
V. First gear bushing
W. Bearing (transmission rear)
X. Shaft snap-ring.
Y. Shim
Z. Nut
AA. Woodruff key
AB. Speedometer drive gear
AC. Shaft snap-ring
AD. Slotted split pin
AE. Output shaft rear retainer
AF. Output shaft
AG. Countergear case side thrust washer
AH. Needle roller bearing
AI. Countergear
AJ. Shaft retaining bolt
AK. Reverse idler gear shaft
AL. Reverse idler gear
AM. Spacer
AN. Counter shaft
AO. Countergear side thrust washer No. 1

*shoulder facing forwards. The first-second synchronizer rings are different from each other and from the third-fourth rings.*

2. Assemble first-second synchronizer mechanism, as above, and fit into reverse gear from the rear.

3. Install second gear and synchronizer ring onto output shaft from rear.

4. Install first-second synchronizer ring onto output shaft, carefully aligning the grooves in the rings with the shaft keys. Check width of grooves before installation. *Do not use force during this installation step.*

5. Install first gear synchronizer ring, first gear and bushing with ball onto output shaft.

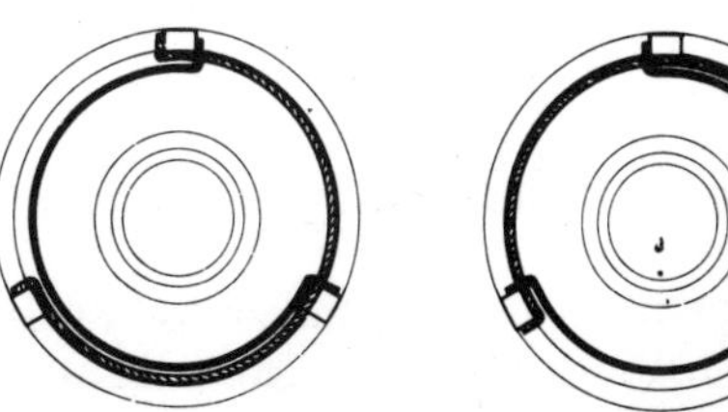

Shift keys and springs as installed.

6. Assemble rear bearing with retainer, shims and locknut, with lock tab to rear of output shaft. Change size of shim pack in order to avoid using the same portion of the lock tab again. Tighten locknut to 60–80 ft. lbs.

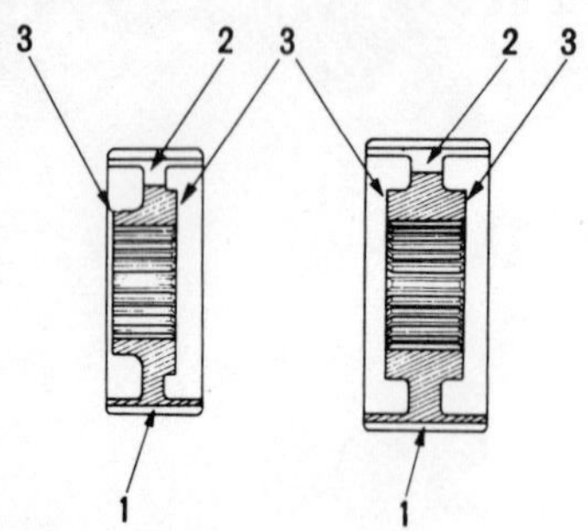


Checking clutch hub.

7. Assemble third gear, synchronizer ring, synchronizer hub and spacer, third-fourth synchronizer mechanism onto output shaft from the front (wide shoulder of hub faces forward).

8. Select the proper snap-ring to obtain correct end-play and install onto output shaft. Snap-rings come in three sizes: 0.079″, 0.083″ and 0.087″.

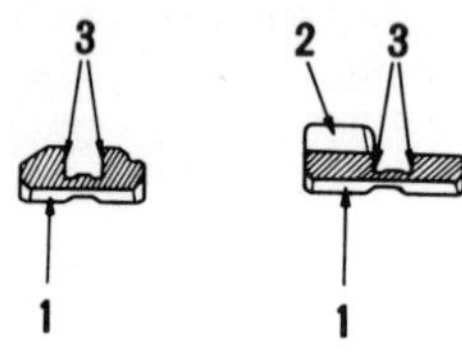


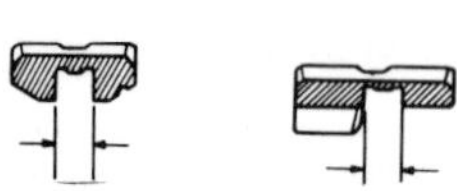

Synchronizer hub groove limit is 0.300″.

9. Fit snap-rings and speedometer drive gear (with Woodruff key) onto rear part of output shaft.

10. Check all gears for excessive end-play.

11. Install input shaft into transmission case.

12. Select front bearing retainer gasket as follows:

a.) If bearing retainer is recessed into case, use gasket part No. 33133-12010 (0.010″ thick).

b.) If bearing retainer protrudes from case, use gasket part No. 33133-22010 (0.030″ thick). Install oil seal into front bearing retainer and tighten retainer bolts to 7–12 ft. lbs.

13. Install needle bearing and synchronizer ring onto input shaft.

14. Assemble output shaft (with gears already installed) into transmission case, aligning rear bearing retainer locating pin with groove in case and also aligning the grooves in the No. 4 synchronizer ring with the shift keys of the third-fourth synchronizer mechanism.

Checking thrust clearance between each gear.

15. Engage reverse and second gears and install first-second shift fork into reverse gear, then rotate fork 180°. Insert first-second shift rail from rear of case and slide into first-second shift fork.

16. Install third-fourth shift fork onto third-fourth synchronizer sleeve and rotate fork 180°. Insert third-fourth shift rail into case through shift fork.

17. Install the reverse shaft shift fork into case by engaging the center of the reverse shift arm. Install the reverse shift fork shaft into case and the reverse shift fork.

18. Secure all shift forks to shift rails with the three roll pins, using a $3/16''$ punch to seat them.

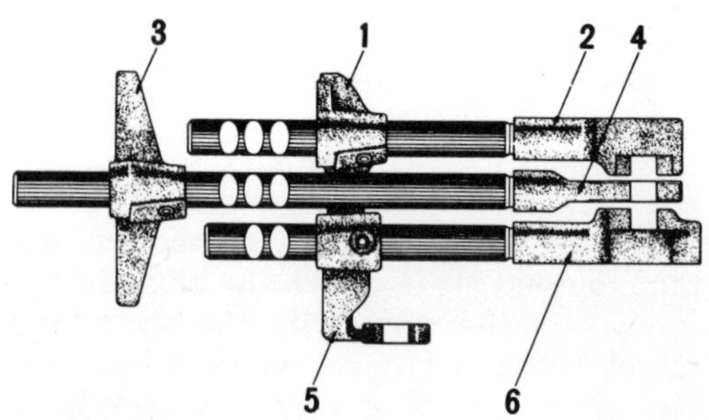


Assembling shift fork.

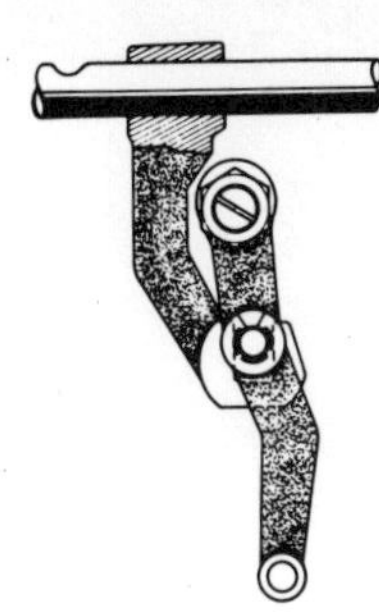

Installing reverse shift fork.

19. Install countergear with needle bearings and thrust washers; check end-play. Washers come in four sizes to allow proper clearance adjustment. Insert countershaft from rear, slotted end of shaft faces rear and lines up horizontally with the case. Install cover and gasket, then tighten bolts to 7–12 ft. lbs.

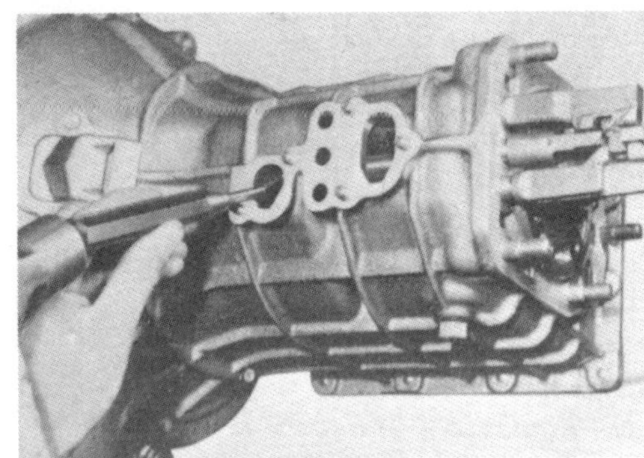

Installing shift fork pins.

20. Engage groove of reverse idler gear with pin of reverse shift arm, then insert reverse idler shaft so that the hole in the shaft lines up with the hole in the front support boss.

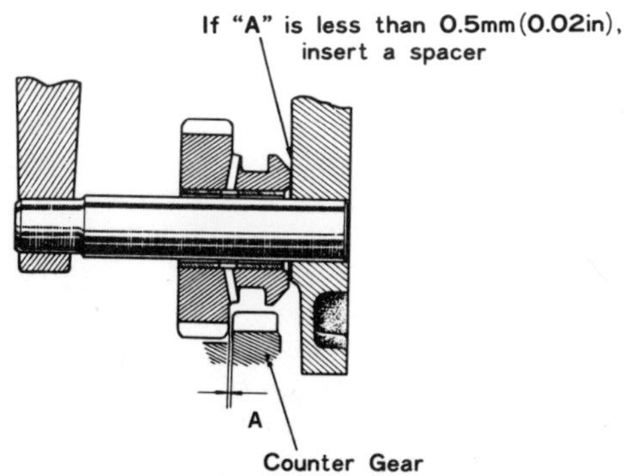


Checking reverse idler gear position.

21. Check end-clearance between reverse idler gear and countergear. Install shims, as needed, to correct fit. Tighten reverse idler shaft retaining screw to 10–13 ft. lbs.

22. Install the three detent balls and springs and tighten cover bolts to 3–7 ft. lbs.

23. Loosen locknut and unscrew reverse shift arm pivot bolt. Adjust clearance between reverse idler gear teeth and teeth of countergear so that there is 0.060″ clearance in neutral. Tighten locknut.

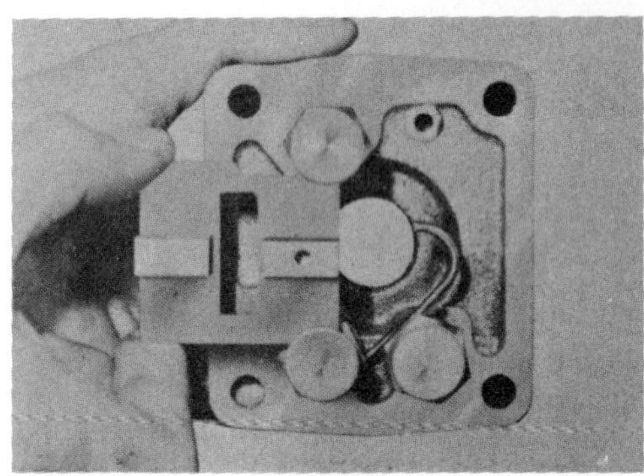

Installing interlock plate.

24. Check clearance between bottom of reverse idler gear groove and top of reverse shift arm. Correct clearance is 0.020–0.060″; adjustable at the pivot. Check that reverse gear does not touch reverse idler gear when first gear is engaged.

25. Install extension housing (with bushing and seal) and tighten bolts to 15–20 ft. lbs.

26. Install speedometer pinion and sleeve (pre-oiled).

27. Grease (or oil) the interlock plate and install onto gear lever retainer plate.

28. Position shift rails in neutral, then bolt gear lever retainer plate to case.

29. Check all clearances and check for smooth gear operation before tightening the cover bolts. Maximum torque on these bolts is 5.0 ft. lbs.

30. Apply light coat of Lubriplate to clutch release bearing sleeve and fork. Install and tighten clutch fork bolt to 14–22 ft. lbs.

31. Test and install back up switch and wires.

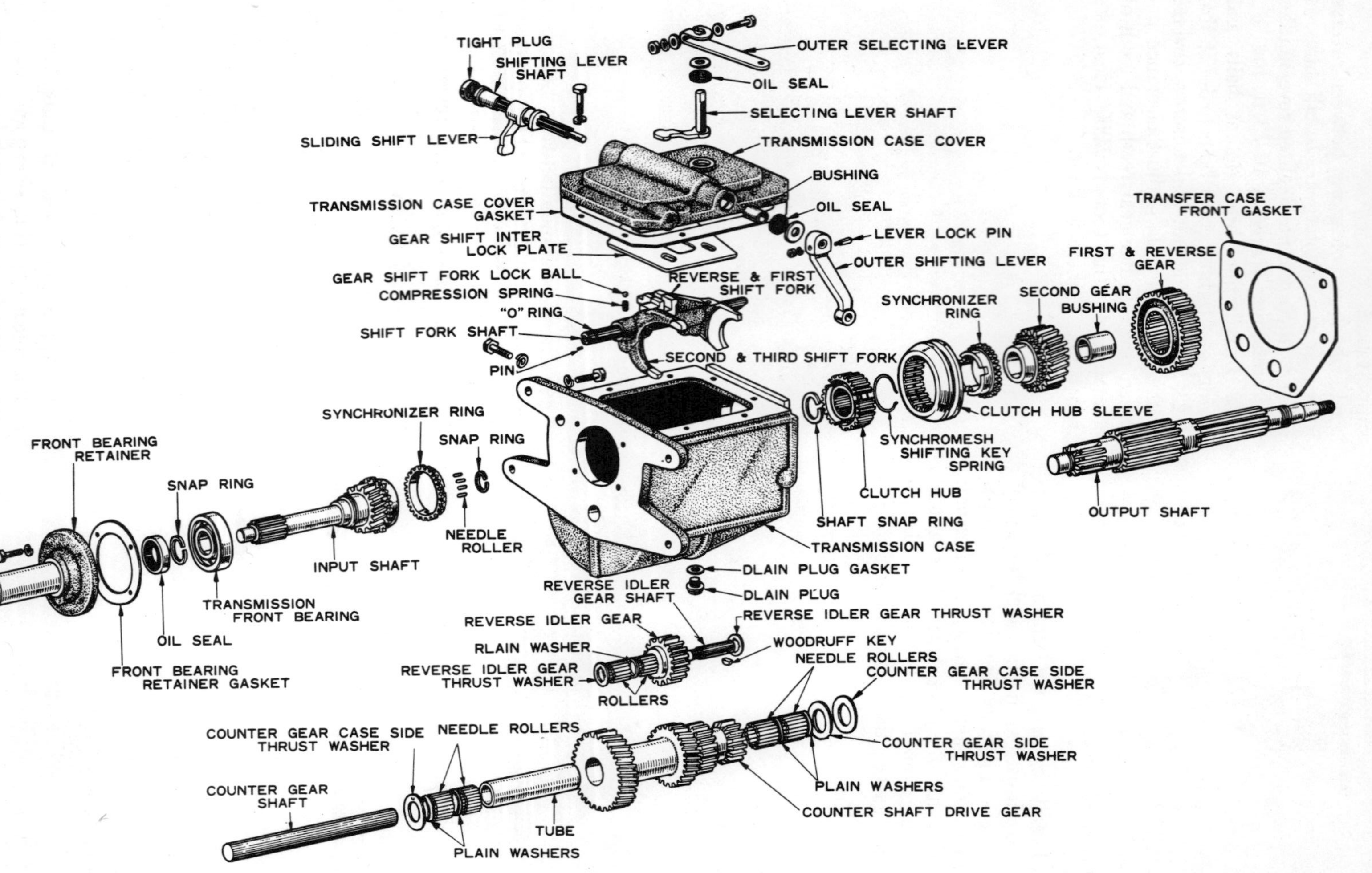


Land Cruiser three-speed transmission is similar to Corona unit.

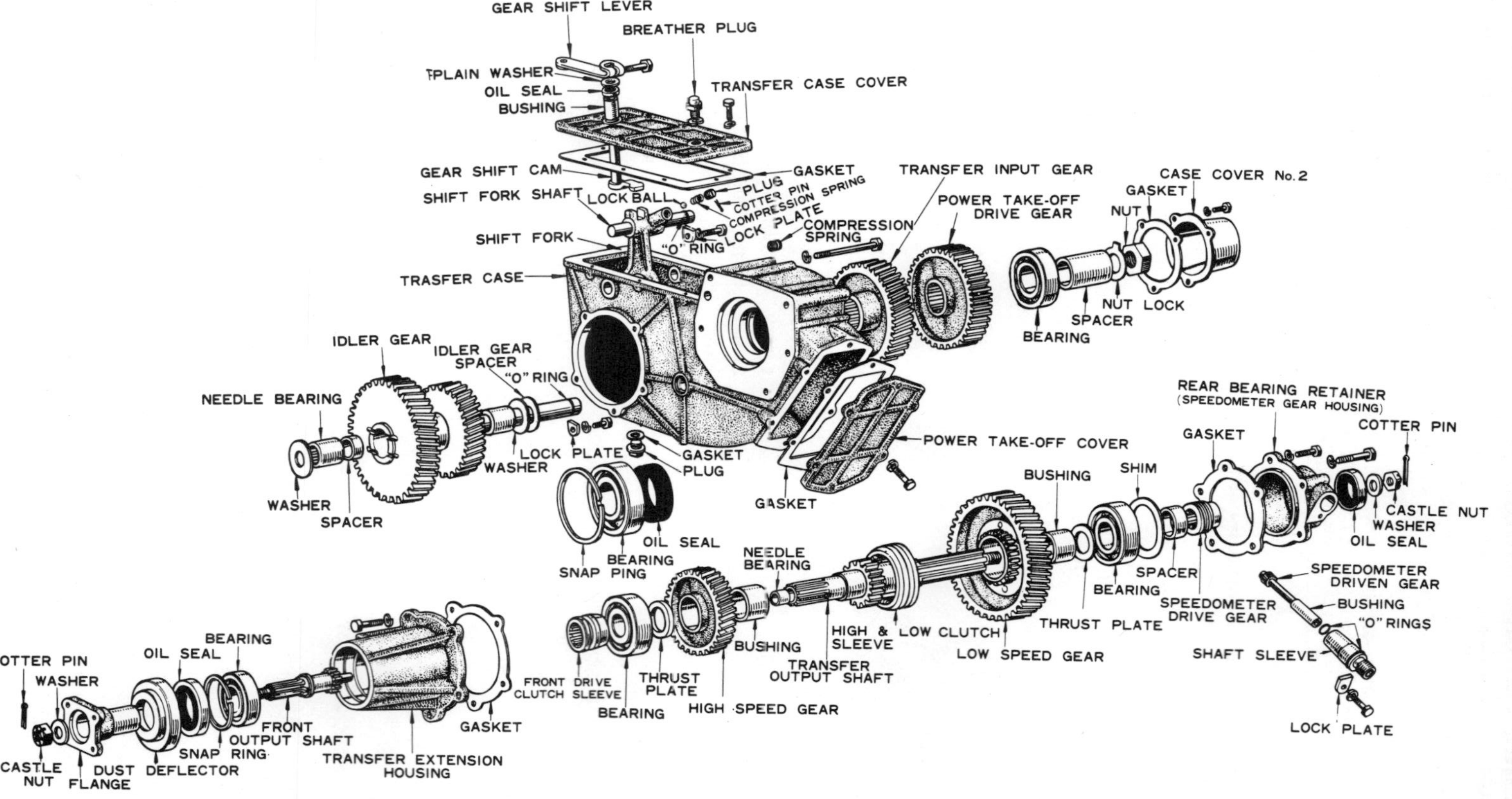


Land Cruiser four-wheel drive transfer case.

## Torque Specifications

| | |
|---|---|
| Case to engine | 36–50 ft. lbs. |
| Case to stiffener plate | 11–16 ft. lbs. |
| Case to starter motor | 25–32 ft. lbs. |
| Extension housing to rear mount | 15–22 ft. lbs. |
| Rear mount to crossmember | 22–32 ft. lbs. |
| Crossmember to body (chassis) | 25–40 ft. lbs. |

### Disassembling Standard Three-Speed Transmission

First, remove the clutch release fork, then the front bearing retainer and case cover. Remove the cotter pin from the straight screw plug, then remove the plug, lock ball and compression spring. Loosen and re-

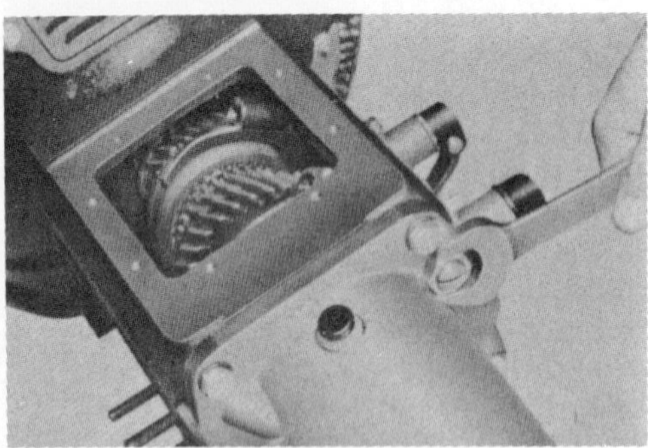

Loosening locknut—three-speed.

move the fork shaft screw plug, then place a brass drift on one end of the fork shaft and drive the shaft out of the case (to the rear). Remove the shift forks and the extension housing. (It helps to move the hub

Removing reverse idler shaft—three-speed.

sleeve to the third gear position.) Remove the synchronizer ring from the input shaft, place a brass drift on the front of the countershaft, and drive the shaft out (to the rear). Remove the input shaft, thrust washers and countergear (it fell to the bottom of the case), then, using the brass drift, drive the reverse idler gear shaft out (to the rear).

Removing shaft—three-speed.

Remove the outer shift lever lock pin, shift levers, cotter pin and interlock support shaft. Unscrew the four shift shaft housing bolts and remove the housing from the case. To remove the 12 rollers in the input shaft, first remove the snap-ring. Using snap-ring pliers, unhook the output shaft snap-ring and pull all components from the shaft. Now, remove the speedometer driven gear from the extension housing, expand the out-

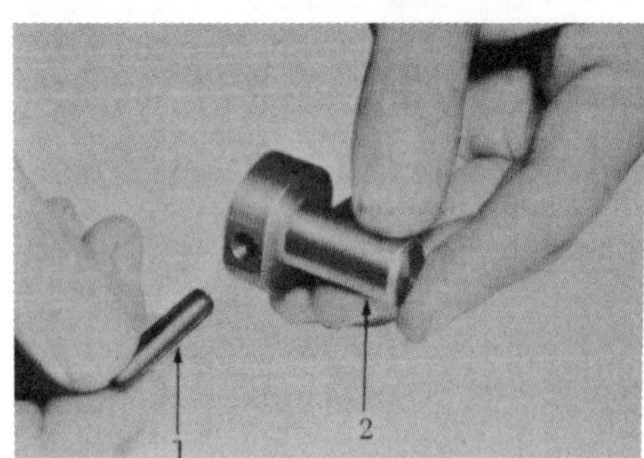


Removing dowel pin—three-speed.

put shaft snap-ring and drive the shaft forward and out of the housing. Clamp the shaft in a vise, remove the snap-ring that holds the speedometer drive gear and remove the gear and oil baffle.

The rear bearing is secured with a snap-ring. Although it is recommended that the bearing be pressed off the shaft with an arbor press, striking one end of the shaft sharply on a hardwood block often is sufficient.

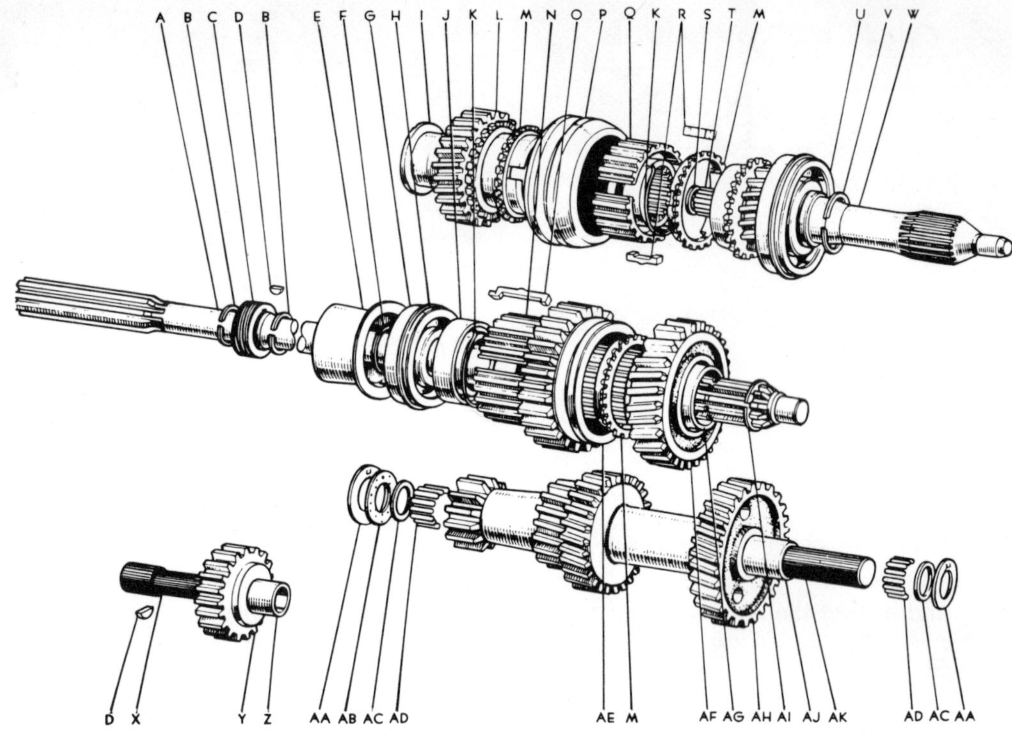


Corona three-speed transmission internal parts.

A. Output shaft
B. Shaft snap-ring
C. Speedometer drive gear
D. Woodruff key
E. Extension housing oil baffle subassembly
F. Shaft snap-ring
G. Bearing
H. Shaft snap-ring
I. Second gear bushing
J. Shifting key retainer
K. Synchromesh shifting key spring
L. Second gear
M. Synchronizer ring No. 2
N. Transmission clutch hub No. 1
O. Synchromesh shifting key No. 1
P. Transmission hub sleeve
Q. Transmission clutch hub No. 2
R. Synchromesh shifting key
S. Hole snap-ring
T. Roller
U. Bearing
V. Shaft snap-ring
W. Input shaft
X. Reverse idler gear shaft
Y. Reverse idler gear subassembly
Z. Solid bushing
AA. Countergear case side thrust washer
AB. Countergear side thrust washer
AC. Spacer
AD. Roller
AE. First and reverse gear
AF. First gear
AG. First gear bushing
AH. Countergear
AI. Shaft snap-ring
AJ. Tube
AK. Countershaft

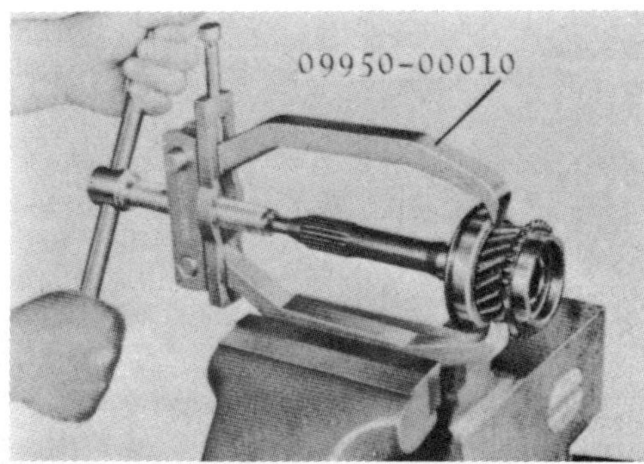


Removing front bearing—three-speed.

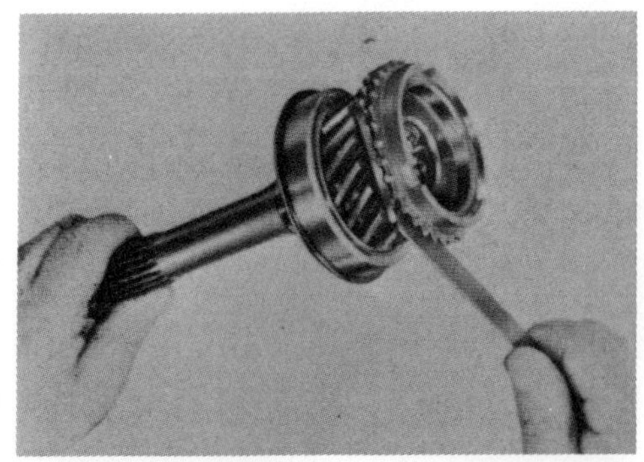

Inspecting synchronizer ring—three-speed.

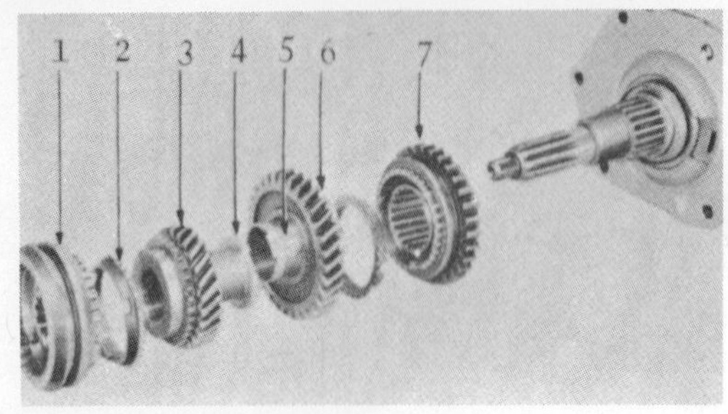


Removing the clutch hub and sleeve—three-speed.

1. Clutch hub and sleeve
2. Synchronizer ring
3. Second gear
4. Second gear bushing
5. First gear bushing
6. First gear
7. Clutch hub, sleeve, first and reverse gear

### Transmission Inspection and Assembly

After disassembly, wash all parts thoroughly and inspect the front and rear bearings for roughness. Wash the bearings thoroughly in gasoline or carbon tet, then apply a few drops of light oil and spin by hand. Any scoring or roughness of the balls indicates an unusable bearing. The front bearing is replaced in the same manner as the rear; remove the snap-ring and press or pull the bearing from the shaft. Check the gears for tooth wear or chipping, then check the synchronizer ring cone for burrs or scoring. The synchronizer teeth are especially susceptible to wear, the result of which is grinding during shifting. Place the ring on its cone and check the clearance between the gear and ring; it should be greater than 0.040″. Check all bushings for abnormal wear and/or scoring, then examine the countershaft and input shaft rollers for pits or roughness. If the rollers are badly scored it is almost impossible to effect a lasting repair without replacing the roller bearing surfaces—the shafts themselves in this case.

To assemble, install the shifting key retainer and the rear bearing onto the output shaft, then select a snap-ring thick enough to reduce the longitudinal play of the rear bearing to the smallest possible value. Assemble the oil baffle, then install snap-ring, speedometer drive gear and its snap-ring. Install the output shaft assembly into the extension housing, securing it with a thick enough snap-ring that play in the housing is kept to a minimum. Now, install the speedometer driven gear and the shaft sleeve.

Install the shifting keys and the first and reverse gear into the clutch hub, with the flat sides of the keys facing the groove in the first and reverse gear. Install the key lock rings with their ends 120° apart (to keep tension equal), then install the completed assembly onto the output shaft, fitting the shifting keys into their retainer in the process. Slide the first gear bushing onto the output shaft; assemble the synchronizer ring and first gear and slide them on next. Slide the second gear bushing onto the shaft, aligning the notches with the first gear bushing; slide second gear onto shaft.

Assemble the three shifting keys and the other clutch hub sleeve and install into

Assembling clutch hub—three-speed.

1. Locking rings
2. Shift keys
3. Clutch hub
4. First and reverse gear

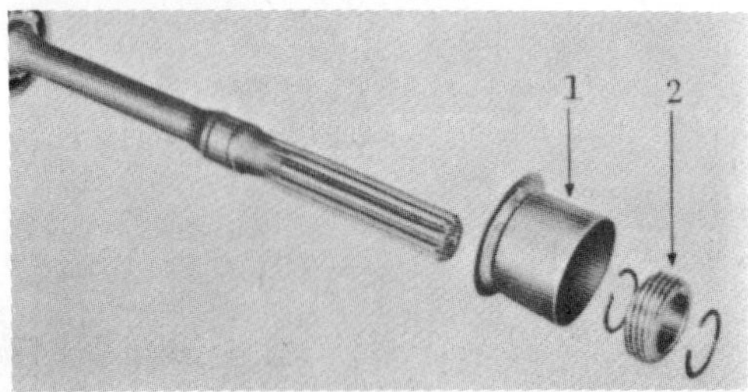


Assembling speedometer drive gear—three-speed.

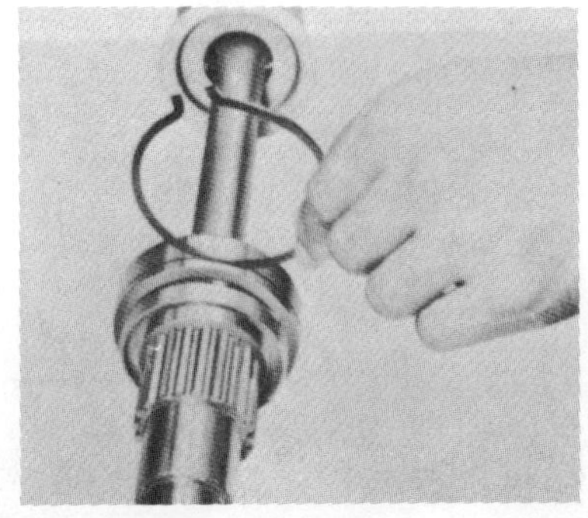

Fitting snap-ring—three-speed.

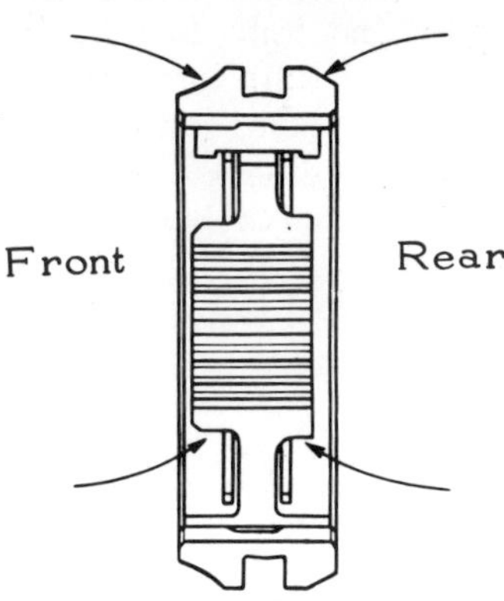


Clutch hub correctly installed—three speed.

clutch hub, installing the key lock rings 120° apart as before, then slide the assembled unit onto the output shaft. Select and install a snap-ring having enough thickness to result in 0.004–0.010″ second gear

Assembling synchronizer rings—three-speed.

Assembling bushing—three-speed.

thrust gap, then pack the input shaft with wheel bearing grease and insert the twelve bearing rollers and snap-ring. Assemble the gearshift lever mechanism and install into transmission case (from the inside), then hook up shift levers. Install the reverse idler gear and shaft (embossed side facing front) and lock the shaft using a Woodruff key. Assemble the countergear and its rollers (23 per end), spacer tubes and thrust washers,

Assembling first gear—three-speed.

Assembling bushing—three-speed.

Assembling second gear—three-speed.

Assembling clutch hub—three-speed.

holding the assembly together with a dummy shaft. Lay the assembly in the bottom of the transmission case, press the front bearing onto the input shaft (using a snap-ring of proper thickness to keep play to a minimum) and install the input shaft into the transmission case. Bolt the front bearing retainer and paper gasket to the front of the case, install Woodruff key into the countergear cut-out, then push countergear shaft through the case and gear, thus displacing the dummy shaft. *NOTE: Make sure the Woodruff key is lined up properly.*

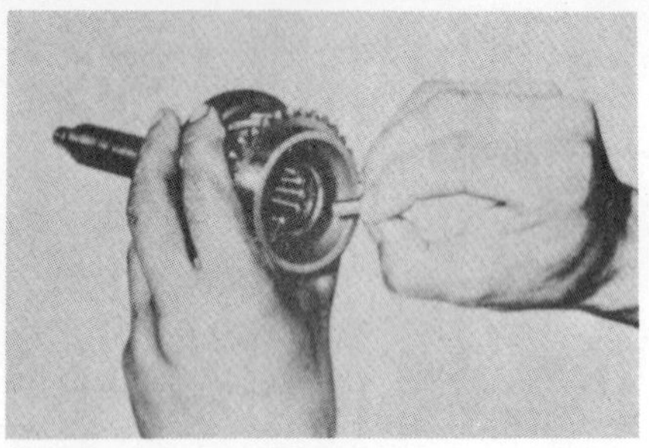

Inserting rollers into mainshaft—three-speed.

Inserting rollers into countershaft—three-speed.

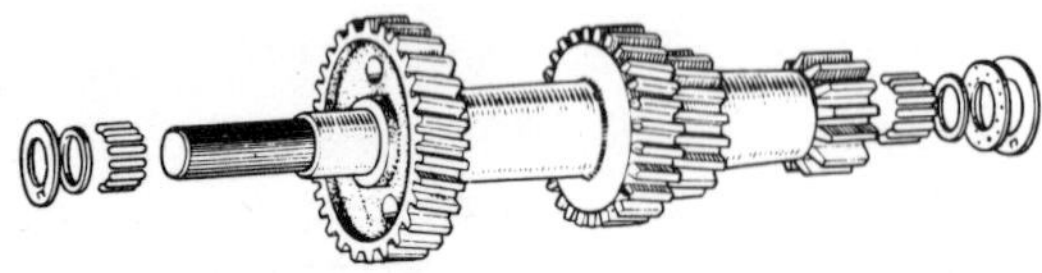

Countergear and shaft components—three-speed.

With the countergear installed, measure its thrust play using a feeler gauge. Specified clearance is 0.002–0.010", which can be corrected using different thrust washers. Install the third speed synchronizer ring onto the input shaft gear, then install the extension housing, lining up all notches and keys. *NOTE: Before installing, position hub sleeve in third gear position.* Check the clearance between the clutch hub sleeve, third gear and second gear; the sum of these clearances must be greater than 0.40". This clearance can be corrected using different gaskets, plus liquid sealer.

Install first and reverse shift fork and second and third shift fork onto first and reverse gear and hub sleeve, respectively. Now, insert the shift fork shaft from the rear, the even grooves toward the front of the transmission. Lock the shaft in place with the screw plug, then insert the lock balls and springs into the forks and screw the plugs in so that only one thread shows

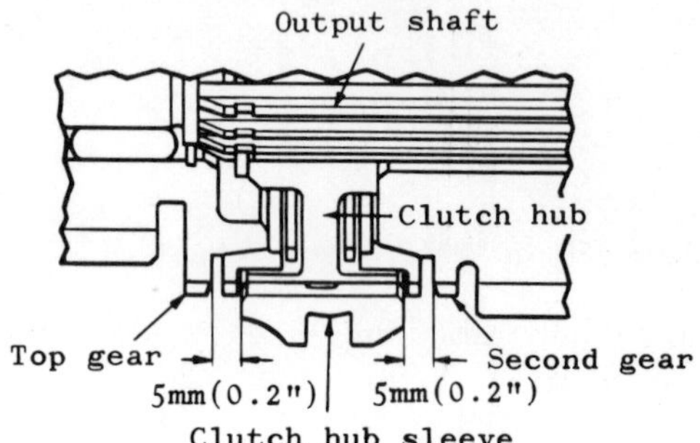


Selecting gasket.

above the fork surface. Secure using cotter pins. Install the case cover, after first making sure the transmission gears move without binding and the shift levers select the proper gears.

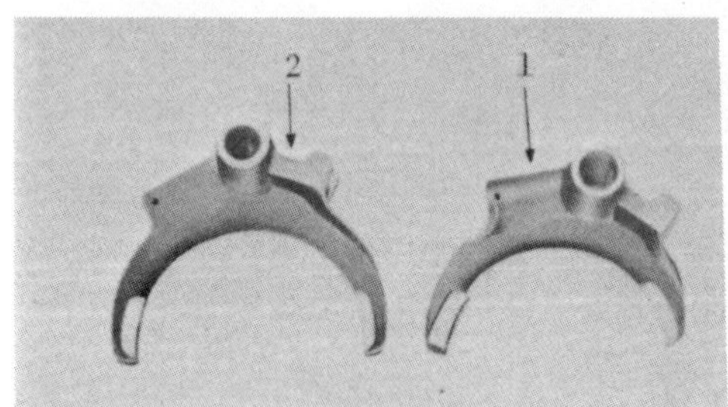


Gearshift forks; (1) is first and reverse, (2) is second and third.

## Disassembling Standard Four-Speed Transmission

Remove all switches and wires, then drain oil. Remove side cover and take out third-fourth shift fork and shaft. Drive pin from fork; catch detent ball. Remove all five lock pins from side cover. Next, remove first-second shift fork and shaft in same manner. Loosen and remove the reverse restrict ball holder, ball and spring. Cut wire and remove shift lever lock bolt, then remove shift and selector lever shaft and the sliding shift lever. Remove reverse shift arm pivot bolt, drive out pin and remove the reverse shift head and shaft (catch the spring-loaded detent ball).

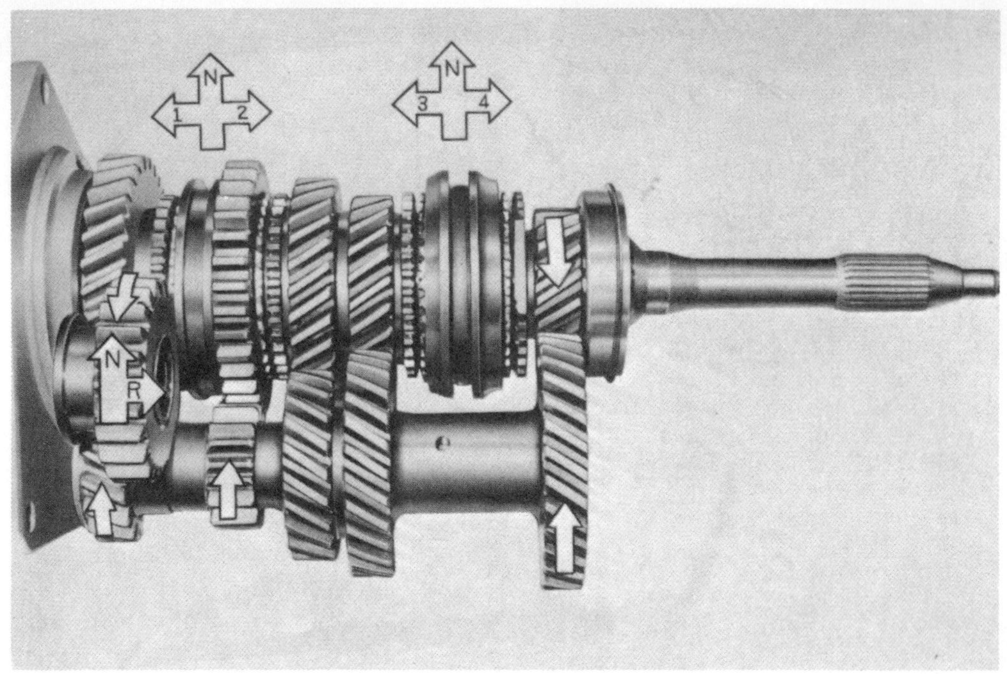


Four-speed transmission power flow.

Remove the front bearing retainer housing (six bolts), and the five bolts from extension housing. Turn housing to expose cut-out for countershaft. Insert dummy countershaft (to keep needle rollers in place) and drop countergear so that output

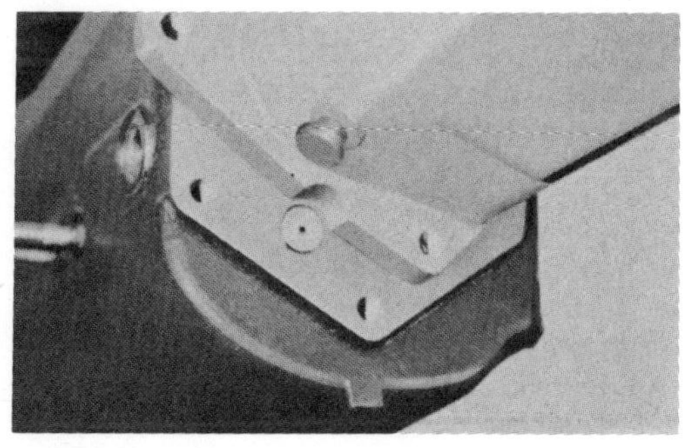

Aligning cutout with countershaft—four-speed.

shaft and all gears can be withdrawn to rear. Remove fourth gear synchronizer, align flat part of input shaft gear with countergear, and drive out to the front. Remove reverse idler gear and shaft, then lift out countergear, along with dummy shaft. *NOTE: There is a Woodruff key in rear of countershaft.*

Remove snap-ring and take off third-fourth synchronizer mechanism. Mark all synchronizer rings if they are going to be

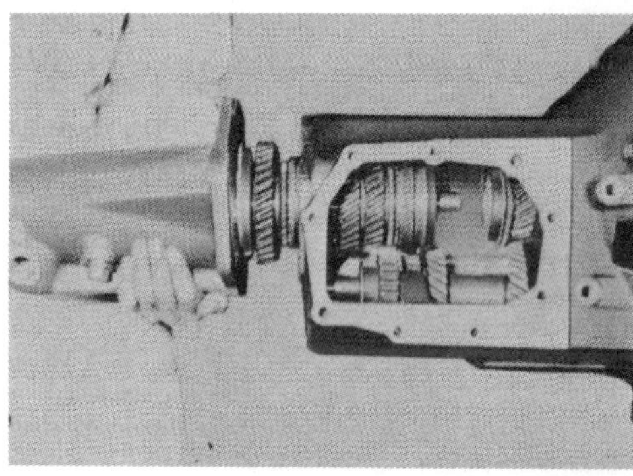

Removing output shaft assembly—four-speed.

used again; first gear ring has a groove, all others are unmarked. Remove third gear, bushing and synchronizer ring. Remove second gear and bushing, then remove reverse gear with clutch hub for first and second gears. Remove speedometer and extension housing. Expand rear baffle snap-ring and press shaft from extension housing. Remove speedometer drive gear and snap-rings, then remove rear bearing snap-ring and press off rear bearing and gear.

### Inspecting the Standard Four-Speed Transmission

Check all gears for wear and damaged teeth. Test bearings for wear and noise. Check synchronizer rings carefully for wear or tooth damage. Hand press synchronizer ring onto gear seat and measure the clearance between; if less then 0.040″, replace ring. Check gear bushings, shift forks and thrust washers for wear.

### Assembling the Standard Four-Speed Transmission

Generally this is the reverse of disassembly. Certain measurements must be taken and clearances adjusted during this process.

*Remote control shift side cover assembly* The clearance between side cover and outer shift lever should be 0.120–0.200″. Use shims, if necessary. Install the pivot pin and arm with the eccentric side of the pin facing the outer side of the side cover, then seal threads on pin with liquid sealer.

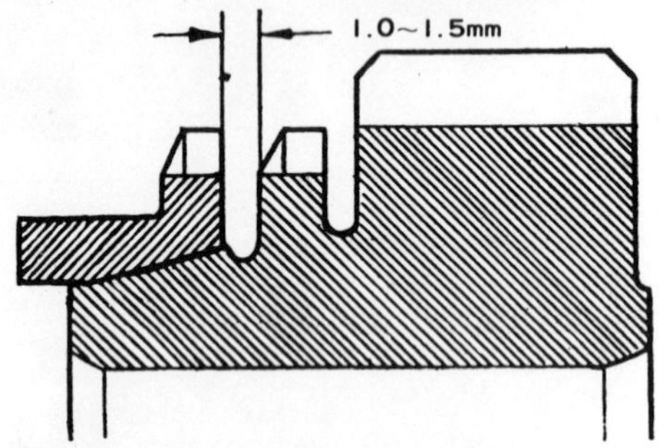

Inspecting synchronizer ring—four-speed.

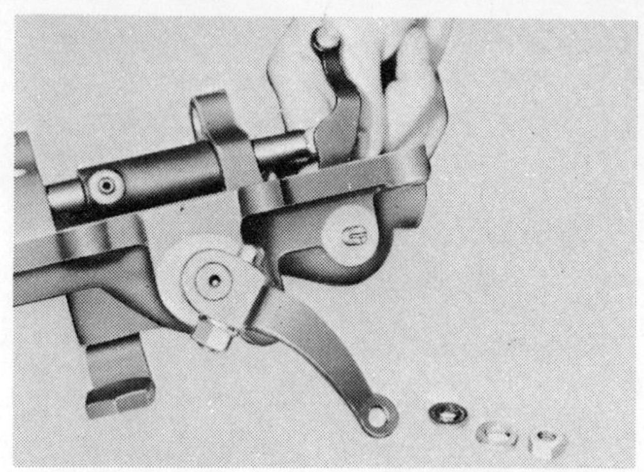
Installing pivot pin and arm—four-speed.

Installing shift arm and pivot pin—four-speed.

*Floor shift side cover assembly* Install reverse shift head shaft lock ball and spring into side cover, depress spring and slide reverse shift head shaft into place. Install reverse shift arm and pivot pin (with sealer on threaded portion) with eccentric side towards cover, then install a washer (inside) and the seal. Lockwasher and nut go on from the outside. (Tighten only finger-tight for later adjustment.) Install shift and selector shafts; lock bolts and wire in place. Install reverse restrict ball, spring and holder, tighten securely, then install slotted pin into reverse fork shaft and head. Install reverse, first and second gear interlock pins, then install first-second shift fork, lock ball and spring. Push down and slide first-second shift shaft into place. Install slotted pin. Install third-fourth interlock pins and the lock ball and springs, as above.

*Extension housing* Place rear bearing onto output shaft and press into place. Select snap-ring to obtain minimum end-play

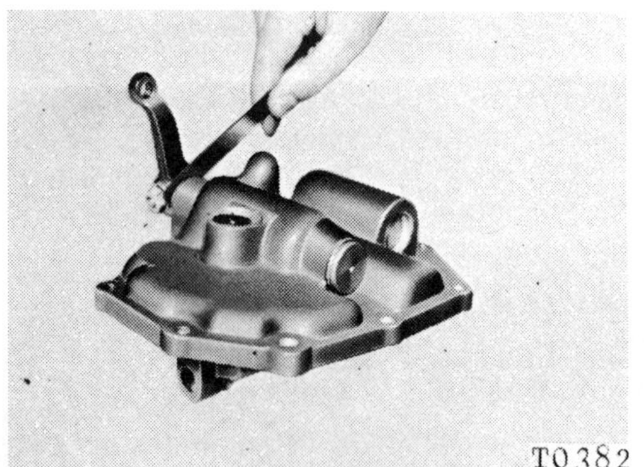

Checking lever clearance—four-speed.

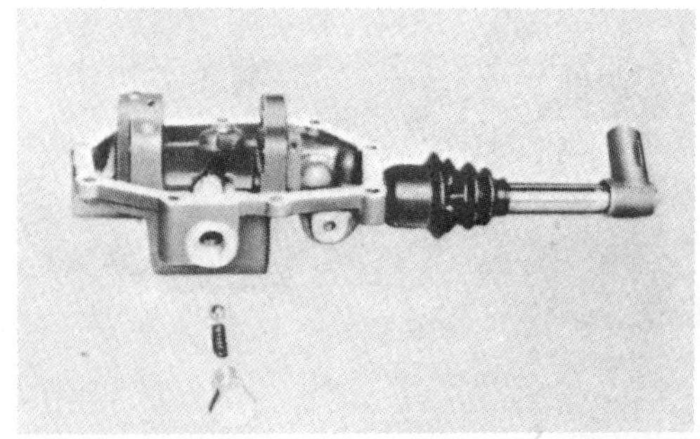
Installing restrict ball and holder—four-speed.

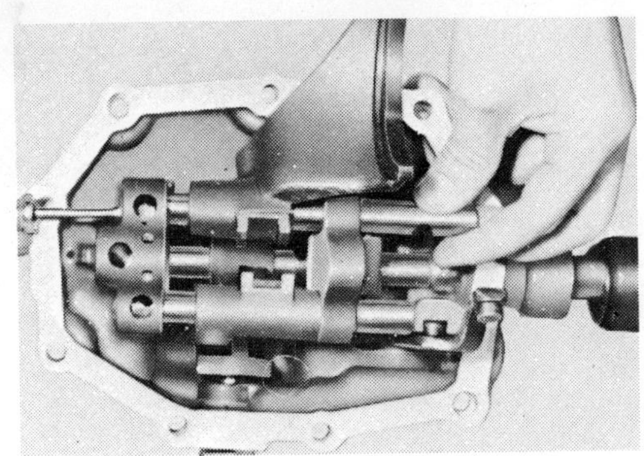

Installing first and second shift fork shaft—four-speed.

(there are two sizes available), then install oil baffle, snap-ring, speedometer drive gear, key and rear snap-ring. Press output shaft into extension housing and select proper snap-ring.

*Main or output shaft and gears* Assemble in reverse order of disassembly. *NOTE: The first gear synchronizer ring is marked with a groove, the first-second synchronizer*

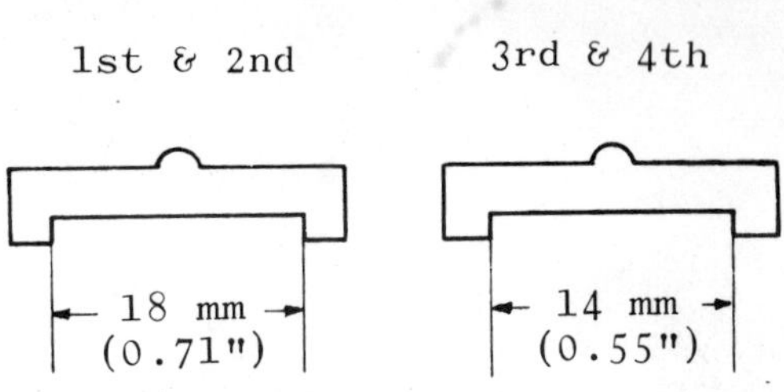


Shift key dimensions—four-speed.

*shift keys are different from the third-fourth keys, and there are 25 needles at each end of the countergear.* Rear extension housing bolts are tightened to 21–28 ft. lbs.; the input shaft retainer bolts to 3–5 ft. lbs. Countergear end-play is 0.002–0.010″.

To adjust reverse pivot pin, first position all gears in neutral. Turn pivot pin clockwise until the reverse idler gear contacts first (counter) gear, then turn pin counterclockwise 90°. Seal and tighten locknut. If no contact is felt, set the pin at 60° from horizontal.

Synchronizer ring grooves—four-speed.

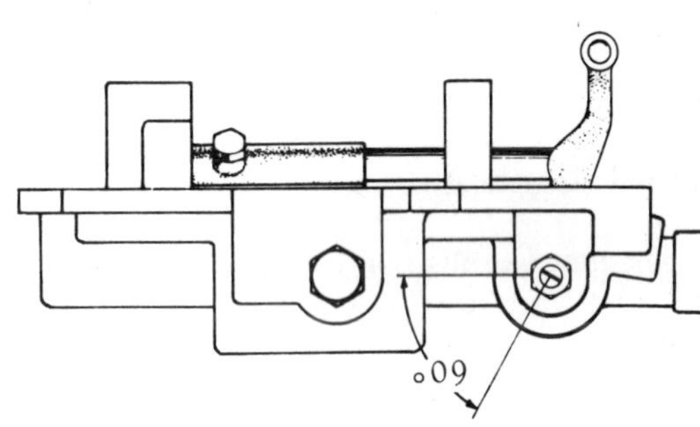


Adjusting pivot pin angle—four-speed.

# Chapter 7
# Automatic Transmission

## General

Two- and three-speed transmissions are currently in use. All late model Crown and all Mark II models use the three-speed transmission, while the Corona and the early Crown use the two-speed (RT) transmission.

The new Corolla two-speed unit is slightly different from the RT type, having only one band and two clutches, whereas the RT type has only one clutch and uses two bands. All (except early RT series) have floorshift controls. The two-speed types are of a design similar to the domestic Powerglide and the three-speed is similar to the Borg Warner transmission.

Coded serial numbers are stamped in the left rear side of the transmission case.
Example of code: 9B–1097
9=1969 B=2nd month (February)
All transmissions use automatic transmission fluid Type A, Suffix A only. No additives are recommended.

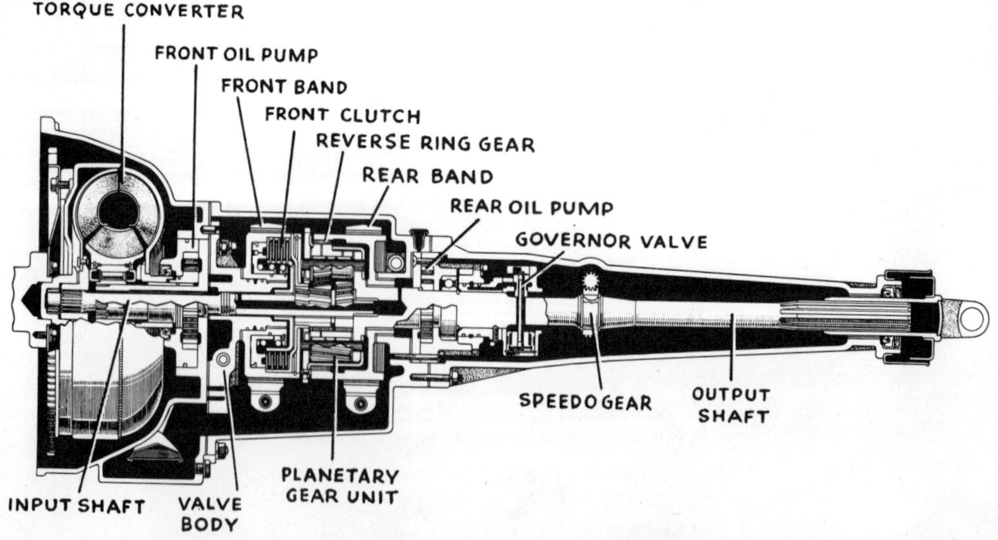


Corona automatic transmission.

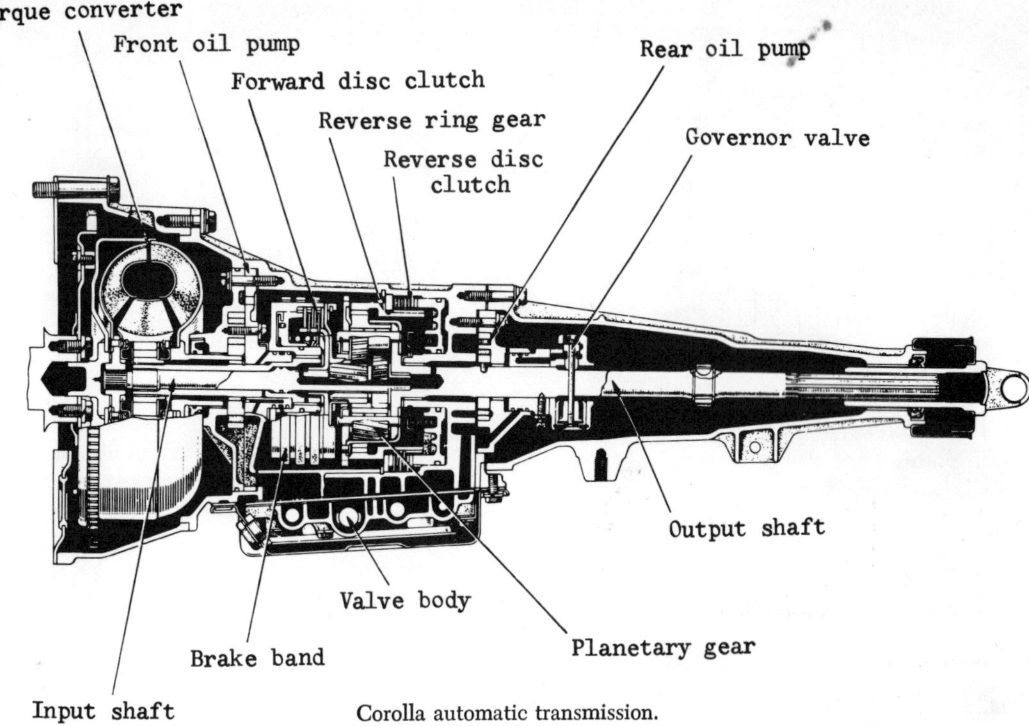


Corolla automatic transmission.

## Principles of Operation

The two-speed transmission consists of:

1. Torque converter
2. Planetary gear unit—with clutches and bands
3. Hydraulic control system—valve bodies.

The torque converter transforms (converts) engine power (torque) automatically and continuously in direct response to varying demands (load and speed). Its components are the *impeller,* driven by the engine, the *turbine,* splined to the transmission input shaft, and the *stator,* mounted on the transmission case by means of a one-way, or free-wheeling "sprag" clutch. The converter is sealed and cannot be drained when installed in the car. Maximum torque conversion is 2.6:1 at stall speed; hydraulic lock-up takes place when turbine speed is 85% of impeller speed. Transmission fluid is pumped from the converter through a cooler, located in the lower radiator tank. The fluid lubricates the gears on its return to the oil pan.

The planetary gear unit consists of a primary (high), and a secondary (low) sun gear, three long primary (high) and three short secondary (low) pinions assembled into one carrier with an internal gear splined to the output shaft. A number of clutches and bands are used to obtain the various gear ratios desired.

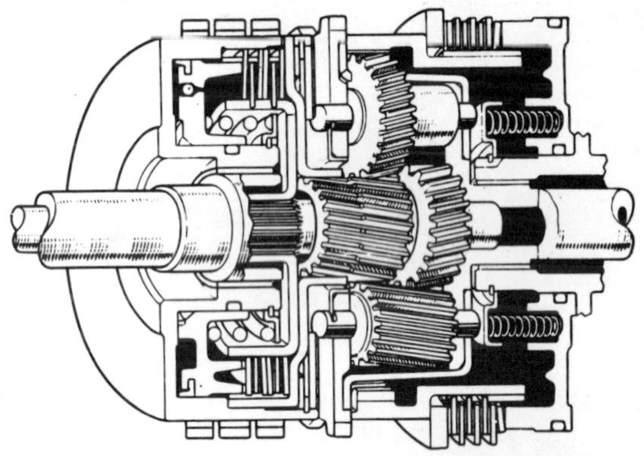

Planetary gear mechanism.

The KE forward clutch has two clutch (drive) discs and four clutch (driven) plates. Engagement is hydraulic, disengagement by compression spring. RT models have three clutch (drive) discs and seven clutch (driven) plates. The clutch is applied and released hydraulically, with a spring assist on release. All clutch plates are slightly dish-shaped for better release. A check ball valve is incorporated in the clutch piston. Application rotates the low sun gear, "D" (high).

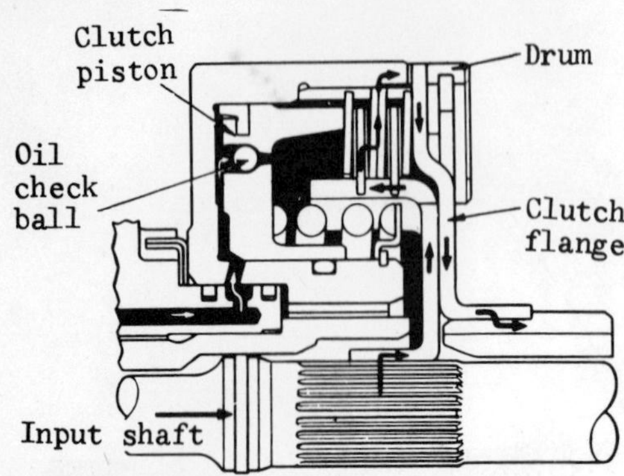

Clutch application.

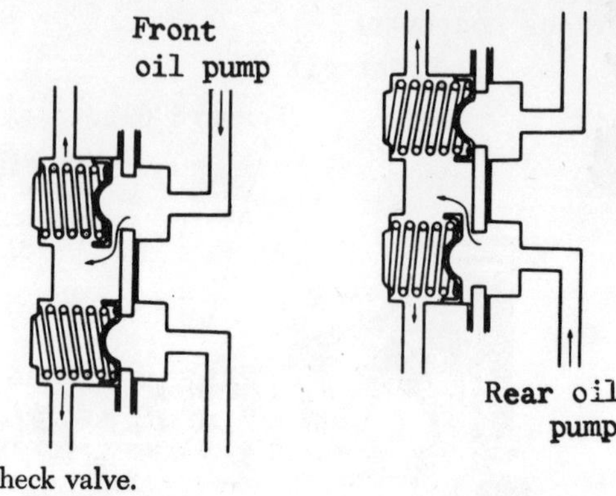

Check valve.

The KE reverse clutch has three discs and four plates (not dished). Applied hydraulically and released by spring pressure, the reverse clutch stops the reverse ring gear.

All low servo cylinders are integral with the housing, band adjustment is external and application and release are hydraulic.

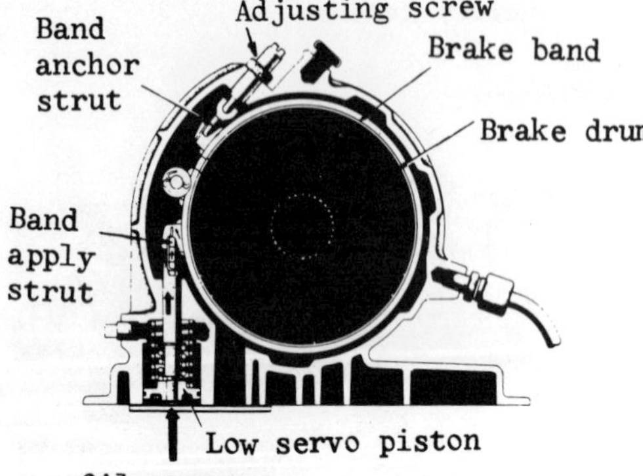

Brake band.

Closing of low band (on forward clutch drum) results in "D" (low).

The RT reverse servo is similar in operation to the low servo; it closes on the planetary ring gear and results in "R" (reverse).

The hydraulic control system consists of two oil pumps and a valve body. Four different hydraulic pressures are utilized to select the proper drive range; all depend upon throttle opening, gear selector position and load requirements (road speed).

The front oil pump, driven by the engine, generates pressure to operate low and reverse drive ranges, circulates fluid to the converter and oil cooler and handles all lubricating demands.

The rear oil pump, driven by the drive shaft, delivers greater pressure than the front pump, although its capacity is lower. It only functions above 25 mph in "D".

The four hydraulic pressures developed by these two pumps are line pressure, throttle pressure, governor pressure and compensator pressure (throttle relay pressure on KE series transmissions).

*Line pressure,* generated by the front or rear pump, is delivered to the pressure regulator valve in the valve body, then to the shift valve. It operates clutches and bands and is normally 50–140 psi.

*Throttle pressure* is line pressure, controlled and regulated by the throttle valve opening. It is normally 0–128 psi.

*Governor pressure* is line pressure, controlled by the governor valve in direct relation to road speed. It ranges from 0–64 psi.

*Compensator pressure* is line pressure, controlled by both throttle opening and road speed. It ranges from 8–64 psi.

*NOTE: Valve bodies of the RT and KE models are completely different and are described separately.*

The Corolla (KE) valve body consists of seven valves, in addition to the output shaft-mounted governor. The manual valve is the equivalent of the shift lever; it opens and closes certain oil passages to obtain desired gears. The check valve, of which there are two, switch the oil flow from front to rear

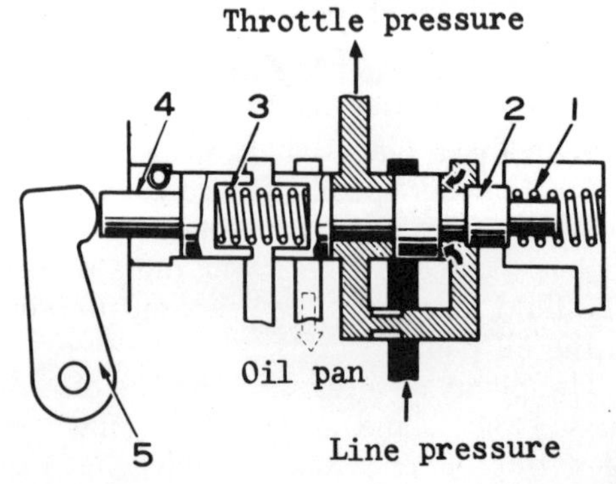

Throttle valve.

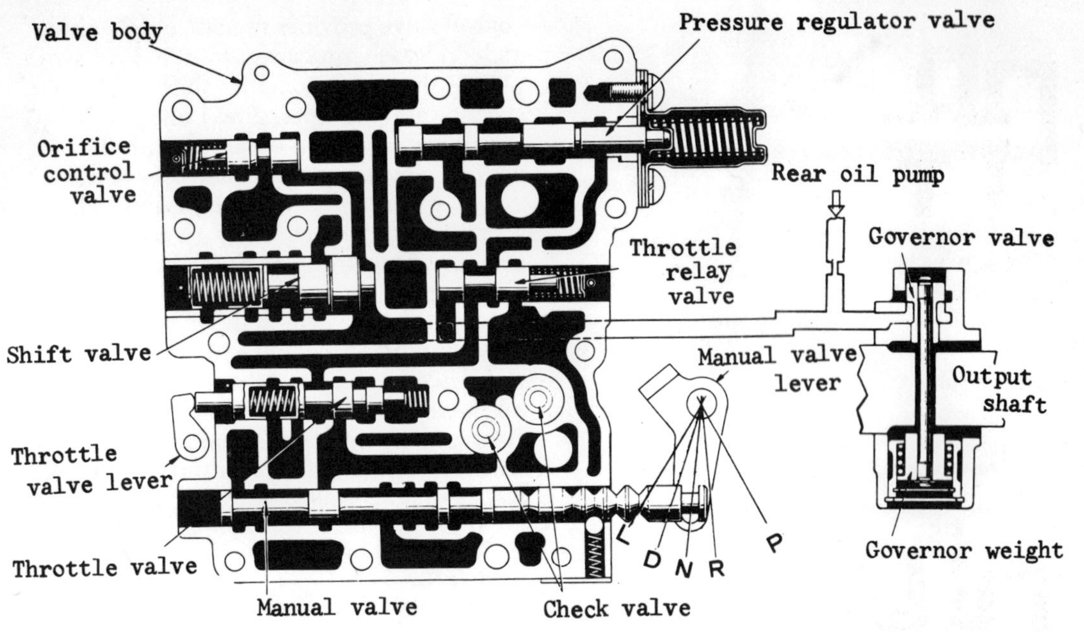


Valve body and governor valve.

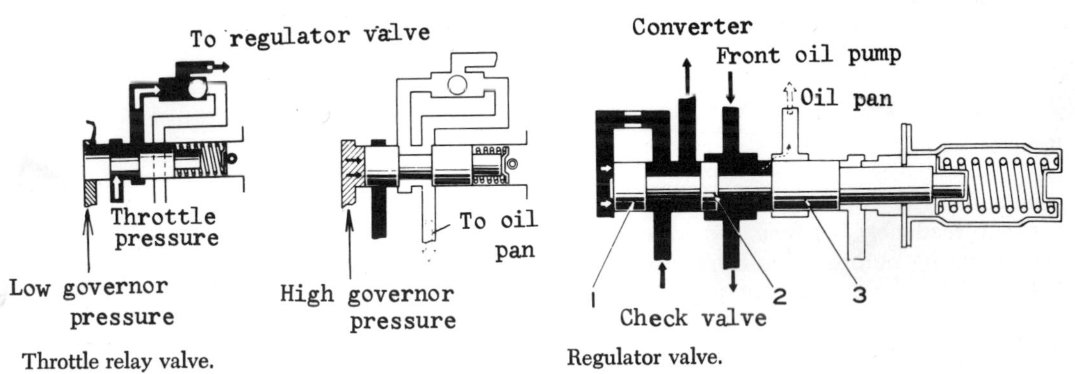


Throttle relay valve.

Regulator valve.

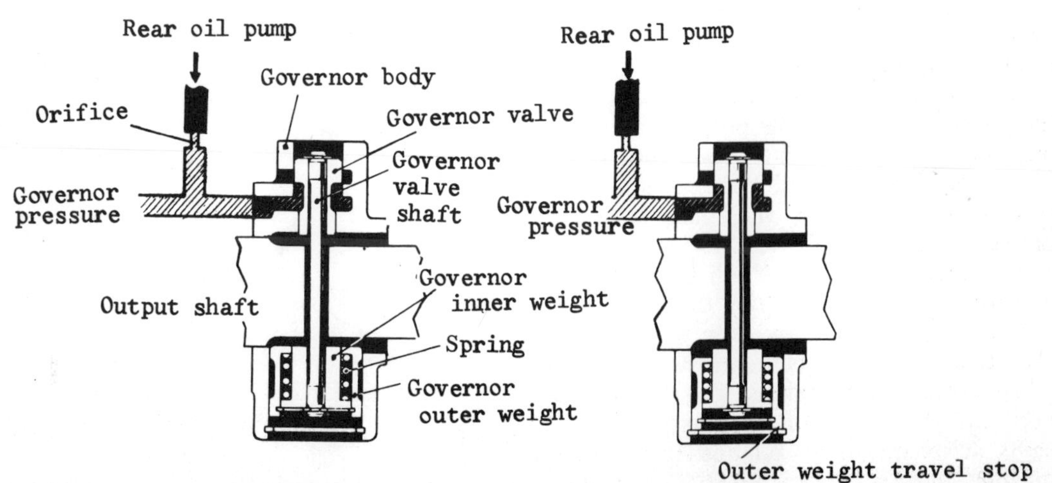


Governor valve.

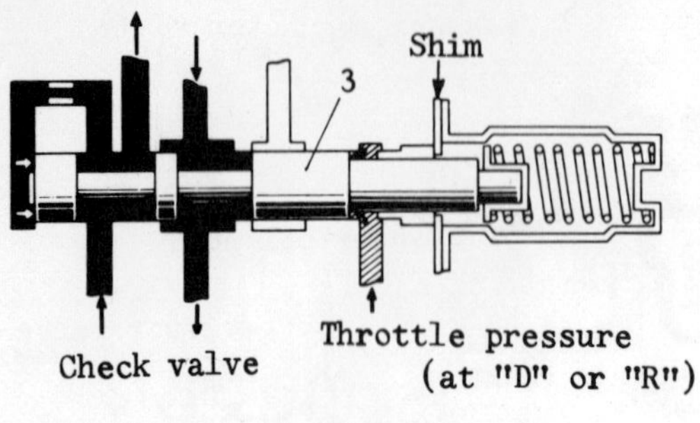


Regulator valve.

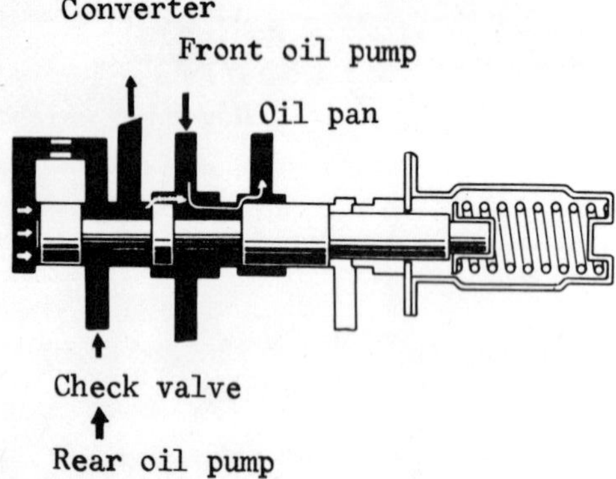


Regulator valve.

pump, and vice-versa, and at the same time prevent feedback between the idling and the operating pumps. The throttle valve is activated by the accelerator pedal; it controls throttle pressure in relation to engine load. It also controls the kickdown by mechanically overriding the hydraulic pressure so that throttle pressure can reach full line pressure. The throttle relay valve shuts off throttle pressure (at high speeds) to the pressure regulator valve. It is controlled by the governor valve and its purpose is to reduce line pressure at high speed, thus preventing hard shifting and reducing unnecessary power losses in the pumps. The pressure regulator valve controls line pressure, in accordance with both engine load and road speed, by changing throttle pressure in "D" and "R", and line pressure in "L". It also prevents converter "drain back" when engine is not running. The shift valve performs the first-second and second-first shifts automatically in relation to throttle opening and road speed in "D" only. Due to valve design, the downshift (second-first) always will take place at a lower speed than the upshift (first-second). The orifice control valve provides smooth, quick "apply" and "release" pressures to the low servo piston during automatic shifts. At high speeds (and high pressures) oil is delivered through an orifice to obtain smooth shifting, and, at lower speeds and pressures, the valve bypasses the restriction and delivers a large amount of oil to ensure quick, smooth engagement of clutch and/or servo.

The governor valve, although physically not part of the valve body, is nonetheless a very important component. Mounted on, and driven by, the output shaft, it regulates oil pressure in direct relation to road speed. Rear pump pressure is controlled by centrifugal force acting on the governor weights and spring.

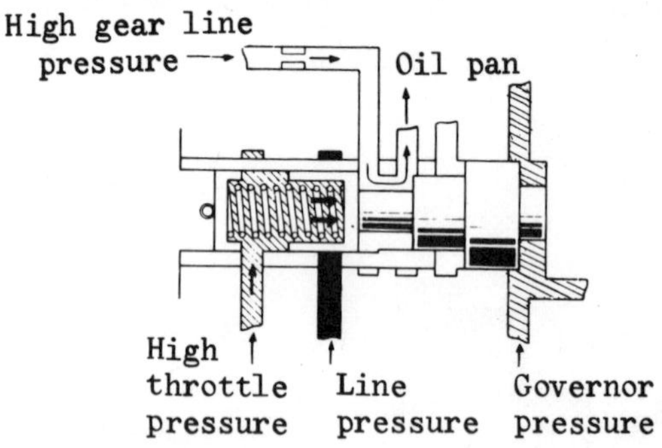


Shift valve.

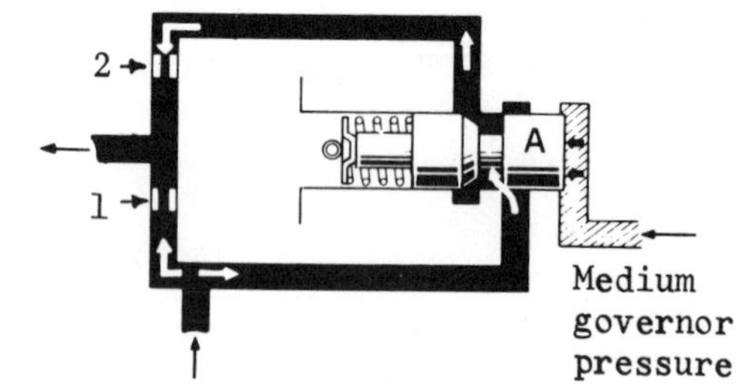


Orifice control valve.

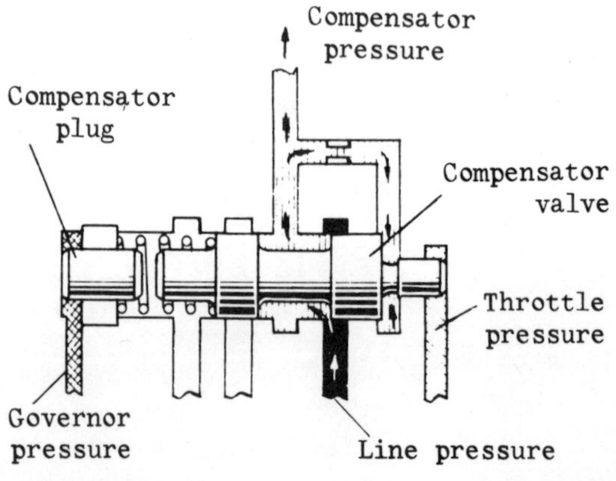


Compensator valve.

### Corona (RT) Valve Body

Different in size and shape from the KE valve body, this unit also has seven valves, in addition to a governor valve. Main differences are with the check valve and compensator valve.

## Operation of Hydraulic Circuits

*"D" (drive) range* Both the low and the high range lines are under pressure, controlled by the compensator valve. In "D" low, the shift valve closes off the high line and pressure is directed to the low servo only. In "D" high, the shift valve, under pressure from the throttle valve, shuts off pressure to the low servo and directs the pressure flow to the forward clutch and the *release* side of the low servo. In the kickdown position, as the accelerator pedal is depressed the throttle valve moves, it shuts off pressure to the shift valve, which then drops back to the low position. Compensator pressure then drops and line pressure is stepped up.

*"L" (low) range* Pressure to the low servo is directed by the manual shift valve and no shift takes place.

*"R" (reverse) range* Pressure to the reverse servo is directed by the manual shift valve and no shift takes place. (On KE models, pressure is directed to the rear clutch.)

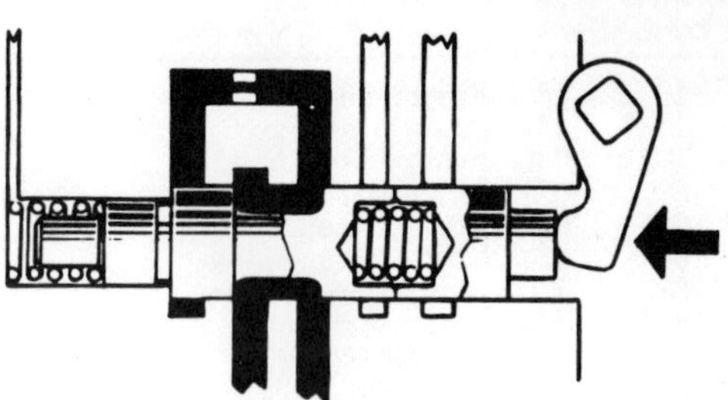

Kickdown operation.

## Hydraulic Line Pressure Tests—Corona (RT)

In order to obtain all the necessary information needed to make correct diagnosis, a series of tests with a 200 psi gauge must be made. There are six pressure points, as shown:

1. Front pump discharge pressure
2. Rear pump discharge pressure
3. Low servo operating pressure
4. Clutch operating pressure (also low servo release pressure)
5. Reverse servo operating pressure
6. Governor pressure (this point is located on the left side of the housing, all others are on the right side)

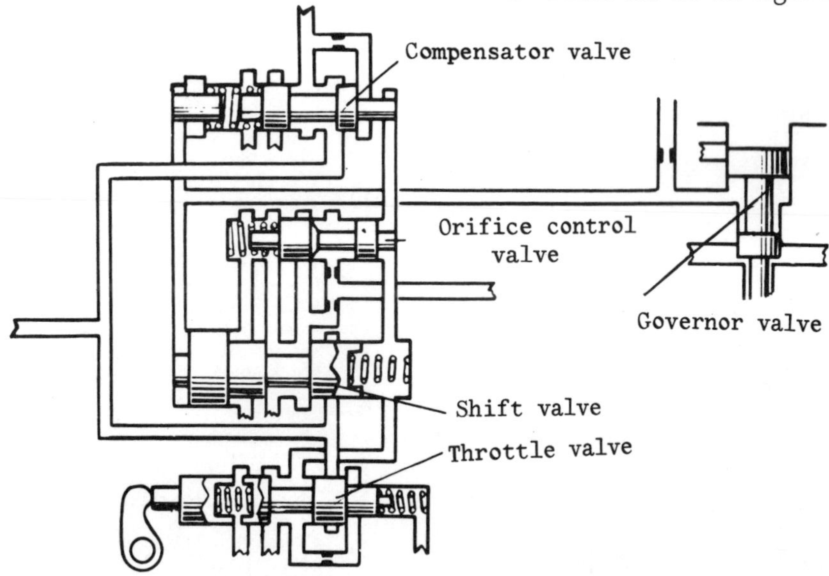


Hydraulic control system schematic.

## Chart AT-1
## Hydraulic Tests—Corona RT

| Test Point | Test Number | Type Test | Brakes | Drive Range | RPM | Speed (mph) | Pressure (psi) |
|---|---|---|---|---|---|---|---|
| 1 | 1* | Front pump output | on | N | 1,500–2,000 | 0 | 122–156 [4] |
| 1 | 2* | Pump crossover | off | D | — | 22–27 | drops to 3 |
| 2 | 3* | Rear pump output | off | D | — | 25 | minimum 34 |
| 3 | 4* | Low servo operation | off | D2 | 1,500 | — | 55–72 [4] |
| 3 | 5 | Low servo operation | off | D1 | 600 | — | 57–78 |
| 3 | 6 | Low servo operation | on | D | 1,500 | — | 116–122 [1] |
| 3 | 7 | Low servo operation | off | L | 1,500 | — | 135–156 |
| 4 | 8* | Clutch operation | off | D | 1,500 | — | 55–72 [2] |
| 5 | 9* | Reverse servo | off | R | 1,500 | — | 135–156 [4] |
| 6 | 10* | Governor | off | D2 | — | 25 | 34–40 |
| 6 | 11* | Governor | off | D | — | 38 | 50–54 |
| none | 12* | Stall Test | on | L, D, R | Max. possible | 0 | [3] |

(1) Throttle rod disconnected at transmission end and held fully open.
(2) This is also equal to low servo release pressure.
(3) Test each range separately; correct speed is 1,950–2,100 rpm.
(4) Difference between front pump and low servo operating pressure should not exceed 10 psi; same for reverse servo pressure.
*Caution: Check transmission fluid level BEFORE testing, or internal damage will result.*
* See chart below for possible problem areas.

## Test Key

| Test Number | Test Indications | What to Check |
|---|---|---|
| 1 | more than 160 psi | 2 |
| 1 | erratic pressure | 2, 13, 14 |
| 1 | less than 120 psi | 3, 13, 14 |
| 2 | no drop; drop and rise | 8 |
| 2 | drops at excessive speed | 8, 12 |
| 3 | more than 10 psi diff. (L) | 4 |
| 3 | more than 10 psi diff. (R) | 5 |
| 4 | less than 34 at idle | 3, 13, 19 |
| 4 | no increase | 2, 6 |
| 4 | less than 25 at kickdown (D) | 14 |
| 8 | less than 50 psi | 11, 12, 18 |
| 9 | less than 120 psi | 5, 10 |
| 10 | less than 30 psi | 14, 18 |
| 11 | less than 45 psi | 14, 18 |
| 12 | engine speed only 1,600 rpm | tune-up needed |
| 12 | engine turns only 1,200 rpm | 20 |

## Chart AT-2
## Automatic Transmission Diagnosis—Corona RT

| Action | What to Check |
|---|---|
| **Gear Engagements** | |
| None | 1, 20, J, E |
| No forward | 1, A, 3, 2, 4, 8, 9, E |
| No reverse | 1, A, 5, 3, 8, E |
| Delayed (all) | 1, A, 3, 5, E |
| Chatter (D) | 4, 9, D, 11, F |
| Chatter (R) | 5, 10, D, F |
| Hard (L) (D) | B, C, 2, 6, F |
| Hard (R) | B, C, 2, 6, F, G |
| **Shifts** | |
| Hard 1–2 | 9, 15, 7 |
| Slip 1–2 | 11, 17, 7, 14, 15 |
| No 1–2 | 1, 17, 14, 18, 6, E |
| Slip (R) | D, 10, 14 |
| Slip (L) | D, 11, 14 |
| Slip (D–high) | D, 9, 4, 14, 15 |
| No kickdown | D, 19 |
| Squeak on kickdown | 15 |
| Incorrect shift point | 19, C, D, 18 |
| **Miscellaneous** | |
| Excessive line pressure | 2, 6, 18 |
| No (D) or (L) after long reverse drive | 3, 12 |
| High fuel consumption | 20, H |
| No push start | 12, 14, 8 |
| Noise | 13, J, 15 |

## Check Points for Charts AT-1 and AT-2

| Code Number | What to Check |
|---|---|
| 1 | Oil level |
| 2 | Stuck pressure regulator valve |
| 3 | Weak front pump |
| 4 | Leaking low servo |
| 5 | Leaking reverse servo |
| 6 | Stuck compensator valve |
| 7 | Stuck orifice control valve |
| 8 | Check valve |
| 9 | Worn low band |
| 10 | Worn reverse band |
| 11 | Leaking front clutch piston |
| 12 | Weak rear pump |
| 13 | Weak pressure regulator valve spring |
| 14 | Internal oil leak |
| 15 | Worn front clutch |
| 16 | Seized front clutch |
| 17 | Worn shift valve |
| 18 | Stuck governor valve weights |
| 19 | Throttle valve linkage |
| 20 | Convertor |
| A | Shift linkage |
| B | Idle speed |
| C | Throttle rod too long |
| D | Throttle rod too short |
| E | External oil leak |
| F | Excessive backlash in drive train |
| G | Motor mounts |
| H | Seized bearings |
| J | Internal transmission damage |

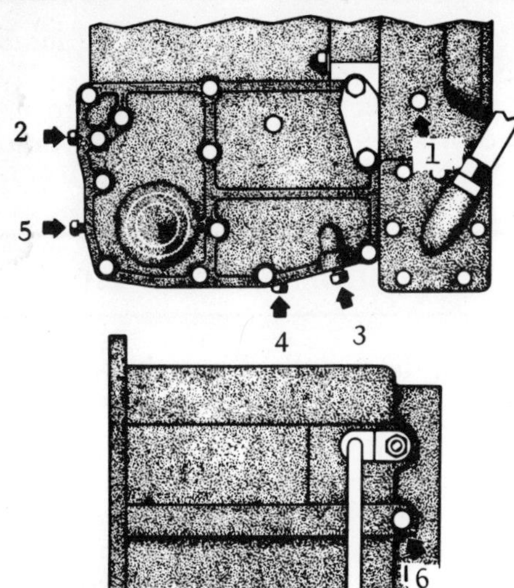


Pressure test points.

1. Front pump discharge pressure
2. Rear pump discharge pressure
3. Low servo piston operating pressure
4. Multiple clutch operating pressure (low servo piston released)
5. Reverse servo piston operating pressure
6. Governor pressure

## Hydraulic Line Pressure Tests—Corolla

There are four line pressure take-off points on the left side of the transmission case. Remove each plug, in turn, and connect a hydraulic pressure gauge of at least 200 psi capacity. Bring engine and transmission to operating temperature and check transmission oil level. Set brakes or jack up rear end of car.

### Forward Clutch (low servo) Release Pressure

L @ idle . . . . 107 psi
D @ idle . . . . 57 psi
R @ idle . . . . 57 psi

Increase engine speed slowly to stall speed (1,950–2,100 rpm); pressure should level off at 121–135 psi. If pressure is too low at idle in all gear ranges, check the following:

1. Front pump worn.
2. Pressure regulator valve spring too weak.
3. Pressure regulator defective.
4. Front pump sucking air (low oil level).
5. Throttle relay valve defective.
6. Oil leaks in pressure or vacuum lines.

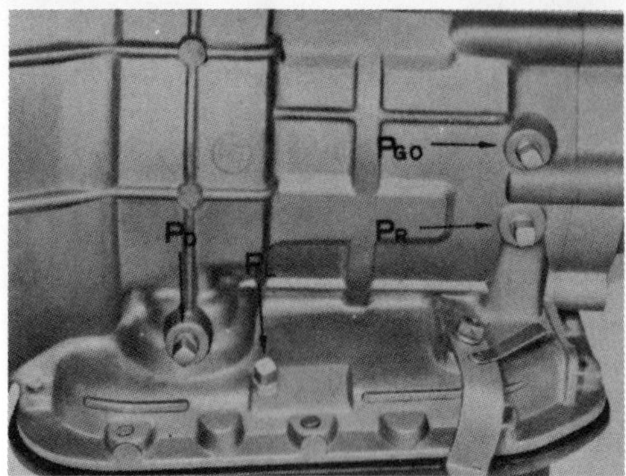


Pressure test points.

$P_D$ Forward multiple clutch operating pressure (low servo piston releasing pressure)
$P_L$ Low servo operating pressure
$P_{GO}$ Governor pressure
$P_R$ Reverse multiple clutch operating pressure

If pressure is *too low* at *full throttle*, check the pressure regulator, throttle relay valve and vacuum and oil lines.

If pressure is only *slightly above or below* standard, adjust pressure regulator valve by adding or removing shims. Shim sizes available are 0.012″ and 0.040″. Adding a 0.040″ shim will lower the pressure by approximately 7 psi, removing a 0.012″ shim will raise pressure 2 psi.

### Governor Pressure

Connect pressure gauge to governor pressure test outlet, engage "D" range and run car at speeds indicated.

13 mph . . . . 17–21 psi
25 mph . . . . 34–38 psi
31 mph . . . . 40–44 psi

If governor pressure is too low at all speeds, suspect:

1. Weak governor valve spring.
2. Stuck or binding governor weight.
3. Excessive wear in rear pump.

If governor pressure does *not* increase, suspect:

1. Stuck governor weight.
2. Stuck E-ring on governor shaft.

### Stall Test

Because this test causes a sharp rise in transmission oil temperature, its duration should be held below ten seconds. Allow sufficient time for the oil to cool before repeating stall test. With rear end jacked up and brakes locked, engage each gear in turn and fully depress the accelerator. Engine should hold steady at 1,950–2,100 rpm. Line pressure taken at the forward clutch outlet should be 121–135 psi.

If pressure is *constant* in all gears, but *below* standard, the engine needs tuning or the stator is slipping (on one-way clutch).

If rpm is *constant*, but *above* standard, the clutches or bands are slipping. Excessive rpm in "L" or "D" range only indicates low band is slipping; in "R" range only, reverse clutch is slipping.

If rpm in all gears is *above* 2,100, but no clutch or band is slipping and the front pump discharge pressure is normal, check the following:

1. Insufficient oil in converter.

2. Converter oil circulation stopped, causing the oil to overheat and generate steam inside the converter (check converter check valve in valve body).

3. Air bubbles due to overheating inside the converter.

If any of the above conditions are *not* caused by a defective valve body, the entire converter assembly must be replaced.

## Transmission Service

### Removing the Corolla Transmission

Drain all coolant from engine and disconnect radiator inlet hose. Disconnect throttle link from carburetor bell-crank (remove air filter if necessary). Remove exhaust pipe flange nuts, then jack up car and support on stands. Drain transmission oil, remove drive shaft and remove exhaust pipe bracket from transmission case. Disconnect exhaust pipe and transmission shift rod

## Chart AT-3
## Automatic Transmission Diagnosis—Corolla

| *Action* | *What to Check* | *Action* | *What to Check* |
|---|---|---|---|
| GEAR ENGAGEMENTS | | SHIFTS—*continued* | |
| None | 1, 2, 3, 18, A, N | Chatter or slipping in R | 1, 3, 19 |
| No L or D | 1, 4, 5, A | Slipping 1–2 (or D2) | 9, 15, 20, 21 |
| No R | 1, 3, A | Slipping 2–1 | 2, 13, 14, 20, 22, B |
| Harsh in L or D | 11, C, E, F | No 1–2 | 9, 13, 15, 16, D, 20, 21 |
| Harsh in R | 12, C, E, F | No 2–1 | 2, 5, 13, 17, 23 |
| | | Incorrect shift points | 16, 17, 22, B, D |
| SHIFTS | | Makes noise in N | H, I, J, K, M |
| Hard 1–2 | 6, 7, 8, 9, B | No start in N or P | L |
| Hard 2–1 | 11, 10, 8, D | Starts in all gears | L |
| Chatter or slipping in L or D | 1, 2, 5 | Maximum speed in gears too low | G |

## Check Points for Chart AT-3

| *Code Number* | *What to Check* | *Code Number* | *What to Check* |
|---|---|---|---|
| 1 | Oil level | 20 | Front pump worn |
| 2 | Low pressure in low servo, worn front pump | 21 | Rear pump worn |
| 3 | Low pressure in reverse clutch | 22 | Throttle relay valve defective |
| 4 | Low servo defective | 23 | Governor weights sticking or valve seized |
| 5 | Low band defective | A | Manual linkage maladjusted |
| 6 | High pressure in front clutch | B | Throttle rod too long |
| 7 | Throttle valve seized | C | Idle speed too high |
| 8 | Orifice control valve defective | D | Throttle rod too short |
| 9 | Front clutch discs worn or burnt | E | Excessive planetary gear backlash |
| 10 | Low band seized or jammed | F | Excessive play in U-joints |
| 11 | High pressure in low servo | G | Engine needs tune-up |
| 12 | High pressure in reverse clutch | H | Worn planetary gears |
| 13 | Improper operation of shift valve | I | Oil pump gears worn or loose |
| 14 | Front clutch discs not releasing | J | Thrust washers worn |
| 15 | Low pressure in front clutch | K | Bushings in transmission case slipping |
| 16 | Low governor pressure | L | Neutral safety switch out of adjustment |
| 17 | High governor pressure | M | Pressure regulator valve defective |
| 18 | Valve body defective | N | Broken transmission shaft/s |
| 19 | Reverse clutch defective | | |

from control shaft. Disconnect throttle link rod from throttle valve lever, then disconnect speedometer drive cable. Remove the four bolts from the rear support and take off the crossmember. (Support the transmission with a suitable jack.) Remove the clamp from the two oil cooler lines and disconnect both lines, then remove the seven bolts that hold the transmission case to the bellhousing. Withdraw the transmission slowly so as not to damage the oil seal. *CAUTION: There will be some oil in the converter, so be prepared with a drain pan.*

### Removing the Torque Converter

Loosen and remove the six bolts that hold the converter to the drive plate. Access is through the special hole provided in the lower bellhousing plate. Rotate the converter by turning the crank pulley.

### Removing the Converter Drive Plate and Ring Gear

Remove the ten transmission housing bolts from the bellhousing and remove the housing. Remove the six bolts that attach the ring gear and drive plate to the crankshaft. It is best to mark both the converter and the drive plate so that they can be installed in their original positions.

### Disassembling the Corolla Transmission

Thoroughly clean and rinse the outside of the transmission case with kerosene. Oil seals and O-rings which are to be used again may be cleaned with transmission fluid only. When scraping off old gaskets be careful not to damage the surfaces of the aluminum case. Rest the transmission on wooden blocks so as not to damage the oil passages on the underside of the case. Do not use rags for wiping or cleaning.

Remove the control rod (three pieces), dust cover and oil filler tube. Remove the front oil pump (six bolts) using a puller, then remove the input shaft. Remove the brake band anchor bolt and withdraw the front clutch and the thrust washer, then remove the brake band and the two struts. Remove the extension housing (six bolts), snap-ring, speedometer drive gear and key. Loosen the locknut and remove the governor body retaining screw. Lock the output shaft, after first engaging "P" (manually), by removing the E-ring from the governor shaft. Remove valve shaft, valve and the governor body. Remove the rear oil pump body (four bolts), drive and driven gears, dowel pin and the pump plate, then remove the planetary carrier with its thrust washers. Remove the reverse ring gear and oil pan. Remove the detent spring seat spring and ball, oil screen and valve body. If the valve body does not come off readily, it may be necessary to disconnect the manual shift lever from the shift valve and gently tap the valve body. Take out the throttle pressure check ball and remove the low servo piston. Remove throttle valve lever and manual valve lever. Remove the snap-ring that retains the clutch pressure plate, then remove the reverse clutch pressure plate, reverse clutch plates and discs, and the reverse clutch cushion spring. With an arbor press and a suitable tool, compress the piston return spring so that the retaining snap-ring can be removed. Slowly release the press, guiding the spring seat past the snap-ring groove. Remove the spring seat and the 16 return springs. Apply air pressure to the piston "apply" hole and remove the piston from the case, centering it by hand.

### Removing the Corona Transmission

Remove air cleaner and disconnect accelerator torque link (early models) or cable (late models), disconnect throttle link rod at carburetor side, then disconnect back-up light wiring at firewall (on early models). Jack up car and support on stands, then drain transmission oil. (Use a clean receptacle so that the oil can be checked for color, smell and foreign matter.) Disconnect all shift linkage. On early models, remove the cross shaft from the frame. Disconnect throttle link rod at transmission side and remove speedometer cable, oil cooler lines and parking brake equalizer bracket. Loosen the exhaust flange nuts and remove the exhaust pipe clamp and bracket. Remove drive shaft and rear mounting bracket, then lower the rear end of the transmission carefully. Support engine with a suitable jack stand and remove the seven bolts that hold the transmission to the engine.

### Disassembling the Corona Transmission

Remove back-up switch and wires, then remove control rod and intermediate shaft lever (early models). Remove left side cover. *NOTE: Push throttle lever all the way to the rear; do not pry the cover off.* Remove right side cover and extension housing, then loosen the two pressure regulator valve cover nuts alternately and remove the pressure regulator spring. *CAUTION: This must be done BEFORE the next operation or the regulator spring will be damaged.* Remove the nuts that hold the transmission case to the housing. Make sure the pressure regulator valve is *fully* pushed in, then separate the case from the housing. There are two dowels, so pull straight back only. Remove input shaft and clutch as a unit. Remove nine of the transmission case side cover bolts, leaving two in place as shown. Hold cover down and slowly remove the two remaining bolts. Lift cover off slowly so that reverse servo spring will not be damaged. A pilot tube, where the regulator spring fits through the cover, makes it necessary for the cover to be lifted straight off. Now remove the low servo piston and spring. Remove anchor bolt cap (on left side), loosen the locknut and unscrew anchor bolt until it is free from the strut. Remove low band, anchor, strut and spring. *NOTE: Mark the low band before removal.*

Loosen reverse band anchor bolt and remove, as above, also marking the band to avoid interchange with low band. Remove snap-rings and speedometer gear from output shaft. Remove the E-ring from the weight side of the governor shaft, then remove the shaft. Cut safety wires and remove governor body and weights. Loosen one lock bolt and remove governor body support. Remove output shaft bearing retainer and snap-ring, then, lightly tapping the output shaft, remove planetary gears and reverse drum towards the front of the case. Now remove reverse band, with all levers and struts. Remove reverse servo piston and rear pump from case, without tilting units. Remove spring and parking pawl. *CAUTION: Do not damage the adjacent sealing surfaces of the case with the sharp ends of the torsion spring.* Remove the manual valve lever shaft from the case, then remove five bolts and ten nuts and lift off the valve body. *NOTE: There are two dowels locating the body. DO NOT PRY VALVE BODY FROM CASE.* Remove the manual valve lever. Remove stator shaft towards rear of case. Remove front pump body towards the front of case. Do not tap on the rear face of the pump body. Remove oil suction pipe through the opening in the right side cover. If necessary, remove all remaining test plugs from the housing.

Removing spring.

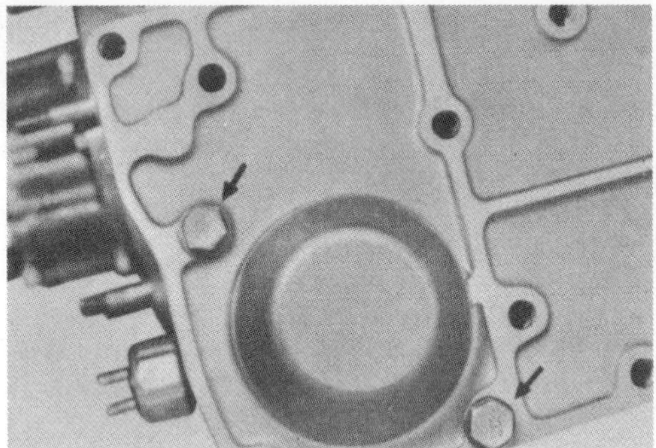

Leave two bolts in place.

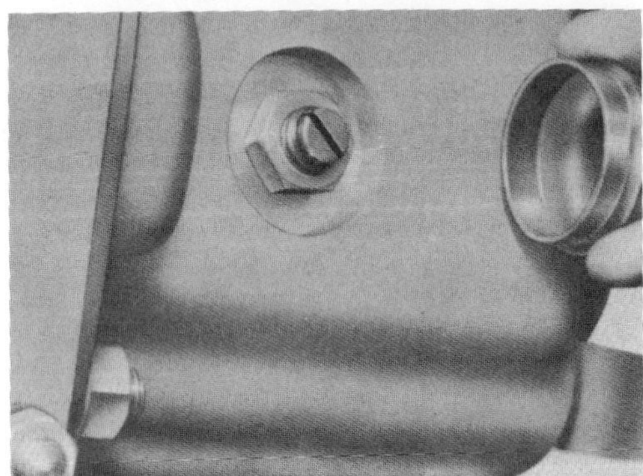

Removing cap.

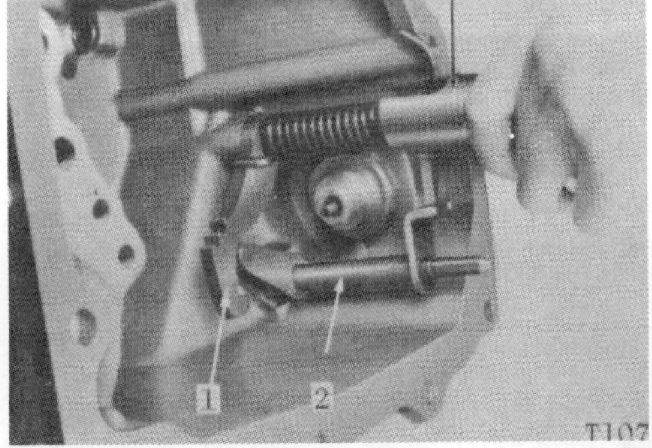


Removing torsion spring.

Removing valve body.

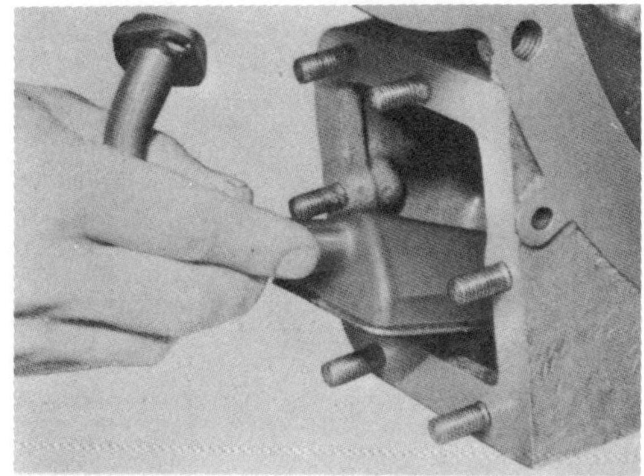
Removing suction pipe.

**Inspecting and Repairing the Transmission**

*Front clutch* While the number of clutch discs and plates is different from the Corolla transmission, the procedures are the same.

*Planetary gears* Same as for the Corolla.

*Low servo piston* Same as for the Corolla, except for the dimensions: return spring free length . . . 1.650″ (1.490″ at 64 lbs., limit 40 lbs.).

*Reverse servo piston* Same as for the Corolla, except dimensions: return spring free length . . . 2.600″ (1.800″ at 25.5 lbs., limit 17.6 lbs.).

Cushion spring free length . . . 0.980″ (0.790″ at 34.7 lbs., limit 17.6 lbs.). *NOTE: Piston rod is secured with two valve keys.*

## Subassembly Inspection and Repairs

### Front Clutch

*NOTE: If clutch discs and plates are to be used again, wash them off with solvent and clean automatic transmission fluid.*

*Disassembling the front clutch* Remove

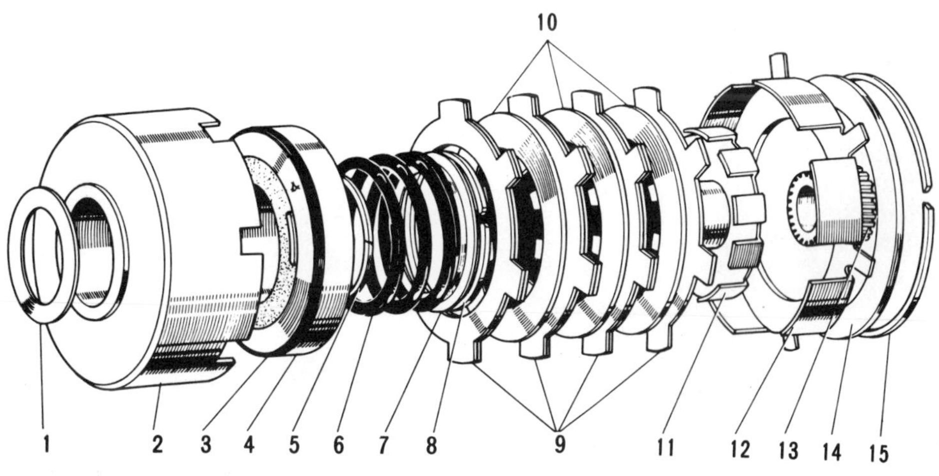

Clutch components.

1. Clutch drum thrust washer
2. Clutch drum
3. Clutch piston oil seal outer ring
4. Clutch piston
5. Clutch piston oil seal inner ring
6. Compression spring
7. Clutch piston return spring seat
8. Shaft snap-ring
9. Clutch driven plate
10. Clutch drive plate
11. Clutch hub
12. Clutch flange
13. Low sun gear
14. Clutch flange retainer
15. Hole snap-ring

snap-ring, flange retainer, clutch flange, hub, plates and discs. Depress spring seat and remove spring. Release pressure gradually and remove the spring seat, carefully guiding it past the groove in the clutch drum. Apply air pressure to remove the piston from the drum. Inspect all parts for signs of wear and/or overheating.

| | *Model RT* | *K* |
|---|---|---|
| Spring free length | 1.970″ | 1.690″ |
| Spring installed length | 0.700″ | 0.910″ |
| at lbs. | 87 | 83–97 |
| Wear limit (lbs.) | 1.380″ @ 60 | 0.850″ @ 70 |

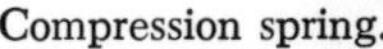

Compression spring.

Assembling clutch plates.

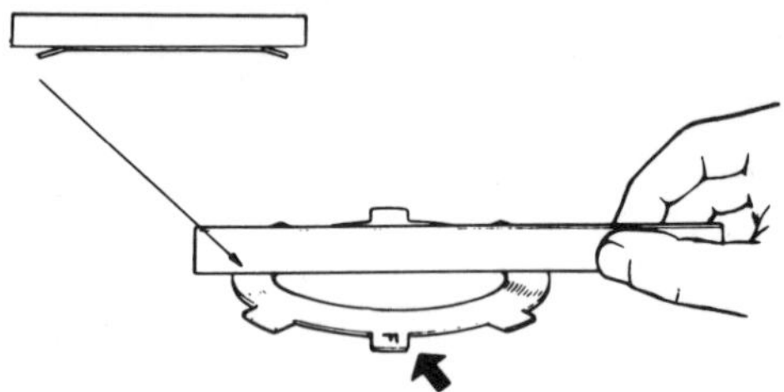

Driven plate "F" mark.

*Assembling the front clutch* Install a new seal into clutch drum. *NOTE: Beware of substituting a reverse clutch seal; front seal diameter is 1.880″, reverse seal diameter is 1.760″.* Install new outer seal onto piston and carefully fit into clutch drum so as not to pinch the seal. Next, install piston return spring and seat with the aid of a press. Make sure snap-ring is locked in place before releasing the press. Place clutch hub onto flange and install clutch disc with the notched lug first, then follow with one disc, two plates, then one disc and one plate. Clutch plates are dished—install with curve away from the piston side. *NOTE: On Corona, install clutch discs and plates as follows (from piston side out): two plates, one disc, two plates, one disc, two plates, one disc, one plate; a total of seven plates and three discs.* Align clutch lugs and install flange onto drum. Install retainer and snap-ring. End-play of the flange should be less than 0.020″. Apply forward pressure to the flange and check play with a feeler gauge; it should be 0.012″ or more.

### Low Servo Piston—Corolla

Press the piston against the rod and remove the E-ring. Withdraw piston, springs, washer and rod. Remove piston ring from piston. Inspect all parts and replace as needed. End gap of piston ring should be 0.004–0.012″; side play of ring in piston groove should be 0.001–0.003″.

Cushion spring (small) free length 0.807″ (0.720″ @ 25–31 lbs. load). Replace if less than 17.5 lbs. Return spring (large) free length 1.680″ (1.400″ at 15–20 lbs.). Replace if less than 11 lbs. *NOTE: Piston should move about 0.080″ against the cushion spring.*

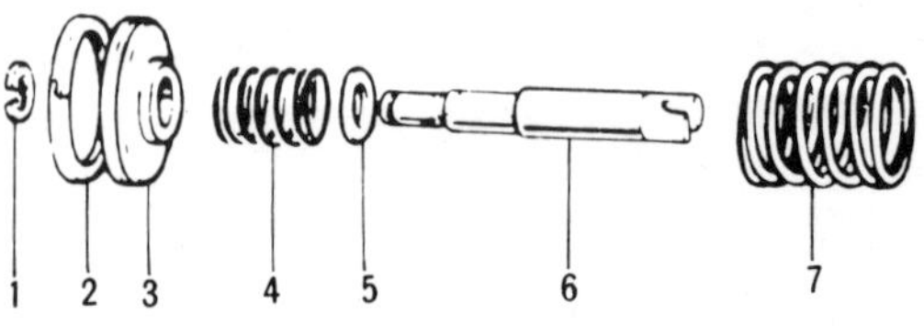

Low servo piston components.

1. E-ring
2. Low servo piston ring
3. Low servo piston
4. Cushion spring
5. Plate washer
6. Low servo piston rod
7. Piston return spring

### Reverse Clutch and Ring Gear

Check same as front clutch; dimensions and specifications are the same. Clutch plates are not dished. Check all springs for distortion and squareness, as well as length and strength. Free length . . . 1.280″ (replace if less than 1.120″); installed length . . . 0.940″ @ 4.15 lbs. Check ring gear for wear or damage. Thrust washer thickness is 0.075–0.079″, limit is 0.067″.

### Planetary Gear

Before disassembling, inspect all gear teeth for smooth meshing. Clamp unit in vise and remove three screws and pinion lock plate (counterclockwise). Use a dummy pin to remove short pinion pin with rollers and washers. Next, remove a long pinion in the same manner. There are 38 rollers (needle bearings) per pinion. Keep pinions, pins and rollers in sets. After removing two sets of pinions, remove the input sun gear and thrust washer. Remove last set of pinions.

Check all gear teeth for wear; check locking gear (park). Carrier bushing wear limit 0.004″; sun gear thrust washer 0.078″ (wear limit 0.067″); pinion thrust washer 0.020″ (limit 0.012″); input shaft diameter 0.392–0.395″ (wear limit for both 0.004″).

Using a dummy pinion pin, install needle rollers into a long pinion. Pack with grease. Install into carrier with upper and lower thrust washers. Fit mating short pinion in same manner. Pinion pin slot must face center. Insert sun gear thrust washer and the sun gear. Install the remaining sets of pinions (the long pinions being installed before the short pinions). All pinion pin slots must face to the carrier center to allow proper engagement of the locking plate, which is turned clockwise to lock. Fasten plate with three screws and lockwashers. After assembling, check the end-play of long and short pinions; 0.006–0.028″. Pinions should have no radial play and should turn freely on their pins.

### Corolla Valve Body

In general, it is not necessary to dismantle the valve body, unless there are good reasons for suspecting a malfunction. No service parts other than springs are supplied, and these must be replaced as a set, not singly.

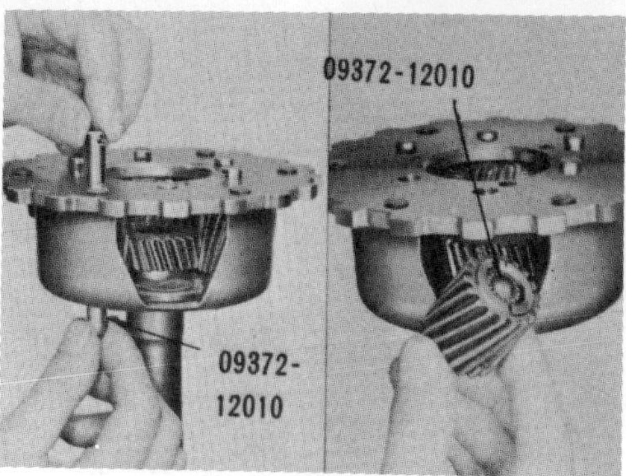


Removing long planetary pinion.

To disassemble the Corolla unit, remove the screws and lift off valve body plate and gasket. Pull out the manual valve and the two check valves and springs. Drive out the three spring retaining pins with a punch (0.096″ diameter), then remove the valves and the springs. Thoroughly clean all parts with clean solvent and allow to air dry. Check all valves for wear and/or damage. Rotate the valves in their bores and, if necessary, dress the valves with very fine crocus cloth (never use sandpaper or emery cloth). The pressure regulator valve must move smoothly in its bore. Check all valves for smooth side surfaces and sharp edges at their ends. Nicks and burrs must be removed. If the bores are damaged, do not hone them—the valve body must be replaced.

There are eight springs of six different sizes:

| *Number* | *Type* | *Free length* | *Pressure @ installed length (lbs.)* |
|---|---|---|---|
| 1 | Pressure reg. valve | 1.93–2.07″ | 1.3–1.4 @1.22″ |
| 1 | Shift valve | 0.945–1.10″ | 3.9–4.5 @ 0.786″ |
| 1 | Throttle relay valve | 0.748–0.860″ | 6.7–7.4 @ 0.531″ |
| 1 | Orifice control valve | 0.570–0.630″ | 1.5–1.9 @ 0.551″ |
| 2 | Throttle valve | 0.610–0.650″ | 4.19 @ 0.591″ |
| 2 | Check valve | 0.670–0.846″ | 0.79 @ 0.610″ |
| | | 0.670–0.886″ | 0.79 @ 0.610″ |

### Assembling the Corolla Valve Body

Assembly is the reverse of disassembly. After assembling springs, check that the throttle valve moves in accordance with the

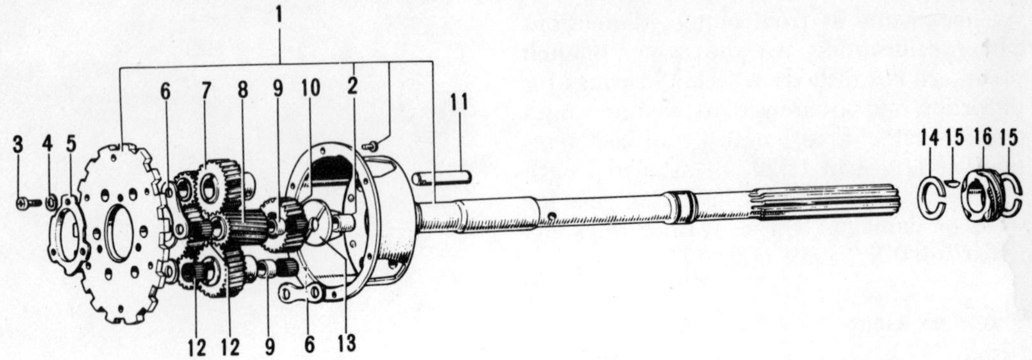

Planetary gear components.

1. Planetary carrier assembly
2. Bushing
3. Screw
4. Washer
5. Planetary pinion pin lock plate
6. Planetary pinion thrust washer
7. Planetary short pinion
8. Planetary long pinion
9. Spacer
10. Input sun gear
11. Planetary pinion pin
12. Roller
13. Washer
14. Shaft snap-ring
15. Woodruff key
16. Speedometer drive gear

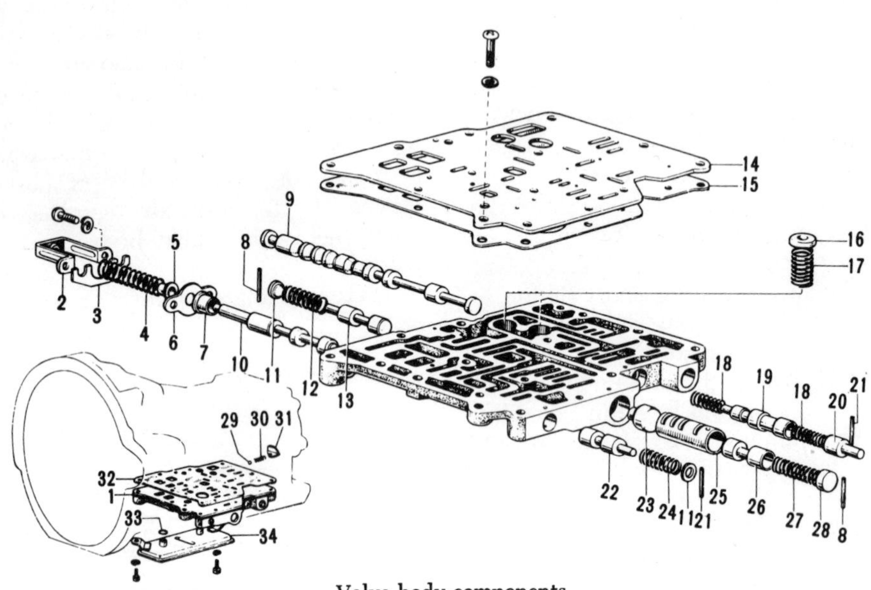

Valve body components.

1. Valve body assembly
2. Pressure regulator spring retainer
3. Pressure regulator shim
4. Spring
5. Pressure regulator valve spring seat
6. Pressure regulator valve sleeve seat
7. Pressure regulator valve sleeve
8. Spring pin
9. Manual valve
10. Pressure regulator valve
11. Orifice control valve spring seat
12. Spring
13. Throttle relay valve
14. Valve body plate
15. Valve body gasket
16. Check valve
17. Spring (2)
18. Spring (2)
19. Throttle valve
20. Downshift plug
21. Spring pin
22. Orifice control valve
23. Shift valve governor plug
24. Spring
25. Shift valve sleeve
26. Shift valve
27. Spring
28. Shift valve spring seat
29. Ball
30. Spring
31. Detent spring seat
32. Valve body plate gasket
33. O-ring
34. Oil strainer

downshift valve plug. Check free movement of *all* valves in their bores with the aid of a small screwdriver or wooden pointed dowel. Now insert the manual control valve and test its movement. Install the two check valve springs and the valves and test their operation and free movement. Install the valve body cover plate with a new gasket—be sure not to cover any oil holes. Tighten screws to 10–12 in. lbs. Clean the oil screen and check for holes or case distortions. Always use new O-rings to prevent the pump from sucking air.

## Corona Valve Body

In general, it is not necessary to dismantle the valve body unless the hydraulic pressure tests have shown a malfunction.

### Disassembling the Valve Body

Remove the check valve, pressure regulator valve and the manual valve. The oil seal rings, thrust washer and port rings are not normally removed unless defective.

### Inspecting the Valve Body

Wash in clean solvent and dry with compressed air. Check face of valve body for distortion. Check valve must be replaced if rusty or bent. Inspect pressure regulator valve for wear, especially scuff marks or nicks. Remove small burrs with a fine oilstone or crocus cloth. Valve must move in and out, as well as rotate freely in its bore. Check bypass hole, then test valve spring (free length 1.890″, limit 1.670″). Inspect manual valve for wear and straightness.

### Assembling the Valve Body

Install pressure regulator valve and manual valve. Check oil seal ring—both ring ends should be seated in the groove. Thrust washer goes on before the seal ring.

Unless previous tests have clearly indicated a defective shift valve body, it is not necessary to dismantle this unit. The shift valve body contains the shift valve, the orifice control valve, the throttle valve, the compensator valve and the throttle valve lever.

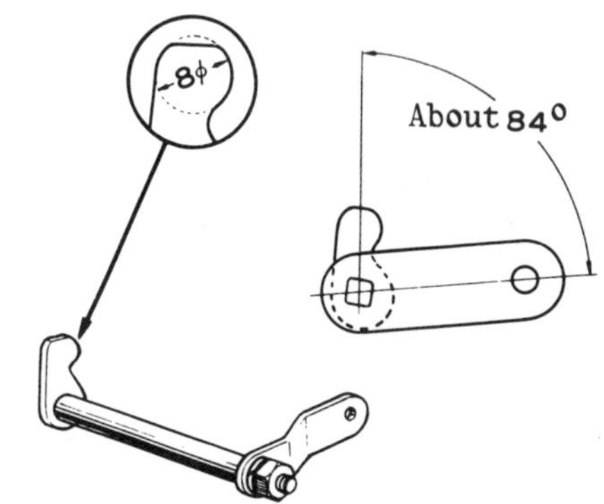


Throttle valve lever.

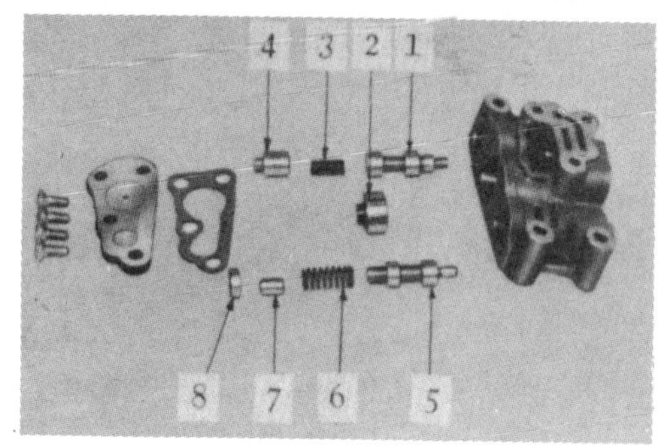


Front side assembly.

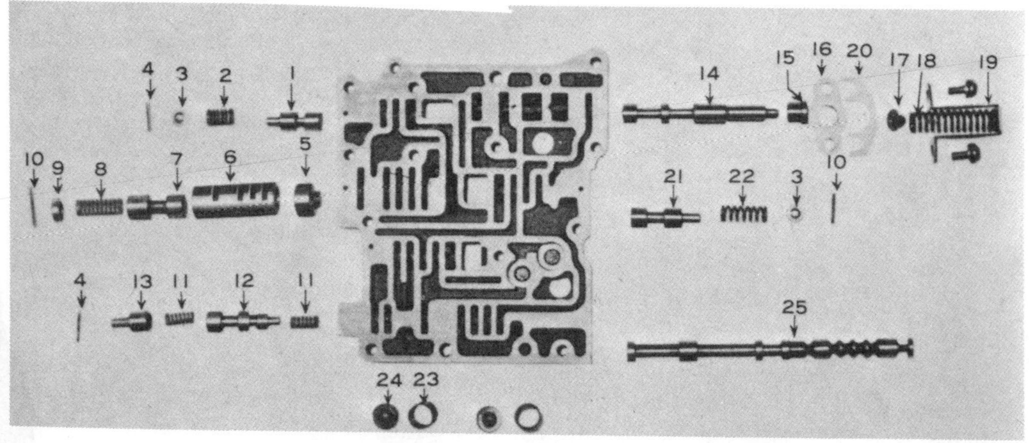


Assembling valve body by the numbers.

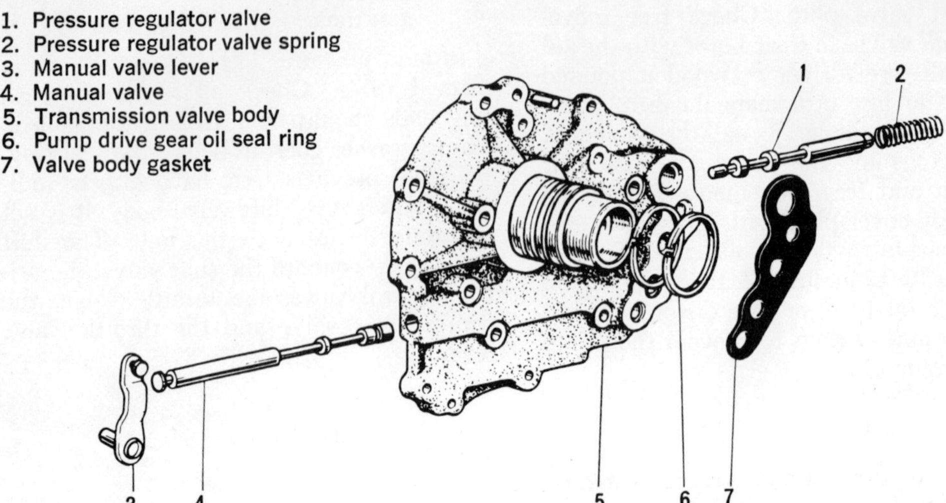


Valve body external controls.

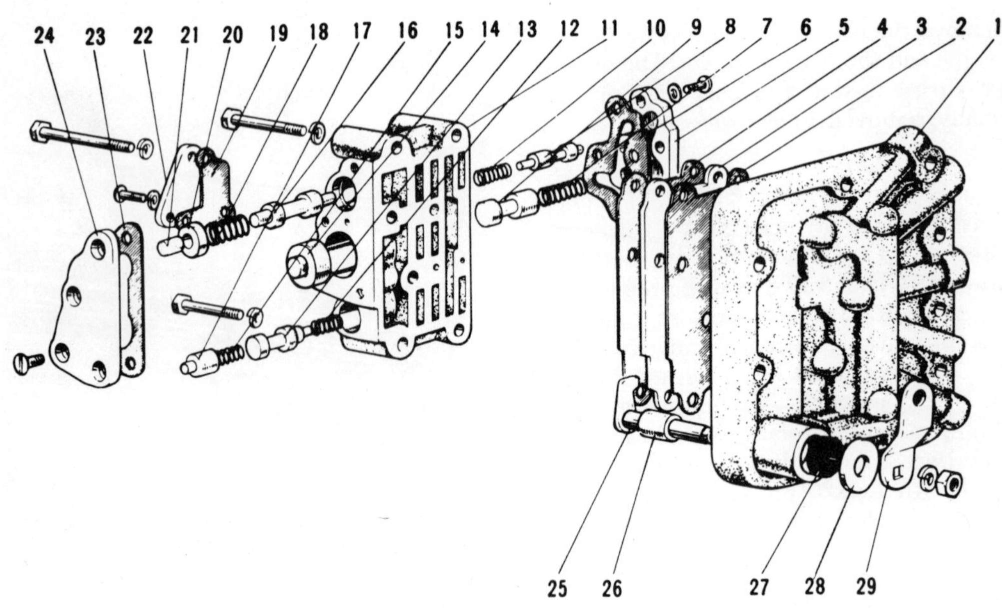


Shift valve components.

1. Transmission housing side cover subassembly L/H
2. Shift valve body plate gasket
3. Shift valve body plate
4. Shift valve body plate gasket
5. Shift valve body rear cover
6. Shift valve body rear cover gasket
7. Shift valve compression spring (black)
8. Orifice control valve
9. Shift valve
10. Orifice control valve compression spring (white)
11. Shift valve body
12. Throttle valve compression spring
13. Throttle valve
14. Shift valve governor plug
15. Throttle valve compression spring
16. Compensator valve
17. Downshift plug
18. Compensator valve compression spring (red)
19. Shift valve body inside gasket
20. Compensator plug sleeve
21. Compensator plug
22. Shift valve body inside plate
23. Shift valve body front cover gasket
24. Shift valve body front cover gasket
25. Throttle valve lever
26. Spacer
27. Oil seal
28. Plate washer
29. Throttle valve outer lever

### Disassembling the Shift Valve

Remove the six mounting bolts from the side cover and remove the shift valve assembly; the Phillips screw should be left alone. Next, remove the rear cover and gasket from the shift valve body and pull out all valves and springs, laying them out in order. Repeat this procedure for front cover; remove the body plate and the two gaskets.

Wash and dry parts with compressed air. Inspect all valves for wear or damage. Clean out all valve bores and look for signs of wear. Valves must slide and rotate freely in their bores. Blow out oil holes and passages in the valve body with air, then test valve springs.

| *Type* | *Color* | *Free Length* |
|---|---|---|
| Shift valve | black | 0.945–1.100″ |
| Compensator valve | red | 0.750–0.960″ |
| Orifice control | white | 0.590–0.670″ |
| Throttle valves (2) | | 0.590–0.670″ |

If the two springs differ more than 0.040″ in length, use the longer at the front of the throttle valve (plug side).

Check the throttle valve lever for wear on the face of the contacting cam.

### Assembling the Shift Valve

Install the throttle valve spring and the throttle plug into the valve body from the front, then install the governor plug into the center bore. Install the compensator valve, the red valve spring, compensator plug and sleeve into the shift valve body and secure with gasket and front cover, tightening evenly to prevent distortion. From the rear of the valve body, install orifice control valve spring (white), orifice valve, shift valve spring (blue) and throttle valve spring, then install rear cover and gasket. After assembling all the valves, test for smooth operation and for overlap of the throttle valve (0.202″). Check the shift valve plate on all transmissions with serial numbers below 9B-1097 and enlarge the hole to 7⁄64″ as shown. (This modification will prevent harsh downshifting.) Now, install the shift valve plate and gaskets onto left side cover. Install the inside cover and gasket and secure in place with one screw only. Place the valve body on the left side cover and install the remaining five screws, tighten evenly to 5–8 ft. lbs., then tighten the Phillips screw on the inside body plate.

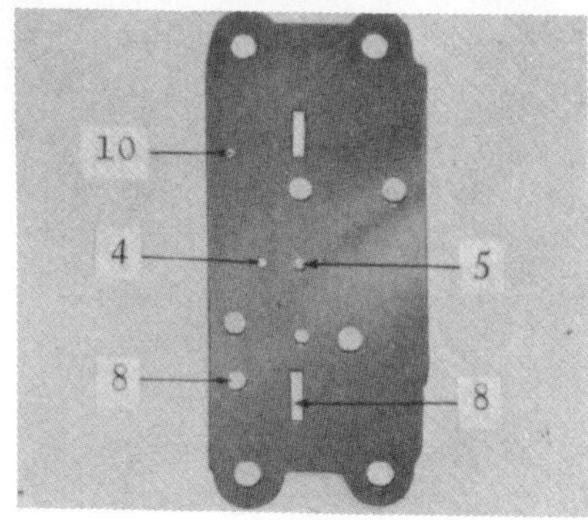

Shift valve body plate, showing modified hole at (5).

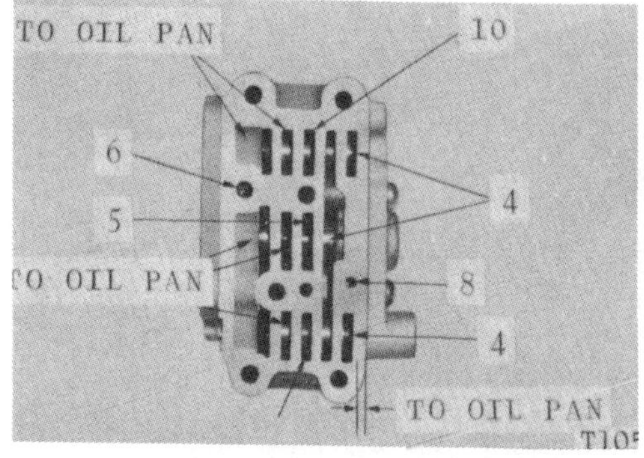

Shift valve body.

Transmission case.

## Corona Front Oil Pump

Pull the pump body from the stator housing and remove the two gears. Wash all pump components and blow dry, using compressed air. Check the pump gears for wear and play (backlash). Clearance between pump body and driven gear is 0.004–0.008″ (limit 0.012″), gear to crescent clearance is 0.008–0.013″ (limit 0.020″).

Place a straightedge across pump body to check gears; clearance should be 0.0016–0.0028″. Replace gears or pump if clearance exceeds 0.012″. Drive gear bushing size is 1.380″.

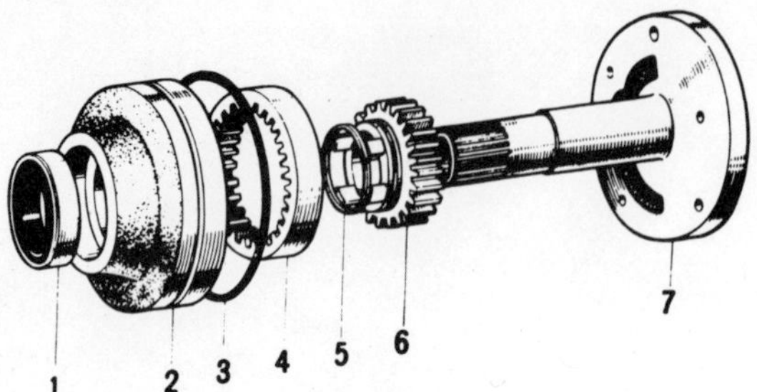


Front oil pump.

1. Front pump body oil seal
2. Front pump body
3. Front pump body O-ring
4. Front pump driven gear
5. Pump drive gear oil seal ring
6. Front pump drive gear
7. Stator shaft

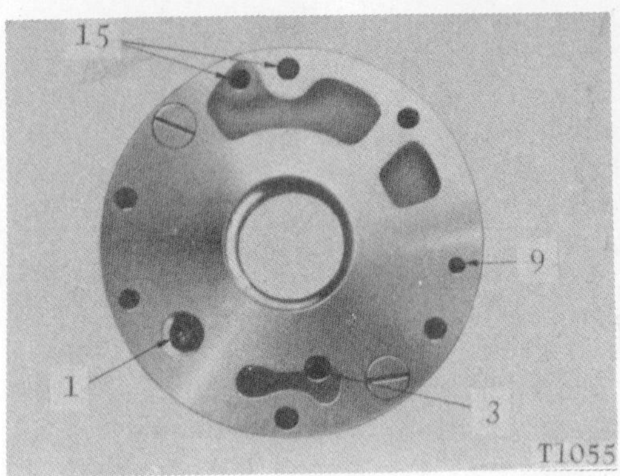


Rear oil pump.

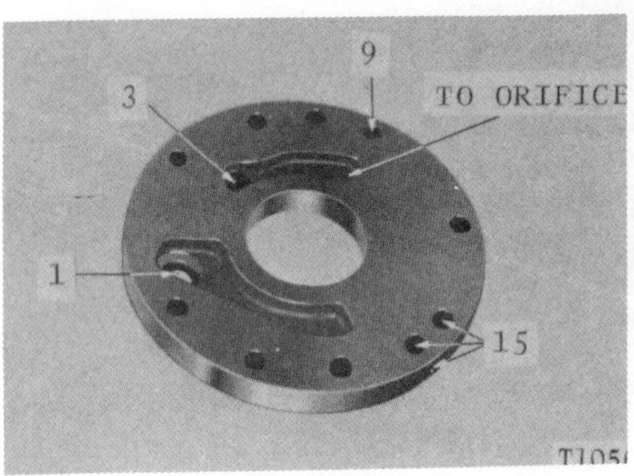


Rear oil pump cover.

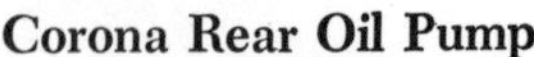

### Corona Rear Oil Pump

Remove the two screws and the pump cover, then remove gears. Wash with solvent and blow out oil passages with compressed air. Check the bearing and, if worn, use a brass punch to drive it out from the pump gear side. Clearance between the driven gear and the body is 0.004–0.007″ (limit 0.012″). Gear to crescent clearance is 0.006–0.011″ (limit 0.020″). Install gears so that the drive gear chamfered side faces forward. Secure pump body with two screws, then install rear bearing retainer and secure with four bolts.

### Corolla Front Oil Pump

Remove the five bolts and disassemble the pump and the stator shaft. Check clutch drum oil seal rings; remove them by unlocking the interlocking ring ends. Check all parts for wear. Stator shaft bushing oil clearance limit is 0.008″. Clutch drum thrust washer thickness is 0.063″ (limit is 0.0551″). In the pump body, examine the check valve ball for free movement. Pump body bushing clearance limit is 0.006″. Check both pump gears for wear or burrs, then check clearance between pump body and driven gear; it should be 0.004–0.008″ (limit is 0.010″). Check clearance between driven gear and pump crescent; it should be 0.010–0.014″ (limit is 0.020″). Check the clearance between gears and face of pump body using a straightedge; it should be 0.001–0.002″ (limit is 0.008″). Replace all parts not within limits. *NOTE: Replace the oil seal each time the pump is removed.*

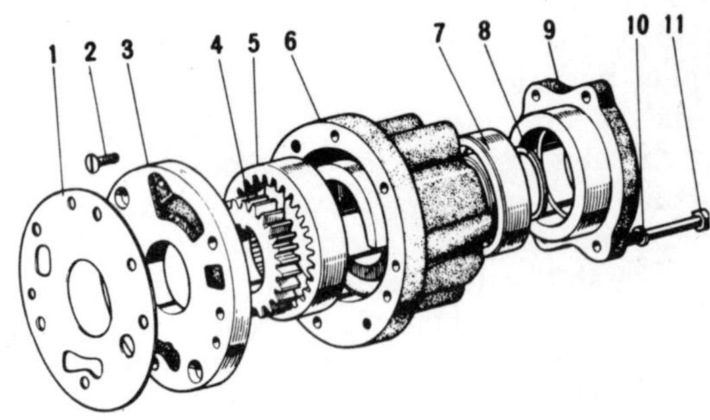


Rear oil pump components.

1. Rear pump cover gasket
2. Screw
3. Rear pump cover
4. Rear pump drive gear
5. Rear pump driven gear
6. Rear pump body
7. Output shaft rear bearing
8. Snap-ring
9. Output shaft bearing retainer
10. Lockwasher
11. Bolt

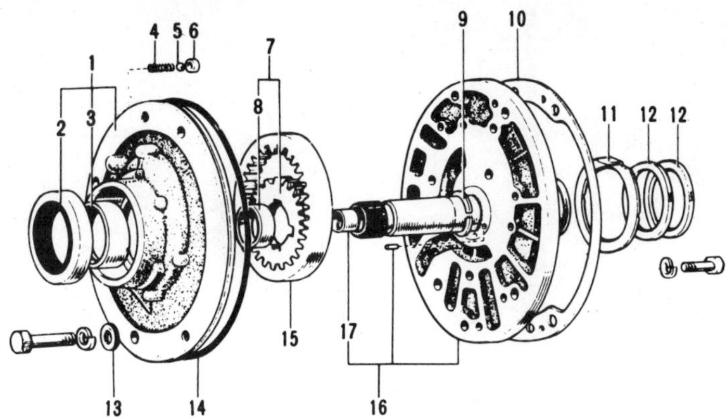


Front oil pump components.

1. Front oil pump body
2. Type "T" oil seal
3. Bushing
4. Spring
5. Ball
6. Lubrication check ball seat
7. Front oil pump drive gear
8. Bushing
9. Shaft snap-ring
10. Front oil pump cover gasket
11. Clutch drum thrust washer
12. Clutch drum oil seal ring
13. Seal washer
14. O-ring
15. Front oil pump driven gear
16. Stator shaft
17. Bushing

Rear oil pump components.

1. Rear oil pump plate
2. Rear oil pump drive gear
3. Straight pin
4. Rear oil pump driven gear
5. Rear oil pump body
6. Bushing

### Corolla Rear Oil Pump

The rear pump is check in the same manner as the front pump; clearances are identical, with the following exceptions:

| | |
|---|---|
| Output shaft diameter | 0.983–0.984″ |
| Bushing diameter | 0.984–0.985″ |
| Clearance | 0.0003–0.0020″ |
| Clearance limit | 0.006″ |

### Governor Valve

A defective governor can severely affect the operation of the transmission. It is therefore recommended that special care be taken when inspecting and installing governor valves.

Remove the two snap-rings from the shaft and withdraw the outer and inner weights. Remove the E-rings and springs, then withdraw shaft and valve. Inspect very carefully; especially check the sliding surfaces and the oil passages. Check the spring; free length 0.957″ (limit . . . 0.787″), installed length 0.512″ @ 1.94–2.16 lbs.

### Rear Extension Housing

This unit contains the speedometer driven gear, drive shaft front yoke bushing and the oil seal and dust shield. Remove the lock bolt and tab and remove the speedometer gear, along with sleeve bushing. Check O-ring on sleeve for leaks. Remove bushing only if it is worn or slipping in its seat. New bushings need no reaming, unless damaged during installation. Align oil groove in bushing with oil passage in housing; standard diameter is 1.500″. The oil seal is really a three-piece assembly consisting of the seal, a dust seal (felt) and a dust shield (metal). Pre-oil (soak) the felt seal prior to installation. Always check drive shaft yoke for signs of wear.

### Manual Valve Lever Shaft

Check the relative positions on the valve lever shaft of the detent and the lever retainer. The included angle must be 62–63°.

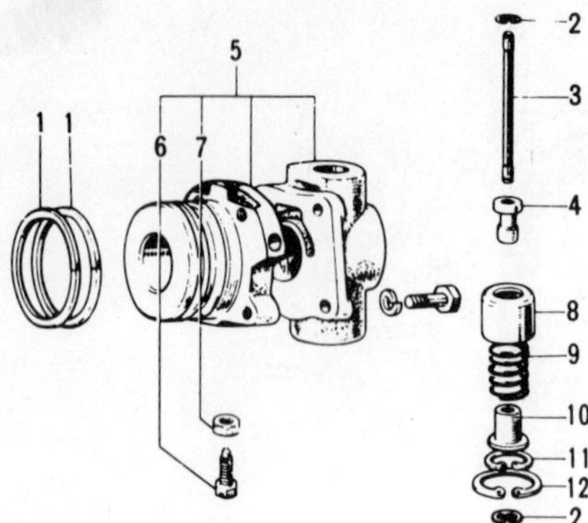


Governor valve components.

1. Governor body oil seal ring
2. E-ring
3. Governor valve shaft
4. Governor valve
5. Governor body
6. Screw
7. Nut
8. Governor outer weight
9. Spring
10. Governor inner weight
11. Hole snap-ring
12. Hole snap-ring

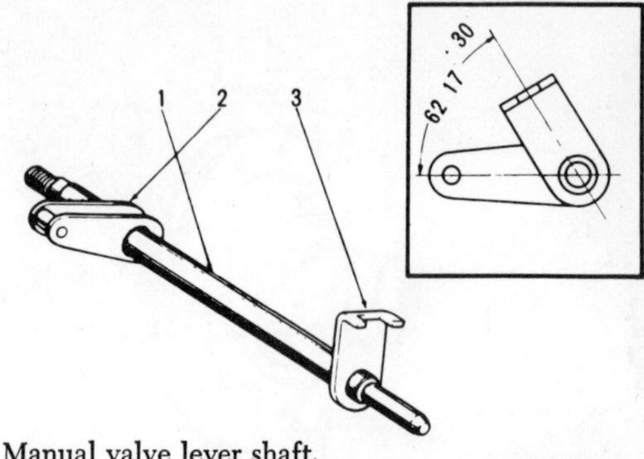


Manual valve lever shaft.

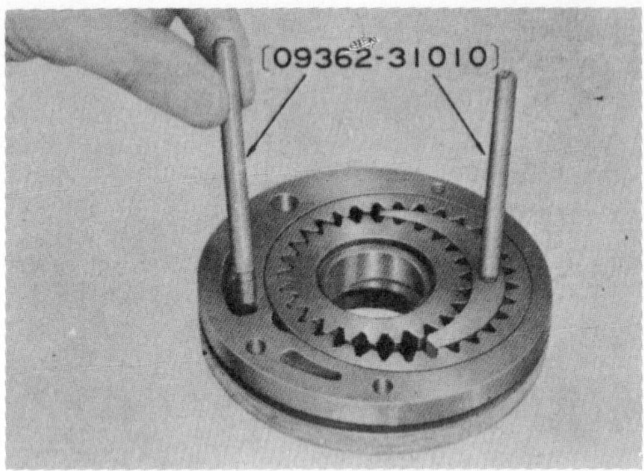


Installing guide pins.

Installing reverse piston.

## Assembling the Corona Transmission

Assemble the front pump and stator shaft to the transmission housing using a new O-ring and gasket. (Use two long guide pins to line up stator shaft and pump body.) Pull the pump body slowly and evenly into the transmission case by alternately tightening the five mounting bolts. Remove these bolts after the pump body is fully seated so that the valve body can be installed. Secure with the same five bolts and the ten nuts on the studs; torque is 5–8 ft. lbs. Install the parking lock pawl shaft (if removed) with the chamfered end first. Install manual valve lever shaft, then fit parking pawl to shaft and install parking pawl tension spring, without damaging the case surface. Install oil pump cover gasket and rear pump and torque the five bolts to 5–8 ft. lbs. (If necessary, use the front pump guide pins to line up the rear pump gears.) Insert the rear servo piston into the cylinder—the use of a ring compressor type tool is strongly recommended here. Install reverse band anchor bolt. Bolt should extend slightly into case. Back off locknut, then install the apply link and lever onto the brake band and connect it to servo piston rod. Screw in the anchor bolt just far enough to keep the band from falling off. Adjust band, as described later in this chapter, then stick the reverse drum spacer to the drum with a liberal dose of Vaseline and install spacer into case. Make sure drum turns freely. From rear of case, install the rear pump drive key at twelve o'clock position and stick in place using Vaseline. Stick the thrust washer to the planetary gear with Vaseline, align the pump drive keyway at twelve o'clock and, from the inside of case, insert the gear into drum and bushing. *CAUTION: When installing planetary gear, support output shaft so that the splined end does not damage the bushing. If necessary, lightly tap the parking lock gear to facilitate installation.* Install the output shaft snap-ring. (Two sizes are available for proper fit.) Assemble bearing retainer to rear pump body. The two oil rings of the governor body support are installed with the slots 120° apart in the rear bearing retainer. Align the hole in the governor support with the hole in the output shaft and tighten the five bolts to 5–8 ft. lbs. Assemble the governor and install the assembly onto the output shaft. Bolts must be wire-locked in place. Install the speedometer drive gear with key and snap-rings. Insert the low servo piston spring into the servo cylinder and, while pushing down on spring, fit the piston with the aid of a ring compressor. *CAUTION: Unless the spring is pushed in and held down, the ring will come off the piston.* Temporarily place a ¼″ flat washer on the low servo piston shaft on the inside of the case and slip a cotter pin through the hole in the piston rod. Install cover gasket, position the spring on the reverse piston and install side cover; tighten bolts to 10–12 ft. lbs. Now, remove washer and cotter pin. Install oil seal onto input shaft and slide the shaft into the clutch. Select correct low sun gear thrust washer and install with oil slots facing the sun gear side; align slots with oil holes in input shaft. The old washer must be examined carefully and, if not worn or damaged, it can be reinstalled. If it is worn, proceed as follows: lay a straightedge across the transmission case and measure the distance between its lower edge and the top of the clutch drum. If this distance is less than 1.310″, use the 0.120″ washer; if greater, use the 0.140″ washer.

Install the pre-assembled input shaft and clutch onto the planetary gear; do not allow the clutch to slip out or become cocked during assembly. Install the low brake band onto the clutch drum (either way) and insert the apply strut tang into its spring. Position the strut (with the thicker side UP) in the notch of the piston rod and insert the other end into its seat on the band. Insert the anchor strut into the anchor and turn anchor bolt IN. Insert the manual valve and pressure regulator valve into the valve body and check for free movement. Remove the manual valve again and install the valve lever shaft into the transmission case, then install valve and lever together. Adjust the valve lever (by bending, if necessary) so that there is no more than 0.020″ clearance between the tip of the lever and the bottom of the groove on the manual valve. Next, bolt the housing to the transmission case. Position the manual valve lever shaft so that it engages the second of the five notches on the parking pawl. Set the manual valve so that it protrudes 1.800″ from the manual valve body housing. Install the reverse thrust washer onto the clutch mounting part of the valve body. Recheck engagement of valve lever retainer and valve lever (62°) through the provided opening in the side cover. Tighten valve lever shaft nut to 20–25 ft. lbs. Install left side cover and tighten to 10–12 ft. lbs. Insert pressure regulator valve spring into the opening at the top right-hand corner of the side cover,

Installing low servo piston.

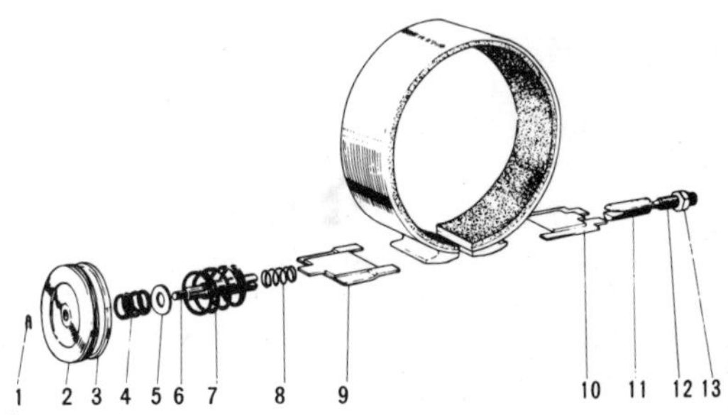


Low brake band components.

1. Snap-ring
2. Low servo piston
3. Servo piston ring
4. Compression ring
5. Plain washer
6. Low servo piston
7. Compression spring
8. Compression spring
9. Low brake band apply strut
10. Low brake band strut
11. Low brake band anchor
12. Brake band anchor bolt
13. Nut

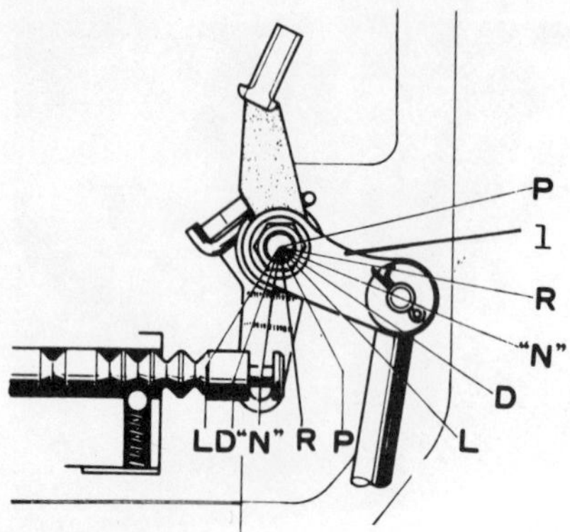


Manual valve lever position.

Adjusting low brake band.

then fit the gasket and spring seat, tightening to 10–12 ft. lbs. Fit O-ring first, then the flange to the oil suction pipe; tighten the two bolts to 5–8 ft. lbs. Mount the extension housing (13–15 ft. lbs.), then install the remaining parts, such as shift linkage, oil cooler lines and fittings, etc. The brake band anchor bolt cap should *not* be fitted until after the low band has been adjusted in the car.

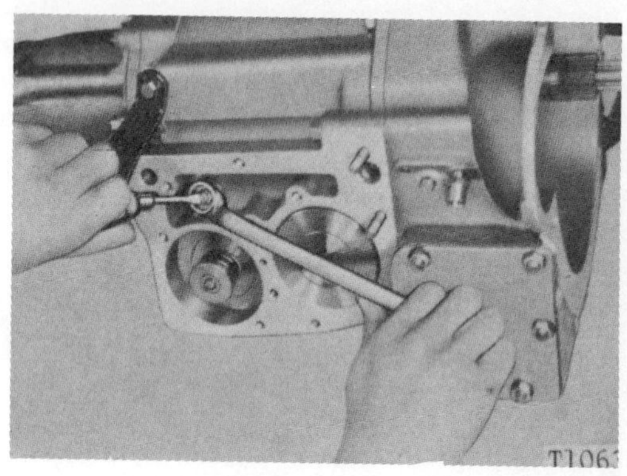

Adjusting reverse brake band.

## Transmission Adjustments

### Corona

*Low band* Screw adjusting bolt in until bottomed, then back off three turns. Tighten locknut.

*Reverse band* Screw adjusting bolt in until bottomed, then back off three and one-half turns.

*Throttle link connecting rod* Adjust rod length so that the kickdown occurs at 28–31 mph with the accelerator pedal fully depressed. The rod must be shortened if kickdown occurs before pedal is fully depressed.

*Neutral safety switch (early type)* Place selector in "D" and adjust switch plate to give 0.040″ clearance between switch and lever. Make sure that the engine does not start in any range but "N" and "P". *NOTE: For late-model switch adjustment, see Corolla.*

### Corolla

*Low servo and band* Loosen locknut on adjusting bolt, tighten the bolt until bottomed, then back off three and one-half turns and tighten locknut.

*Throttle link connecting rod* Loosen the rod locknuts and adjust rod length so that

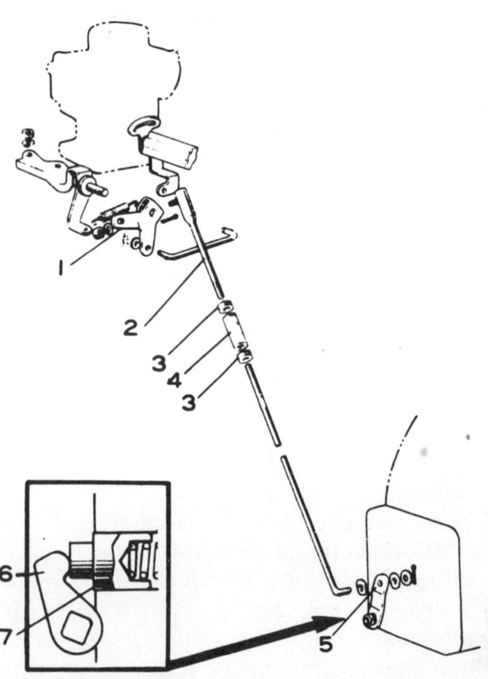


Connecting rod components.

pointer lines up with transmission case mark with the throttle butterfly fully opened and the accelerator pedal fully depressed.

*Neutral safety switch* Place selector in "N", then loosen locknut (2) and adjust control rod length so that shift lever pin rests firmly against the "N" detent on the plate. Make sure that the back-up lights operate in "R" and that the engine will not start in any range but "N" or "P".

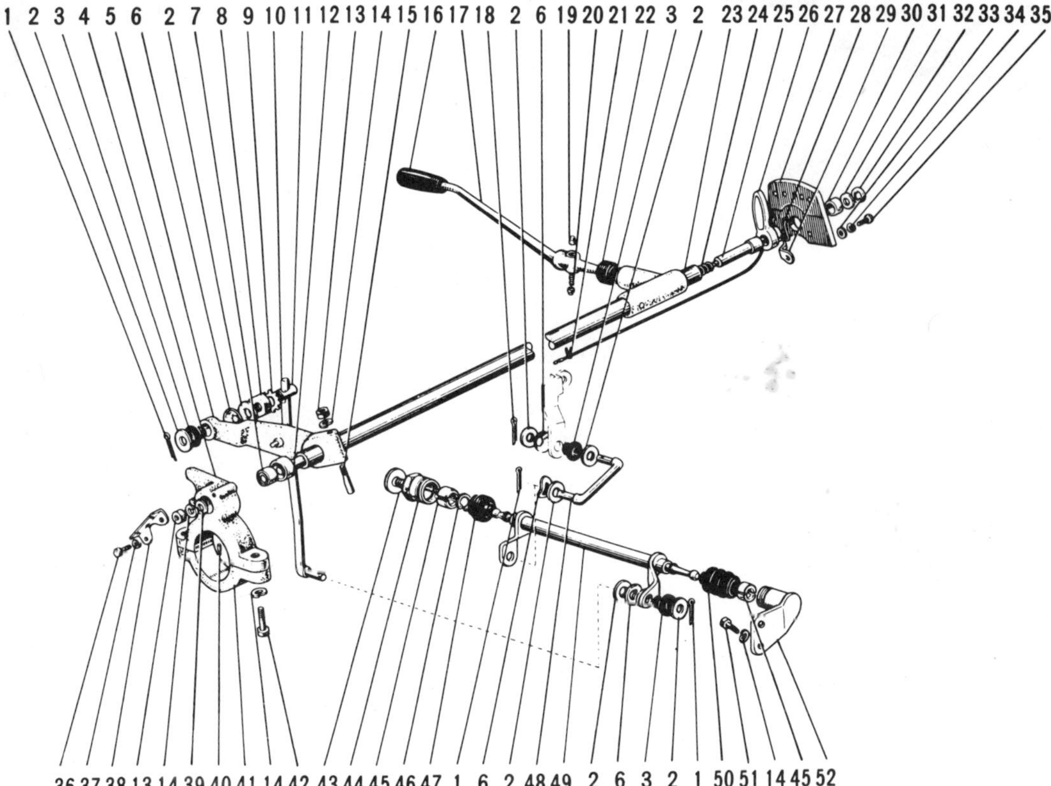


Shift lever and related components.

1. Cotter pin
2. Plain washer
3. Bushing
4. Control shaft lower bracket
5. Control shaft bracket
6. Wave washer
7. Lower bracket bushing
8. Hexagon nut
9. Toothed washer
10. Transmission control rod 1st.
11. Connecting rod swivel
12. Lower bracket bushing cover
13. Nut
14. Lockwasher
15. Lever lock pin
16. Shift lever knob
17. Shift lever
18. Cotter pin
19. Shift lever pin
20. Compression spring
21. Indicator light wiring retainer
22. Shift lever housing dust cover
23. Control shaft
24. Compression spring
25. Contral shaft upper piece
26. Control position
27. Bulb
28. Control position indicator plate
29. Control position indicator retainer
30. Indicator light ground plate
31. Upper control shaft piece bushing
32. Plain washer
33. E-ring
34. Plain washer
35. Lockwasher
36. Screw
37. Lockwasher
38. Safety switch bracket
39. Plain washer
40. Pin
41. Lower bracket clamp
42. Bolt
43. Wave washer
44. Cross shaft support No. 1
45. Cross shaft support bushing
46. Hole snap-ring
47. Cross shaft dust cover
48. Transmission control rod 2nd
49. Cross shaft
50. Cross shaft dust cover
51. Bolt
52. Cross shaft support

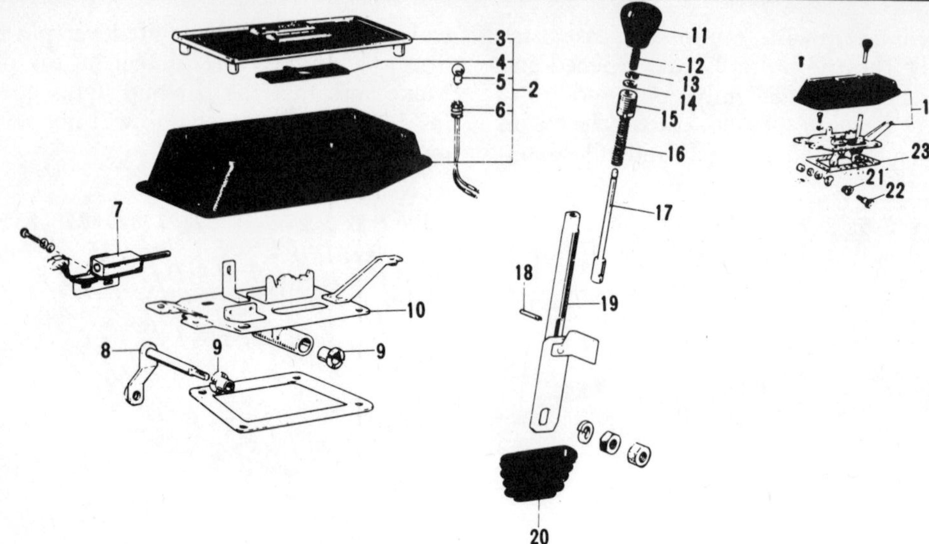


Console shift lever and components.

1. Transmission floorshift assembly
2. Position indicator housing assembly
3. Position indicator upper housing
4. Slide cover
5. Bulb
6. Indicator light wire
7. Neutral safety switch
8. Control shaft
9. Bushing
10. Shift lever plate
11. Shift lever knob
12. Spring
13. E-ring
14. Plate washer
15. Shift lever bushing
16. Spring
17. Detent rod
18. Pin
19. Shift (selector) lever
20. Shift lever boot
21. Bushing
22. Connecting rod swivel
23. Shift lever plate seat

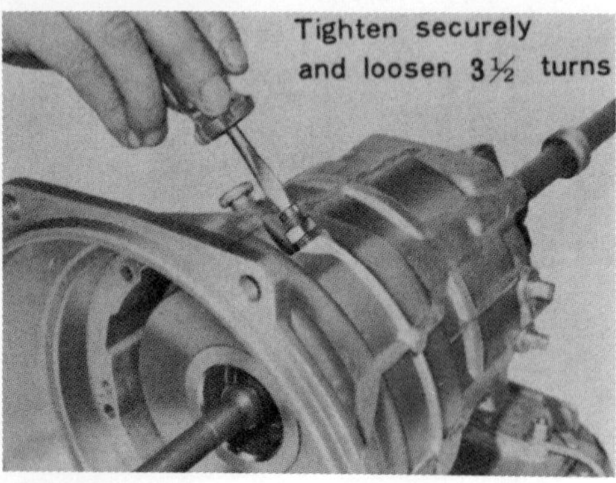


Adjusting low brake band.

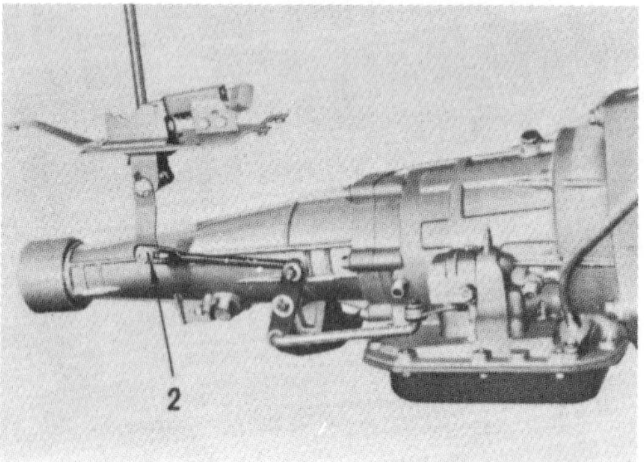


Adjusting shift lever.

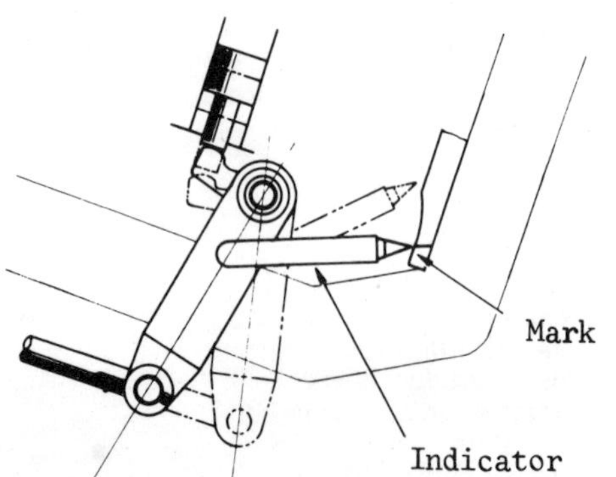


Indicator position.

Transmission removal, sequence of operations.

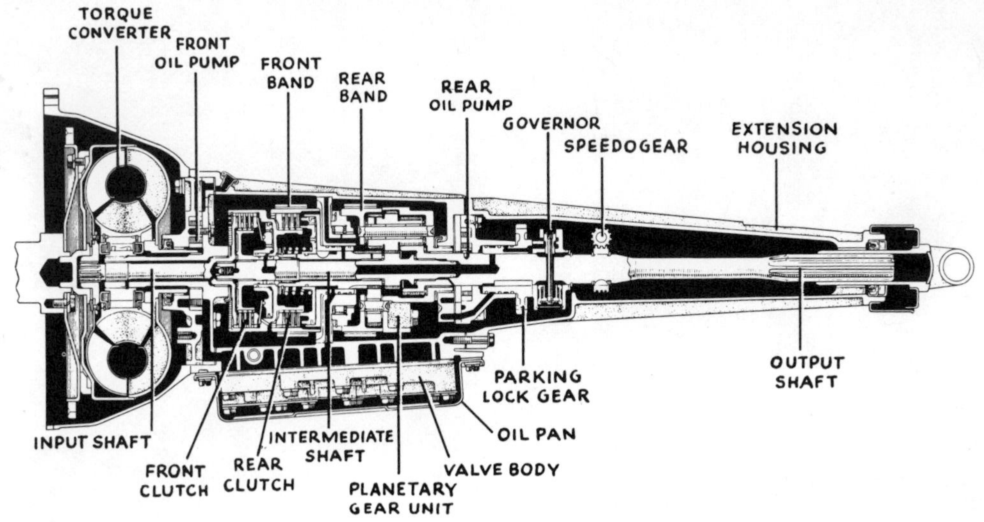


Crown and Mark II automatic transmission.

## Crown and Mark II Three-Speed Transmission

Early Crown models have remote control shift linkage, late Crowns and all Mark II models are equipped with a console-type floorshift. The three-speed transmission uses a system of two clutches and two bands to give three forward speeds plus reverse. Ratios are D1 and Low, 2.400; D2, 1.479; D3, 1.000 and Reverse 1.920. (Basically, this type transmission is similar to the domestic Borg Warner unit.)

### Removing the Transmission

Follow the numbered steps in the illustrations. In addition, disconnect torque rod from carburetor, all radiator and oil cooler hoses and disconnect battery cables.

### Disassembling the Transmission

Drain oil and clean off the case before beginning disassembly. *NOTE: Do not pry on the aluminum transmission case, as surfaces are very soft and are easily damaged. If two housings do not separate easily, tap them with a plastic mallet. Do not use gasoline to clean parts or use rags or wipers that leave lint.* Disconnect or remove in sequence, the following: parking rod, extension housing, speedometer gear and snap-ring, governor body, snap-ring, governor shaft and E-rings, governor valve, rear

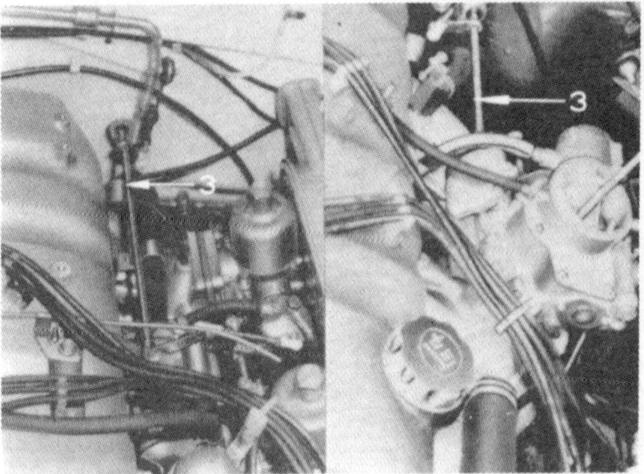


Transmission removal, sequence of operations.

pump body and gears, rear pump drive pin and cover plate, oil pan, oil tubes, valve body, rear servo and center support bolts. Then remove rear brake band, strut, front oil pump, front clutch and thrust washers, second sun gear thrust washer, rear clutch and front band (mark band). Remove intermediate shaft and second sun gear needle bearings (2), then loosen rear band adjusting bolt and loosen two outer center support bolts. Remove center support, rear band and planetary gear unit in one assembly, then remove control shaft lever, manual control valve lever pin and throttle valve lever and parts.

### Inspecting the Transmission

Wash all parts in clean solvent or transmission oil. Check all oil passages and tubes with compressed air (gently), including the oil cooler lines. Inspect oil seals, bushings,

Transmission removal, sequence of operations.

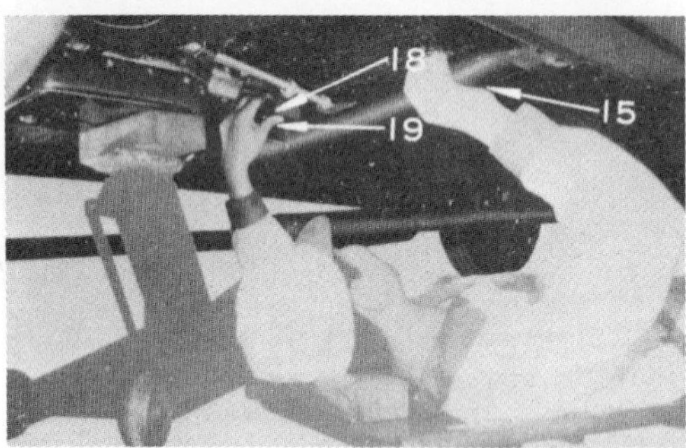

Transmission removal, sequence of operations.

thrust washers, gears, clutches, bands, piston and oil rings, servos, levers and the housing itself. Look for distortion, scuffing, wear (shiny areas indicating scuffing), gouges, nicks, dents, or burrs.

### Transmission Subassemblies

#### Front Clutch

To disassemble, first remove the input shaft snap-ring, then the input shaft and washer. Remove clutch hub, discs and plates (keeping them in order), then remove the snap-ring and diaphragm spring with set ring. Apply compressed air to the clutch "apply" hole to remove clutch piston. Inspect the shaft splines and teeth for wear or burrs, then check clutch discs and plates for signs of overheating or distortion. The clutch piston reed valve opening should be 0.030–0.045″; the height of the clutch diaphragm spring 0.252″ (limit 0.197″).

To assemble, place rings on clutch drum and piston and carefully install piston into drum without cutting the seal rings. Install diaphragm spring and set ring and secure with snap-ring. Install pressure plate (flat side up), then clutch discs and plates. Temporarily install the outer snap-ring and measure the thickness of the input shaft base plate then, using a gauge block of equal size, measure the free-play between clutch pack and underside of the snap-ring. Free-play should be 0.014–0.030″. Clutch plates are available in 0.063″ and 0.055″ sizes to ob-

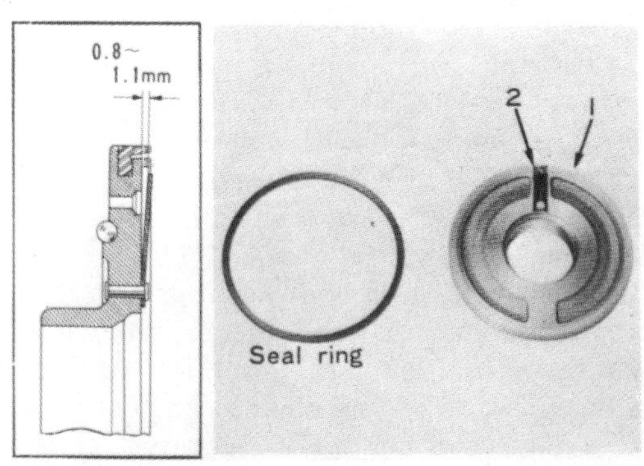

Clutch piston inspection.

tain correct clearances. Having selected the correct size clutch pack, reassemble with clutch hub. Stick thrust washer onto inside of input shaft (with Vaseline) and assemble with snap-ring. Be sure all snap-rings are properly seated.

### Rear Clutch

Remove the snap-ring, clutch flange, three discs and six plates (keeping them in order), then depress the piston return spring and remove snap-ring. Remove the needle bearing, clutch piston (with air pressure at hole in rear of drum), then remove seal-rings and O-rings.

The return spring free length should be 1.810″ (limit 1.650″). Clutch plates are installed with the notch to the right of the oil return hole in the clutch drum.

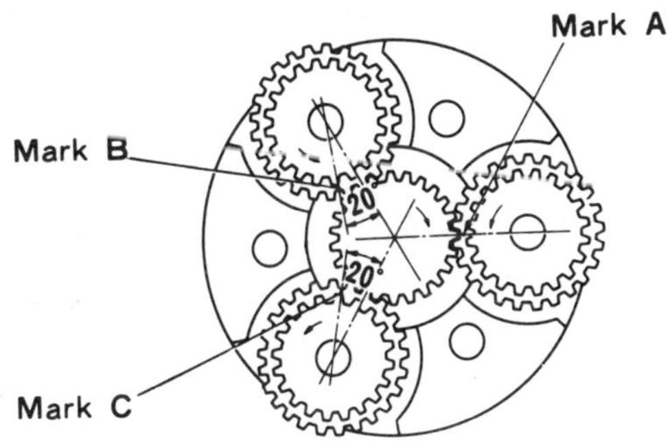


Long pinion installation position.

### Planetary Gear Unit

Remove center support and one-way clutch from outer race. Remove snap-ring and outer race from drum, then strip planetary gear. Difference between this unit and the Corona unit include the riveted pinions, which must be cut away from the carrier and the drum (bolted to the carrier with three bolts). Before disassembling, check marks on pinions (A, B, and C). If no marks exist, punch mark pinions and sun gear for correct installation.

Inspect all parts for wear, nicks, dents or other damage. Check one-way clutch sprags, then install pinions and needle rollers and align marks as shown. Stake securely in three places (two on groove of carrier to prevent pin rotation). Check output shaft for free rotation. Fit outer race to drum with snap-ring and install one-way clutch. If correctly installed, it should turn only in a counterclockwise direction. Check for free movement of oil check ball inside front of intermediate shaft, then check brake bands for signs of cracking.

### Front Servo

Remove snap-ring and drive out piston by applying compressed air to the apply hole in the cylinder. Remove spring retainer, piston rod, washer and spring. Drive out pin (¼″ punch) and remove lever. Separate inner and outer pistons and seals and inspect them for wear.

1. Brake band
2. Band anchor
3. Band apply lever
4. Band apply strut
5. Band apply bolt
6. Straight pin
7. Front servo body
8. Spring
9. Front servo release tube
10. Front servo piston rod
11. Plate washer
12. Spring
13. Straight plug
14. Front servo piston
15. O-ring
16. Front servo piston cylinder
17. Hole snap-ring
18. O-ring
19. Spring retainer
20. Front servo apply tube

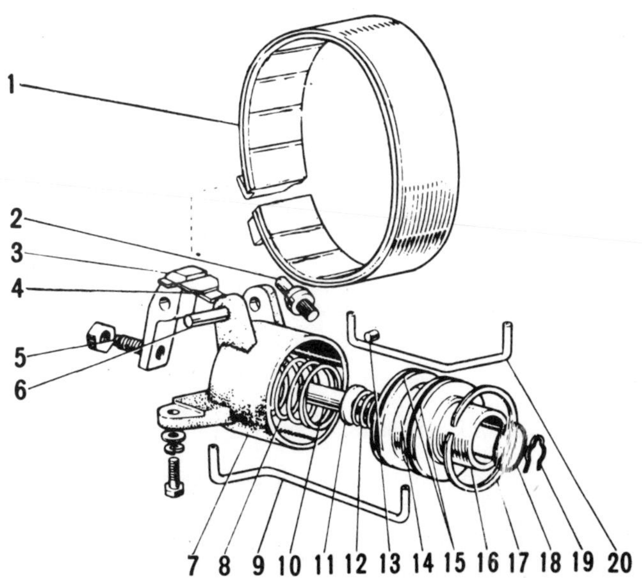


Front servo components.

### Rear Servo

Unhook torsion spring (by hand), then disassemble as above. Check mounting part of servo for squareness or distortion where it bolts to the transmission case.

### Valve Body

Do not disassemble unless a careful diagnosis has shown the cause of trouble to be in the valve body. Do not wash or clean valve body prior to disassembly. Remove pressure regulator valve spring (16) (hold down while unscrewing), seat (15), and retainer (14), then remove screws (one is shorter), cover (1) and gasket (2). Remove all valves and springs. Using needle-nose pliers, remove spring pin (28) and downshift plug (22).

Inspect all valves for damage or wear. Valve edges should be clean and sharp, and valves should rotate freely in their bores.

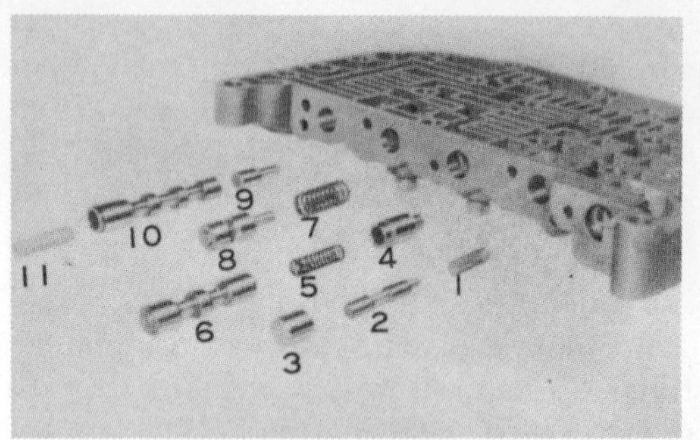


Valve body assembly sequence.

Assemble the valve body in sequence as illustrated.

### Governor

This unit is slightly different in shape and size from the one used in Corona models, but it is similar in operation; the parking lock gear is part of the governor support body in this application and spring free length is 0.728″ (limit 0.610″).

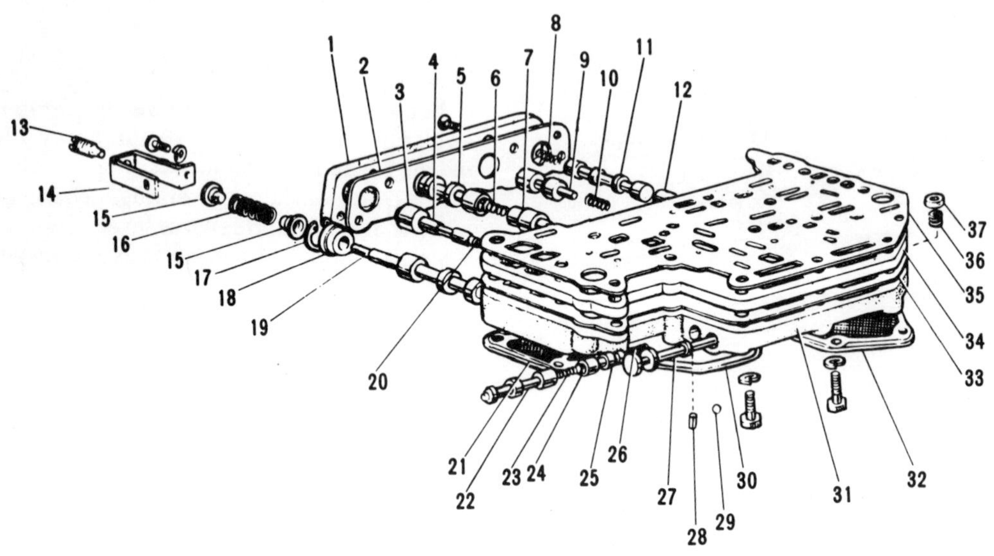


Valve body components.

1. Valve body cover
2. Valve body cover gasket
3. Throttle relay plug
4. Throttle relay valve
5. 2–3 shift valve
6. Spring
7. Throttle modulator valve
8. Spring
9. Orifice control valve
10. Spring
11. 1–2 shift valve
12. 1–2 shift valve low plug
13. Adjusting bolt
14. Pressure regulator valve spring retainer
15. Pressure regulator valve spring seat
16. Spring
17. Hole snap-ring
18. Pressure regulator valve sleeve
19. Pressure regulator valve
20. Spring
21. Front oil strainer
22. Downshift plug
23. Spring
24. Spacer
25. Throttle valve
26. Spring
27. Manual valve
28. Spring pin
29. Reverse shift restrict ball
30. Line pressure tube
31. Valve body
32. Rear oil strainer
33. Valve body plate No. 2 gasket
34. Valve body plate
35. Valve body plate No. 1 gasket
36. Spring
37. Check valve

## Valve Spring Specifications

| No. | Items | Outer diameter mm. | Outer diameter inches | Free height Standard mm. | Free height Standard inches | Free height Limit mm. | Free height Limit inches |
|---|---|---|---|---|---|---|---|
| 1 | 1–2 shift valve spring (blue) | 7.2 | 0.284 | 26.0 | 1.02 | 23.0 | 0.91 |
| 2 | Orifice control valve spring | 11.0 | 0.433 | 25.8 | 1.01 | 23.0 | 0.91 |
| 3 | 2–3 shift valve spring | 7.6 | 0.299 | 26.0 | 1.02 | 23.0 | 0.91 |
| 4 | Throttle relay valve spring | 6.6 | 0.260 | 19.0 | 0.75 | 16.0 | 0.63 |
| 5 | Pressure regulator valve spring | 11.4 | 0.448 | 48.8 | 1.92 | 46.0 | 1.81 |
| 6 | Throttle valve front spring (yellow) | 8.6 | 0.338 | 22.5 | 0.89 | 21.0 | 0.83 |
| 7 | Throttle valve rear spring (yellow) | 6.5 | 0.256 | 17.5 | 0.69 | 16.0 | 0.63 |
| 8 | Check valve spring | 9.5 | 0.374 | 16.4 | 0.65 | — | — |

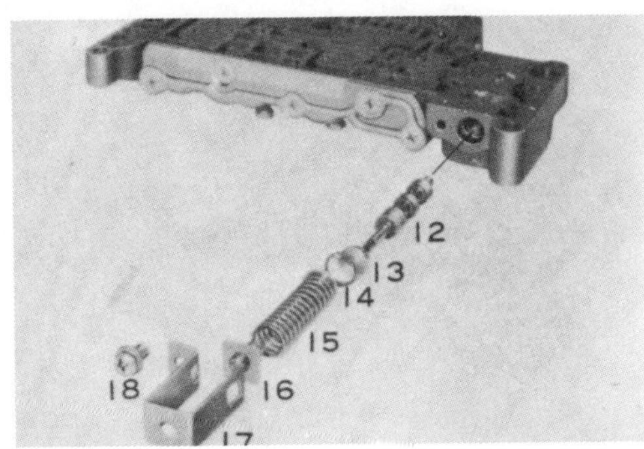

Regulator valve assembly sequence.

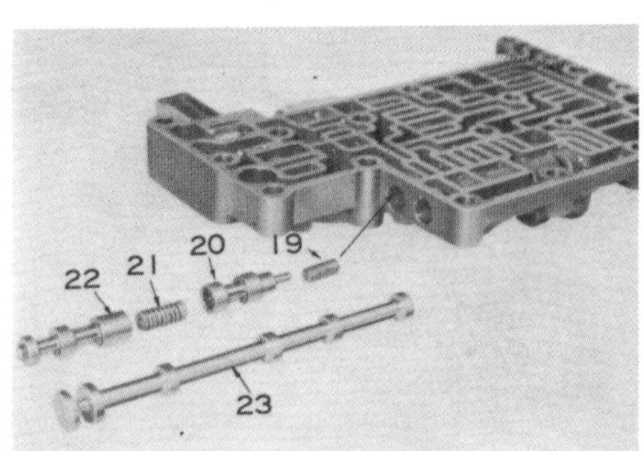

Valve body assembly sequence.

FRONT AND REAR PUMPS

Remove five bolts and tap stator support on bench to disengage it from housing. Mark both gears for reassembly and check all parts for damage and wear.

## Pump Clearances

| | | Front | Rear |
|---|---|---|---|
| Driven gear to body | Limit | 0.012″ | 0.010″ |
| Driven gear to crescent | Limit | 0.020″ | 0.020″ |
| Driven gear to body surface | Limit | 0.008″ | 0.008″ |

### Assembling the Transmission

Blow off all components with compressed air; prior to installation dip them in clean transmission oil. Soak brake bands and clutch plates for two hours in ATF prior to installation. Use no rags at any time and make sure any bristles left over from wash brush are removed. Assemble throttle valve lever in sequence illustrated, then assemble manual control valve lever shaft detent ball and spring. Align hole in lever with hole in shaft and drive in pin. Work lever through all positions. Install planetary gear unit, rear band, one-way clutch and center support. First install rear band into rear drum and rotate center support counterclockwise onto the planetary gear. Stick thrust washer to case with a glob of Vaseline (thrust washer is good as long as the oil groove is still visible), then back off rear band anchor bolt and check band position with regard to anchor strut. Align oil holes in center support with oil passages in transmission case and install planetary gear, with center support and O-ring into case. Secure two outer support bolts lightly in case in order to line up the center support.

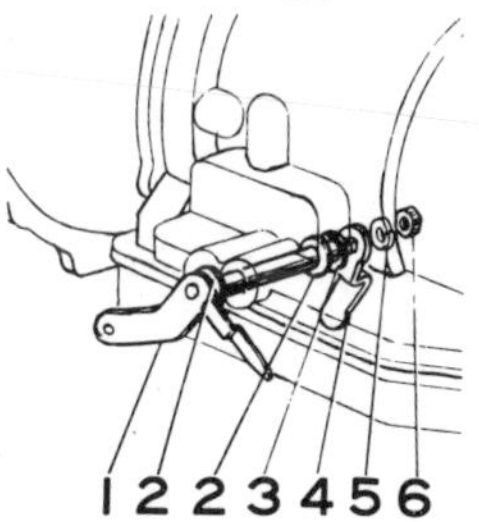

Throttle valve lever.

1. Throttle valve lever
2. Plate washer
3. Wave washer
4. Throttle valve inner lever
5. Lockwasher
6. Nut

1. Extension housing gasket
2. Stud bolt
3. Extension housing
4. Extension housing cover gasket
5. Extension housing cover
6. Type "T" oil seal
7. Seal washer
8. No. 2. dynamic damper
9. Dynamic damper bracket
10. No. 1 dynamic damper
11. Extension housing dust deflector
12. Bushing
13. Type "T" oil seal
14. Dust seal
15. Dust seal retainer
16. Seal washer
17. Speedometer driven gear
18. Bushing
19. O-ring
20. Speedometer shaft sleeve
21. O-ring
22. Speedometer sleeve lock plate
23. Parking lock pawl shaft
24. Parking lock pawl
25. Torsion spring
26. Spacer
27. Parking lock lever
28. Spring pin
29. Torsion spring
30. Plate washer
31. Plate washer
32. Parking lock shaft

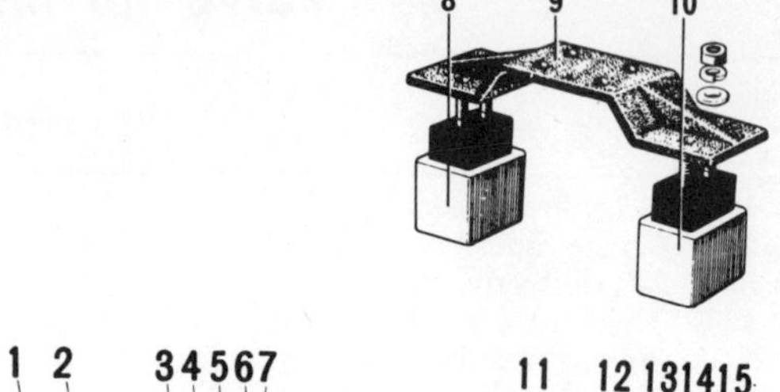


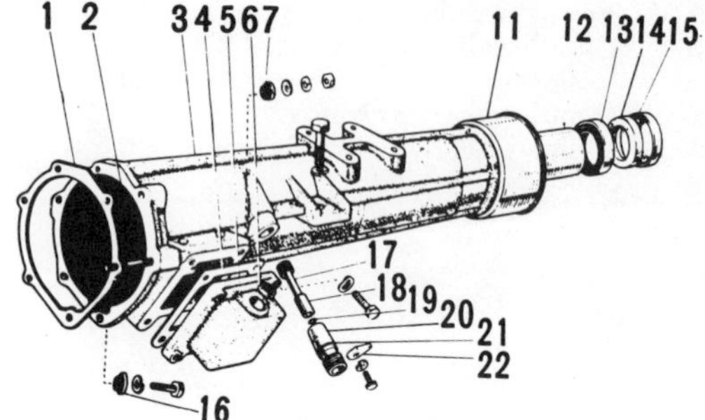


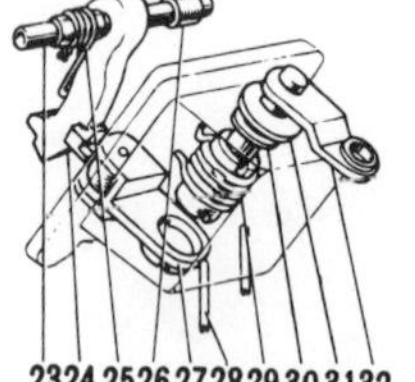


Extension housing components.

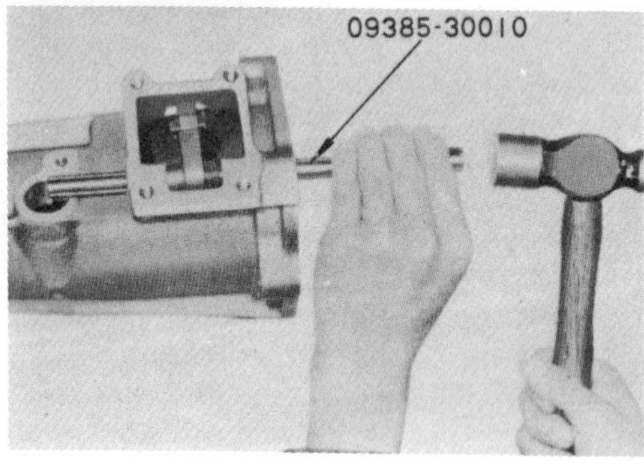


Removing shaft.

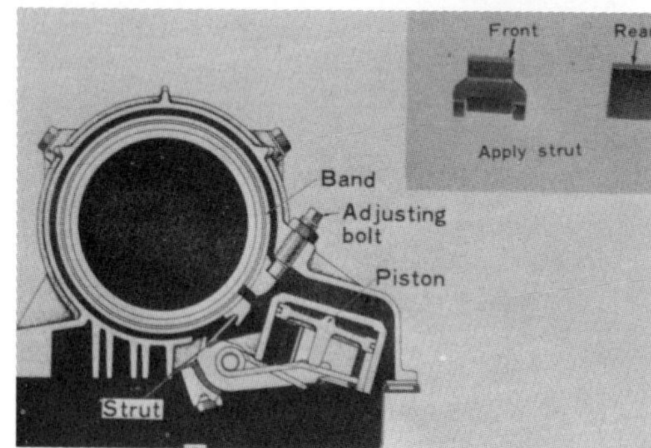


Installing rear band.

Install oil ring at nose end of intermediate shaft, fit thrust bearing, then slide assembly into planetary gear. *NOTE: If the pinions are not lined up correctly the intermediate shaft will not fit into the planetary.*

Install rear clutch thrust washer onto front clutch, with oil groove on washer facing front clutch side, then hold front band in place and install both clutch assemblies into case. Install rear servo; the shorter of the three bolts fits into the outer hole, one of the other two bolts (1.42") serves as the third center support locating bolt. Install front servo and front band. Take care to install the strut correctly.

Installing check ball.

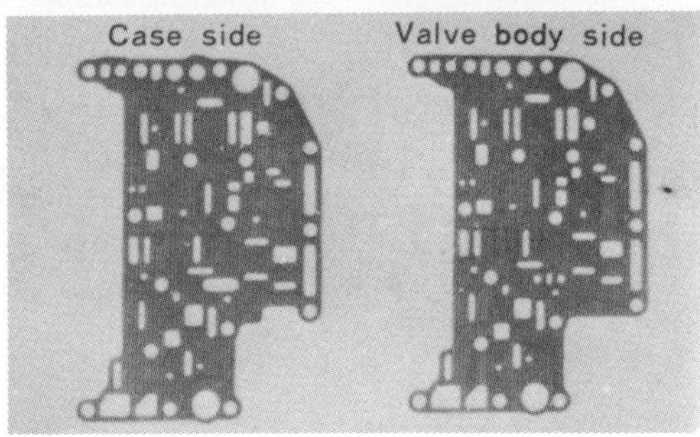


Gasket.

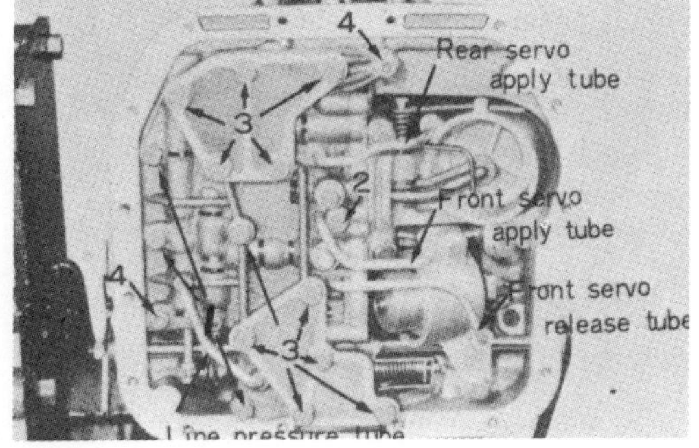


Hydraulic lines in valve body.

To install valve body, first insert throttle pressure check ball into case, then install valve body plate with its two gaskets as shown. Align manual valve with manual valve lever and secure valve body to case. *NOTE: The 15 valve body bolts are of different lengths.* Install oil tubes and lightly tap them into place.

Install front oil pump carefully without cocking or damaging the O-ring. Secure clutch drum thrust washer to rear of stator support with Vaseline. Do not dislodge thrust washer; tighten slowly and evenly. Now refer to your notes on the end-play of the input shaft (measured prior to disassembly). If end-play was within limits (.019–.035″), use the old washer; if not, washers are available in 0.078″ and 0.063″ sizes. Select for proper fit as necessary.

To adjust the rear band, tighten screw to 10 ft. lbs., then back off one full turn (360°) and secure locknut. The front band is adjusted in the same manner. Tighten screw to 10 in. lbs., then back off to obtain 0.118–0.120″ clearance (slightly smaller than a ⅛″ drill bit). Rotate input shaft and check for brake band drag.

Install oil pan and gasket; tighten pan bolts to 4–6 ft. lbs. Install rear oil pump cover gasket and plate, keeping oil holes lined up. Install pin to output shaft, then align slot in oil pump drive gear with pin and slide gears and pump into position.

Install governor body support and key and assemble governor in reverse order of disassembly. Install speedometer drive gear with key and snap-rings, then install extension housing. Place manual valve in "P", place parking lock pawl in "lock" position and hook up linkage. Install control rod to manual valve lever shaft, then install rear engine mounts (long on left, short on right side). Check free rotation of input and output shafts and tighten all bolts to specifications.

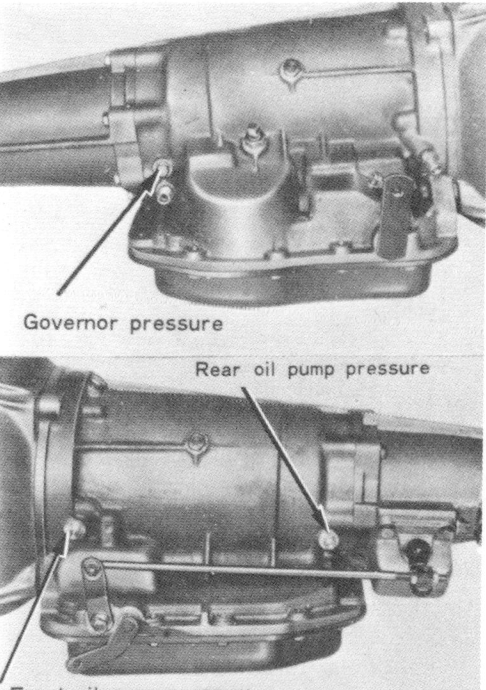


Pressure test points.

## Oil Pressure Tests

Check oil level (hot) but do not overfill. Set parking brake securely and block front wheel (or raise rear wheels). Bring oil to operating temperature. Connect oil pressure gauge (200 psi) to pressure test points shown.

By shifting the gear selector into all gear ranges it is possible to test pressure regulator and throttle relay valve operation by measuring front and rear pump discharge pressures.

# Chart AT-4
# Automatic Transmission Diagnosis—Crown and Mark II

| Action | What to Check | Action | What to Check |
|---|---|---|---|
| Gear Engagements | | Slipping | |
| None | 1, 7, 6, 12, 20 | Starting in D | 24, 2, 8, 27 |
| Delayed | 1, 2, 9, 28 | In D2 | 2, 3, 7, 10, 27 |
| No reverse | 1, 4, 5 | In D3 | 2, 3, 7, 27 |
| No forward | 1, 2, 8 | 3–2 | 9, 14a |
| No D2 | 1, 2, 3 | Under acceleration | 2, 8, 17a |
| No L | 1, 2, 5 | | |
| Harsh | 21, 22, 11, 18, 28 | | |
| Shifts | | Noise | |
| No 1–2 | 15, 16a, 3 | Mechanical | 25, 26, 8 |
| No 2–3 | 16a, 17, 4, 10, 14a | Hydraulic | 7, 10 |
| No 3–2 | 17, 16, 3, 14a | No push start | 10 |
| No 2–1 | 15a, 16, 13a | | |
| None | 13, 14, 15, 16, 17 | | |
| Harsh | 11, 19, 23,28 | | |

# Check Points for Chart AT-4

| Code Number | What to Check | Code Number | What to Check |
|---|---|---|---|
| 1 | Oil level low | 15 | Modulator valve pressure high |
| 2 | Front clutch not operating | 15a | Modulator valve pressure low |
| 3 | Front band not operating (servo) | 16 | Governor valve pressure high |
| 4 | Rear clutch not operating | 16a | Governor valve pressure low |
| 5 | Rear band not operating (servo) | 17 | Throttle valve pressure high |
| 6 | Pressure regulator stuck | 17a | Throttle valve pressure low |
| 7 | Front pump pressure low | 18 | Orifice control valve pressure high |
| 8 | One-way clutch slipping | 19 | Front band worn (slipping) |
| 9 | Internal oil leaks | 20 | Parking pawl locked or jammed |
| 10 | Rear pump pressure low | 21 | Idle speed too high |
| 11 | Line pressure excessive | 22 | Throttle valve pressure low |
| 12 | Manual valve maladjusted | 23 | One-way clutch defective |
| 13 | 1–2 shift valve pressure high | 24 | Line pressure low |
| 13a | 1–2 shift valve pressure low | 25 | Worn planetary or pump gears |
| 14 | 2–3 shift valve pressure high | 26 | Converter (stator) clutch defective |
| 14a | 2–3 shift valve pressure low | 27 | Throttle connecting rod too long |
| | | 28 | Throttle connecting rod too short |

*Front pump:* full throttle in D, D2, L . . . 130–150 psi
in R, N and P . . . 185–210 psi

*Governor:* check at varying vehicle speeds:

18 mph . . . . 24.2 psi
35 mph . . . . 38.4 psi
52 mph . . . . 63 psi

*Rear pump* at 35 mph in D, pressure should be 70–85 psi.

*Stall test* at full throttle (see front pump) engine should turn 1,950–2,150 rpm. If pressure is good but engine speed low, the engine needs tuning, the carburetor valve is not opening fully or stator clutch is slipping in torque converter. If engine speed exceeds specifications in D, D2 and L only, the front clutch is defective. If engine speed exceeds specifications in R only, the rear clutch is defective.

## Floorshift Lever—Crown and Mark II

To remove the floorshift lever, disconnect it at transmission and remove the four bolts that hold the console to floor. Disconnect the wiring for neutral safety and back-up switch and lift console off.

When assembling, install the spring pin (14) with the slot facing upwards. Tighten the wire adjusting nut so that pin-to-plate

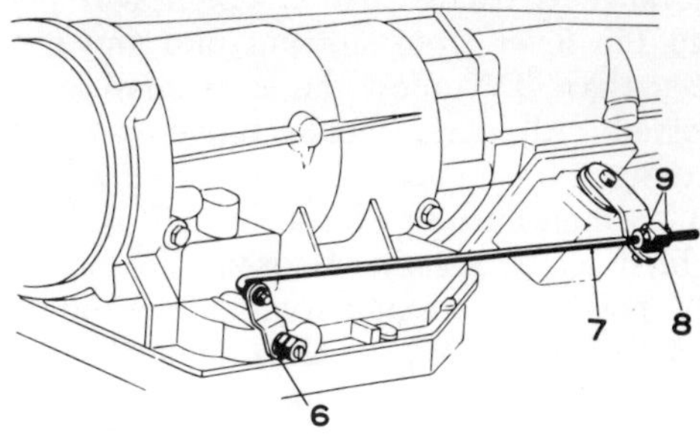


Park rod.

1. Shift lever
2. Connecting rod swivel
3. Control rod
4. Manual valve lever
5. Manual valve lever shaft
6. Control shaft LH lever
7. Parking lock rod
8. Parking lock rod swivel
9. Nut

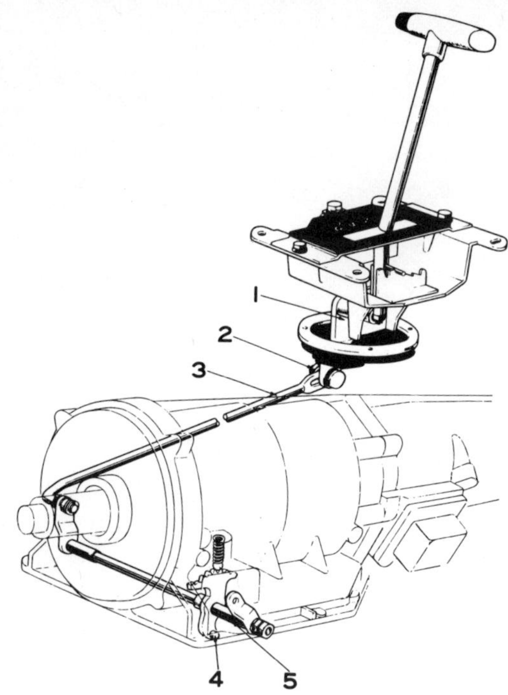


Floorshift lever control linkage.

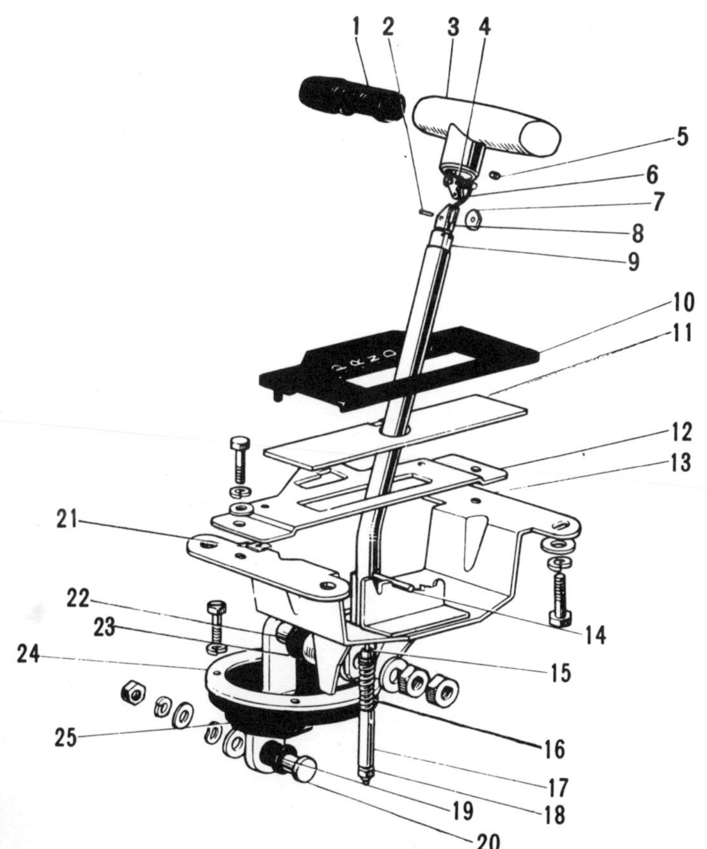


1. Shift lever knob button
2. Straight pin
3. Shift lever knob
4. Wire pull lever
5. Retaining bolt
6. Shift lever wire
7. Wire pulley
8. Wire guide
9. Shift lever
10. Control position indicator
11. Slide cover
12. Position indicator support
13. Shift lever plate
14. Spring pin
15. Shift lever spring seat
16. Compression spring
17. Detent sleeve
18. Lock nut
19. Bushing
20. Connecting rod swivel
21. Spring nut
22. Control shaft
23. Bushing
24. Shift lever boot retainer
25. Shift lever boot

Floorshift lever and related components.

clearance is 0.020–0.040″, which will prevent the lever from shifting into any gear other than "D" unless the shift knob is depressed. All parts should move smoothly without interference.

Check all bushings for wear and play and tighten as necessary. Loosen the locknut (2), position the manual valve lever on the transmission in "N", put the selector lever in "N" and lock the swivel locknut. Check the "P" position and, if necessary, adjust as follows: loosen the locknuts (9) and check all bushings for play and wear. Place the selector in "P" and engage the parking lock shaft (10) by hand. Secure the locknuts. The engine should start in "P" and "N" only. If not, adjust the neutral safety switch as previously described.

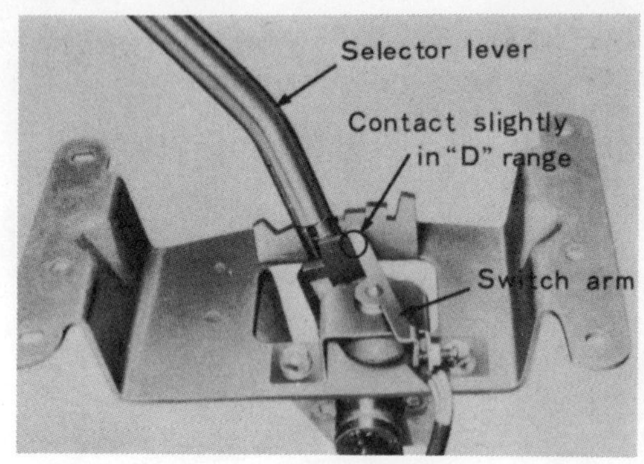

Switch in installed position.

# Chapter 8
# Brakes

## General

All models are equipped with four-wheel hydraulic brakes and mechanically operated parking brakes acting on rear wheels only. All late models are equipped with dual (tandem) master cylinders, in accordance with federal standards, and Corona and Crown are additionally equipped with a brake pressure control valve. Some Crown models have power assisted front disc brakes. A common warning light is connected to both parking brake lever and hydraulic system pressure switch.

*Corolla* Twin leading shoe type with two wheel cylinders per wheel; rear brakes are of the leading-trailing type with only one wheel cylinder per wheel.

*Corona* Front and rear are self-adjusting with one wheel cylinder per wheel.

*Crown* Front brakes are disc type and rear are leading-trailing type.

*Land Cruiser* Front and rear are of the leading-trailing type with two single-acting wheel cylinders in front and two double-acting cylinders in rear.

## Service

### Removing the Brake Drum and Shoes

All brakes are removed in a similar manner. Jack up car (or wheel) and remove hubcap and grease cap. Pull cotter pin from wheel bearing locknut and remove locknut. Temporarily install grease cap and remove wheel and drum as a unit. (This prevents bearings from dropping onto the floor.) Next, remove brake shoe retainers, self-adjusting cables, all springs and the shoes. Mark shoes for later identification (leading or trailing). Strip wheel cylinders and catch the escaping brake fluid. Cylinders need not be removed from backing plates

## Brake System Specifications

| *Model* | | *Corona 2R* | *Corona 3R* | *Corolla* | *Crown* | *Land Cruiser* |
|---|---|---|---|---|---|---|
| Brake drum diameter (in.) | | 9.00 | 9.00 | 7.87 | 9.00 | 11.40 |
| Brake disc diameter (in.) | | — | — | — | 10.80 | — |
| Master cylinder bore (in.) | | 0.7500 | 0.7500 | 0.6250 | 0.7500 | 1.0000 |
| Wheel cylinder bore (in.) | Front | 0.8125 | 1.1250 | 0.7500 | 2.2500 | 1.1250 |
| | Rear | 0.6250 | 0.7500 | 0.6875 | 0.7500 | 1.0000 |

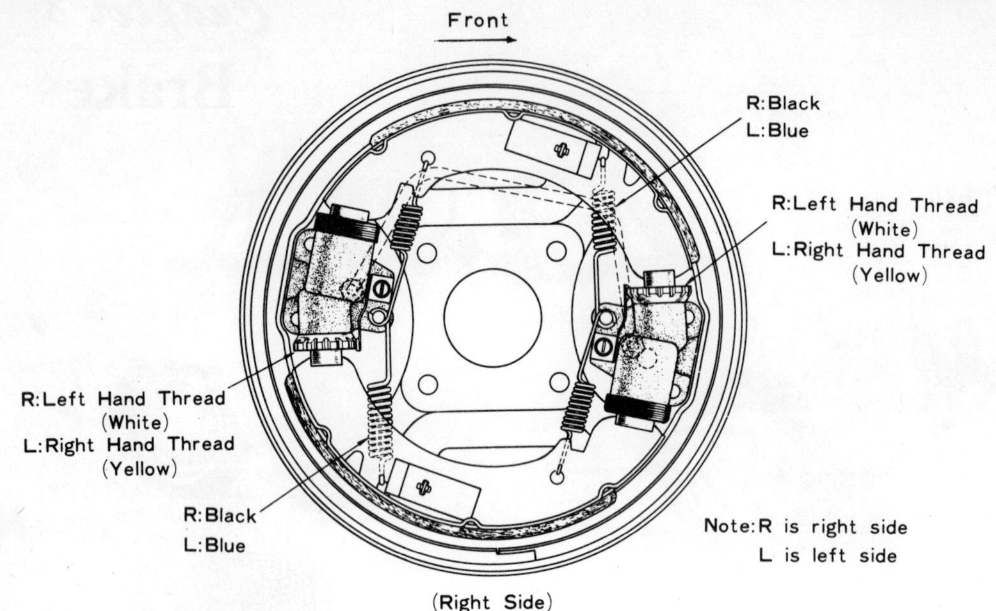


Corolla front brakes.

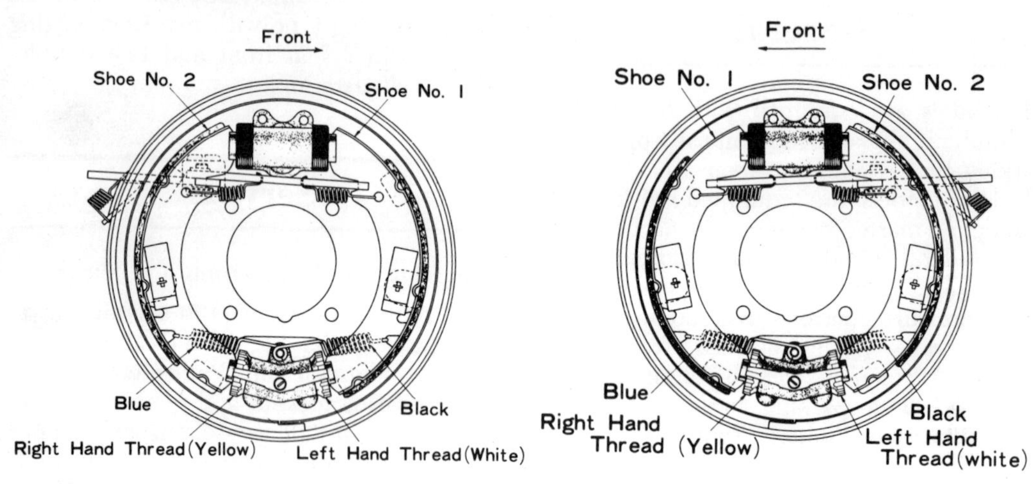


Corolla rear brakes.

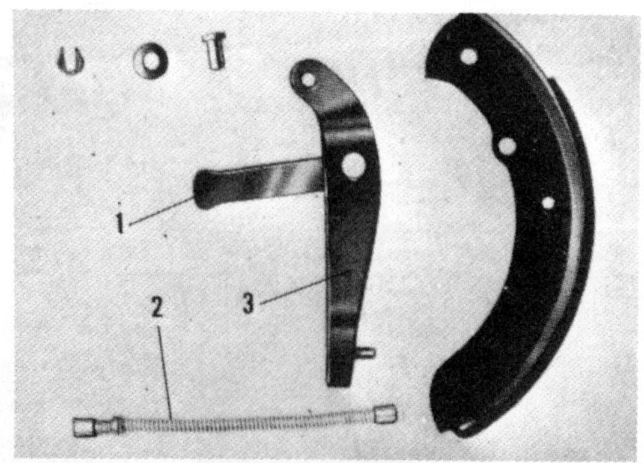


Parking brake lever.

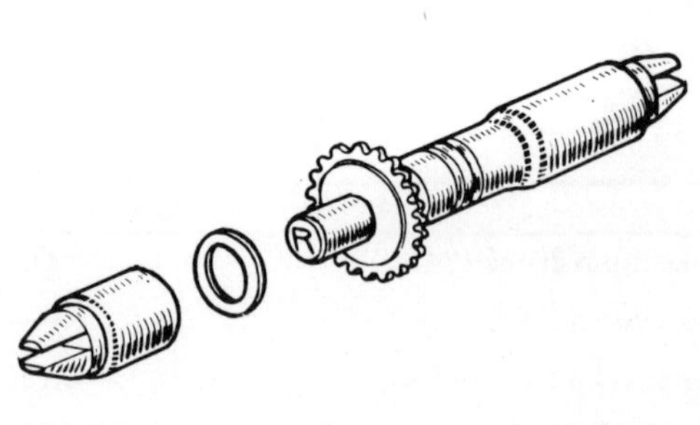


Star wheel adjuster.

## Brake Diagnosis Chart

| *Condition* | *Mechanical* | *Hydraulic* | *Vacuum* |
|---|---|---|---|
| Low Pedal, long travel | F G I M f e | T | b |
| Spongy Pedal | I | P Q U | |
| Hard Pedal | A F G K V a | R T U W | b c d g |
| Fading Pedal | I | P Q S T W | |
| Grabbing or Pulling | A D E G H I K L N V X Y Z a | R W | b |
| Noise | F G H I J K L M N | | |
| Chattering | D G I L N O | | |
| Dragging (slow or incomplete release) | a e f A B C F G H K L V | R U T W | K |

A—Pedal linkage binding. Check by bleeding one wheel cylinder using light pedal effort only.
B—Parking brake cables and linkage dirty or sticking.
C—Parking brake improperly adjusted (too loose or too tight).
D—Wheel bearing loose.
E—Front wheel alignment; uneven tire tread.
F—Brake shoe improperly adjusted. Automatic self adjusters corroded, broken or distorted.
G—Brake linings (or pads) worn, distorted or oily.
H—Shoe return spring weak, broken or incorrectly installed.
I—Drums cracked, worn too thin (beyond limit), scored or glazed (hard spots) or out-of-round.
J—Weak hold-down springs.
K—Brake shoe support plate ledges worn or grooved.
L—Support plate loose, worn or distorted.
M—Disc brake pad knock back (loose or worn wheel bearings or steering parts).
N—Caliper not aligned with disc or loose on bracket.
O—Disc (rotor) has excessive lateral runout or one-sided wear.
P—Hydraulic fluid airlocked; low grade fluid (boiling point too low).
Q—Hoses and lines weak or soft, expanding under pressure.
R—Hoses and lines kinked, collapsed, dented or clogged.
S—Hoses and lines having loose connections, ruptures or other damage causing leakage.
T—Master cylinder primary cup worn or damaged, bore rough, worn or cracked.
U—Master cylinder check valve faulty or compensator port blocked.
V—Wheel cylinder frozen or seized.
W—Wheel cylinder cups swollen, worn or damaged seals, bores rough or corroded.
X—Wheel cylinders mismatched (in size).
Y—Unequal tire pressure.
Z—Rear wheels (both) grabbing because pressure control valve defective
a—Power unit valve pushrod linkage binding.
b—Corrosion, lack of lubrication in power cylinder. Control valve, power cylinder, piston or diaphragm defective.
c—Vacuum lines loose, broken or collapsed. Low engine manifold vacuum.
d—Vacuum check valve defective (sticking).
e—Power unit hydraulic check ball stuck or clogged, pushrod improperly adjusted.
f—Air trapped in hub (rear) cavity of master cylinder; inspect master cylinder boot.
g—Air filter dirty or clogged.

for overhauling. On rear brakes, the parking brake lever must be disconnected in order to remove the shoes. Unless necessary, do not disengage the cable from its seat in the lever.

### Inspecting the Brakes

Check condition of lining and shoes; replace if worn to less than 30% of original thickness or if burnt, glazed or oily. (Burnt lining, although it still may retain its normal thickness, has lost its braking properties and will crack and peel off.) Check brake drums for uneven wear, scoring, bell-mouthed wear, glazing or hard spots. Factory drum refinishing limit is 0.080″ for all models except F series, which is 0.120″. Observe state inspection limits in all cases. Contour grind new brake shoes for a better fit. Check shoes closely and remove all sharp edges from metal which might contact the backing plate. Shoes are bonded and replacement lining must conform to federal safety standards.

### Wheel Cylinders

Remove boots, pistons and cups and closely inspect bores for signs of wear, scoring and/or scuffing. When in doubt, replace or hone wheel cylinders with a special brake hone, using clean brake fluid as lubricant. Wash residue from bores using clean fluid; never use oil or any other solvent on any brake components. Blow dry with air and install with fresh brake fluid. General limit of honed cylinder is 0.005″ oversize. (Do not try to save money by reusing brake components such as cylinders and cups.)

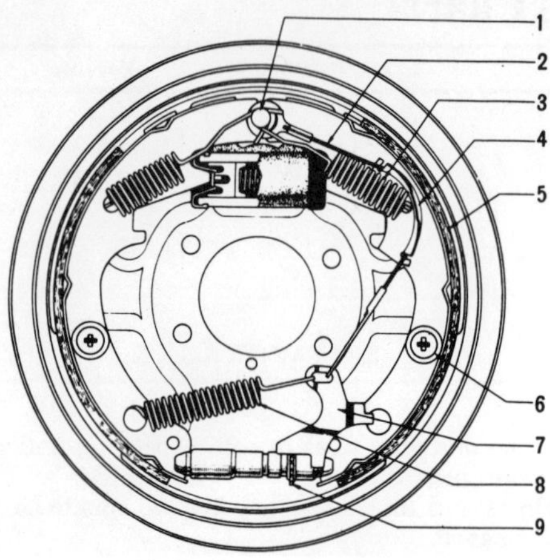


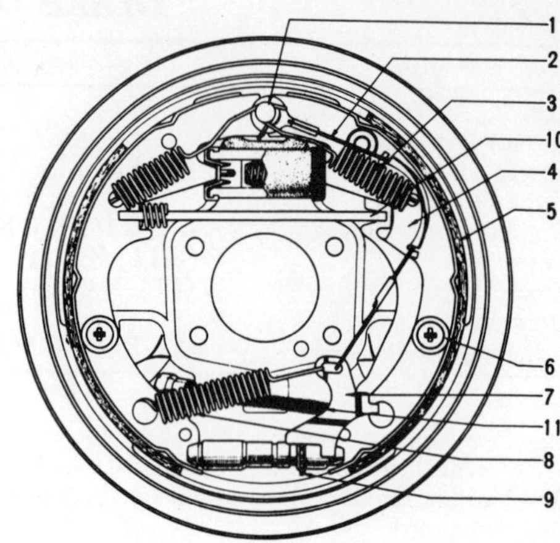


Corona brakes with self-adjusters.

1. Anchor pin
2. Self-adjuster cable
3. Anchor pin-to-No. 2 shoe spring
4. Cable guide
5. No. 2 shoe assembly
6. Shoe hold-down spring cup
7. Self-adjuster lever
8. Adjuster spring
9. Adjusting screw
10. Parking brake shoe
11. Parking brake cable

The self-adjuster screws should be taken apart and all dirt and rust removed with a wire brush. Lightly coat with Lubriplate before assembly; components should turn freely.

**Installing the Brakes**

After cleaning the backing plates and applying a light coat of Lubriplate at the points of contact between shoes and plate, install the wheel cylinder (already assembled). Position the brake shoes and secure them with the hold-down springs and pins. Hook eye of black spring onto anchor pin of rear shoe and hook other end to front shoe. *NOTE: With self-adjusters, coat cable guide with Lubriplate and install onto rear shoe.*

**Brake Adjustment**

Brake shoes must be adjusted so that there will be slight contact with the drum but no binding or dragging of shoes.

*Corolla front* Remove plugs from backing plate and with adjusting tool or a thin screwdriver turn wheel cylinder adjusting nut until wheel locks (turn tool away from center of wheel), then back off about four notches until wheel rotates freely.

*Corolla rear* Move tool to tighten brakes (there are two adjusters on each front and rear wheel); back off four notches.

*Crown front* Disc brakes; need no adjustment.

*Crown rear* Move adjusting tool *away* from center of wheel to tighten, then back off about nine notches.

*Corona front and rear* Self-adjusting type.

*Land Cruiser front* Each shoe must be adjusted separately (there are two adjusters per wheel). Tighten each shoe until locked, then back off five notches.

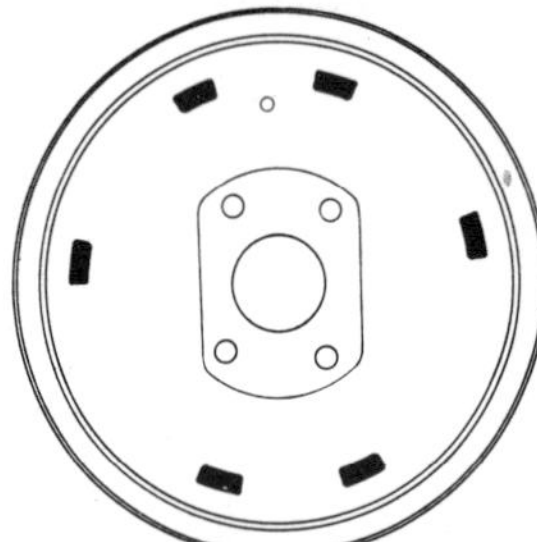

Lubrication points.

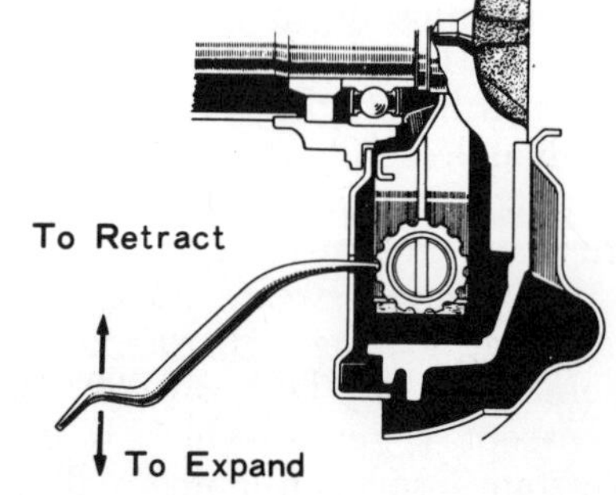


Front brake adjustment.

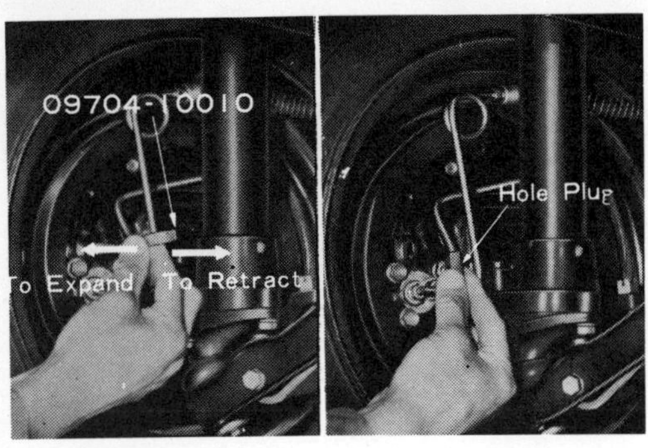


Rear brake adjustment.

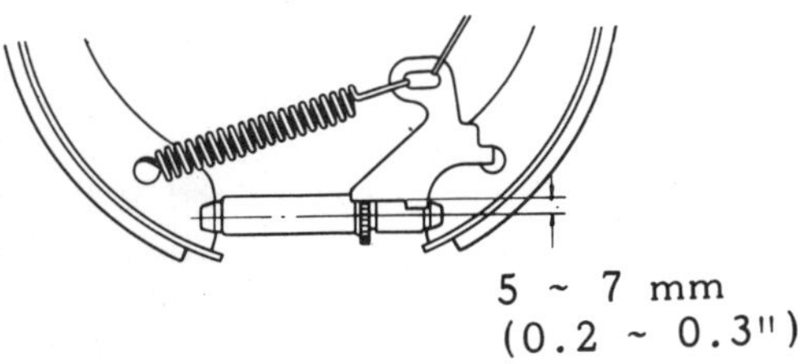


Self-adjuster lever position.

### Self-Adjusters

Self-adjusters have both left- and right-handed threads and great care must be taken to install them correctly. Adjusters are stamped "L" and "R" for easier identification.

Corolla adjusting bolts are color-coded for easy identification; LH threads are WHITE, RH threads are YELLOW.

Attention also must be paid to the color-coded individual springs on Corona; primary springs are BLACK, secondary springs are BLUE. Springs must be carefully checked and installed; mixed up pull-back springs result in severe malfunctions and eventual failure.

## Brake Pressure Control Valve

To prevent rear wheel lock-up during panic stops, a control valve has been incorporated into the brake system. Its function is to reduce brake pressure to the rear wheel cylinders, in proportion to pedal pressure, in a fixed ratio. A defective valve causes partial or total brake failure (in case of leaks or ruptured lines). Valves must be replaced as an assembly if defective.

To test the valve, connect a T-fitting and hydraulic pressure gauge to master cylinder rear outlet line (gauge should read to at least 2,000 psi) and connect a second gauge (1,200 psi) to the rear brake line at wheel cylinder. Apply pedal pressure and check readings against graph.

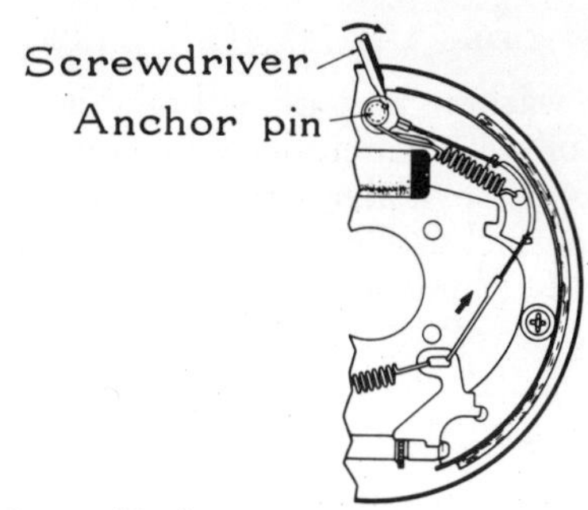


Checking self-adjuster action.

## Master Cylinder

A number of master cylinders are used on all models. Early types are of the single cylinder design, while later models all have a dual (tandem) type master cylinder which has a separate system for front and rear brakes. Warning switches also are incorporated; should pressure in either of the two systems drop below 80 psi, these switches cause a warning light to go on. Power assisted disc brakes act on front wheels only.

### Removing the Master Cylinder

Remove reservoir cap and float and drain as much fluid as possible before removal. *CAUTION: Brake fluid will cause paint damage if not immediately rinsed off.* Disconnect brake lines and wires from warning switches (where fitted), unhook brake pedal return spring, disconnect clevis pin and disengage pushrod from pedal. Remove all bolts that hold cylinder to firewall, then lift out the master cylinder.

### Disassembling the Master Cylinder

Remove the reservoir caps and floats and unscrew the bolts that hold the reservoir to the main body. (Later models have integral reservoirs.) Remove warning switches (where fitted), then remove from rear of cylinder, in order, boot and snap-ring, stop plate (washer), piston No. 1 with spacer, cylinder cup, spring retainer and spring. Remove end plug and gasket from front of cylinder, then remove the front piston stop bolt from underneath, pull out the spring and its retainer, piston No. 2, spacer and cylinder cup. Remove the two outlet fittings, washers, check valves and springs. Remove the piston cups from their seats on the pistons only if they are to be replaced.

### Inspecting the Master Cylinder

After washing all parts in brake fluid and rinsing off with water, dry with compressed air. Inspect cylinder bore for wear, scuff marks or nicks. Cylinders may be honed slightly, but limit is 0.006″. In view of the importance of the master cylinder, it is recommended that it be replaced rather than overhauled.

### Assembling the Master Cylinder

Reverse the sequence of disassembly. Absolute cleanliness is important, and all parts must be coated with clean brake fluid. Bleed the master cylinder and make sure all lines are tightened correctly and do not leak. Use fluid that meets 70-R-3 specifications (for standard brakes) and use the special disc brake fluid for disc brake equipped cars.

## Disc Brakes

Installed only on Crown front wheels, these units are of the self-adjusting, stationary caliper type with two wheel cylinders per side. Repairs should be limited to replacing brake pads, as overhaul of internal caliper components requires special tools not easily available.

### Replacing the Disc Brake Pads

Jack up car and remove wheel, then remove E-ring from retainer pin and remove keeper plate. Hook onto pad backing plate and pull pad from caliper. Using a flat bar, push the wheel cylinder pistons back into the housing as far as they will go. This will cause the fluid level in the master cylinder to rise; therefore either open the bleed screw at each side of the wheel cylinder while pushing in on the piston or drain brake fluid out of the master cylinder to prevent overflow.

Thoroughly clean all wheel cylinders before installing new pads. Slide new pad onto pin protruding from wheel cylinder piston, so that the slot in the pad backing plate is fully engaged. Pads are marked "#1" and "#2" and are enscribed with an arrow, which points in the direction of the forward rotation of the wheel. Install plate, retainer pin and E-ring, then refill master cylinder to correct level and adjust brakes by repeated application of the pedal until a firm and high pedal is obtained. *DO NOT attempt to drive the car before the pads are fully seated.* Disc brakes are bled in the same manner as drum brakes.

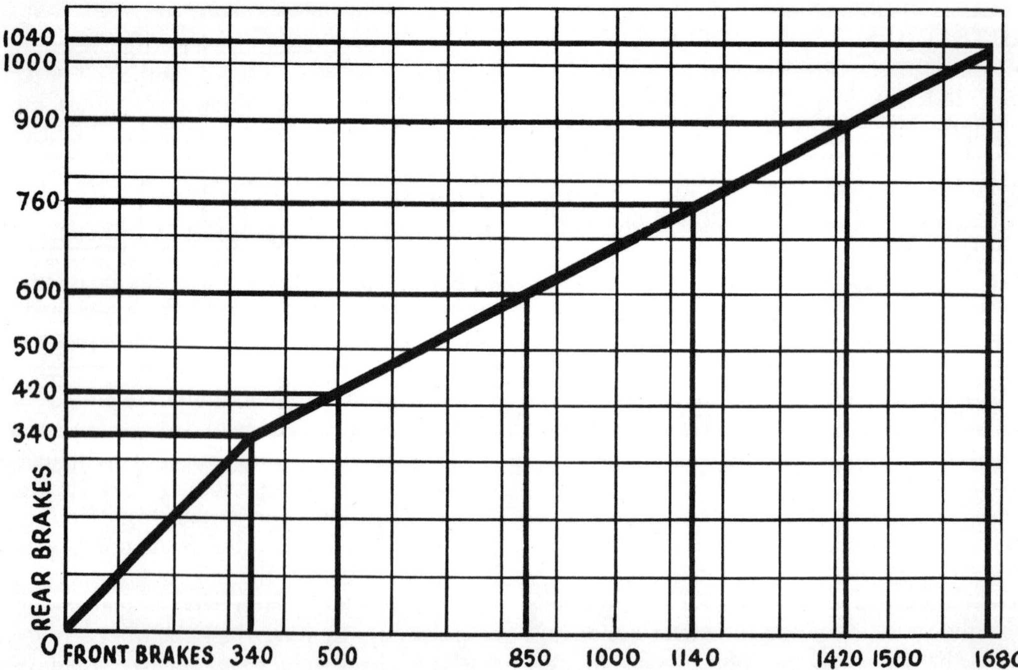


Brake pressure control valve—reduction ratios.

# Brake Shoe Pull-back Springs

| Model | Front Free Length | Front Installed Length | Front Lbs. Pull | Rear Free Length | Rear Installed Length | Rear Lbs. Pull |
|---|---|---|---|---|---|---|
| Corolla | P—2.740″ | | | 1.630″ | | |
| | A—2.680″ | | | 2.680″ | | |
| Corona | 5.728″ | 6.280″ | 46 | 3.660″ | 4.070″ | 16 |
| | S—6.020″ | 6.810″ | 38 | 6.020″ | 6.810″ | 38 |
| Crown | * | | | P—3.660″ | 4.070″ | 16 |
| | | | | A—6.020″ | 6.810″ | 38 |
| Land Cruiser | 7.460″ | 8.070″ | 33 | 3.660″ | 4.070″ | 16 |

P—Piston side of wheel cylinder
A—Adjuster screw side
S—Self adjusters
* Disc brakes

Note: All spring dimensions are measured between insides of spring ends (hooks).

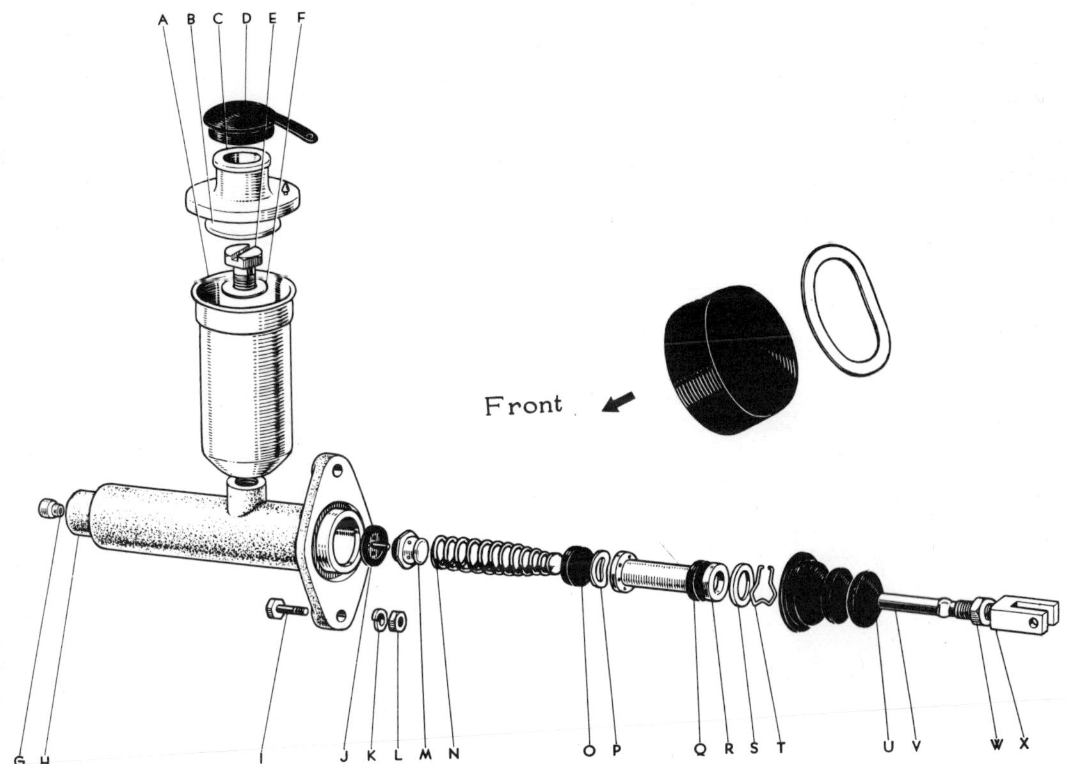


Single circuit master cylinder components.

- A. Master cylinder reservoir
- B. Master cylinder reservoir float
- C. Reservoir cap
- D. Reservoir filler cap
- E. Master cylinder reservoir set bolt
- F. Reservoir set bolt washer
- G. Union seat
- H. Master cylinder body
- I. Bolt
- J. Outlet check valve seat gasket
- K. Spring washer
- L. Nut
- M. Outlet check valve
- N. Piston return spring
- O. Cylinder cup
- P. Piston cup spacer
- Q. Cylinder cup
- R. Master cylinder piston
- S. Plate washer
- T. Hole snap-ring
- U. Master cylinder boot
- V. Master cylinder pushrod
- W. Nut
- X. Cylinder pushrod clevis

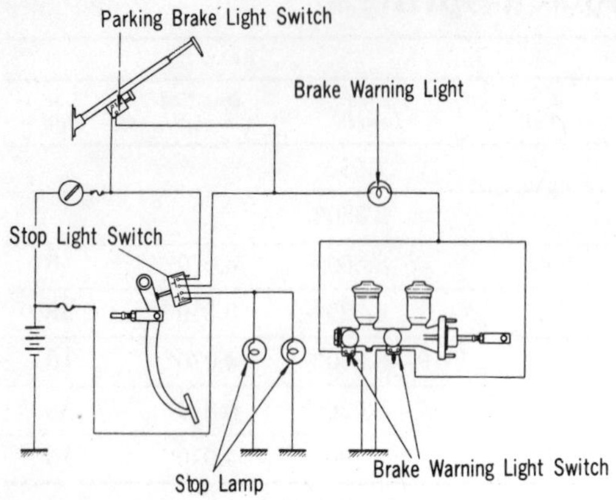

Brake warning light circuit.

## Power Brake Booster

Crown, Mark II and Land Cruiser models are equipped with booster brakes. Manifold vacuum is utilized to operate a booster diaphragm, which assists braking by applying pressure to the wheel cylinders. The system consists of three separate components: vacuum booster, vacuum control valve and hydraulic cylinder. An additional check valve, located in the booster end plate, maintains maximum vacuum in the system at all times.

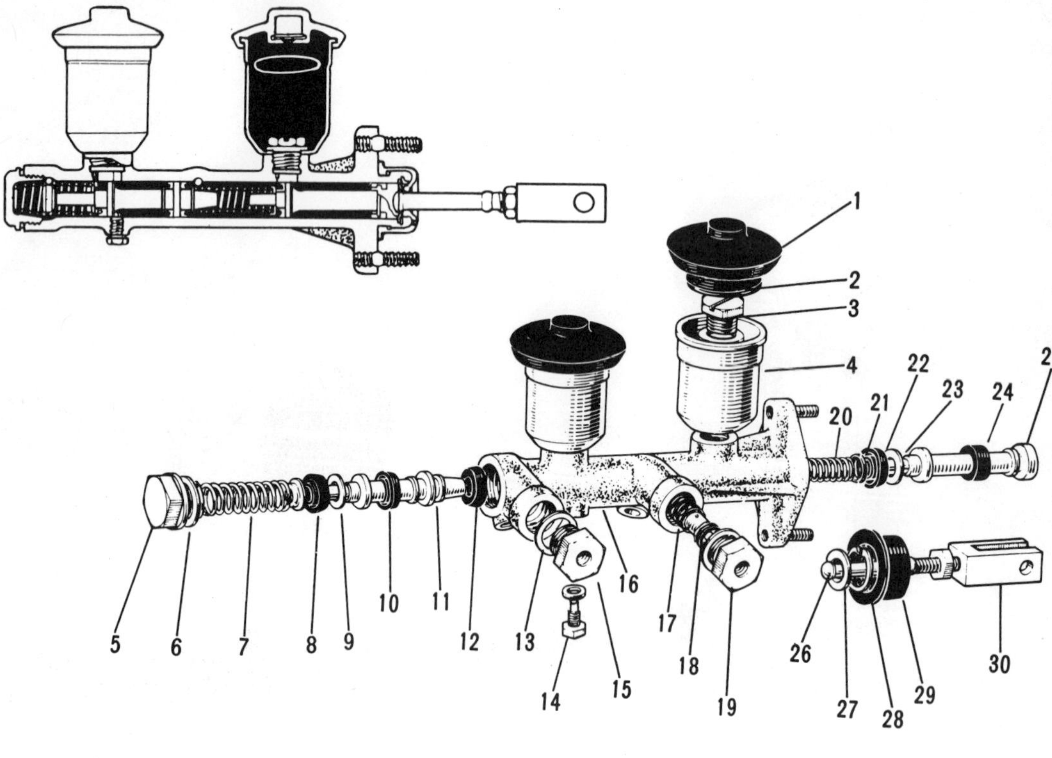

Dual circuit master cylinder components.

1. Reservoir filler cap
2. Reservoir float
3. Reservoir set bolt
4. Master cylinder reservoir
5. Master cylinder plug
6. Gasket
7. Compression spring
8. Cylinder cup
9. Piston cup spacer
10. Cylinder cup
11. Master cylinder piston No. 2
12. Cylinder cup
13. Gasket
14. Piston stop bolt
15. Valve plug
16. Tandem master cylinder body
17. Compression spring
18. Master cylinder outlet check valve
19. Valve plug
20. Compression
21. Piston return spring retainer
22. Cylinder cup
23. Master cylinder piston cup spacer
24. Cylinder cup
25. Master cylinder piston No. 1
26. Master cylinder pushrod
27. Master cylinder piston stop plate
28. Hole snap-ring
29. Master cylinder boot
30. Master cylinder pushrod clevis

### Brake Diagnosis Guide—Power Brakes Only

*Test 1* With engine stopped and transmission in neutral, depress pedal several times to deplete all vacuum reserve in the system. Depress pedal, hold with light pressure and start engine. If the vacuum system is operating, pedal will tend to fall away under foot pressure and less pressure will be needed to hold the pedal in the same position. If no action is felt, the vacuum system is faulty and must be checked (see diagnosis chart).

*Test 2* With engine running at medium speed and brakes off, turn off ignition, immediately releasing the throttle (this will build up vacuum). Wait at least 90 seconds, then apply brakes. If there is enough vacuum assist for two applications, power booster is working. If there is no power assist, or if only one application is possible, the vacuum check valve is faulty or there is a vacuum leak.

### Parking Brake

All passenger cars except the Corolla have a dash-mounted L-shaped handle which operates the parking brake. The Corolla employs a floor-mounted straight lever-type handle. Parking brake cables cannot be removed without first removing rear wheels and brake drums. Land Cruiser parking brake acts on the rear drive shaft by means of a special brake drum.

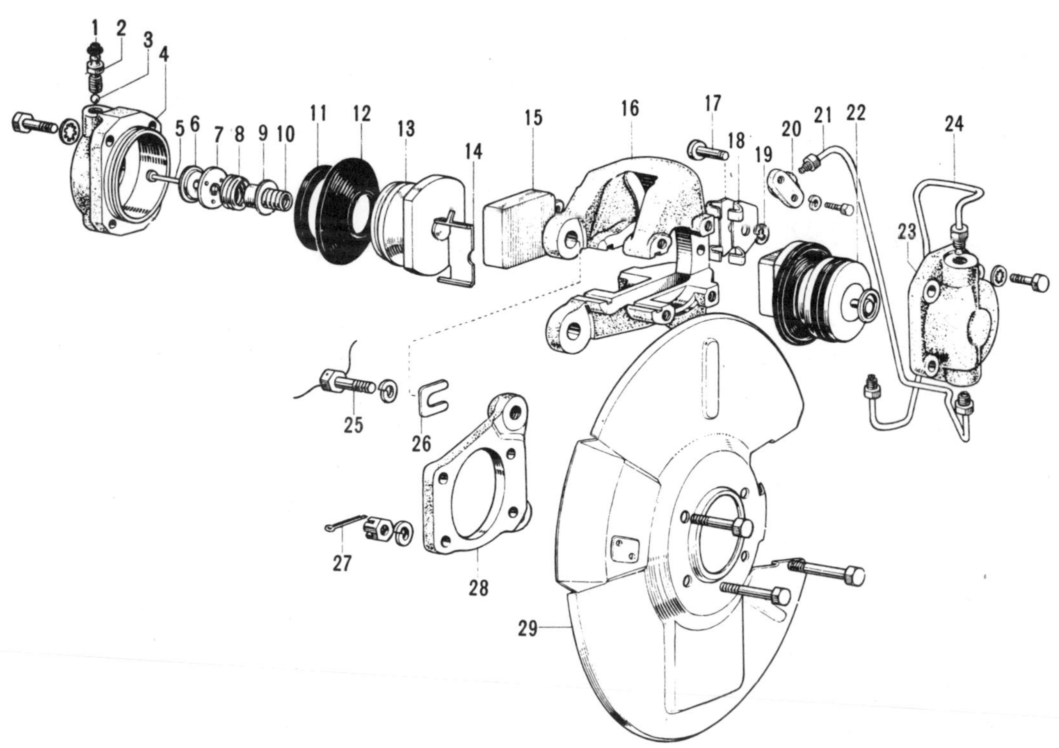


Disc brake components.

1. Bleed plug cap
2. Bleed plug
3. Ball
4. Disc brake cylinder No. 2
5. Pin
6. Retract pin cap
7. Spring retaining plate
8. Compression spring
9. Bushing housing
10. Retract bushing
11. Piston seal
12. Cylinder boot
13. Disc brake piston
14. Pad support plate
15. Disc brake pad
16. Disc brake caliper
17. Pin
18. Keep plate
19. E-ring
20. Two-way connector
21. Wheel cylinder front tube
22. Disc brake piston
23. Disc brake cylinder No. 1
24. Cylinder bridge tube
25. Head with hexagon bolt
26. Caliper support shim
27. Cotter pin
28. Caliper support bracket
29. Disc brake front dust cover

### Adjusting the Parking Brake

*Corolla* Remove the adjusting cap (plastic) and adjust No. 1 cable so that there are at least five, but no more than nine, notches (teeth) of lever travel when the brake is fully applied.

*Corona* Loosen the brake warning switch bracket and push parking brake lever all the way down. Reset the switch so that it will come *on* as soon as the lever is moved one notch. Release the parking brake lever fully, then loosen the parking brake pull rod locknut at the equalizer bar and adjust until the front cable has no more slack. Tighten locknut and test adjustment by pulling parking brake lever; it should have a little play at the start and should travel from eight to thirteen notches during application.

*Crown* Same adjustment procedures as Corona.

*Land Cruiser* Jack up rear wheels and turn the parking brake adjuster located at the bottom of the brake plate counterclockwise until the brake is fully locked, then back off one or two notches so that the drum can rotate freely.

### Stop Light Switch

Switches are of the mechanical type, actuated by the brake pedal. Adjust so that switch will come *on* as soon as pedal travel exceeds free-play. Make sure that some play is left for the master cylinder pushrod; at least 1⁄16″ but not more than ⅛″. To adjust, loosen locknut at clevis and turn pushrod until desired clearance is obtained between pushrod and master cylinder piston. Check the height of the pedal and adjust by setting the stoplight switch (which in this case acts as a pedal stop). All passenger cars have 5.5–6.0″ clearance from top of pedal pad to slanted section of floor. On Land Cruiser models, distance from pad to vertical section of firewall should be 6.7″.

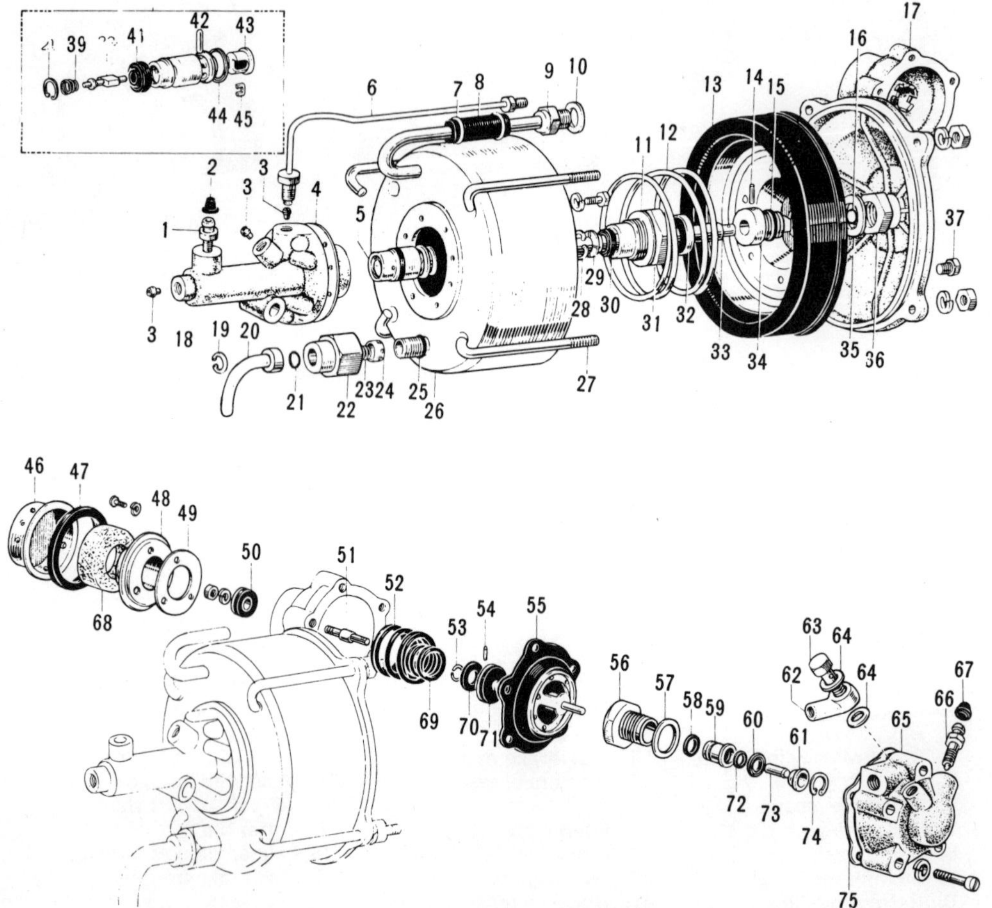


Power brake booster components.

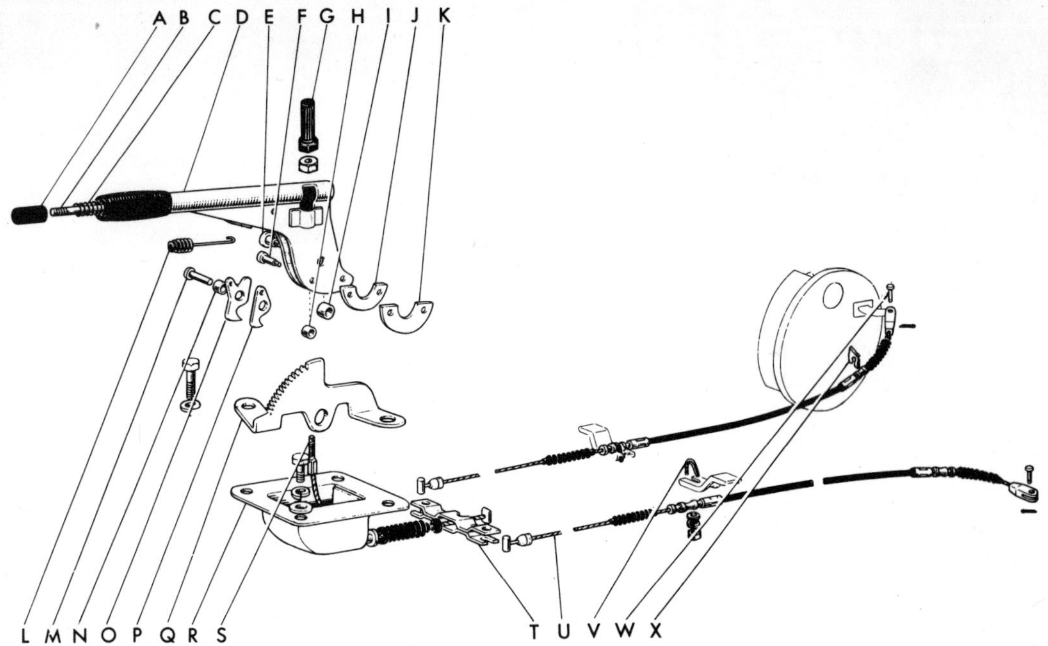


Parking brake components; Corolla.

A. Parking brake release rod knob
B. Parking brake pawl release rod
C. Compression spring
D. Parking brake lever
E. Lever pivot pin
F. Pin
G. Wire adjusting cap
H. Spacer
I. Spacer
J. Parking brake cable guide
K. Parking brake cable guide support
L. Tension spring
M. Pin
N. Spacer
O. Parking brake pawl No. 2
P. Parking brake pawl No. 1
Q. Parking brake lever sector
R. Parking brake lever boot
S. Parking brake cable No. 1
T. Parking brake equalizer
U. Parking brake cable No. 2
V. Cable clamp
W. Pin
X. Cable clip

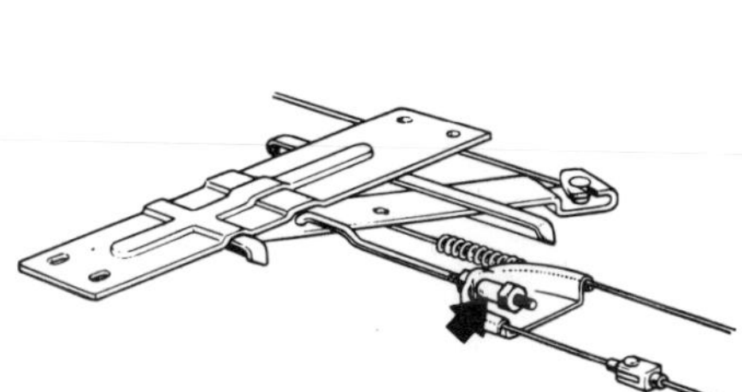

Corona parking brake adjusting bolt.

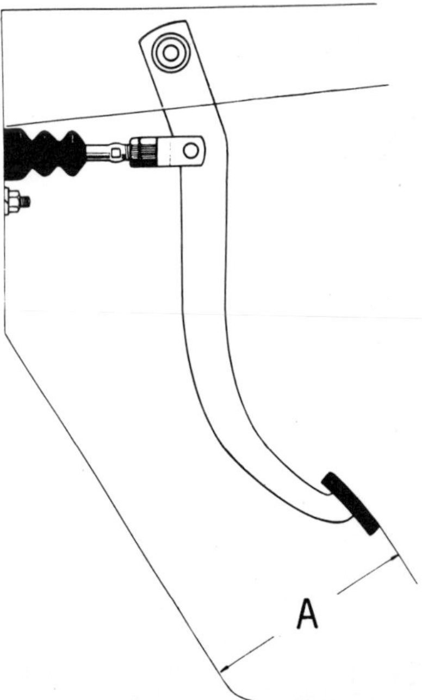


Brake pedal adjustment.

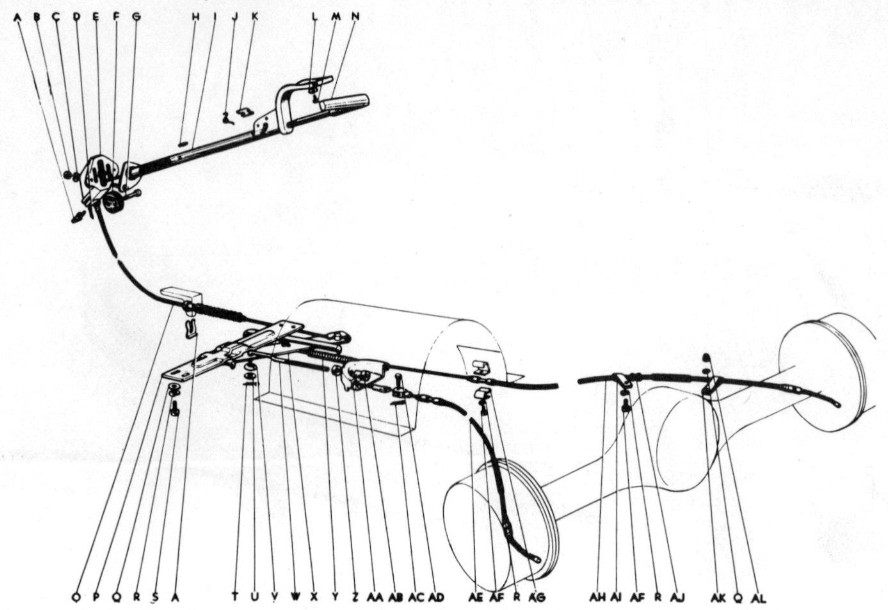


Parking brake components; all except Land Cruiser and Corolla.

A. Clip
B. Nut
C. Wave washer
D. Cotter pin
E. Pulley bracket
F. Wire pulley
G. W/hole pin
H. Parking brake plunger pin
I. Parking brake plunger guide
J. Torsion spring
K. Parking brake pawl
L. Toothed washer
M. Screw
N. Parking brake plunger
O. Parking brake No. 1 cable
P. Equalizer support bracket
Q. Plate washer
R. Spring washer
S. Bolt
T. Cotter pin
U. Plate washer
V. Wave washer
W. Parking brake pull rod
X. Parking brake intermediate lever
Y. Tension spring
Z. Nut
AA. Parking brake equalizer
AB. Nut
AC. Cotter pin
AD. W/hole pin
AE. Parking brake No. 3 cable
AF. Bolt
AG. Cable retainer
AH. Parking brake No. 2 cable
AI. Clamp
AJ. Bushing
AK. Cable guide
AL. Nut

*Chapter 9*

# Differential and Drive Shaft

## Differential

All rear axles are hypoid, semi-floating type with Hotchkiss drive (semi-elliptic rear springs). Limited slip differentials are available as optional equipment on Crown models only.

### Differential Diagnosis

Because rear axle adjustments and repairs are not to be taken lightly, correct diagnosis is of greatest importance. Transmitting engine torque through a set of gears to the rear wheels will always produce a certain amount of noise which is normal. Noise produced by the engine, transmission gears, tires, wheel bearings, exhaust system, drive shaft or even the wind can be mistaken for rear axle noises. Rear axle noises are usually related to road speed rather than to engine or transmission speed. To isolate suspected rear end troubles, check the following:

1. Check tire pressures and rear axle oil level.
2. Drive car long enough to warm up the rear axle and the rear axle oil.
3. In neutral, run the engine at varying rpm; if the noise remains it does not come from the rear axle.
4. Certain tire tread patterns, or tire wear, can produce objectionable noises. Check this by driving over different road surfaces; if the noise changes, the rear axle is not to blame. *NOTE: Switching tires from side to side sometimes helps.*
5. Worn, loose or damaged wheel bearings can be easily confused with axle noise. Wheel bearing noise is usually more noticeable when coasting at lower car speeds. Gentle application of the brakes will usually change this noise. Alternately turning left and right—which preloads the wheel bearings—causes a defective wheel bearing to become even noisier.
6. Rear axle noise can be classified either as GEAR noise or BEARING noise. Gear noise is recognized as a high-pitched whine or resonating sound, more pronounced at certain speeds and usually limited to a narrow speed range under drive (accelerating load), coast (decelerating load) or float (maintaining speed) conditions. Axle bearing noise is usually constant with the pitch (tone) related to car speed.

Drive pinion bearing noise is higher pitched than differential side bearing noise. Pinion bearing noise is usually heard at low speeds (20–30 mph).

Differential side bearing noise is lower in pitch because the bearings are turning at the same speed as the road wheels (in a straight-ahead position), which does not vary when turning left or right or when the brakes are applied gently.

Rear axle backlash produces a noise similar to that made by universal joints or a loose fit of universal joint on the transmission splines. It may be due to excessive clearance between the differential gear and pinion, or a loose fitting differential shaft in the case. Excessive drive gear and drive pinion clearance will also cause excessive backlash; however, gear noise is usually present in this case, as well as the backlash noise.

Another axle condition to be considered is a knocking or clucking noise heard when coasting at low speed, which can be caused by a loose fitting differential gear in the differential case bore. Lightly applying the brakes will usually reduce this sound. Noise produced by poor universal joints has a very similar sound, but generally CANNOT be reduced by a slight brake application. When noise is the result of worn bearings, the gears do not have to be replaced unless

Removing backing plate nuts.

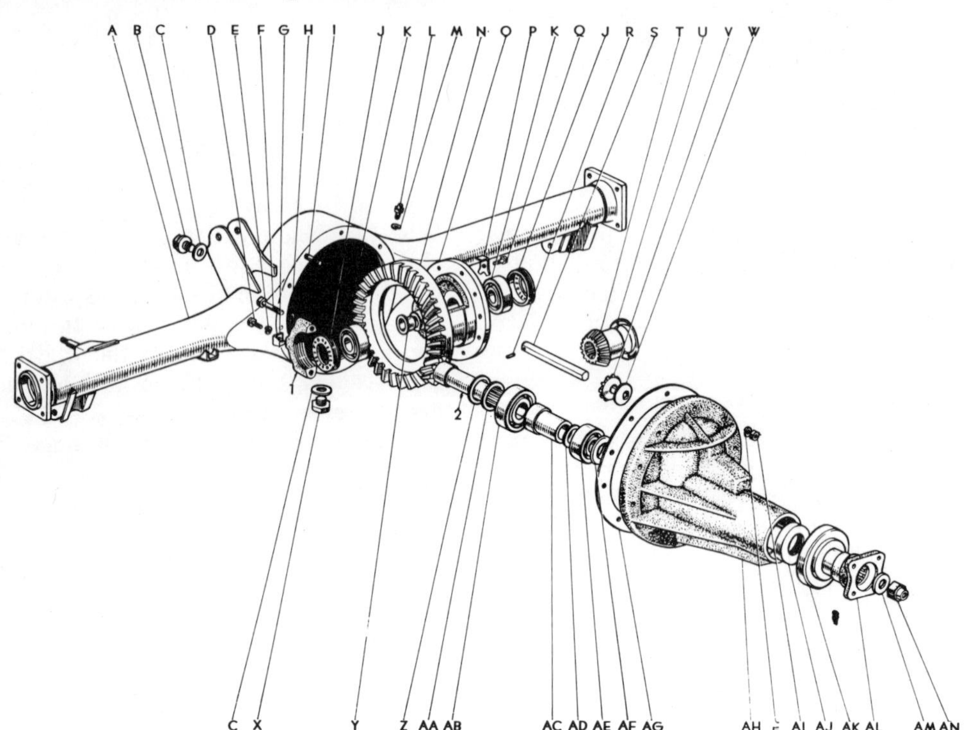


Differential components.

A. Housing assy
B. Filler plug
C. Gasket
D. Bolt
E. Lock washer
F. Hexagon bolt
G. Bearing adjusting nut lock
H. Lock washer
I. Stud
J. Bearing adjusting nut
K. Bearing
L. Breather plug
M. Lock washer
N. Ring gear and drive pinion 1 and 2
O. Case
P. Lock plate
Q. Bolt
R. Lock pin
S. Pinion shaft
T. Side gear
U. Thrust washer
V. Pinion
W. Thrust washer
X. Drain plug
Y. Oil reservoir
Z. Spacer
AA. Shim
AB. Bearing
AC. Spacer
AD. Shim
AE. Bearing
AF. Oil slinger
AG. Gasket
AH. Carrier
AI. Nut
AJ. Oil seal
AK. Dust deflector
AL. Universal joint flange
AM. Flat washer
AN. Nut

inspection shows them to be damaged. Differential gear noises heard only under certain conditions, such as during wheel balancing, are to be considered normal.

**Removing the (Rear Axle) Differential Carrier**

Jack up the car and remove the rear wheels, drain the oil and remove the brake drums. Remove the four nuts that hold the backing plate (access is through the service hole in the axle flange), then remove the axle shaft with an impact puller. (The backing plate comes off with the axle.) Remove the other axle shaft in the same manner, then disconnect the drive shaft at the pinion yoke. Remove the differential carrier nuts and remove the carrier assembly from the housing, then install the drain plug.

**Disassembling the Differential Carrier**

Thoroughly wash and rinse the carrier—blow dry with compressed air. Securely clamp the carrier in a vise or suitable stand. Apply a light coating of mechanic's blue (or lipstick) to the teeth of the ring gear. Applying a slight drag on the ring gear to avoid backlash, rotate the pinion in a smooth and continuous manner to obtain a good tooth pattern on the ring gear. Next, attach a dial indicator gauge to the carrier base and check the ring gear backlash. Also check ring gear runout at this time. If the tooth pattern obtained is correct, and the backlash and runout are within limits, any gear noise must come from the spider or side gears.

With the dial indicator gauge set up on the carrier, check the backlash between spider gears and side gears. Excessive backlash usually is due to either worn thrust washers or a worn spider shaft. If every-

Checking ring gear runout.

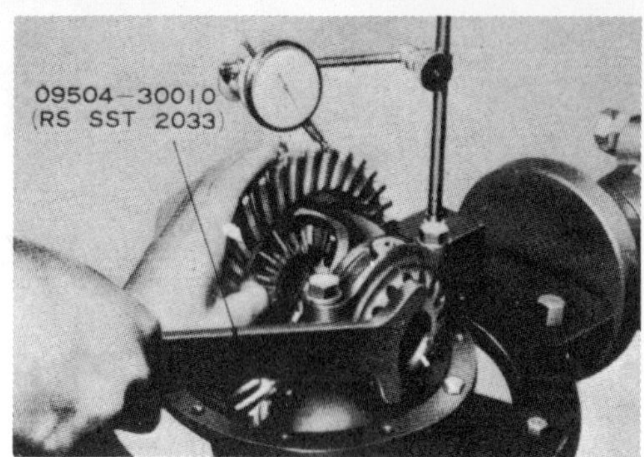


Adjusting backlash.

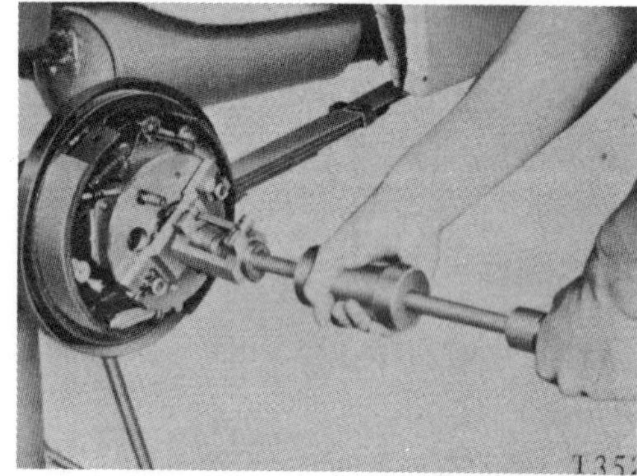

Removing rear axle shaft.

Applying red lead or lipstick to gear teeth.

Removing differential carrier.

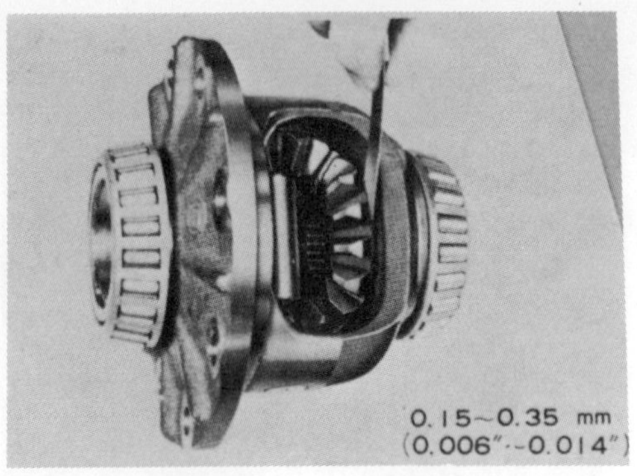


Checking side gear thrust clearance.

Checking side play.

thing checks out within specifications, test the preload on the differential drive pinion nut. Punch mark both pinion and nut in their original positions, then LOOSEN the pinion nut about ½ turn and torque to specifications. If the punch marks line up again (within 60°) the pinion preload was correct.

Punch mark both the carrier and the side bearing caps for identification, remove locknuts and take off caps. Remove the differential case assembly from carrier. Do not mix the bearing cups; paint mark them for identification. Remove differential pinion nut (do not let the pinion drop out), then remove pinion spacer, yoke and oil seal.

With a brass punch, drive out the pinion bearing cups. *NOTE: This should be done*

## Rear Axle Specifications

| *Model* | | *K* | *RT* | *MS* | *F* |
|---|---|---|---|---|---|
| BACKLASH (in.) | | | | | |
| Ring gear and pinion | | .004–.006 | .005–.007 | .005–.007 | .006–.008 |
| Side gears, spider gears | (2)<br>(4) | .001–.006 | .002–.008<br>.001–.008 | ** | ** |
| Side gear to case ** | | | | .006–.014 | .006–.014 |
| Axle shaft end-play | | .002–.014 | .002–.014 | | .002–.018 |
| RUNOUT (in.) | | | | | |
| Ring gear | | .0016 | .0016 | .0020 | .0040 |
| Differential case | | .0016 | .0016 | .0020 | .0040 |
| Axle shaft (center) | | .0015 | .0015 | .0020 | .0025 |
| TORQUE (ft. lbs.) | | | | | |
| Ring gear to case | | 45–55 | 50–60 | 50–70 | 72–87 |
| Side bearing cap | | 40–47 | 37–52 | 50–70 | 65–80 |
| Carrier to housing | | 15–22 | 20–25 | 20–25 | 30–40 |
| Case cover to case | | | 18–26 | 18–26 | |
| Spider shaft lock bolt | | | 11–16 | 11–16 | |
| Differential pinion nut | | 95–110 | 125–130 | 115–145 | 145–175 |
| PRELOAD (in. lbs.) | | | | | |
| Pinion bearings | New* | 2.8–4.8 | 7.0–9.2 | 7.0–9.2 | 12–15 |
| | Old* | 1.0–2.8 | 4.8–7.0 | 4.8–7.0 | 4.8–8.2 |

* Without oil seal and differential gears installed.

*only when the bearings are to be replaced.* Press or pull off the drive pinion rear bearing. Avoid damaging the flat spacer behind the bearing. Measure the spacer thickness and note the measurement for future use. Remove both side bearings from the differential case and mark them "L" and "R" for identification. *NOTE: Remove side bearings only if they must be replaced.*

Punch mark differential case and cover, then remove cover bolts and cover (where fitted). Remove spider shaft and pinions, side gears and all thrust washers. *NOTE: Some differential types have four spider pinion gears; punch mark the gears before removal so they can be correctly reinstalled.*

### Inspecting the Differential Carrier

Check all bearing cones and cups for wear. Inspect tooth surfaces of all gears carefully and inspect all thrust washers for wear and signs of slipping in their seats. Check all gear shafts for scoring, wear or distortion. Finally, inspect the case and carrier housing for cracks or other damage. Also check case for signs of wear at the side gear bores, bearing cap and mounting hubs.

### Assembling the Differential Carrier

Wash and clean all parts before installation. Lightly oil all bearings and gear shafts, except ring gear and drive pinion teeth. Place the side gears and the spider gears, with their thrust washers, into the differential case. Insert the spider shaft and align the lock pin holes in case and shaft. Fit the case cover in place and install lock pin (bolt) and tighten cover bolts to specification; check play. If the side bearings were removed, install them now. If the ring gear was removed, install it now. Tighten bolts in symmetrical sequence to avoid distortion and runout.

Install drive pinion bearing cups into carrier housing, using a suitable installing tool. Make sure cups are seated solidly. Assemble drive pinion rear bearing to drive pinion and insert into carrier housing. Install spacer and front bearing to drive pinion; install yoke and tighten nut to specifications. (Drive pinion oil seal is NOT installed at this point.) The drive pinion preload is measured in in. lbs. (not ft. lbs.). Adjust preload by changing the length of the bearing spacer (between front and rear bearings) until the required preload is obtained.

Place the previously assembled differential case into position in the bearing hubs and put the caps into position as marked (L and R). Set the case so that there will be the least amount of backlash between ring gear and pinion (in order to save time adjusting). Install the adjusting nuts (also marked L and R) and take care not to cross-thread them. Finger-tighten the bearing caps until the threads are lined up correctly, then tighten slowly.

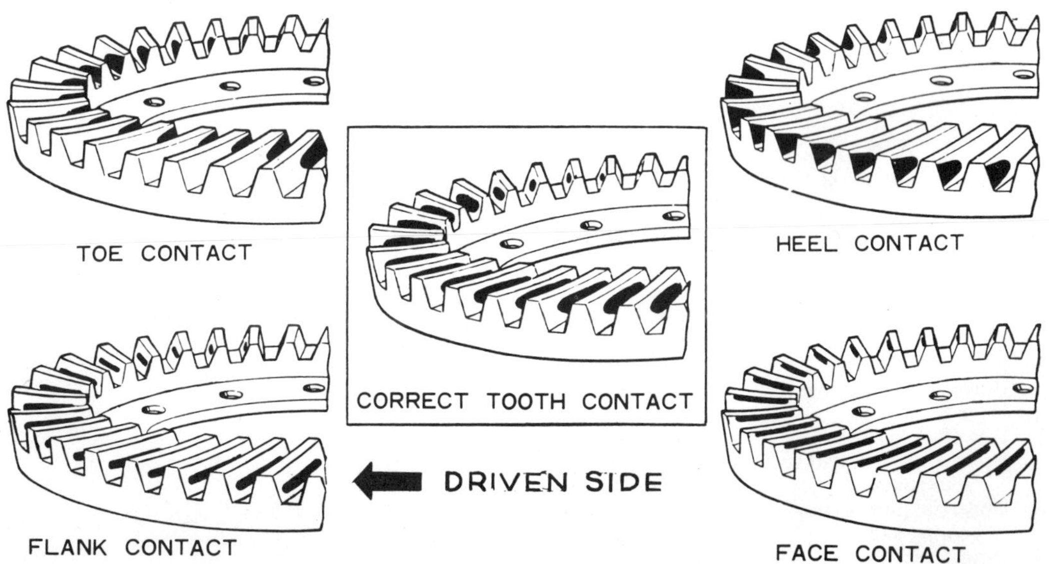


Ring gear tooth pattern.

### Differential Side Bearing Preload Adjustment

Back off the right-hand adjusting nut (ring gear teeth side) and screw in the other nut until almost no backlash is felt. Attach a dial indicator gauge so that it reads at right angles to the back of the ring gear, then screw in the right-hand adjusting nut until the gauge indicates that all side play has been eliminated. Tighten the adjusting nut another one or one and one-half notches (depending on the fit of the lock tabs). Recheck the preload on the drive pinion as before; this time the specifications are different (see table). If too loose, readjust side bearing preload; if too tight, adjust the ring gear backlash.

### Ring Gear and Pinion Backlash Adjustment

Install dial indicator gauge so that it contacts the ring gear teeth at right angles. Adjust the backlash to specifications. If too great, adjust by loosening the bearing cap bolts slightly and screwing the right-hand adjusting nut (ring gear teeth side) OUT about two notches. Tighten the left-hand adjusting nut the same amount. *NOTE: One notch of the adjusting nut equals about 0.002″ of backlash.* Recheck the backlash, then tighten the bearing cap nuts.

### Ring Gear and Pinion Tooth Pattern Test

Using a dial indicator gauge, recheck all runout dimensions (ring gear back, ring gear outer circumference and differential case). Apply a thin coat of mechanic's blue, red lead or even lipstick to the ring gear teeth. Rotate the gear several times, applying a light drag to the ring gear. Rotate gear in both directions. Inspect tooth pattern. There are four basic tooth patterns: heel, toe, flank and face. Most often the tooth pattern obtained will be a combination of two of these patterns and the adjustments must be made accordingly.

*Heel contact* Move the drive pinion IN by increasing the thickness of the spacer (between pinion head and rear bearing). Readjust backlash by moving ring gear away from pinion.

*Face contact* Adjust same as above.

*Toe contact* Adjust by moving the drive pinion OUT by reducing the thickness of the spacer. Readjust backlash.

*Flank contact* Adjust same as toe contact.

Continue assembling as follows:

Remove drive pinion nut and install seal into differential carrier housing, then install oil slinger, dust shield and yoke and retorque the pinion nut as specified. Install the differential carrier assembly into the

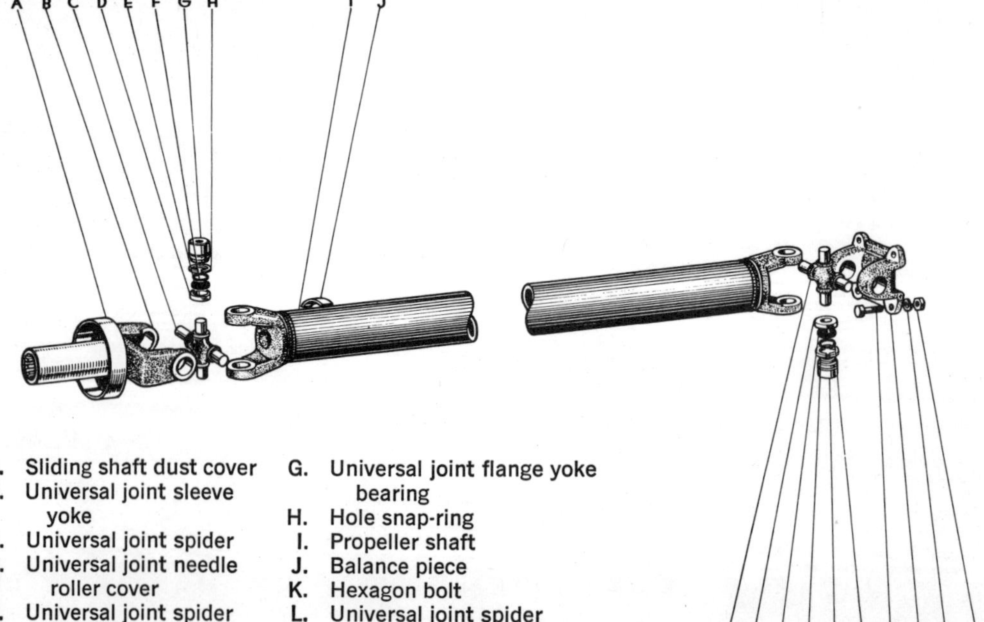


A. Sliding shaft dust cover
B. Universal joint sleeve yoke
C. Universal joint spider
D. Universal joint needle roller cover
E. Universal joint spider bearing seal
F. O-ring
G. Universal joint flange yoke bearing
H. Hole snap-ring
I. Propeller shaft
J. Balance piece
K. Hexagon bolt
L. Universal joint spider
M. Lockwasher
N. Nut

Drive shaft and universal joints.

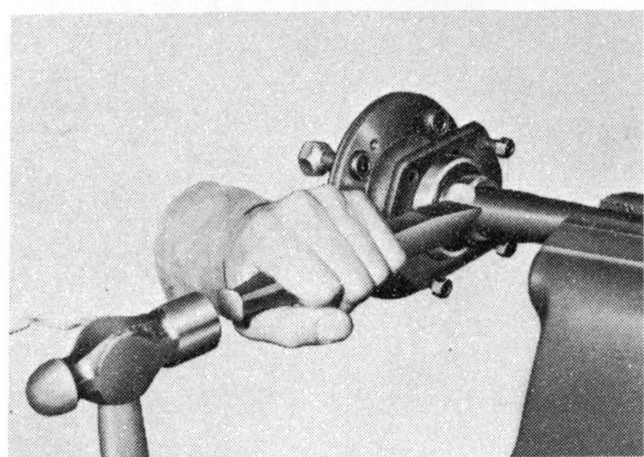

Removing bearing inner retainer.

axle housing. Apply Permatex to the new gasket and tighten to specifications. Connect the universal joint flange to the yoke and tighten securely, then insert the two axle shafts and secure backing plates. Refill with proper grade oil and secure filler and drain plugs. Slide front yoke of drive shaft into transmission and secure rear universal to rear flange, then remove jack stands.

#### Disassembling the Axle Shaft

Remove axle shaft as previously described. Using a cold chisel, split the axle bearing retainer (or grind it off) and pull off the bearing, oil seal and grease catcher. The hub bolts then can be pressed out. Install nut to prevent thread damage. *NOTE: The axle inner oil seal should be replaced only if it leaks.*

#### Assembling the Axle Shaft

Press in the new hub bolts, then assemble the outer retainer, spacer and bearing to the shaft by pressing them into place. The inner retainer must be preheated to about 300° F. and quickly installed so that it will seat properly.

Removing universal joint bearing cup.

Assembling universal joint.

Measure the thickness of the backing plate and select gasket to match as follows: the combined thicknesses of gasket and plate should total 0.120″ ± 0.003″. Apply Permatex to both sides of bearing retainer gasket and rear axle end gasket and install both onto the axle shaft, then place the axle shaft into the axle housing without damaging the oil seal. Whenever possible, use NEW nuts to secure the backing plate to the axle housing; tighten to specifications. *CAUTION: Do not mistake the top for the bottom of backing plate end and retainer gaskets.* Bleed brakes and reconnect parking brake. Check oil level; use hypoid SAE 90.

## Drive Shaft

The most common problems with drive shafts concern the universal joints. Seldom do drive shafts need to be replaced (other than in collision cases) and balancing a drive shaft is rarely necessary (other than for competition).

#### Removing the Drive Shaft

Jack up rear end of car and support on stands. Remove the four bolts from the rear yoke and slide the drive shaft out of the transmission. Plug hole with a clean rag to prevent oil leakage.

#### Disassembling the Drive Shaft

Punch mark both yokes and drive shaft for correct reassembly. Remove the snapring from inside the yoke, then, with the help of two sockets (9/16″ and 1¼″) press out the bearing cups, one at a time.

1. Differential case cover
2. Differential side gear
3. Differential side gear thrust washer
4. Straight pin
5. Right clutch member
6. Differential pinion
7. Left clutch member
8. Differential case
9. Differential ring gear

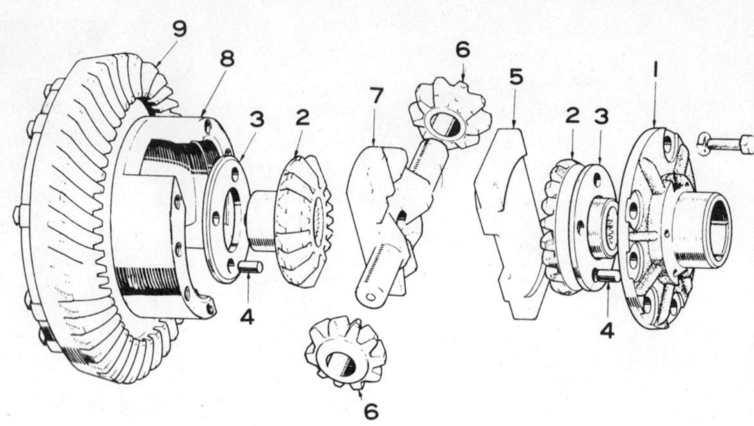


Limited slip differential.

### Inspecting the Drive Shaft

Inspect the cup bores for out-of-round (wear) condition. Inspect front yoke and splines for wear and rust, then check that welded balance weights are still in place. Inspect needle rollers and spider (cross) for signs of wear. Replace all worn parts.

### Assembling the Drive Shaft

Install the grease seals on the spider (soft side UP). Pack cup and needle rollers with grease and install seal into cup, then fit snap-ring into groove on cup and install assembly on spider. Place spider into yoke bore from inside, and press into place in vise. Repeat on other cups.

Select snap-rings so that there is less than 0.002″ play. Snap-rings come in four sizes; always use the same size snap-ring for both sides.

### Installing the Drive Shaft

Lightly oil the splines of the front yoke and carefully insert into transmission so as not to damage the oil seal. Connect the rear yoke flange to the yoke and tighten the four bolts.

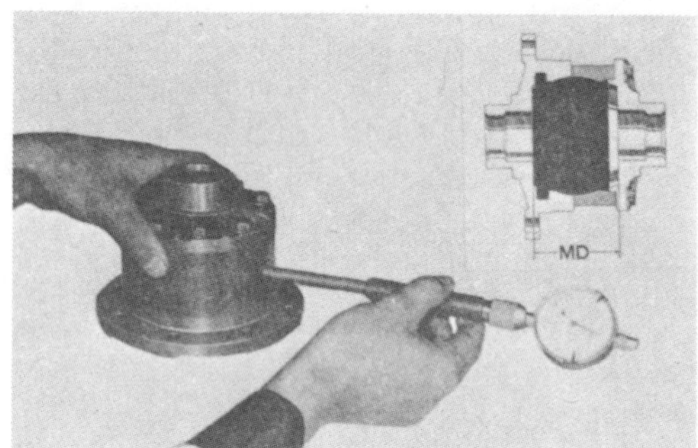


Checking mounting distance (M–D).

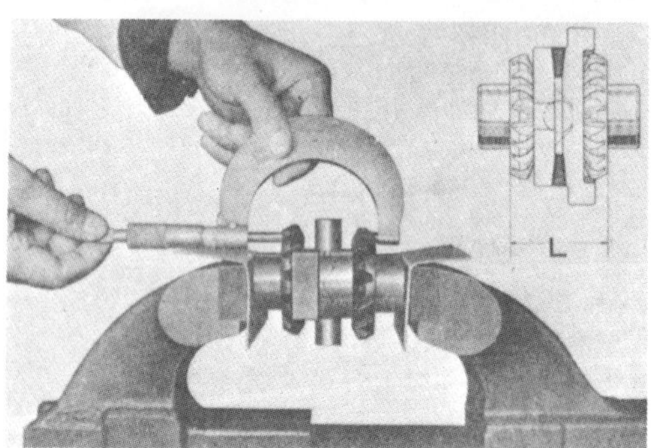


Checking clearance (L).

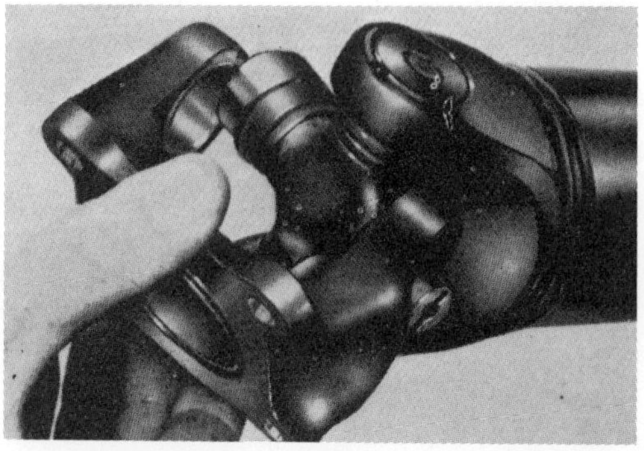

Installing yoke.

## Limited Slip Differential

In this type differential when torque is applied to the right clutch member, the design of the interlocking teeth of both clutch members creates a separation force which tends to drive the two members apart. This, in turn, forces the side gear against the differential case and, due to the special design of the side gear thrust washers, additional friction is created between the side gear and the differential case to assist in transmitting driving power to both axle shafts. (Power flow is actually through the case and thrust washer into the side gear and from there to the axle shaft.)

Check the component parts in the same manner as for standard type differential. Ring gear runout limit is 0.004″, case to cover torque is 29–36 ft. lbs. Check the inside dimensions (M–D) of the differential case and check the outside dimensions (L) of the assembled side gears and clutch members. Divide the difference by two; this is the thickness of the thrust washers to be used MINUS the side gear to case clearance of 0.001–0.004″. (Deduct one-half of this from each washer.)

### Special Assembly Procedures

Wash the differential case, case cover and bolts in cleaning solvent to remove all traces of oil or grease. (Use trichloroethylene or carbon tetrachloride.) Coat the contact surfaces of the differential case, case cover and all bolts with a quick-drying primer.

Insert the dowel pins into the case and the cover, select the proper thrust washers and assemble right and left clutch members and side gears. *NOTE: Thrust washers are identified by stamped letters "A" through "F". When using a "B", "D", or "F" washer, position it with the thin side towards the ring gear.* Apply non-drying Permatex to the case bolts and assemble cover to case. Torque bolts to 15–25 ft. lbs. *NOTE: Allow case assembly to dry for three hours at room temperature. In cold weather, warm the case to about 85–120° F.*

Fill with hypoid SAE 90 oil—1.27 qts. *CAUTION: Do not use any of the special oils available for domestic type non-slip differentials.*

# Chapter 10
# Steering and Suspension

## Steering

Corona steering is of the recirculating ball type having needle bearings on the sector shaft. Steering ratio is 20.8:1; Mark II has a variable ratio of 19.5–21.5:1. Crown models have a variable ratio of 20.5–23.6:1. Land Cruisers use a sector roller and worm with a 21:1 ratio, Corollas use sector roller and worm with a 18.1:1 ratio. All use two sintered bushings on the sector shaft except Corolla.

### Steering Wheel Removal

Disconnect horn and turn signal wires under dash panel. Depress horn ring and remove by twisting counterclockwise. Remove spring, take off steering column nut and lift off horn contact seat. Punch mark steering wheel position on shaft and remove wheel using a puller. (This should be done carefully, especially on late models with the collapsible steering column.) Remove screws and turn signal switch assembly from housing. Remove upper (remote shift) shaft E-washer and ring. Remove contact (horn) ring housing and pull off the upper column bearing.

On Crown models having remote shift and automatic transmission, the shift indicator is connected to the shift lever by a small wire attached to a plastic bushing. Use extra care during removal, as this bushing is very fragile. To remove wheel, turn signal lever must be turned to the left.

### Steering Column

Crown and Land Cruiser models have a two-piece steering column. Crown models use a sliding block arrangement, while two universal joints and a sliding splined center shaft are used on Land Cruisers. Later models are equipped with a collapsible column.

#### Inspecting Steering Wheel and Column

There is little to inspect on the wheel except the horn contact plate, and the spring-loaded contact pin and roller on some models. Only on Corollas must the entire steering be removed for repairs, other models allow for separate disassembly of steering gear box and/or column as needed.

#### Installing the Steering Wheel and Column

Proceed in reverse order of disassembly. Torque wheel housing nuts to 3–5 ft. lbs.; steering wheel nut to 15–22 ft. lbs.

### Removing Corolla Steering Assembly

For removal, it is necessary first to remove the entire manifold section and also to loosen the front exhaust pipe hanger. Disconnect the wiring harness at the steering column, then remove horn button by lifting it straight up. Remove contact spring and punch mark steering column and nut. Remove wheel nut and pull wheel off using a puller, then position turn signal lever to right and remove the switch retaining screws and switch. Loosen the steering column attaching screws under the turn signal switch and remove the switch assembly from the housing. Remove the steering housing clamp from the column tube, without completely dismantling it. *NOTE: At this point it will be possible to drive off the upper collar and bushing with a suitable punch.* Remove package tray, steering column clamp bolts and clamp. Under the hood, disconnect wires from temperature and oil pressure sending switches; also disconnect speedometer cable from steering gear box. Jack up car and place stands under front jacking points.

Punch mark sector shaft and pitman arm and remove arm with puller, then remove the splash shield from underside of the engine. Remove the three bolts that hold the steering box to frame, then remove entire steering assembly by pulling it out from under the car (towards the front).

On early Corona models, first remove front seat, then remove steering wheel and contact housing as follows: first depress and turn the horn ring counterclockwise to disengage, then disconnect all harness connections at column and disconnect dimmer switch wiring. Remove clutch and brake pedals and steering column hole cover plate. Remove upper and lower steering column clamps and back up switch from engine side of column, then disconnect both shift rods at control arm in engine compartment. (Mark them for identification.) Jack up car

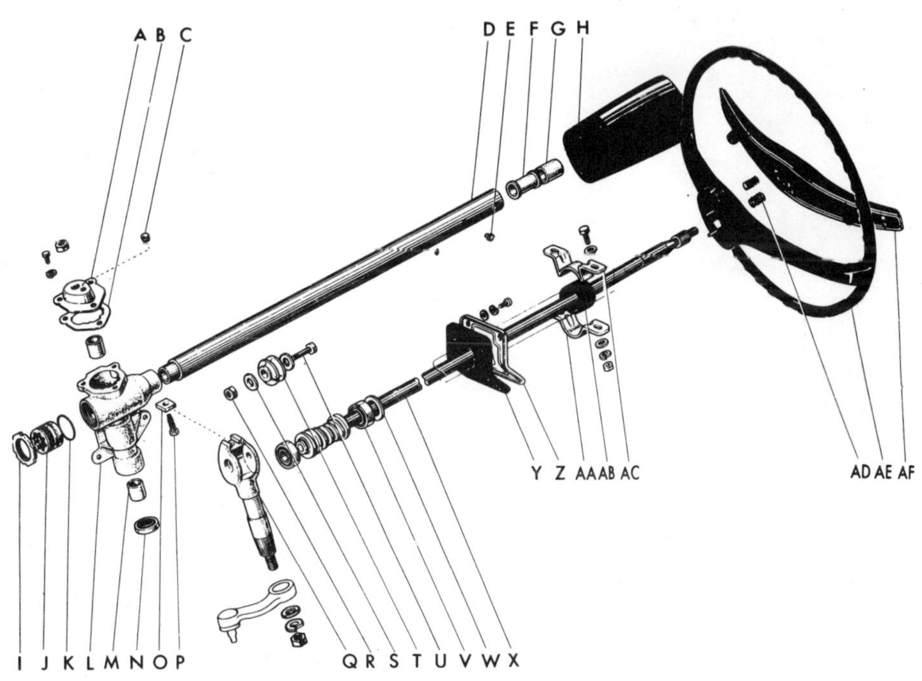


Corolla steering assembly.

A. Sector shaft end cover
B. Sector shaft end cover gasket
C. Steering gear housing oil plug
D. Steering column tube
E. Steering housing clamp
F. Bushing
G. Collar
H. Steering housing
I. Worm bearing adjusting lock nut
J. Worm bearing adjusting screw
K. O-ring
L. Steering gear housing
M. Bi-metal formed bushing
N. "S" type oil seal
O. Sector shaft thrust washer
P. Sector shaft adjusting screw
Q. Steering sector shaft
R. Hexagon nut
S. Shim
T. Steering sector roller
U. Steering sector roller shaft
V. Radial ball bearing
W. Shim
X. Steering main shaft
Y. Steering column weather seal
Z. Steering column opening cover plate
AA. Steering column lower clamp
AB. Grommet
AC. Steering column upper clamp
AD. Compression spring
AE. Steering wheel
AF. Horn button

and place stands under crossmember. Remove pitman arm with suitable puller, after marking its position on sector shaft. Remove the bolts that secure the steering box to frame and pull out steering (towards inside of car). Remove the control shaft from the steering column tube.

Later models do not have remote control shift levers and are simpler to remove; raise at lower edge and lift up and out. To remove on early Crown models having remote shift and combined horn and signal rings, first remove seat assembly. Remove steering wheel and clutch and brake pedals, then disconnect harness at steering column. Disconnect dimmer switch wires; remove steering column hole cover and upper and lower steering column clamps. Remove back up switch from engine side of steering column and disconnect both shift rods at control shaft side. Jack up car and support under front crossmember, then remove the two bolts and nuts from the intermediate shaft and disconnect the flexible coupling. Remove the steering column clamp screws and clamp. (On RS41L and MS45L models,

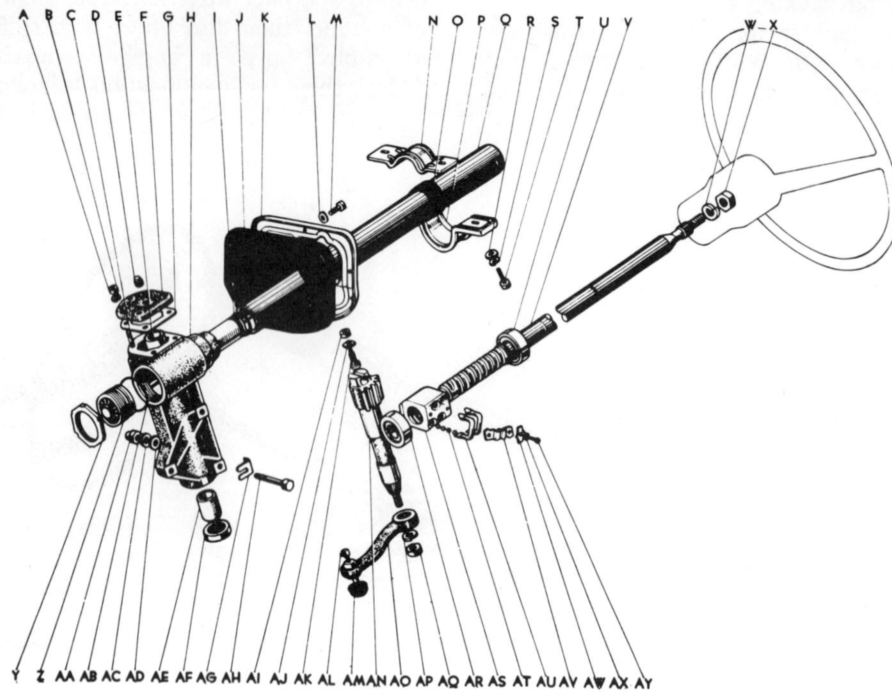


Corona steering assembly.

A. Nut
B. Spring washer
C. Stud bolt
D. Breather plug
E. Bimetal formed bushing
F. Sector shaft end cover
G. Sector shaft end gasket
H. Steering gear housing
I. O-ring
J. Steering column hole seal
K. Steering column hole cover
L. Plate washer
M. Bolt
N. Steering column upper clamp
O. Steering column clamp grommet
P. Steering column lower clamp
Q. Steering column tube
R. Plate washer
S. Spring washer
T. Bolt
U. Bearing
V. Steering mainshaft
W. Spring washer
X. Nut
Y. Worm bearing adjusting screw locknut
Z. Worm bearing adjusting screw
AA. Nut
AB. O-ring
AC. Wave washer
AD. Plate washer
AE. Bimetal formed bushing or needle roller bearing
AF. Type "S" oil seal
AG. Steering post adjusting shim
AH. Bolt
AI. Nut
AJ. Sector shaft thrust washer
AK. Sector shaft adjusting screw
AL. Grease fitting
AM. Steering link joint dust seal
AN. Steering sector shaft
AO. Pitman arm
AP. Spring washer
AQ. Nut
AR. Bearing
AS. Mainshaft ball nut
AT. Ball
AU. Mainshaft ball guide
AV. Mainshaft ball guide clamp
AW. Ball guide clamp screw lock plate
AX. Spring washer
AY. Pan screw

also remove the package tray and the instrument panel lower cover plate.) Disconnect the radio and antenna switches. Remove the four bolts that hold the jacket to the dash panel and pull the steering towards the inside. Avoid spilling oil on the upholstery.

On Land Cruiser models, remove the three screws that hold the center cover of the wheel pad, then remove wheel with puller. Unbend lock tabs at upper coupling and separate the two steering column shafts. Disconnect wiring harness connections at steering column side, then remove back up switch (engine compartment). Remove steering column hole cover bolts and steering column clamps. Withdraw jacket, hole cover plate and steering assembly towards interior of car.

**Disassembling the Corolla Steering Column**

Clamp steering gear box in vise and remove the end cover bolts. Slacken the sector shaft adjusting locknut and remove the end cover. Drain oil and remove the sector shaft, then remove the worm bearing adjusting locknut and screw with a special wrench to avoid damage. Remove the O-ring from between the adjusting screw and the outer ball race. With a lead hammer (to avoid damaging the threads) drive out the steering column, together with the bearings. *NOTE: Do not mix the bearings and races during this step.*

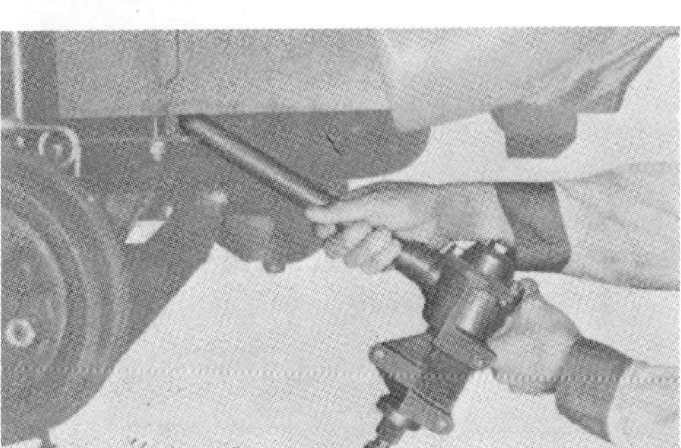

Removing steering gear box.

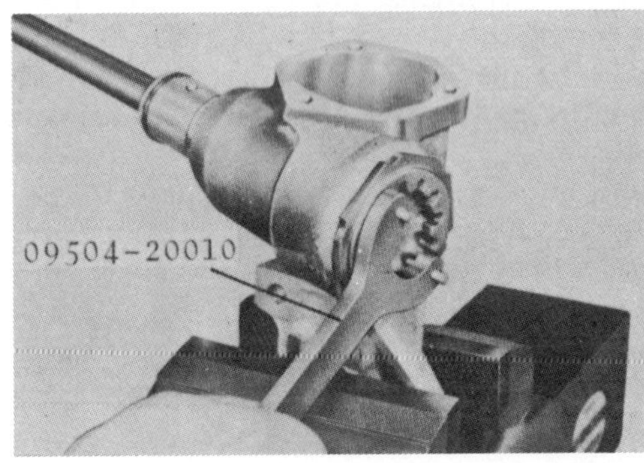


Removing adjusting screw.

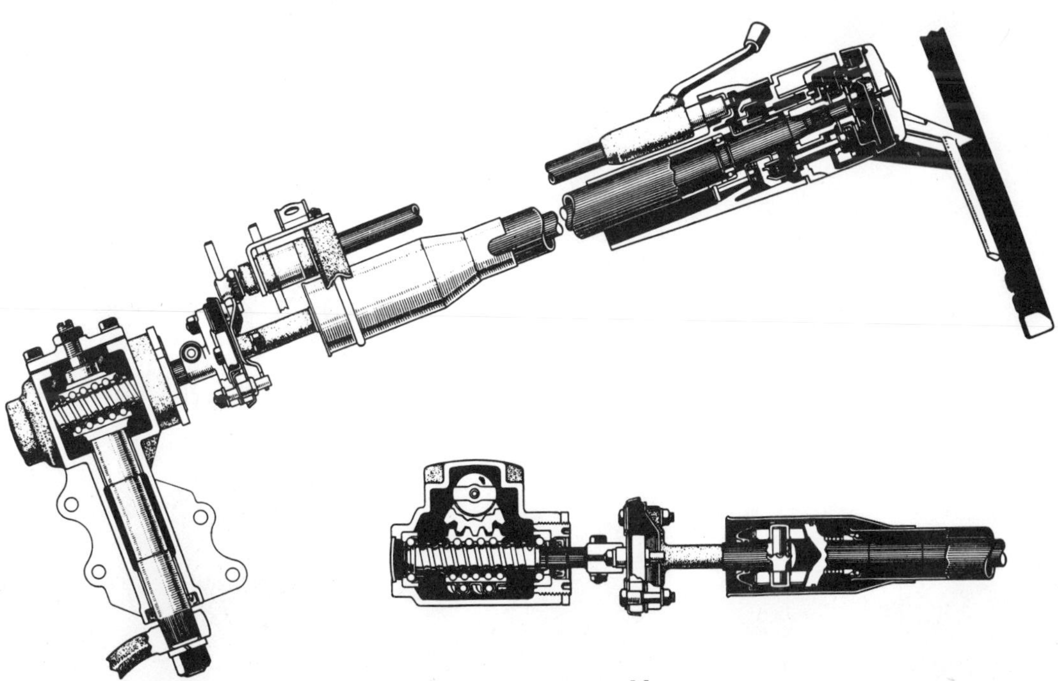

Crown steering assembly.

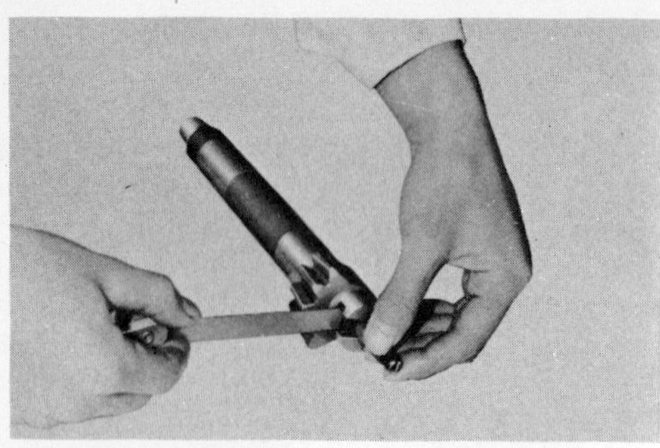

Selecting thrust washer.

## Front Suspension

Suspension is of conventional design with unequal wishbones and coil springs, similar to domestic types. Land Cruiser models have regular semi-elliptic springs supporting the front drive axle. On Corona and Crown models, the entire front suspension unit can be dismounted by removing four rubber-insulated bolts and disconnecting brake lines, steering linkage and sway bar.

## Coil Spring Specifications

| | Spring Capacity (lbs.) | | |
|---|---|---|---|
| *Model* | *Corona* | *Crown* | *Crown* (MS41) |
| SPRING COLOR | | | |
| Red | 1131–1157 | 1584–1617 | 1504–1544 |
| Yellow | 1158–1184 | 1618–1639 | 1545–1584 |
| White | 1185–1210 | 1640–1660 | 1585–1623 |
| Blue | 1211–1236 | 1661–1694 | 1624–1663 |

Spacer is 0.125″ thick on all models.

COIL SPRING COMBINATIONS

| *LEFT SIDE* | *RIGHT SIDE* |
|---|---|
| Blue | Yellow |
| White + S | Red + S |
| White + S | Yellow |
| Yellow + S | Yellow |
| White + S | White |

Note: S = spacer

### Front Suspension Removal (One Side)

Jack up car and place on stands. Remove wheel and upper shock absorber nut, then remove lower shock absorber bracket and withdraw shock absorber. Disconnect stabilizer bar and steering linkage at lower arm

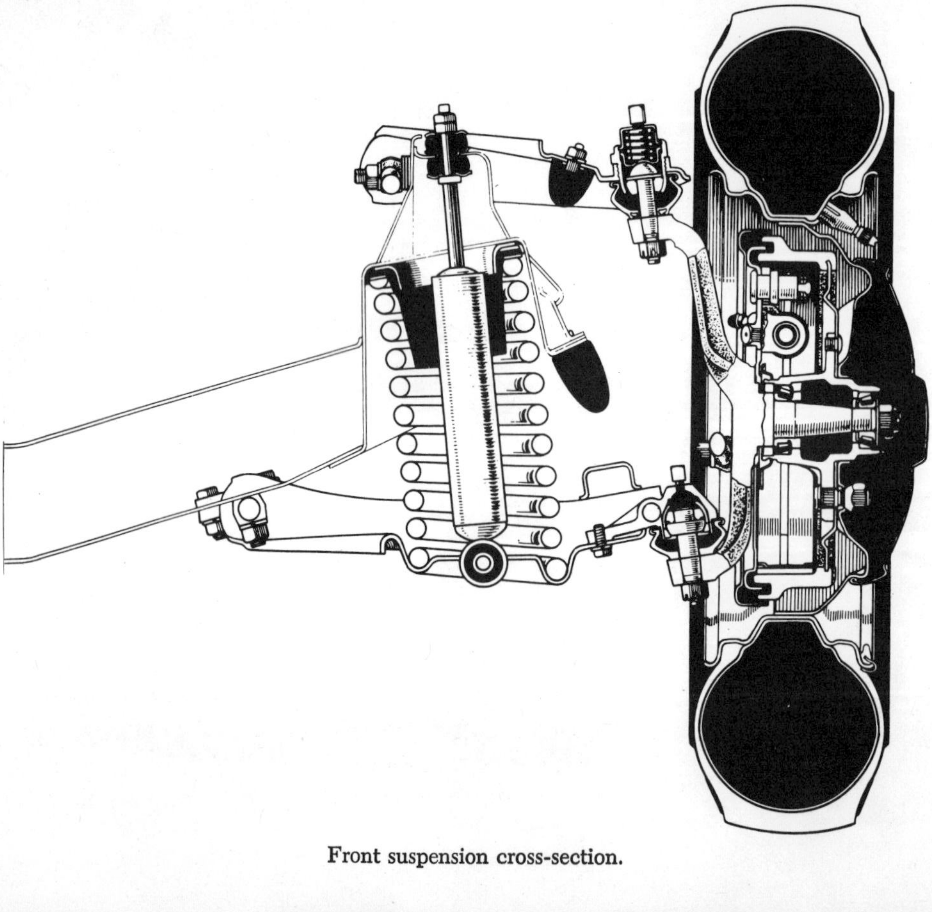

Front suspension cross-section.

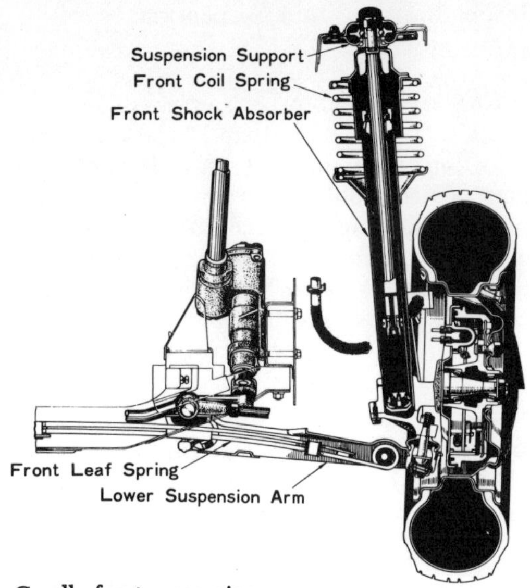


Corolla front suspension.

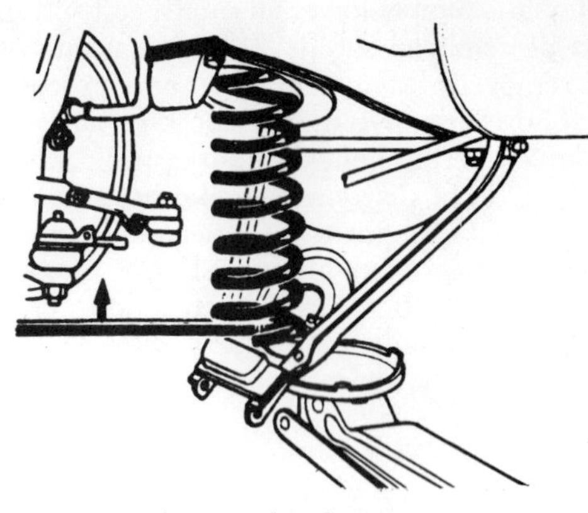

Lowering A-frame and coil spring.

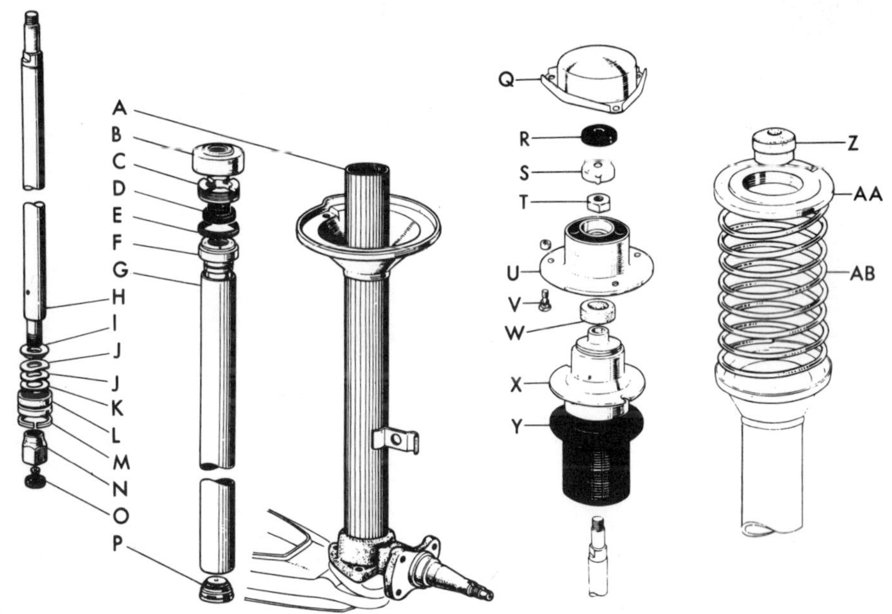


Shock absorber components.

A. W/steering knuckle shell
B. Shock absorber upper cap
C. Shock absorber ring nut
D. "D" type oil seal
E. Gasket
F. Shock absorber rod guide
G. Shock absorber cylinder
H. Shock absorber piston rod
I. Non-return valve stopper No. 1
J. Non-return valve spring
K. Non-return valve
L. Shock absorber piston
M. Shock absorber piston ring
N. Piston nut
O. Shock absorber piston valve
P. Shock absorber base valve
Q. Suspension support cover
R. Absorber cushion
S. Bearing dust cover
T. Nut
U. Front suspension support
V. Serration bolt
W. Suspension support dust seal
X. Bumper front seat
Y. Shock absorber dust cover
Z. Front spring bumper
AA. Front spring upper seat
AB. Front coil spring

only and place jack under lower arm so that the bolts can be removed from the lower ball joint. Slowly lower jack until coil spring can be removed safely. If spring need not be removed, leave it in place and proceed as follows: remove upper ball joint nut and remove steering knuckle from upper control arm. Do not disconnect brake hose unless necessary. To remove upper and lower control arms from chassis, simply remove the mounting bolts from each, taking care to keep the adjusting shims marked for later assembly and alignment.

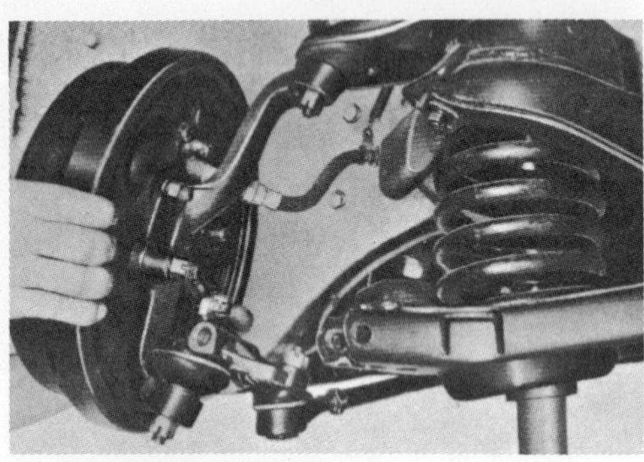

Disconnecting steering knuckle.

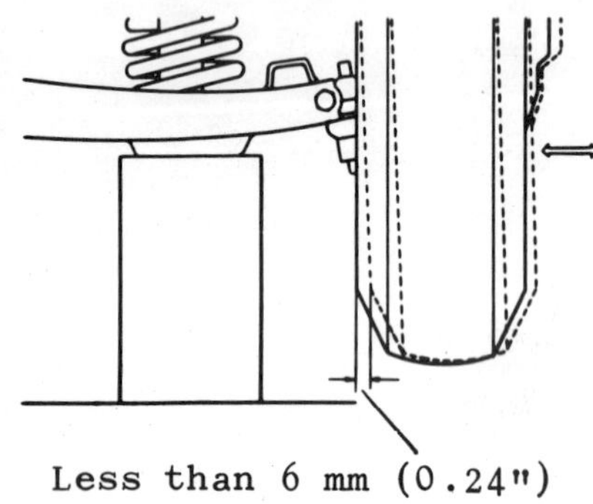


Checking ball joint side play.

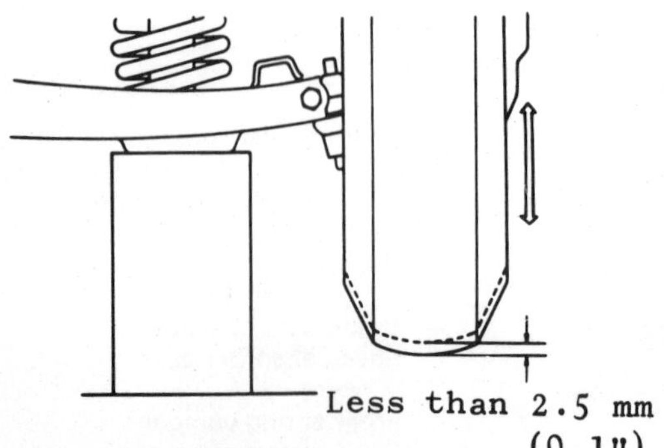


Checking ball joint vertical play.

**Inspecting the Front Suspension (One Side)**

Check shock absorber for leaks. Replace shock if there is more than 1" slack in either direction, or if the outer case is dented or bent. Check control arm pivot bushings and replace bushings if necessary. Also check control arms for damaged or worn threads. Check coil spring for distortion and cracks, compare to spring specifications. Check spring insulator and replace if cracked or deformed.

**Installing the Front Suspension (One Side)**

Assemble the upper and lower control arms and pivot bushings, turning each pivot bushing an equal amount. Assemble upper ball joint to arm. Insert spring into seat and, using a pry bar, work spring into the lower arm. Place jack under lower arm and slowly

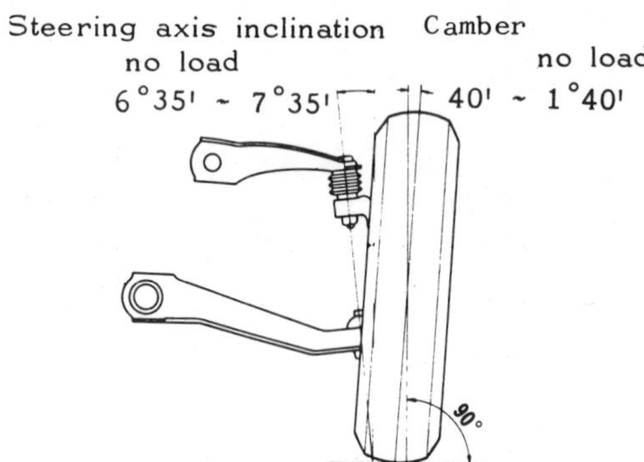


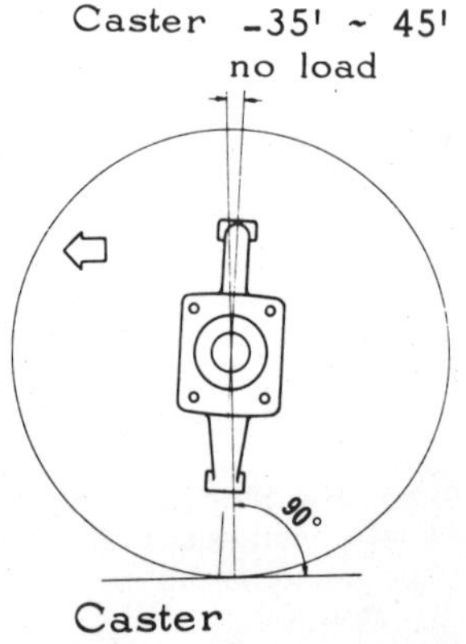

raise until spring is compressed enough to allow the lower ball joint to be connected and tightened. Make sure spring is seated properly at both ends. *NOTE: It may be necessary to remove the spring rebound damper to facilitate installation.* Now, insert the shock absorber and tighten at both ends.

**Inspecting the Ball Joint Without Removal**

*Upper ball joint* Disconnect from steering knuckle and check free-play by hand. Replace if ball joint is noticeably loose.

*Lower ball joint* Jack up car under lower control arm, then check play of wheel. Replace ball joint if play at wheel rim exceeds 0.1″ vertical motion or 0.25″ horizontal motion. Make sure dust covers are securely glued to ball joints.

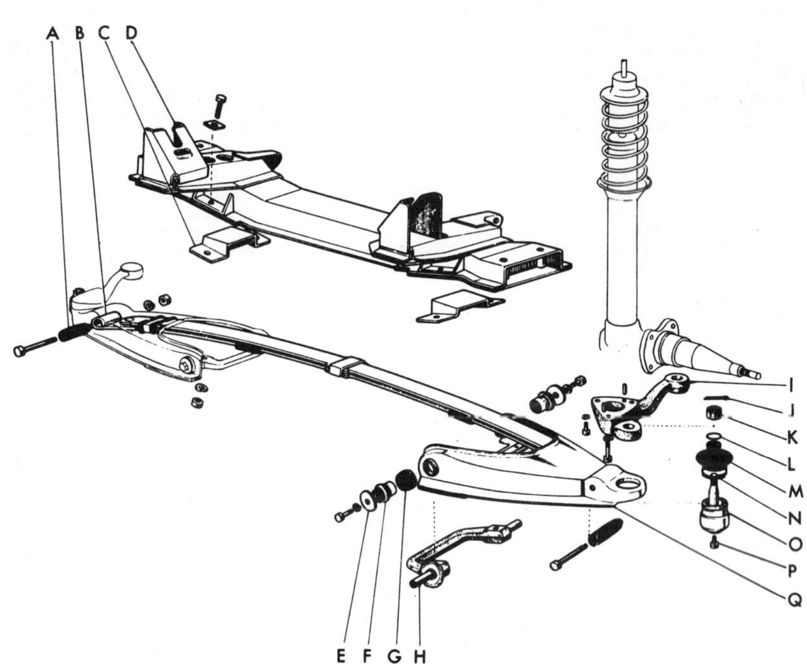


Corolla front axle components.

A. Front spring bushing
B. Front spring leaf
C. Front spring seat
D. Front suspension crossmember
E. Plate washer
F. Lower arm bushing
G. Lower arm strut bushing
H. Lower arm shaft
I. Steering knuckle arm
J. Cotter pin
K. Castle nut
L. Ring
M. Lower ball joint dust cover
N. Set ring
O. Lower ball joint
P. W/head tapered screw plug
Q. Suspension lower arm

## General Conversion Table

| *Multiply by* | *To convert* | *To* | |
|---|---|---|---|
| 2.54 | Inches | Centimeters | .3937 |
| 30.48 | Feet | Centimeters | .0328 |
| .914 | Yards | Meters | 1.094 |
| 1.609 | Miles | Kilometers | .621 |
| .645 | Square inches | Square cm. | .155 |
| .836 | Square yards | Square meters | 1.196 |
| 16.39 | Cubic inches | Cubic cm. | .061 |
| 28.3 | Cubic feet | Liters | .0353 |
| .4536 | Pounds | Kilograms | 2.2045 |
| 4.546 | Gallons | Liters | .22 |
| .068 | Lbs./sq. in. (psi) | Atmospheres | 14.7 |
| .138 | Foot pounds | Kg. m. | 7.23 |
| 1.014 | H.P. (DIN) | H.P. (SAE) | .9861 |
| —— | To obtain | From | Multiply by |

*Note:* 1 cm. equals 10 mm.; 1 mm. equals .0394″.

MILLIMETERS TO INCHES

| *Inches* | | *MM.* |
|---|---|---|
| 1/64 | .016 | .396 |
| 1/32 | .031 | .793 |
| 3/64 | .047 | 1.190 |
| 1/16 | .063 | 1.587 |
| 5/64 | .078 | 1.984 |
| 3/32 | .094 | 2.381 |
| 7/64 | .109 | 2.778 |
| 1/8 | .125 | 3.175 |
| 9/64 | .141 | 3.571 |
| 5/32 | .156 | 3.968 |
| 11/64 | .172 | 4.365 |
| 3/16 | .188 | 4.762 |
| 13/64 | .203 | 5.159 |
| 7/32 | .219 | 5.556 |
| 15/64 | .234 | 5.952 |
| 1/4 | .250 | 6.350 |

| *Inches* | | *MM.* |
|---|---|---|
| 17/64 | .266 | 6.746 |
| 9/32 | .281 | 7.143 |
| 19/64 | .297 | 7.540 |
| 5/16 | .313 | 7.937 |
| 21/64 | .328 | 8.334 |
| 11/32 | .344 | 8.730 |
| 23/64 | .359 | 9.127 |
| 3/8 | .375 | 9.525 |
| 25/64 | .391 | 9.921 |
| 13/32 | .406 | 10.318 |
| 27/64 | .422 | 10.715 |
| 7/16 | .438 | 11.112 |
| 29/64 | .453 | 11.508 |
| 15/32 | .469 | 11.905 |
| 31/64 | .484 | 12.302 |
| 1/2 | .500 | 12.700 |

| *Inches* | | *MM.* |
|---|---|---|
| 33/64 | .516 | 13.096 |
| 17/32 | .531 | 13.492 |
| 35/64 | .547 | 13.890 |
| 9/16 | .563 | 14.287 |
| 37/64 | .578 | 14.683 |
| 19/32 | .594 | 15.080 |
| 39/64 | .609 | 15.477 |
| 5/8 | .625 | 15.875 |
| 41/64 | .641 | 16.271 |
| 21/32 | .656 | 16.667 |
| 42/64 | .672 | 17.064 |
| 11/16 | .688 | 17.462 |
| 45/64 | .703 | 17.858 |
| 23/32 | .719 | 18.225 |
| 47/64 | .734 | 18.625 |
| 3/4 | .750 | 19.050 |

| *Inches* | | *MM.* |
|---|---|---|
| 49/64 | .766 | 19.446 |
| 25/32 | .781 | 19.842 |
| 51/64 | .797 | 20.239 |
| 13/16 | .813 | 20.637 |
| 53/64 | .823 | 21.033 |
| 27/32 | .844 | 21.429 |
| 55/64 | .859 | 21.827 |
| 7/8 | .875 | 22.225 |
| 57/64 | .891 | 22.621 |
| 29/32 | .906 | 23.017 |
| 59/64 | .922 | 23.414 |
| 15/16 | .938 | 23.812 |
| 61/64 | .953 | 24.208 |
| 31/32 | .969 | 24.604 |
| 63/64 | .984 | 25.002 |
| 1 | 1.000 | 25.400 |

(10 mm. = 0.3937″)

# Distributors

U.S.A.

Toyota Motor Distributors, Inc.
Main Office: 2055 West 190th Street
Torrance, California 90501
Phone: (213) 770-1730

Eastern Office: 50 Polito Avenue
Lyndhurst, New Jersey 07071
Phone: (201) 935-1550

Mid-Southern Toyota Distributors, Inc.
1640 North LaSalle Street
Chicago, Illinois 60614
Phone: (312) 943-5900

Southeast Toyota Distributors, Inc.
1501 S. Federal Highway
Pompano Beach, Florida 33062
Phone: (305) 946-2200

# Motor Imports

U.S.A.

Division of Service Motor Co., Ltd.
518 S. King Street
P. O. Box 2788
Honolulu, Hawaii

CANADA

Canadian Motor Industries
2000 Eglington Avenue E
Scarborough, Ontario
Canada
Phone: 751-4040

# U.S. Parts Depot

### Torrance, California 90501

Toyota Motor Distributors, Inc. Parts Depot
2055 West 190th Street
Phone: (213) 770-1730

### Lyndhurst, New Jersey 07071

Toyota Motor Distributors, Inc. Parts Depot
50 Polito Avenue
Phone: (201) 935-1550

### Houston, Texas

Toyota Motor Distributors, Inc. Parts Depot
5600 Hartsdale Drive
Phone: (713) 785-3550

### Chicago, Illinois 60649

Mid-Southern Toyota Distributors, Inc.
7744 S. Stony Island Avenue
Phone: (312) 374-2500

### Jacksonville, Florida 32207

Southeast Toyota Distributors, Inc.
709 Tallyrand Avenue
Phone: (904) 353-0983

# Regional Offices

U.S.A.

### Los Angeles, California

Toyota Motor Distributors, Inc.
2055 West 190th Street
Torrance, California 90501
Phone: (213) 770-1730

### San Francisco, California 94111

Toyota Motor Distributors, Inc.
Suite 211, World Trade Center
Phone: (415) 781-7452

### Denver, Colorado 80211

Toyota Motor Distributors, Inc.
2785 N. Speer Blvd.
Phone: (303) 433-6489

### Portland, Oregon 97232

Toyota Motor Distributors, Inc.
2717 N. E. Broadway
Phone: (503) 288-6756

### Houston, Texas 77036

Toyota Motor Distributors, Inc.
5600 Hartsdale Drive
Phone: (713) 785-3550

### Salt Lake City, Utah 84117

Toyota Motor Distributors, Inc.
50 West Third South
Phone: (801) 363-5544

### Lyndhurst, New Jersey 07071

Toyota Motor Distributors, Inc.
50 Polito Avenue
Phone: (201) 935-1550

### Boston, Massachusetts Area

Toyota Motor Distributors, Inc.
Room 212
886 Washington Street
Dedham, Massachusetts 02026
Phone (617) 326-2884

### Chicago, Illinois 60614

Mid-Southern Toyota Distributors, Inc.
1640 North LaSalle Street
Phone: (312) 943-5900

### Pompano Beach, Florida 33062

Southeast Toyota Distributors, Inc.
1501 S. Federal Highway
Phone: (305) 946-2200

CANADA

### Vancouver, British Columbia

Canadian Motor Industries
1345 West Georgia Street
Phone: (604) 683-1352

### Montreal, Province of Quebec

Canadian Motor Industries
1744 Cote Des Neiges
Phone: (514) 342-2520

### Halifax, Nova Scotia

Canadian Motor Industries
P.O. Box 199